Alternatives to Assimilation

BRANDEIS SERIES IN AMERICAN JEWISH
HISTORY, CULTURE, AND LIFE

Jonathan D. Sarna, Editor

Leon A. Jick, 1992
The Americanization of the Synagogue, 1820–1870

Sylvia Barack Fishman, editor, 1992
*Follow My Footprints: Changing Imagies of Women in
American Jewish Fiction*

Gerald Tulchinsky, 1993
Taking Root: The Origins of the Canadian Jewish Community

Shalom Goldman, editor, 1993
Hebrew and the Bible in America: The First Two Centuries

Marshall Sklare, 1993
Observing America's Jews

Reena Sigman Friedman, 1994
*These Are Our Children: Jewish Orphanages in
the United States, 1880–1925*

Alan Silverstein, 1994
*Alternatives to Assimilation: The Response of Reform
Judaism to American Culture, 1840–1930*

Jack Wertheimer, editor, 1995
The American Synagogue: A Sanctuary Transformed

Sylvia Barack Fishman, 1995
*A Breath of Life: Feminism in
the American Jewish Community*

Alternatives to Assimilation

THE RESPONSE OF REFORM JUDAISM TO AMERICAN CULTURE, 1840–1930

❖

Alan Silverstein

Brandeis University Press
Published by University Press of New England
Hanover and London

Brandeis University Press
Published by University Press of New England,
Hanover, NH 03755
© 1994 by the Trustees of Brandeis University
All rights reserved
Printed in the United States of America
5   4   3   2
CIP data appear at the end of the book

For My Parents
Sol and Doris Silverstein

Contents

Preface

My interest in the history of the American synagogue commenced during my undergraduate years of study at Cornell University. Two professors, David Brion Davis and Walter Lafeber, stimulated my pursuit of Americana; and one faculty member, Gerd Korman, served as both a mentor and friend, guiding me into the field of American Jewish history.

During my graduate school years, the building blocks of this volume were crafted in the Columbia University classrooms of David Rothman and Walter Metzger. In particular, Professor Metzger recommended that I apply the conceptualizations of American social history to the evolution of the Reform temple in the United States.

At various points throughout the extended period of research and the writing of *Alternatives to Assimilation*, I experienced the involvement of several faculty members at the Jewish Theological Seminary. I am indebted to Ismar Schorsch for valuable insights during the early stages of this effort, to Jack Wertheimer for relentless stylistic demands, to Naomi Cohen for valuable substantive recommendations, to Neil Gillman for encouragement, and to Stephen Garfinkel for assistance in bringing this process to a conclusion.

I also am greatly appreciative to Dr. Cynthia Eller for her careful reading and indispensable input, and above all to Professor Russell Richey, Associate Dean for Academic Programs at Duke University Divinity School. Russell Richey was my primary source of advice and evaluation in assessing the American cultural setting in which both Protestant and Jewish religious institutions were shaped. He was always available for guidance, encouragement, and friendship.

In addition, I am thankful to the professional staff of the Brandeis University series of which this book is a part. In terms of academic affairs, this monograph benefitted substantially from the insights of numerous scholars who served as readers, most notably Jonathan Sarna, series editor, and Malcolm Stern, whose sudden death was a source of great sorrow. As for the production of the book, I express my admiration to David Caffry, Mary Crittendon, and the many other members of the staff of University Press of New England, whose efficient and cooperative spirit brought this manuscript into print.

Furthermore, I express my appreciation for the graciousness and helpful nature of the archivists of the four temples examined in this study—Keneseth Israel (Philadelphia), Emanu-El (San Francisco), Temple Sinai (New Orleans), and Bene Yeshurun (Cincinnati). Equal gratitude is due the staffs of the American Jewish Archives (Cincinnati), American Jewish Historical Society (Waltham, Massachusetts), Western Jewish Historical Society (Berkeley), and the United States Census Bureau regional office (Philadelphia).

Finally, I am grateful to my wonderful family—to my father-in-law and mother-in-law, Sol and Cili Neufeld; to my children, David and Rebecca; and to wife, Rita—for their love and for encouraging me to devote so much time to this project. In particular, I am indebted to my parents, Sol and Doris Silverstein.

My father systematically read and offered advice with regard to every aspect of this volume. Dad instilled in me a deep love for learning, for history, and for writing. His example has been the inspiration for me to write *Alternatives to Assimilation*. Of equal magnitude was the legacy of values imparted to me by my mother. Mom taught me to maintain a spirit of optimism and confidence independent of the magnitude of the challenge at hand. Her teachings fortified me with the stamina to bring this task to completion. I am delighted to dedicate this book to my parents, for their love and support.

A.S.

Alternatives to Assimilation

Introduction

The religious lives of most American Jews are exhibited within Reform, Conservative, and Orthodox congregations. The contemporary synagogue in the United States provides an elaborate array of activities for its membership. Religious services are adapted to meet the aesthetic and spiritual needs of affiliates. Distinctive prayerbooks, liturgies and approaches to decorum are evident. Sisterhoods and Brotherhoods (Men's Clubs) conduct educational, recreational, and social events for an adult clientele. Children are involved in age-appropriate youth groups and religious school classes. The professional staff includes one or more rabbis, a cantor, an educational director, and often a youth director and an executive director as well. The synagogue or temple is programmatically and ideologically linked to a national congregational body of like-minded houses of worship. Full-time personnel frequently are alumni of affiliated national training institutions and are members of national professional associations. Prospective members are recruited via brochures, newspaper advertisements, and aggressive marketing techniques.

This nearly universal pattern within synagogue life was not always present. On the contrary, Jewish immigrants to America in 1840s, for example, encountered an institutionally simpler religious life, one modest by European Jewish standards. Individual synagogues were solely houses of worship. Sisterhoods, Brotherhoods, youth groups, and synagogue-based religious schools were not part of temple life. Moreover, congregations were isolated, lacking national bodies linking Jewish congregations to one another or professional associations linking the leadership. Nationwide training institutions were not part of American Jewish life. Rabbis were virtually nonexistent, as were teachers, *chazzanim*, and other ritual officiants. Upon his arrival in Baltimore from Europe in 1849, Rabbi Abraham Rice observed:

I dwell in complete darkness, without a teacher or companion. . . . The religious life [of Jewry] in this land is on the lowest level, most people eat foul food and desecrate the Sabbath in public. . . . Under these circumstances my mind is perplexed and I wonder whether it is even permissible for a Jew to live in this land.[1]

What were the origins of these institutional innovations not present at all prior to the Civil War and yet now assumed to be indispensable to synagogue life? The emergence of the Reform movement in American Judaism has been chosen as the appropriate vehicle for this assessment of cultural change. Both in terms of temple life and national denominational innovation, Reform Judaism was the pacesetter for the Conservative and Orthodox movements. As early as the conclusion of the First World War, at the local and nationwide levels Reform's successful adaptations to the American scene were consciously being emulated by its institutional rivals within American Judaism.

Two distinct approaches characterize existing evaluations of the history of the Reform movement in American Judaism. The earliest monographs described the Reform movement solely as a theological orientation toward Judaism transplanted from Germany to the United States. Attention was focused exclusively upon elites and upon religious beliefs. Studies centered on rabbinic leadership, ritual debates, and ideological platforms and remained limited to the orbit of Central European and subsequent American Jewish life. The cultural impact of the general American environment and the social influences emerging from local temples and laity were largely ignored.[2] In contrast, recent scholarship has concentrated on social and cultural changes that made United States society receptive to Reform and helped mold a uniquely American version of Reform Judaism. These efforts have placed the evolution of many aspects of the Reform movement into the context of temple life. Rather than addressing the thoughts of elites alone, this newer research into social history stresses changes emanating from the congregational level.[3]

This study continues the effort to assess the impact of the American environment upon the emergence of the Reform movement. Whereas some Reform ideas arrived in the United States from Germany, the American ambience recast these ideologies into a unique institutional blend. In part, organizational models that characterized America's Reform temple by 1930 can be traced both to the Jewish tradition's advocacy of religious education and to notions imported from like-minded coreligionists in Central Europe.[4] However, since the structural patterns of Reform, Conservative, and Orthodox congregations as well as urban churches in the United States often evolved in parallel fashion, more than ideology must be addressed. Large cultural influences should be sought, trends that impacted simultaneously upon Jewish and Christian religious institutions. Therefore, this volume will concentrate on the interaction of a rapidly changing American ambience with Jews in the United States of varied liturgical and ritual proclivities.

Alternatives to Assimilation seeks to further previous studies of the history of American Judaism in the following ways. First, it will examine the impact of global cultural trends upon American society at large, upon American Christian religious institutions, and then ultimately upon the Reform movement in American Judaism. In which decades of American history did British institutional models of organizations prevail? At what points in time did German concepts of institutional innovation dominate American secular and religious life? At which juncture in America's cultural evolution did a distinctive American approach predominate? In answering these inquiries, we can identify three stages in this process of cultural accommodation; hence the tripartite structure of the work.

1. 1840–1880, The Anglo-American Stage: Becoming a National Union of Congregations

2. 1880–1900, The German Stage: Expanded Roles of Temples and of the Union

3. 1900–1930, The American Stage: Adapting to Corporate Culture

Second, we will assess changing demographic factors that motivated synagogue leaders to alter their objectives. To do so, this assessment will explore the social history of the Reform movement in American Judaism, history from the bottom up, by addressing the concerns of its laity and of its affiliated congregations. At each stage in the molding of American Reform, we will highlight the dynamic interplay between the local temple and emerging national bodies. One chapter in each of the three parts of this book will examine these cultural stages of adaption by concentrating on case studies of one large temple in the first major city to arise within each of the four geographical regions of the United States.

East, Philadelphia's Keneseth Israel
West, San Francisco's Emanu-El
South, New Orleans' Temple Sinai
Midwest, Cincinnati's Kehillah K'doshah B'nai Yeshurun

Although sizable metropolitan temples are not necessarily representative of every aspect of the life of Reform Jews, the decision to select large institutions for this investigation is based upon the disproportionate influence that national lay leaders affiliated with major urban temples exerted upon the Reform movement. The annual *Proceedings of the Union of American Hebrew Congregations* reveal the almost total control that lay leaders from "cathedral congregations" exhibited within the Union. Their rabbis were the Jewish professionals most commonly consulted by national reform agencies. Their laity were the Union's officers, the vast majority of its Executive Board, the primary participants in UAHC Committees, a plurality of attendees at the yearly General Council, and the most generous monetary contributors to the Reform movement's fiscal coffers. From 1878 to 1898, for example, among the 105 members of the Executive Board, only 4 resided in small Jewish communities such as Quincy, Illinois. The other 101 Board members were congregants in large temples throughout more than twenty large cities in the United States. During that same period of time, only nine men occupied the coveted offices of UAHC President, Vice President, Secretary, or Treasurer. All but one were members of large temples in Cincinnati or New York City. In like fashion, influential congregations in major cities hosted all fifteen sessions of the General Council that occurred during the nineteenth century.[5]

Since national lay leaders to the Reform movement came to policy gatherings shaped by the experiences encountered within their own "cathedral congregations," the trends emerging within major urban temples should be considered as crucial in assessing local pressures for institutional innovation by the UAHC. In this context, chapters 1, 3, and 5 will assess the extent to which the organizational modification of American synagogue life as evident among the four temples was an outgrowth of the sociological realities affecting the "Jews in the pews." Subsequently for each stage of development, chapters 2, 4, and 6 will reflect upon the response by Reform's national congregational bodies to pressures generated by congregational adaptation, as well as the impact of UAHC innovation in furthering local temple goals. The simultaneous consideration of denominational bodies at their national level interfacing with their affiliated temples offers a bipolar view of the evolution of a unique American Reform Judaism.

Third, in this study new quantitative data have been gleaned from census records and from temple archives. Previously unused statistical data also have been extracted from the proceedings of national and local bodies. These materials will permit the examination of patterns regarding the ages, ethnic backgrounds, occupations, family and household sizes, and marital patterns among the affiliated members of neighborhood temples. The data also address related concerns such as rabbinic salaries and mobility, trends of affiliation within the UAHC, attendance at its annual Councils, committees and fund-raising campaigns, and age, ethnicity, and family background among Reform rabbis.

Fourth, changes within temple life and at the national level are refined beyond the vague notion of "Americanization." The evolution and accommodation of the Reform movement to its environment will be measured against broad "megatrends" within American history such as denominationalism, professionalization, rationalization, and ethnic conflict, plus the changing roles of women, adolescents, and children in the United States. This effort places the Reform movement into the context of general American history. When possible, attention also will be accorded to institutional parallels between U.S. Protestants and Jews. Topics explored will include the Social Gospel, the Institutional Church, church extension, circuit preaching, denominational colleges, Sunday School education as well as the publication of religious tracts, books, and newspapers. This volume will assess to what degree the Reform movement in American Judaism became an allied American religious body, structurally more akin to Christian groups in the United States than to the institutional life of Jews in Europe or Mediterranean countries. As historian E. Brooks Holifield has written:

To note such parallels [between Christian and Jewish religious institutions] is not to deny the profound differences, but the similarities require further refinement of the notion of Americanization. When we want to understand why some long-settled Protestant congregations and some immigrant Jewish congregations adopted similar reforms at roughly the same time— . . . for example, becoming social centers as well as communities of worship—then we need an interpretive theme larger than Americanization to clarify the transitions.[6]

Finally, several guiding questions prevail throughout all three periods under consideration. How did everchanging cultural and social influences alter rabbinic function and status? What identifiable demographic factors among the laity of the Reform movement evolved from 1840 to 1930? Were temple members aging and if so, how did temple function change to accommodate this reality? What was the socioeconomic level exhibited by temple members? Did they exhibit distinctive patterns of ethnicity as well? How did the programmatic agenda of the local temple change to keep pace with the rapidly shifting American cultural scene? At what point in time and under what circumstances did temples add religious schools, women's and men's auxiliaries, and young adult activities? In what fashion did the UAHC, the Hebrew Union College, the Central Conference of American Rabbis, and ultimately the National Federations of Temple Sisterhoods and Brotherhoods adapt to cultural innovations? At what point did the Union of American Hebrew Congregations perceive itself as leading a religious movement open only to Jews comfortable with Reform Judaism, thereby stimulating the creation of rival Conservative and Orthodox movements?

PART ONE

❖

1840–1880

Anglo-American Influences

❖ I ❖

Local Synagogues as Voluntary Associations

During America's colonial era, individual churches within each town profoundly influenced religious, civic, and family life. Affiliation with a colonial church was indispensable for Christian settlers. Churches transmitted religious values to the next generation, provided for the needs of the indigent, conducted informal social and business linkages, and offered collective input to civic officials.[1] Similarly, membership in the colonial synagogues was a virtual requirement for North American Jews. Like their medieval European antecedents, colonial congregations functioned as a total *kahal kodosh*, an all-encompassing "sacred community." The *kahal kodosh* provided a wide range of services: public prayer and kosher food, a mikveh, matzah for Passover, a cemetery and burial plots, marriage and other rites of passage, education for youngsters, and holy day worship services. Colonial synagogues tended to each local Jewish family's social, religious, and economic needs.

The successful outcome of the Revolutionary War changed this relationship dramatically. Legal ties between the nascent United States and its former "mother country" were severed. The newly ratified Constitution separated church and state, casting local houses of worship adrift. Affiliation by the "unchurched" could no longer be assumed, and congregations entered a competitive environment. In the post-Revolutionary period, no longer did the church or synagogue have any civil function or presence. The congregation had become "a *voluntary association*, supported by private donation. . . . for the nurture and worship of a self-selected group of . . . believers [emphasis added]."[2]

In an atmosphere of freedom where one was free to affiliate or not, American rates of church membership plummeted from nearly 100 percent in 1750 to barely 7 percent forty years later. Churches and synagogues were forced to become activists; they were thrust into a "free marketplace of souls." They hoped to persuade members to join their voluntary association with the marketing techniques used by voluntary clubs within the realms of politics, culture, and recreation. This distinctively American pattern of appealing to "voluntas," self-interest or free will, was concretized during the nineteenth century. As Alexis de Tocqueville, the astute foreign observer of the U.S. scene, reflected during his visit in 1831, "Americans of all ages, all conditions, and all dispositions, constantly form [voluntary] associations . . . associations of a thousand kinds—religious, moral, serious, futile, general or restricted, enormous or diminutive.[3]

American synagogues too felt pressured to adapt to the new voluntarism. This effort contrasted sharply with Jewish life in the Central European areas from which most American Jews had come. In the German states, the local Jewish community (*kehillah*) was officially recognized by the government. Affiliation was mandatory, and communal taxation by the *kehillah* was enforced by the secular authorities.[4] In a totally different atmosphere of voluntary associations, efforts to recruit the unaffiliated majority of American Jews dominated the life of the four sample temples treated in this study (Keneseth Israel [KI] of Philadelphia, Kehillah K'doshah B'nai Yeshurun [KKBY] of Cincinnati, Emanu-El of San Francisco, and Temple Sinai of New Orleans). The temple sought to define the needs of potential members and offered to fill them. Early American synagogues aspired to emulate local church successes in offering newcomers "a ready-made community of like-minded and like-believing, in which they could immediately establish a sense of belonging and enter a network of trustworthy acquaintances and safe institutions."[5]

The Laity

Ethnic Profiles

In the mid-nineteenth-century Irish and German Catholics, in a fashion similar to immigrant Protestants, gravitated to ethnic churches reflecting their national backgrounds. American Jews in the period prior to 1880 also reflected this pattern. Ethnic diversity often caused the formation of new synagogues. "Since the ritual of Germany and Poland differed and congregations offered not only places for worship but places for fellowship, German, Polish, Bohemian, Russian, and Lithuaniuan Jews all formed separate congregations when enough of them clustered."[6]

German Jews predominated largely by default, because the composition of the Jewish population was primarily of central European national origin.[7] Local American Reform temples were dominated by a diverse yet decisive German-speaking majority in the 1840 to 1880 era. A distinction must be made between the two major migrations of so-called "German" Jews. The years 1836 to 1848 saw a large group of Rhineland and southern German Jews arrive in the United States. After the failure of the Revolution of 1848, an even larger Jewish migration occurred from Prussia. These post-1848 immigrants were largely Posen Jews who followed the Polish ritual and were dubbed "Poles" by the other Germans until the arrival of the massive post-1880 Jewish immigration from Eastern Europe (Russia, Poland, Romania, etc.) transformed the earlier arrivals into "Germans."[8]

United States immigration data quantify this ethnic pattern within early-nineteenth-century American Jewish life. In the thirty-year period before 1848, the growth of the United States Jewish population was estimated to have been from 3,000 to 50,000. The overwhelming percentage of the Jewish immigrants were of Central European origin. Although U.S. immigration figures from this period do not specify religion, government data recorded a total of only 700 Christian or Jewish immigrants from Russia, 400 from Poland and fewer than 100 from Romania during the era from 1818 to 1848. Perhaps many of these Eastern European immigrants were Jews, but the collective number of Jewish immigrants from Eastern Europe in this thirty-year span could not have exceeded 1,000. In this same time period, a tiny number of Jews came to the United States from France, from England, and from Holland; virtually none arrived from anywhere else. In contrast, several hundred thousand German-speaking emigres settled in the United States.[9] By the simple process of elimination, the dramatic rise of the American Jewish population must have been due primarily to German Jewish immigration.

Between 1848 and 1878, as American Jewry's ranks were assumed to have increased from 50,000 to 230,000, the German Jewish ethnic element continued to predominate. Larger and larger numbers of Eastern Europeans immigrated into the United States throughout these three decades. Yet in total, only 33,000 Russians (Jewish or Christian) entered this country, with 13,000 arrivals from Poland, and fewer than 1,000 from Romania. These are modest figures compared to the staggering totals for German immigration to America at this time. German immigration figures exceeded 2,300,000 persons, with an additional 54,000 Central Europeans coming to the United States from Hungary and Austria.[10] From 1848 to 1878, it is conceivable that many of the 47,000 Eastern European immigrants to America were Jews. Nonetheless, most of the apparent 180,000 increase in the U.S. Jewish population are attributable either to Central European newcomers or to the children of earlier Jewish immigrants from Germany and nearby lands.

Some mid-nineteenth-century American synagogues had more of a universal German flavor than others. Local diversity of prayerbooks, *minhag* (customs), and ethnicity prevailed. As historian Hasia R. Diner has cautioned:

Historians who universalize from the German experience, who assume that the years 1820–1880 constitute a "German" era in American Jewish history, and who attribute Jewish religious, economic, and social developments in America to Germanness, not only simplify but ignore the sweep of geography and culture from which Jews came to mid-nineteenth century America.[11]

During this pre-1880 period, the presence of limited numbers of Eastern European and other non-German Jews within local Reform congregations was not yet a source of social discomfort.

The patterns of national origin among the memberships of the sample temples reflected the diverse trends within the American Jewish population at large. In the mid-nineteenth century, founders and members were exclusively male. All nineteen of the Philadelphia founders and all ten Cincinnati founders located in the 1850 census were of German birth. In larger and later samples of data traced to the San Francisco (1860) and New Orleans (1870) synagogue founders, some significant variation to this trend did appear. In San Francisco's Emanu-El, for instance, although twenty-two of twenty-seven founding members located in the census archives did come from Germany, two others were Frenchmen, one was English, one was Polish, and the final founder among the twenty-seven was a native of Louisiana.[12]

The founders of Temple Sinai in French-speaking New Orleans showed an even larger departure from the Germanic norms of Philadelphia and Cincinnati. Only thirty-four of forty-seven among the Temple Sinai sample were Germans, while nine came from France, and one each from Posen, Bohemia, Austria, and New York City. The 1870 census subdivided the earlier category of "Germany" for thirty-two members of the New Orleans sample. Among this group, twenty-one came from Bavaria, eight from Prussia, and one each from Baden, Württemberg and Hesse-Darmstadt. The 1860 census offered similar statistics regarding the San Francisco population. Of the thirteen Bay Area residents for whom such data are available, seven were natives of Bavaria, with three Prussians, and one each from Hanover, Saxony, and Baden.[13]

The wives of the founders of these sample congregations frequently were of Central European descent as well. According to the data culled from the 1850 census, all but three (two from Pennsylvania and one from

Massachusetts) of the nineteen spouses in the Philadelphia sample were of German birth. In Cincinnati, only two of the nine recorded wives were non-Germans, one being born in France, and the other in Ohio. Yet given the shortage of prospective brides in mid-nineteenth-century America's hinterland,[14] variety of national origins was evident among the San Francisco and New Orleans wives.

Among the nineteen females married to the German founders in the San Francisco Emanu-El congregation, all but one were of German extraction; the final woman in question hailed from Poland. All five of the non-German San Francisco founders had non-German mates, two from France, one from England, one from South Carolina, and one from Louisiana. An even greater diversity of national origins was exhibited by the Temple Sinai (New Orleans) founders. Only half of the thirty-two German males had married German-born women. Of the others, nine found hometown women from Louisiana, five chose French women as their wives, and two others met spouses from Mississippi and South Carolina. The marital patterns of the nine Frenchmen among the New Orleans founders divided equally into thirds, three marrying women from Germany, three from France, and three from Louisiana. As for the final four New Orleans non-German founders, the Bohemian and the Austrian married women from their native lands, while the Posen and New York males found wives from Louisiana and South Carolina, respectively.

Age Distribution

Mid-nineteenth-century voluntary associations sought members from all stages of life. Yet the average age of the founders of our sample congregations was quite young, in the low to middle thirties. Mid-nineteenth-century American immigrant groups were youthful since young adults proved to be the most likely candidates for emigration out of central Europe and other parts of the European continent. United States census data consistently showed that two-thirds of the pre-Civil War American population were under age thirty, and three-fourths under age forty.[15] These sample temples were no exception. In the census data: Kehillah K'doshah B'nai Yeshurun (Cincinnati) founders averaged 34.1 years of age; Keneseth Israel (Philadelphia) 37; Emanu-El (San Francisco) 31.2; and Temple Sinai (New Orleans) 36.8.

The concentration of very young men involved, however, was even more prominent than these averages imply. The Cincinnati sample, for instance, revealed that eight of the ten men were between twenty-five and thirty-five years of age. Of the nineteen Philadelphians, eleven were in their thirties, and two others were even younger. In both the Cincinnati and Philadelphia congregations, the 1850 census information was several years after the actual founding of these synagogues[16] (1841 for K.K. B'nai Yeshurun in Cincinnati, and 1846 for Keneseth Israel in Philadelphia), so at the actual time of their inception, these men were an average age of thirty-three for Philadelphia, and twenty-five for Cincinnati. The San Francisco situation was by far the most homogeneous. Of the twenty-five founders located in the 1860 census, twenty-three were of ages ranging between twenty-two and thirty-five. These founders were even younger at the actual time of Emanu-El's creation nine years earlier. New Orleans' Temple Sinai represented the sole exception to this consistent pattern of youthful founders. Of Temple Sinai's forty-six organizers, twenty-two were in the twenty to thirty-nine age category, sixteen others were in their forties, seven were in their fifties, and one was sixty-one years old. This departure reflected the reality that this Temple emerged in 1870, a later period of greater age diversity. Since synagogues as voluntary associations sought to affiliate any prospective member, a wider age range appeared precisely at a time when America's demographic patterns had changed.

Consistent with the social mores of nineteenth-century America, the founders of these early Ashkenazic congregations found wives younger than themselves. On the average, the differences in age between husband and wife were 6.2 years for Cincinnati, 9.9 for Philadelphia, 8.1 for San Francisco and 5.1 for New Orleans. As was true with the husbands, the average age of female spouses in the census data did not adequately describe the remarkable youth of these wives of synagogue leaders at the times that their shuls arose (some were not yet married). In Cincinnati, seven of the ten women had not passed their thirtieth birthday at the 1843 establishment of K.K. B'nai Yeshurun. When Keneseth Israel's founders first assembled, seventeen of the nineteen wives or fiancees were in the nineteen to thirty-five age bracket. Of the twenty-two San Francisco mates, twenty-one had not reached age thirty-nine at the time of Emanu-El's first organizational meeting, with sixteen of them ranging from ages thirteen to twenty-nine. Even New Orleans' Temple Sinai, with its older group of founders, included thirty-three of its forty-five wives under age thirty-nine.

The prevalence of young couples with young children among the memberships of these temples created a need for effective synagogue-based religious schools. Neighboring Protestant church Sunday schools offered a role model in this regard. As Isaac Leeser, the most prominent Jewish religious leader in antebellum America, lamented in the mid-1840s:

If we look abroad upon society around us, we cannot help seeing evidence of the spirit of propagation which is abroad in the land. . . . Even the Friends, whose tenets are to have no creed, have their *schools, to impress upon the minds of their children the religion.* . . . [emphasis added] Unitarians, Universalists, Catholics, Protestants, have all their primary and high schools. . . . But Judaism seems to be neglected.[17]

The strength of Christian religious schools was attributable to the American Sunday School Union (ASSU) and the emphasis put on the Sunday School by Protestant national religious bodies. Envious rabbis and Jewish parents may well have pressured for a similar nationwide structure for U.S. Jews.[18]

Occupational Patterns

In additional to ethnic and age considerations, related business interests forged a network of trustworthy acquaintances. These interpersonal bonds were forged more by economic realities than by selective recruitment. In the three sample congregations within America's hinterland, opportunities for entrepreneurial initiatives enticed pioneers to venture forth. In each case, a pattern of merchandising emerged. In contrast, Philadelphia was an East Coast urban center accessible to less venturesome immigrants, so the clientele affiliated with its congregations were more diversified.

Many original members of Kehillah K'doshah B'nai Yeshurun (KKBY) in Cincinnati for instance, shared occupational involvements. At least fifteen of the twenty-four founders whose occupations appeared in the 1850 Cincinnati City Directories earned their living in "dry goods" and/or "clothing" at the "wholesale" or "retail" level. Among the remaining nine members, two worked as "clerks," and one each as a tailor, a shoemaker, a jeweler, a peddler, a barkeeper, an auctioneer, and a butcher. Some of their places of business included:

Bloch and Frenkel Clothiers (Lazarus Bloch, Benedict Frenkel)
Levi Freidman and Co. Clothier
Goodheart and Ackerland Clothiers (Abraham Goodheart)
Lewis Levy Clothier
Isaac Trost and Brother Clothier
A. and I. Wolf Clothing Store (A. B. Wolf, Sr., and Daniel Wolf)
Friedman and Miller Clothiers (Solomon and Joseph Friedman)
Simon Himmelreich Clothing Store
F. Goldschmidt and Co. Wholesale and Retail Dry Goods (Abraham Fechheimer)
J. and A. Goodheart Dry Goods (Julius Goodheart)
Henry Sacks and Brothers Wholesale Dry Goods
Isaac and Henry Wertheimer Dry Goods Store

The origins of this Cincinnati congregation linked primarily young clothing/dry goods merchants bonded by common religious, ethnic, age, and commercial concerns.

The more diversified occupations of Philadelphia's Keneseth Israel (KI) founders were divisible into the categories of businessmen and craftsmen. Of the former group, the census takers vaguely classified eleven of the nineteen as either "merchants" (five), peddlers (four), or "dealers" (two). Unlike the Cincinnati case study, none of these occupational descriptions indicated the nature of the items sold, peddled, or "dealt with." Because they lack greater specificity, the data fail to reveal potential links between the occupational patterns of the Philadelphia and Cincinnati membership samples. As for craftsmen, the census data identify three shoemakers, two tailors, a cordwinder, a watchmaker, and a "laborer." These young artisans probably were not affluent, nor were the four peddlers among the "businessmen." Unlike in (Cincinnati) K.K. B'nai Yeshurun's membership of middle- or upper-middle-class business people, the founders of Philadelphia's Keneseth Israel included both upwardly mobile as well as the less well-to-do.

San Francisco's Emanu-El founders displayed occupational patterns more similar to the case study in Cincinnati than that of Philadelphia. All but two (an attorney and the congregation's "sexton") of the twenty-five men whose occupations were traceable in the census records and 1860 City Directory engaged in some substantial merchandising venture. Of the twenty-five men, seven described themselves as "clothiers" or "dry goods" dealers, five were "general importers" or "jobbers," and five others simply appear as "merchants." The remainder of the twenty-five included two "cap makers," two "jobbers in tobacco/cigars," a "broker and commercial merchant," and one "dealer in fancy goods." In contrast to the less affluent circle of members at Philadelphia's Keneseth Israel, absent from Emanu-El were "peddlers" and simple craftsmen (shoemakers, tailors, watchmakers, and laborers). Among the businessmen involved in this congregational venture in San Francisco were:

David Samuels, Dry Goods
L. S. Ackerman, Dry Goods
Martin Heller and Brother, Commercial (Clothier)
Louis A. Cohen, Merchant
Lazard Godchaux, Dry Goods
I. and H. Levy, Dry Goods
William Scholle and Brothers, Importers
Augustus Wasserman, Importer
A. Tandler and Co., General Importers (Dry Goods)

Moses Frank, Importer and Jobber
J. Seligman and Co., General Importer (Henry Seligman)
Louis Tichner, Merchant
John L. Woolf, Merchant
J. L. Lang, Merchant
Samuel Shonewasser, Merchant
I. E. Bloch, Merchant
David Abrams, Cap Maker
August Kline and Forchheimer, Hats
M. Cohen, (Cigars) Merchant
M. Mayblum, Importer (Cigars and Tobacco)
Charles Emanuel, Fancy Goods
G. Goodman, Broker and Commercial Merchant[19]

As in the Cincinnati case study, the lives of San Francisco founders reflected demographic patterns exhibited by Jews residing outside of America's northeastern urban areas. The San Francisco Jews were linked by age and ethnicity, as well as by occupational choices. Most were aspiring merchandising businessmen.

The founders of New Orleans' Temple Sinai also exhibited an economic profile similar to their coreligionists in the Cincinnati and San Francisco samples. In the New Orleans sample, only one (Max Dinkelspiel, an attorney) out of eighty-two identifiable occupations could not be directly categorized as a sizable commercial undertaking. As in Cincinnati and San Francisco, the most common occupations were twenty-seven clothing and/or dry goods wholesalers, retailers, and importers. Given New Orleans' centrality to the cotton trade in the South, second in frequency of businesses were twelve "cotton factors and commercial merchants." Other popular merchandising pursuits existed among temple founders: nine were wholesale and/or retail dealers in groceries and produce, seven general "commercial merchants," four boot and shoe dealers, four tobacco and cigar merchants, plus three each for merchandisers of crockery, hats, and notions. The remaining nine individuals included two jewelers, one importer of watches, a "broker," an "agent," a "harbormaster," a "metal goods dealer," a "photographic gallery owner," and a "druggist." Of particularly unique interest was the interstate nature of some of these wholesale and import businesses. At least twelve of Temple Sinai's founders were either partners and/or agents of firms with representatives permanently based in New York City. A thirteenth firm had ties to Boston. These firms included:

Meyer, Deutsch (NYC), and Weis, cotton factors and commercial merchants
E. Lehman (NYC), Neugass, and Co., cotton factors and commercial merchants

Loeb (NYC), Friedlander, and Co., importers and dealers in dry goods
Simon, Loeb, and Joseph (NYC), importers/dealers in dry goods
Roos and Frank (NYC), Co., clothing
L. Lehman (NYC), Beer and Co., wholesale dealers in foreign and domestic dry goods
Fischer (NYC) and Rose, importers wines, liquors and cigars, fruit and cheese
Jacobowsky (NYC), Hart, and Co., saddlery, harness, saddlery hardware wholesale
Joseph Magnes (agent), Guardian Mutual Life Insurance Co. of NYC
Louis Stern and Brother (Meyer Stern-Boston), auctioneers, commercial merchants[20]

Except for the Philadelphia case study then, the founders of these early Ashkenazic congregations primarily engaged in commerce, notably dry goods, on a large scale. They often expanded beyond retail endeavors into wholesale and even import trade, forming partnerships with relatives, friends, and occasionally business associates on the East Coast. Whereas the large immigrant Jewish population of mid-nineteenth-century Philadelphia included a wide spectrum of socioeconomic levels, the Jewish communities of other urban regions of the United States were homogeneously middle or upper class. German and other recent European Jewish immigrants who penetrated into the interior of the United States in this era did so because of more lucrative business opportunities. They did not venture into America's west simply to be peddlers or craftsmen. They relinquished the emotional security of residing in more populous Jewish areas in order to be in business for themselves. The same entrepreneurial spirit that led these individuals to initiate economic ventures also inspired their efforts to forge a new type of synagogue and to advocate a nationwide Jewish union.

Synagogue Life and Personnel

Religious Reform

Reformers within the Jewish communities of Central Europe adopted the aesthetics of Western culture and relinquished those of the East. To achieve Protestant standards of dignity and decorum, Reform Jews within Central Europe introduced a series of innovations. Notably, they adopted the use of the organ at synagogue services, along with a mixed (male and female) choir, prayers in the vernacular, the abbreviation of the Hebrew litany of Psalms, and the discarding of the traditional skullcap and prayer shawl. Traditional *davening* was replaced with solo, choir, or congregational singing with instrumental accompaniment, interspersed with readings in the vernacular by individuals, or with the participation of the congregants. To the neo-Orthodox in Germany, the Reformers' efforts were *hukkat hagoyim* (mimicry of the non-Jews), an abandonment of the Jewish tradition. Bitter strife was the result.[21]

Conflict and resulting synagogue splits and secessions emerged within American Jewish life as well. Initially modeling themselves after similar groups within Germany,[22] so-called Reform *vereinen* (societies) of German Jewish immigrants evolved into new congregations in mid-nineteenth-century America's East and Midwest. This process occurred at Baltimore's Har Sinai (1842), New York's Emanu-El (1845), Albany's Anshe Emeth (1850), Cincinnati's K.K. B'nai Yeshurun (1845) and Bene Israel (1855), and Chicago's Sinai (1861). The ideological justification of leniency in religious practice seemed an ideal match for the pragmatism of American life.

During the pre-Civil War years, ritual reforms slowly began to be introduced into American synagogue life. By the 1860s, liturgical liberalization was common. Among the four sample congregations, one from each geographical region of the country, the broad dispersion of this process is evident. At the opening of its new building in Cincinnati in 1865, KKBY installed family pews instead of traditional separate seating for men and women. In 1866, KKBY's Rabbi Isaac Mayer Wise initiated a late Friday evening Sabbath service to accommodate worshippers who had to work Saturday. In 1866, Keneseth Israel of Philadelphia prohibited men from wearing hats during the prayer services as was traditional, opting for the Protestant practice of remaining bareheaded. On 21 March 1869, the board of directors of KI eliminated congregational singing for the *kiddush* and the *kedushah* prayers. On 15 December of that year, in harmony with Christian patterns, KI ended altogether the chanting at services by the traditional *chazzan*. Singing and music would now be left entirely to the choir and organist.[23]

In San Francisco's Emanu-El, similar trends emerged. In 1861, the congregation introduced a late Friday evening service, mixed gender seating and the abolition of the *tallit* (prayer shawl) and hat at services. That same year, a public ceremony of "confirmation" for teenagers was linked to the holiday of Shavuot. (Confirmation was borrowed from the Christian life-cycle sequence and intended to replace the *bar mitzvah*.) Three years later, a new abridged prayerbook was approved that eliminated much of the Hebrew liturgy, adding readings in the vernacular (both German and English), and placed the modern rabbinic sermon at the center of public religious worship. In concert with Protestant practices of the era, women received equality with men in many religious obligations and practices.[24]

The pace of liturgical changes in American Jewish synagogue life accelerated. Some sixteen years later, Isaac Mayer Wise's *American Israelite* observed:

> Now among the three hundred American [Jewish] congregations, there are not fifty who adhere to what used to be called orthodoxy. With all the noise and pretensions from that quarter, they have organs and mixed [men and women] choirs . . . abridged rituals [of public prayer] without prayers for the bodily resurrection, the coming of the messiah, the returning to Palestine, and the restoration of bloody sacrifices; family pews for men and women, sermons and hymns in the vernacular.[25]

Pride in reform was evident in the opulence and magnificence of the buildings constructed in the mid-1860s by prominent American temples. In 1864, Keneseth Israel (Philadelphia) launched the "Moorish vogue in synagogue building in the United States," imitating the lavish style of the famous Temple in Kassel, Germany. That same year, Cincinnati's K.K. B'nai Yeshurun opened its new, Moorish-style "Temple" with both elegance and extravagance. Two years later, Emanu-El (San Francisco) completed its two massive bulbous domes. These golden globes loomed garishly atop its new and massive building reflecting the "general Oriental revival" of American architecture.[26]

In part, these imposing structures testified to the rapid pace of congregational membership growth. The facilities also indicated a desire to accommodate ancient Judaism to contemporary American life. The grandeur of these Moorish edifices was a statement of acculturation. It marked the effort to move from the neutral image of "congregation" to the more explicit concept of Reform "temple" previously reserved solely for *the Temple* in Jerusalem of old. Constructing a large and ornate "temple" was a public affirmation to non-Jewish society. It indicated the replacement of an ill-regarded foreign word "synagogue" with a word, "temple," that is well known and respected within Western Christendom. In the dedication sermon in 1866 at the opening of his congregation's new building, Rabbi Isaac Mayer Wise distinguished between the "perpetual mourning" of the synagogue and the "gladness" of worship within a "temple."

> Let happy hearts be united into one grand chorus, and worship the God of our fathers with solemn hymns and exulting psalms. . . . this is the object of our divine worship, the first object of this temple, and a leading principle of modern Israelites.[27]

As early as 1810 the use of the word "temple" had "become common in Germany due to its frequent use in France as a universal designation for a house of prayer, especially for those of non-Catholics.[28] By their choice of terminology, the members of these Reform congregations publicly repudiated the traditional Jewish hope for the messianic restoration of *the Temple* (of ancient times) in Jerusalem. In the process they projected civic loyalty: in the revised prayerbooks, the American Jew no longer prayed for his or her ultimate return to the land of Israel, but instead, as devoted citizens, regarded the United States as "Zion" and their local congregation as their "temple." Unlike the other three sample congregations, when Temple Sinai was established in New Orleans in 1870, it was created immediately as a Reform congregation and thus assumed the title "temple" as part of its original name.[29]

Increasing affluence and a desire for acceptance among America's Jews of the mid-nineteenth century made these ritual, architectural, and ideological changes widespread. To facilitate this process, congregational leaders sought a national body to publish prayer books, train reform-minded rabbis, and create a nationwide deliberative process regarding future adaptations. In the terminology approved by Isaac Leeser and Isaac Mayer Wise in 1848, American Jewry needed "a plan of union [for the synagogues of America].[30]

Modern Rabbinic Leadership

The premodern German rabbi had been the *rosh yeshivah* (head of the local academy of Jewish learning) and sometimes also a participant in the local *bet din* (rabbinic court). His coercive powers served to arbitrate disputes within the Jewish community. As part of the effort to prove Jewry worthy of "emancipation" (modern citizenship), Jews in Germany recast the rabbinate into the mold of the modern German Protestant ministry. Like his Lutheran and German Reformed counterparts, the German rabbi found his place within one specific congregation. Within the confines of the synagogue, the rabbi's charge was to portray Judaism in a modern idiom both for Jews and gentiles. His primary weapons for this formidable task were the congregational religious school for children and the modern sermon in the vernacular for adults. By according prominence to public preaching, congregations dramatically altered the focus of the traditional Jewish public prayer experience. This expanded sermonic role was traceable to trends within the world of German Protestantism.[31]

Accustomed to religious innovation within their native Germany (and France as well), German Jewish immigrants to the United States in the 1840s through 1870s arrived with revised conceptions both of the synagogue and of the rabbinate. Substantial changes were unachievable due to the pitiful lack of suitable American rabbis, particularly in the 1840s and 1850s. A few competent, self-taught Jewish religious leaders did appear on the scene before this time. Most noteworthy were Gerson Mendes Seixas and Isaac Leeser, in New York City's and Philadelphia's Sephardic congregations, respectively. The first formally trained rabbi in America, Abraham Rice, did not arrive until 1840.[32] Religious school teachers were almost equally scarce, as were cantors, *mohelim* (ritual circumcisors), and *shochtim* (ritual slaughterers of animals for kosher meat). Only the very largest mid-nineteenth-century American Jewish communities obtained the services of even partially or informally trained individuals.

For the young German Jewish merchants and "dealers" who settled in places like Cincinnati, New Orleans, and San Francisco, let alone more remote sections of America, random individuals who chanced upon the scene provided limited Jewish religious leadership. Most mid-nineteenth-century U.S. Jewish areas

were ministered to by a variety of functionaries, most of whom were completely incompetent as religious leaders and preachers. Innumerable "shochtim" and "hazanim" floated from one city to another, frequently acting as rabbis, sometimes going into business. . . . congregations were always advertising for rabbis, and nondescript functionaries were always seeking new positions. A typical notice of the period proclaimed, "Hazan wanted, a situation as Shochet, Hazan and teacher, and if necessary to act as Lecturer in the German language, being duly qualified for any of the above offices."[33]

An upgrading in the dismal quality of the American rabbinate occurred within the larger communities in the late 1840s, 1850s, and 1860s, when a first wave of formally trained Central European rabbis arrived in the United States. Among the four sample congregations, this group of more effective clergymen included Isaac Mayer Wise (K.K. B'nai Yeshurun in Cincinnati), Samuel Hirsch (Keneseth Israel in Philadelphia), Elkan Cohen (Emanu-El in San Francisco), and James Gutheim (Temple Sinai in New Orleans). Like modern Protestant-style rabbis within Germany, these leaders served a specific congregation. They acted as resident preacher, primary school teacher and superintendent, officiant at life-cycle functions, and communal representative of the local Jewish community. Their tasks harmonized with Central European Jewish trends. Their rabbinic role in the United States was not only shaped by events within the German states, but also by the status accorded to Protestant congregational ministers in American urban areas.

The center of communal religious affairs in nineteenth-century Prot-estantism had shifted from the community at large to the individual church. The American Christian clergyman like the Reform rabbi, became the employee of a specific local congregation whose trustees could hire, supervise, and if necessary fire their spiritual leader. No longer was he the religious spokesman for an entire community; instead, he became "one of several preachers from his own or other denominations . . . [serving] only his specific spiritual constituency."[34] The ability of the local church to attract or retain members become intertwined with the effectiveness of the pastor.

Lay leaders of religious institutions sought popular preachers to compete with weekend streetcar trips to parks, beaches, resorts, the theater, and sporting events. This growing range of material pleasures and cultural diversions was a by-product of urbanization and industrialization. Sunday (or Saturday for Jews) was no longer sacrosanct, set aside as "the Lord's Day." The preacher and his church had to compete in an open marketplace of enticements. Thus, the goal of sermons and public lectures by the clergy in the 1840s and beyond was to "market" religion effectively. People were less open to prayer and more prone to opt for recreational leisure-time activities such as public speaking.[35]

By the 1860s, the preaching of eloquent clerical orators became quite popular. Admired clergy served as speakers for general educational forums such as those conducted by the Lyceum and Chautauqua societies. "Because of his power in the pulpit, the preacher was not only in demand as a popular lecturer but was also regarded as an authority on a wide variety of subjects."[36] The preachers addressed a wide array of everyday problems. In the absence of opportunities for ongoing contact with other impressive orators, and with expensive prices charged by theaters, the weekly sermon in a church or a synagogue became an event of local importance. For many Americans, the sermon transcended the worship service itself, often attracting Jews and gentiles alike. Seeking to compete effectively in this arena, synagogue leaders longed for a national mechanism to provide eloquent American Jewish pulpit orators.

The American Synagogue Sermon

As Isaac Mayer Wise recalled toward the end of his life, until the arrival of Isaac Leeser in America in 1824, Jewish "preaching was done [in the United States] but exceptionally and only on certain occasions, and then it was not considered an integral part of the ritual." The first sermons accepted as legitimate parts of the Jewish prayer service were those of Isaac Leeser (beginning in 1829), as well as of Reverend Posnansky in Charleston, Reverend Braun in Baltimore and Dr. Merzbacher in Manhattan during the 1840s. Weekly preaching within an American synagogue did not take place until the ascendance of Rabbi Isaac Mayer Wise to his pulpit in Albany, New York, in 1846. The first English-language schedule of sermons by an American Jewish clergyman was by James Gutheim in Cincinnati in 1848. In 1850, Rabbi Wise added English orations to his growing repertoire, printing a "philosophical, dogmatic sermon [in English] on the theology of Moses." This highly publicized milestone "launched a new era of [American] Jewish preaching." Men like Leeser, Samuel Isaacs and, Henry Jacobs joined Gutheim, Wise, and other rabbis in alternating sermons in German and English every other Sabbath.[37]

Initially, rabbis followed strict German Jewish guidelines: They expounded upon moral or theological notions derived from verses within the weekly Torah portion. Nonetheless, the more informal approach of the American Christian pulpit quickly surfaced in Jewish settings. In his initial years as a congregational rabbi in Albany, Isaac Mayer Wise, for example, realized that Germanic "logical and rhetorical addresses were beyond the people and a special pulpit diction incomprehensible to them." He acknowledged that an American preacher had "to speak as though you are teaching, possibly an upper class (high school)." He "determined to do this. . . . I shall moralize, I shall thunder; it will do no harm. I had transformed myself completely [in style] into the American orator of that time."[38] Rabbis possessing a mastery of these Anglo-American sermonic techniques as yet were rare within Jewish life in the United States.

The arrival of Morris Raphall from England to New York City's B'nai Jeshurun congregation marked a dramatic moment in the history of the American rabbinate. Raphall was touted as "the foremost expounder of the Jews to the non-Jews in England." As part of its successful recruiting effort to bring this prominent English-language Jewish preacher to B'nai Jeshurun, the synagogue committed itself to a magnanimous annual salary of $2,000. This sum was eight times greater than the average rabbinic compensation of that time. Raphall quickly demonstrated his value, as "throngs of Christians and unaffiliated Jews came to hear him preach at his regular services."[39] The sermonic achievements of Rabbi Raphall marked a new plateau for the American rabbinate. Raphall's fame created even more pressure for a national system to train and to supply suitable Jewish clergymen.

Rabbinic Careers

The earliest group of rabbis who served our sample congregations were men who did not have a lasting impact upon their synagogues. Either they lacked stature, or their tenure of office was too brief. This pre-Raphall list of American Jewish clergy included (Philadelphia) Keneseth Israel's

Samuel Naumberg (1852–1856) and Solomon Deutsch (1856–1860); (Cincinnati) K.K. B'nai Yeshurun's H. A. Henry (1849–1851) and A. L. Rosenfeld (1851–1853); and (San Francisco) Emanu-El's Max Welholf (1851–1854). Among influential Jewish religious leaders of the Raphall genre whose presence could attract throngs of worshippers were David Einhorn (1861–1866) and Samuel Hirsch (1866–1885) of Keneseth Israel in Philadelphia; James K. Gutheim of K.K. B'nai Yeshurun in Cincinnati (1846–1849) and Temple Sinai in New Orleans (1872–1884); Isaac Mayer Wise (1854–1900) of K.K. B'nai Yeshurun in Cincinnati; and Julius Eckman (1854–1856) and Elkan Cohn (1860–1889) of Emanu-El in San Francisco.

Like their constituents, these men hailed from Central European countries: Hirsch and Cohen were from Prussia, Gutheim was born and raised in Westphalia, and Wise emigrated from Bohemia. Prussian-born Hirsch and Cohen had gained private *smicha* (ordination) as well as doctorates from German universities (Hirsch at Leipzig, Cohen at Berlin). Gutheim, in contrast, was largely self-taught. Wise's partial ordination and university "credential" remain the subject of historical speculation.[40] Both Hirsch and Cohen served as full delegates to some proceedings at the German (Reform) Rabbinical Conferences in the mid-1840s. All four Jewish religious leaders came to America well aware of the issues dividing German Jewry about the nature of the rabbinate and of synagogue practices.

Morris Raphall was recruited away from his English pulpit by New York City's B'nai Jeshurun. Similarly, two of the four rabbis engaged by the sample congregations were recruited from abroad. They were in demand because of their rabbinic reputation as orators, scholars, and religious leaders. Upwardly mobile Jews and Christians wanted ministers and rabbis whose stature reflected their mounting aspirations. It "became increasingly important to have a minister [or rabbi] of high social standing. . . . [Therefore] Episcopalians and others frequently [enticed them to leave lesser congregations or] imported them from Europe."[41] Cincinnati's K. K. B'nai Yeshurun sought Isaac M. Wise, who had already served effectively in Albany, New York (1846–1854). Emanu-El of San Francisco pursued Elkan Cohn, who had occupied a pulpit in Germany and then followed Wise to Albany (1854–1860). Temple Sinai of New Orleans recruited James Gutheim, who served in Cincinnati (1846–1849), in New Orleans (1849–1868), and as "Associate Rabbi" of Emanu-El of New York City (1868–1872). Keneseth Israel of Philadelphia engaged Samuel Hirsch, the Chief Rabbi of Luxembourg from 1843 to 1866. Like Rabbi Raphall and prominent Protestant clergy of the time, these four men impressed their prospective future lay leaders. They were married, family-oriented clergymen, suitable to be leaders and role models for their emerging communities. They were also potential "princes of the pulpit." In contrast to the uniformly youthful ages of their laity, these rabbinic leaders assumed their positions at the four sample congregations at the diverse ages of thirty-five (Wise), forty (Cohen), fifty-one (Hirsch), and fifty-five (Gutheim).

Recruiting a Rabbi

An attractive rabbinic presence was critical to persuading prospective members to affiliate with a mid-nineteenth-century synagogue. Competition was fierce for the limited number of desirable candidates. One common technique for locating a rabbi was to place advertisements in Rabbi Ludwig Philipson's *Allgemeine Zeitung des Judentums* in Germany and in Isaac Mayer Wise's *American Israelite*. Notices also appeared in other Jewish periodicals in Central Europe and in the United States. Interested parties would be screened by a cadre of respected rabbinic authorities. Screeners might include Rabbis Philipson or Leopold Stein in Germany or American religious leaders of long standing, such as Rabbis Wise and Gutheim.[42] Negotiations began in earnest once serious candidates emerged either through this screening process or through similar recommendations.

In 1854, for instance, at San Francisco's Emanu-El, congregation President Henry Seligman set out to engage the services of a suitable English-speaking rabbi. As Emanu-El's chronicler Fred Rosenbaum recorded:

it was [Isaac Mayer] Wise's friend and like-minded colleague . . . James Gutheim . . . whom Seligman invited to assume the Emanu-El pulpit; however Gutheim had been serving the Jewish community of New Orleans for several years, and chose to remain at his post. For the Emanu-El pulpit . . . [Gutheim then] suggested Dr. Steinberg, his former classmate at the seminary of Muenster . . . but he too declined to come. Steinberg was aware that another German rabbi, already in America, was much interested in the Emanu-El position, and he felt it undignified to compete with him. . . . That was the scholarly Julius Eckman who became San Francisco's first congregational rabbi [in 1854].[43]

Once a synagogue decided to hire a specific individual, laymen faced a dual challenge. They had to reach an accord with the preferred candidate, plus secure a release from existing contractual obligations to his current congregation. Recognizing the scarcity of American Jewish preachers able to lecture in both German and English, Jewish religious leaders bargained for substantial concessions. In 1854, Isaac Mayer Wise obtained a lifelong contract, exemption from the ordeal of a trial sermon, and a six-month period of grace to allow the rabbi to "mull over" this major decision.[44]

Similarly in 1870, the officers of Temple Sinai in New Orleans had been in active communication with James G. Gutheim during the arduous months of forming a new synagogue. Having already served a different New Orleans synagogue effectively from 1849–1868 (save for a three-year exile to Alabama during the Civil War), Gutheim was a known and coveted religious leader. He was willing to be coaxed into abandoning his "associate rabbi" position in Manhattan to return to the adulation that he had enjoyed in the Crescent City. Delays in these negotiations involved details regarding salary as well as Gutheim's insistence upon being hired on a long-term basis premised "upon good behavior." Gutheim also requested "a stipulation in the contract that either party to the contract may give six months notice to vacate the office."[45] Specific information regarding the recruitment of Samuel Hirsch by Keneseth Israel and Elkan Cohen by Emanu-El of San Francisco is not available. Their fine reputations as pulpit orators made these two men widely respected by colleagues and deserving of similarly accommodating conditions of recruitment.

Given the shortage of effective preachers for the growing number of American synagogues, the retention of a rabbi remained a challenging task. In 1854, Isaac Mayer Wise's Albany temple tried to ward off overtures made to him by Cincinnati's K.K. B'nai Yeshurun. So, too, in 1858 did a Louisville synagogue unsuccessfully seek to lure Rabbi Wise away from the Queen City. Comforting words by his Cincinnati lay leaders as well as a $600 pay raise dissuaded Wise from accepting the Louisville offer. More dramatic was the short-lived success of New York City's Anshe Chesed in 1873 in gaining Wise's verbal assent to relocate permanently to the East Coast. K.K. B'nai Yeshurun thwarted this agreement with a series of emergency general congregation meetings and a negotiating team that dealt directly with Rabbi Wise. Ultimately, general persuasiveness sweetened by a $2,000 pay increase changed Wise's decision. The episode resulted in an official declaration by the congregation's board of trustees:

We hold that as no congregation has a right to remove from office for a trivial cause a rabbi who had faithfully and conscientiously performed his duties, so no rabbi, except for the promotion of a great principle, has a right to leave his congregation as long as it unanimously claims his services, insists upon his continuation in office for life and provides properly for him and his family.[46]

A similarly impassioned expression of loyalty to a rabbi was a proclamation by gentile leaders in New Orleans in 1868 who urged James Gutheim not to accept the associate rabbi position offered to him by New York City's Emanu-El:

We regard your removal from us not merely an irreparable loss to your church and people, but a calamity to this city and state, as we cannot afford at this time such men as you. We must sincerely hope, therefore, that some satisfactory arrangement may be made for your remaining permanently among us.[47]

Rabbinic Salaries

Like Rabbi Morris Raphall, each of the four key rabbis in the sample received generous salaries reflecting high status and desirability to their communities. Hired in Albany in 1846 for $250 per year, Isaac Mayer Wise was offered a $1,500 salary as an enticement to come to Cincinnati in 1854. Rabbi Wise's compensation mounted to $4,000 by 1873, and grew to $6,000 the following year to ward off the recruiting efforts of Manhattan's Anshe Chesed. James Gutheim's willingness to return from New York City to his former community of New Orleans in 1872 as part of the effort to launch Temple Sinai as a new congregation was rewarded by a $6,000 salary. Samuel Hirsch's initial agreement with Keneseth Israel of Philadelphia in 1866 included a $3,000 compensation plus a $2,500 guaranteed annual income upon disability or retirement. Already in the 1850s, San Francisco's Emanu-El founders committed themselves to an allocation of $3,500 for their rabbi. These salaries compared very favorably to skilled craftsmen, doctors, and lawyers and to salaried professionals in this era, whose income rarely exceeded $1,000 annually. Plus, in each of the four cases, the rabbis received generous fringe benefits, notably free housing in a "parsonage" (synagogue-owned or -rented facility).[48] Rabbinic compensation continued to improve. Twelve years prior to the end of the century, the *American Israelite* boastfully reflected:

A quarter of a century ago and even now in many places he (the rabbi) was the ill-paid servant of a congregation which was ruled over by a few dominant spirits, to whom he was forced to bow and paid court if he wished to retain his position. . . . The poor Rabbi, who was generally from some small town in Poland, Hungary or Bavaria, ignorant of the customs of this country, burdened with a family and serving a people who were prejudiced against him for his place of birth, had a really hard time of it . . . half contemptuous pity being usually his best reward, and one year his usual term of office. . . . But what a wonderful change has taken place. . . . Today the rabbi of even mediocre ability can command a position of from 2 to $3000 a year and upward . . . [respected as] a member of one of the learned professions.[49]

The value of an effective rabbi to the vitality of a local congregation became widely acknowledged. The challenge, particularly for Jewish leaders in America, was the shortage of satisfactory candidates. While churches grew rapidly due to an abundant supply of ministers and missionaries, synagogues in all but the most desirable locations suffered without adequate rabbinic leadership. As Isaac Leeser complained as early as the 1840s:

> it requires no great experience to convince anyone, that among the English-speaking Jews at least, including England and her dependencies, no less than the United States of North America, there is hardly such an institution as a Jewish ministry.
>
> Where are the preachers who are to be the leaders of the people? Where the ecclesiastical chiefs who are to instruct?
>
> What does anyone think would be the fate of Protestant Christianity without the constant appeal to the fear and reason of its professors from the ten thousand pulpits which scatter information and admonition many times during every week? Who does not discover in the army of religious orators, a most powerful arm for the upholding of any system?[50]

Adequate training and dispersing of congregational rabbis was a critical need which marked another basic reason why American Jewry sought to organize itself on a national scale.

The Education of Children

Day School Format

In the mid-nineteenth century, full-day religious education was provided by some American Christian groups. Roman Catholics, "who were immigrating to the United States in large numbers before the Civil War, realized that they could not change the Protestant atmosphere of the public schools . . . so they established parochial schools." Day schools also were attempted by the Lutheran denominations, as well as by some Presbyterians, motivated by the secularization of public education.[51] The formation of Jewish day schools was motivated in part by similar concerns regarding Protestant missionizing. In 1843, Isaac Leeser warned that "we are in great error if we suppose that Christian teachers do not endeavor to influence actively the sentiments of their Jewish pupils."[52]

KKBY's Talmud Yelodim Institute (TYI), established in 1849, set a goal of teaching the entire range of subjects offered in Cincinnati's burgeoning public school system. In addition, TYI included Hebrew and German materials appropriate to Jewish religious training. TYI conducted its classes Monday through Friday, using Saturday afternoon for additional

Jewish subjects. The program targeted children from ages six through twelve. The affairs of TYI were conducted by its own board of education as well as a slate of officers elected by KKBY's annual meeting.

With the appointment of Isaac Mayer Wise in 1854 as KKBY's rabbi and TYI's first "superintendent," substantial responsibility shifted from lay leaders into his hands. Nevertheless, Rabbi Wise's educational efforts remained under the ultimate jurisdiction of the TYI Board. For example, when complaints surfaced at the KKBY Annual Meeting of 1857 accusing Wise of neglecting his school responsibilities, the TYI Board imparted this concern directly to Rabbi Wise. In spite of his subordinate status, Wise retained the authority to arrange classes, to establish the placement of students, to choose teachers, and to alter the curriculum. As "superintendent," Rabbi Wise submitted monthly reports to TYI board of education meetings and attended when called upon.[53]

Within a few years of assuming his position, Isaac Mayer Wise extended TYI's range of instruction. He added a supplementary program for children aged twelve through fifteen who were attending full-day public secondary schools. This upper-level Talmud Torah offered two hours of instruction each Saturday and Sunday, with two additional sessions during the week. The new program limited its scope to "Jewish religion, Hebrew literature and additional tools for 'higher Jewish learning.'" Wise's dream was to develop TYI's adolescent division into a preparatory program for an anticipated Jewish college.[54]

The full-day TYI program maintained high academic standards. It followed the customary American educational pattern of annual public examinations. As with most schools of that era, discipline remained an ongoing concern. The goal was to train respectful American citizens. Full or partial scholarships became available to deserving indigent or orphaned children through a "special fund assessed to all KKBY members, from tuition and from special donations, occasionally supplemented by bank loans." The school's secular studies teachers were generally of high caliber and received comparatively attractive salaries, ranging between $500 and $1,000. Rabbi Wise and a few knowledgeable laypersons attended to the Jewish instruction. The absence of qualified teachers of Judaism was a problem even for the best-situated and most affluent of congregations, let alone for synagogues with less funds and scattered within America's vast interior.[55]

The mid-nineteenth-century Jewish day school in Cincinnati and elsewhere was doomed by the emergence of improved public school systems. Public schools eliminated the more offensive trappings of Protestant sectarianism, notably New Testament scripture readings, moralizing, and the fervent observance of Christian holidays. As early as 1857, the minutes of TYI's board of education reveal Rabbi Wise's recommendation of shifting the entire program to weekends, given the precipitous decline in TYI's enrollment. With the administrative disruptions and patriotic fervor generated by the Civil War, day schools of all faiths declined. Tax-supported public schools became favored training grounds for American civic pride. Despite considerable reluctance among the laity of KKBY, TYI became a supplementary "religious school" in 1867.[56] Pleased with this affirmation of the goal of Americanization, Rabbi Wise reflected:

It is our settled opinion here that the education of the young is the business of the State, and the religious instruction, to which we add the Hebrew, is the duty of the religious bodies. Neither ought to interfere with the other. The secular branches belong to the public schools, religion in the Sabbath schools exclusively.[57]

The abandonment of congregational day schools created a pattern of diluted religious education for Jewish children reared within the United States. Not until nearly a century later did some middle- and upper-middle-class American Jews reconsider full-day school Jewish education for their sons and daughters.

Supplementary Synagogue Schools

The idea of a Jewish education in American life supplementary to and separated from secular studies programs was originally derived from the Old World *cheder*. In Europe the *cheder* was the domain of the *melamed*. He had some Judaic knowledge and often little if any experience in or aptitude for elementary education. Memories of excessive discipline and of smashed knuckles ingrained in the minds of Jewish immigrants to America a need for a better Jewish education for their children. For those American Jews unwilling to commit their offspring to a full-day Jewish school environment, a United States version of the *cheder* would not then suffice. Moreover, neighboring Christian churches had led the way through the development of the so-called Sunday school. By linking Sunday schools to local church membership, Christian education also contributed to increased rates of affiliation among young Christian families.[58] Jewish leaders were envious of Christian successes. They began to view the Sabbath school as a possible solution for their own membership recruitment problems, and for their efforts to "save" the Jewish children of the community from the overtures of Christianity.

In 1838, Rebecca Gratz established the first Jewish Sunday school in the United States in Philadelphia, the home base for the national Christian Sunday school movement. Miss Gratz's speech on the eve of the school's opening admitted: "We have never had a Sunday school in our congregation [Philadelphia's Mikveh Israel] and so I have induced our ladies to follow the example of other [Protestant] religious communities."[59] Lacking satisfactory Jewish instructional materials in the English language for the first few years, Gratz's school "was forced to use at least one of the Christian Sunday school textbooks." Rebecca Gratz's successful efforts led to the establishment of similar schools in Charleston, Savannah, New York, and Richmond. Gratz's Sunday school was organized on a community-wide basis. Her program was open to any Jewish child, and not limited merely to sons and daughters of those affiliated with a congregation.[60]

In the era from 1850 to 1870, supplementary schools arose within many Jewish congregations. By the 1860s, for instance, Emanu-El of San Francisco sent out a brochure marketing its supplementary school program. As with KKBY's TYI in Cincinnati, Emanu-El's rabbi served as superintendent. He administered to the ongoing functions of the school, addressed the student body at least once a month on some "religious or moral topic," maintained a registry of enrollment and absenteeism, and conducted teachers' meetings minimally once every two months.[61]

Likewise, in Philadelphia's Keneseth Israel, the role of the post-Civil War rabbi had become so pervasive within the supplementary synagogue school that "the School Board was not allowed to make decisions without him [the Rabbi] being present, and should it happen that they . . . [did] not come to an agreement . . . [the issue was to] be brought before the Board of Directors [of the entire Congregation] and the decision . . . [was] theirs."[62] Teachers were constantly reminded of their duty to comply with the rabbis' directives. The superintendent periodically addressed the restricted KI Board meetings when important school matters had to be discussed.

Although dependent on meager textbooks and limited facilities, supplementary synagogue school curricula spanned the gamut of Judaic studies. Subjects included Hebrew reading, translation of the prayers and Bible history, and religious instruction in the Protestant-like "catechisms" (lists of standardized Jewish "beliefs"). At San Francisco's Emanu-El, classes extended Saturday from 2:00 P.M. until 4:00 P.M., on Sundays from 10:00 A.M. until noon, as well as additional hours during the week for students requiring assistance in Hebrew reading. Eligibility for Sunday classes was linked to the fulfillment of required attendance at a number of Saturday morning services.

As with the full-day Jewish schools, strict rules for discipline and against excessive absenteeism dominated the policies of the synagogue *Talmud Torah*. In Emanu-El, for instance, teachers had a moral duty "to practice such discipline" as would be applied by "a kind, firm, judicious parent," while scrupulously avoiding *cheder*-like corporal punishment and "all appearance of indiscreet haste in the discipline of their pupils."[63] Ultimate authority rested in the hands of the rabbi. Penalties included delayed dismissals and expulsion. Punishment could be applied not only for misconduct, but also for repeated unexcused absences or tardiness, disorderly conduct in the processions organized for entering or dismissal from classrooms and, especially, for damage inflicted upon school property. Disregard for American civic standards of behavior, characteristic of the *cheder*, were no longer to be tolerated. Instead, children were to learn the full gamut of Jewish studies, reared in harmony with prevailing U.S. standards for good citizenship. The graduates of these synagogue supplementary schools were groomed to excel as Americans and as Jews.

In both the Jewish day school and in the synagogue supplementary program, the educational success of the undertaking depended upon staffing and materials. The scarcity of congregational rabbis to serve as superintendents of the programs was a nationwide problem. In addition, the lack of satisfactory faculty remained a perennial drawback. The absence of suitable textbooks and curricula sabotaged many ambitious congregational school initiatives. American Jewry needed to emulate their Christian neighbors by addressing these concerns on a national basis.

Conclusion

As antebellum synagogues competed within America's "free market place of souls," they encountered a U.S. citizenry facing a new series of choices. Should they or should they not join a house of worship or remain unchurched and seek fulfillment elsewhere? If they chose to become members, should they align with Protestantism, Catholicism, or Judaism? Within these larger religious communities, which denomination was their preference? In confronting the reality of such "voluntas" (free will), synagogues had to compete for members with secular clubs as well as with Christian missionaries. Each rival realm offered a potent challenge to temple leaders.

The Young Men's Christian (YMCA) and Young Mens' Hebrew Associations (YMHA) plus fraternal lodges, such as the Free Masons, the Odd Fellows, and B'nai Brith, provided stiff competition. In the 1840s, B'nai Brith lodge membership, for example, "conferred a sense of community on men seeking roots in an alien environment. It gave them a psychological shelter, a buffer for their self-respect that was constantly threatened by the harsh reality they encountered in America."[64] The lodges provided a "secular synagogue," a sense of belonging and of mutual assistance, yet one devoid of theological or liturgical commitments.

The Society for Ameliorating the Condition of the Jews, established in 1820 as a focal point for Protestant proselytizing, also challenged local Jewish congregations by engaging in aggressive outreach to rootless Jews.[65] Christian missionaries sought to recruit vulnerable persons isolated either within America's hinterland, in impersonal urban areas, or within conditions of dependency and deviance, such as orphans, widows, the homeless, the insane, the blind, the deaf, the aged, and the ill. The Society also concentrated on Jewish children attending public schools or in public asylum. Within these exposed settings, zealous Christian missionaries baptized dying patients and other vulnerable persons who had no relatives to protect them. Protestant missionizing tracts, sermons, bible translations, newspapers, and itinerant preachers created an atmosphere of siege for American Jewry.

Faced with formidable rivals for the loyalties of Jewish immigrants, temple lay and rabbinic leaders were handicapped by the fragmentation of American Judaism in the mid-nineteenth century.

Duplication and overlapping abounded. Petty bickering and personal rivalries precluded effective cooperation. . . . Clubs and fraternal orders jealously guarded their territory, and barriers against fellow Jews who differed in cultural background or economic status were common. Even charities divided according to land of origin.[66]

Regardless of the institutional advances achieved by local temples in recruiting rabbinic orators, adding a synagogue school, and offering ritual reform, the limitations of localism were intolerable to an influential leadership group of rabbis and laity alike. They needed future rabbis and educators, school textbooks, and liturgical publications. To combat the bold initiatives of thriving lodges and Christian missionaries, the needs of local congregations created pressure for organizing American Judaism on a nationwide scale.

❖ 2 ❖

A National Religious Union:
The First Decade of the Union of
American Hebrew Congregations

In the era from 1840 to 1870, Christian congregations functioned in a fashion similar to the four sample synagogues. Churches offered their laity a sense of belonging, an accommodating religious ideology, a modernized ministry, and a church-based religious school. Like their Jewish neighbors, lay leaders in Protestant houses of worship clamored for assistance at the national level, to more adequately "missionize" the frontier. To achieve these goals on a nationwide scale, the American Protestant majority imported from Great Britain the organizational innovations associated with "denominationalism."

The word "denomination' implies that the group referred to is but one member of a larger group, called or denominated by a particular name. The basic contention of the denominational theory of the church is that the true church is not to be identified in any exclusive sense with any particular ecclesiastical institution. . . . No denomination claims to represent the whole church of Christ. No denomination claims that all other churches are false churches.[1]

Beyond its pluralistic nature, denominationalism provided an organizational framework that nineteenth-century American Methodists, Presbyterians, Episcopalians, Baptists, Congregationalists, Lutherans, Unitarians, and other Christian groups were quick to adopt. Each denomination created its own *national religious union*: "a voluntary association of like-hearted and like-minded individuals who [were] . . . united on the basis of common beliefs for the purpose of accomplishing tangible and definable objectives, in particular, propagation of its point of view."[2] These nationwide Protestant bodies were governed by congregational representatives. A national union offered a sense of belonging to a country-wide religious movement. The individual parishioner could gain a broad religious identity simply by joining a local affiliated church. For example, if a person became a member of a neighborhood Methodist congregation, by extension he automatically felt a part of American Methodism. Religious identification became portable. This portability was well suited to an era in which residents frequently moved from one area of economic opportunity into another.

By 1840, to be a bona fide American religious movement meant to be organized as a national religious union. The union's nationwide authority remained rooted in local churches, since it consisted of congregational representatives and offered each local church some degree of autonomy. In addition, the national union provided each congregation with a common liturgical, doctrinal, and hymnodal grammar, a standard for life and practice. That grammar allowed a Methodist for example, who moved to a new community to feel "at home" in the local Methodist church. The union also offered a network of auxiliary (missionary) societies, to persuade "the unchurched" to consider church membership.

To this end, each national religious union concentrated upon "practical projects" such as the production and distribution of printed materials. They each issued religious tracts for adults, inexpensive English-language Bible translations, curricula and materials for local church Sunday schools, and the weekly publication of national religious newspapers. Their affiliated colleges trained contemporary-style ministers and religious educators. Largely because of these organizational ventures, the percentage of church members among America's rapidly burgeoning population rose impressively from 6.9 percent in 1800 to 15.5 percent by 1850.[3] In absolute numbers, this increase involved growth by the hundreds of thousands. In 1848, an envious Isaac Leeser wrote in the pages of *The Occident* (his national Jewish newspaper):

Look at the Christian churches, who have all the advantages of numbers, wealth, organization, bishops, conventions, and whatever else needs to consolidate power and to encourage adhesion to popular creeds . . . their Boards of Foreign and Domestic Missions; their male and female missionaries and teachers . . . the large number of books, tracts and bibles. . . . Is it any wonder that they flourish?[4]

This was a period of time during which many Jews and Christians were reassessing their attitudes toward one another. "Christians often attended the many banquets and balls given by Jewish congregations and charities. . . . Some Christians even sent their children to Jewish day schools, because they were generally known for their high standards of education."[5] Given this growing affinity between American Jews and their neighbors, how did these American religious models for organizational life shape the effort to create a Union of (all) American Hebrew Congrega-

tions? In what ways were the terminology and programmatic objectives of
this Hebrew union initially similar to those of parallel Protestant unions in
the United States? What uniquely Jewish goals emerged as well? How did
these institutional ideas relate to the persistent clash between American-
izers such as Isaac M. Wise and Isaac Leeser with Germanophiles like
David Einhorn?

The Founding of the Union of American Hebrew Congregations (UAHC)

Early Advocates of Union

From 1840 to 1870, Isaac Leeser, Isaac Mayer Wise, and other Ameri-
canizers openly sought both to defend American Jews against Christian
missionizing and to co-opt what they regarded as the common features
proven successful among the American Protestant religious unions. Isaac
Leeser was born in Westphalia, Germany in 1806. An avid reader with a
flair for writing, Leeser had neither advanced training in secular studies
nor formal rabbinic training. Although Leeser mastered those unpunctu-
ated biblical selections reprinted in the *Occident*, and his correspondence
included some hebrew letters, apparently he did not rely primarily upon
traditional rabbinic commentaries. According to Isaac M. Wise, Leeser
explained to friends and colleagues that he "cared but little what different
[ancient and medieval] rabbis may have written, for his Judaism was laid
down [primarily] in the Bible, the prayerbook and general custom."[6]
Whether or not he actually possessed biases against classical Jewish texts,
as early as 1829 Isaac Leeser gained national prominence by introducing
preaching to the American Jewish pulpit.
  Like most German Jews who came to the United States before direct
overseas links between Central Europe and the United States began in the
1840s, Leeser's immigration to America included several months in
England. He arrived in the United States as a young adult, and went to the
home of his uncle and mentor, an Anglophile, Zalma Rehine in Richmond,
Virginia. Leeser's appointment in the late 1820s as the minister of
Philadelphia's Mikveh Israel, a Spanish-Portuguese synagogue, placed him
further within the British cultural orbit. For the next quarter of a century,
Isaac Leeser's model for synagogue practice was the Bevis Marks
Sephardic congregation in London. During his tenure at Mikveh Israel,
Leeser consistently sent doctrinal inquiries to the office of Britain's
Sephardic Chief Rabbi.[7] In 1841 (5th of Tebet 5601) for example, when
faced with the quandary of whether to allow an uncircumcised deceased
Jewish child to be buried in Mikvah Israel's cemetery, Isaac Leeser sent a

letter of inquiry to Reverend David Meldolo, rabbi of London's Bevis Marks congregation. The inquiry commenced with the phrase, "the station you occupy as the head of the Portuguese Jews of England encourages us to take the liberty of laying before you the following question." Ongoing correspondence between Leeser and Meldolo continued throughout the 1840s and into the following decade.[8] The institutional models of England became Isaac Leeser's primary point of organizational reference.

As an immigrant in search of acceptance by Americans, Leeser astutely observed that antebellum American organizations repeatedly borrowed English institutional models. British cultural dominance derived not only from the historical links created during the colonial era but also from British control of transatlantic trade, early nineteenth-century industrial technology, and the English-language world of print. Organizational concepts spread across the Atlantic Ocean through the numerous British journals that were imported or copied for distribution in the United States. Following the linkage of passenger boat travel between Liverpool and New York in 1816, British immigrants as well as American travelers to England reported their findings in the pages of American newspapers, novels, and nonfictional books. The influence of the British Isles was evident in the rise of American free public schools, penal institutions, the abolitionist movement, women's rights crusades, hospital reform and in the U.S. acceptance of national religious unions for its churches.[9] As Leeser concluded:

America is more allied to England than with any other country; there prevails between them an identity in the origin of the people and the laws; the language is the same in both, and the intercourse between them is daily becoming more rapid, certain and intimate. If this is undeniably the case in commercial and political relations, it is not the less so in religious concerns.[10]

Isaac Leeser advocated the institutional trappings held in common among America's diverse denominations as the organizational approaches suitable to Jewish religious life in the United States. He established the *Occident* as a unifying newspaper,[11] and projected himself to the public as if he were *the* "denominational" leader. He sought to publish religious tracts: a Jewish Bible translation that appeared in 1845 and anticipated volumes that might be produced by his call for an American Jewish Publication Society. Furthermore, Rabbi Leeser strove to develop materials for aiding Jewish Sabbath schools. Most importantly, in a fashion parallel to each Protestant denomination, Leeser championed the need for a Jewish college intended as a training institution for rabbis, teachers, and educated laity.

Isaac Leeser expressed keen interest in the progress of the American affiliate of the "Church of England," the Episcopalians. Both of Leeser's places of residence in the United States, Richmond and Philadelphia, boasted strong Episcopalian churches. In each community, Episcopalians constituted the "social and intellectual elite." In Leeser's private life, he had close ties with several Episcopal clergymen, especially Dr. Joseph Jacquett, an Episcopalian minister in Philadelphia, with whom Leeser coedited a *Biblia Hebraica* in 1848. Leeser's personal vision of a national American Jewish union articulated from 1841 through 1845, included a two-tiered Episcopal-style governance. An "ecclesiastical" council of clergy (rabbis and chazzanim) paralleled the "superior ecclesiastical" body of Episcopalianism's High Chamber of Bishops. Leeser's "lower" chamber of "deputies" (congregational lay and rabbinic delegates) correlated with the Episcopalian General Convention.

In an Episcopalian manner, Isaac Leeser advocated a "federative union" for Jewish congregations. Cooperation or conformity was required only for practical tasks, such as the improvement of religious education. As a federation, the union would not require assent from member congregations on either doctrine or liturgy. In 1845, Leeser wrote:

Let it be understood, once and for all, that a union of Israelites, does not take from any synagogue its independence; each community can retain its prayerbook, its mode of reasoning, of raising of revenue, and of internal government . . . a federative union.

[the "union"] shall not interfere directly or indirectly in the internal affairs of the congregations, except to offer their advice when anything should be undertaken in opposition to the law and the commandment, and to judge between contending parties . . . such should arise in our congregations.[12]

In the late 1840s, Leeser's interest in a national religious union brought him into contact with a valuable ally, Rabbi Isaac M. Wise. Rabbi Wise's sustained efforts ultimately brought this vision to fruition in the 1870s. Isaac M. Wise arrived in the United States in 1846 from Bohemia, then under Austrian rule. Thus, he escaped from the intense Jew-hatred and narrow economic options available to Jews within Central Europe. In appreciation of the tolerance of U.S. society and its abundant opportunities for employment, Wise became an advocate of Americanization and American religious organizational techniques. "The Jew must be Americanized," he wrote, "for every German book, every German word reminds [the Jew] . . . of the old disgrace [anti-Semitism]."[14]

Wise's frustration with the weakened condition of his native Bohemia instilled in him an intuitive appreciation for unity and organizational strength. Furthermore, as a Reform Jew, Rabbi Wise committed himself to the "mission" of "unifying" all humankind in accepting the liberal Jewish view of the worship of God. "To bring about this sublime unity [of all of mankind]," preached Isaac Mayer Wise, "God has selected the people of Israel from all the nations to be the bearers of divine truth, and to diffuse the bright light of religion among mankind." In the September 1847 edition of the German-Jewish journal *Allgemeine Zeitung des Judentums*, Wise wrote: "It is . . . desirable that only one school should exist, for 'Union' is the significant word to which the Western continent has given such an important meaning in world history."[15]

As an immigrant enamored of American culture, Wise was impressed by Isaac Leeser. Leeser was a clergyman who had successfully integrated into the predominantly Protestant civic life of the United States. The initial encounter between these two rabbis was both indirect and unintentional. Articulating his own concept of American Jewish "union," Wise delivered two English-language lectures on this topic to a small group of his Albany supporters in 1847. "Without asking Wise's consent," one of these supporters, "a certain Mr. Koschland," sent a printed text of these remarks to Leeser. Isaac Leeser was so pleased at the prospect of an ally in the pursuit of "union" that he published the address in his newspaper *Occident*. Within a few weeks, the two men met in person. As Wise later reflected, "in one-half hour we understood each other thoroughly . . . in a few hours we were very friendly." Wise commenced "exchanging letters with Isaac Leeser relative to a plan for the unification and elevation of American Jewry." Several months later, early in 1848, Leeser obtained Rabbi Wise's cosponsorship in a public call for "a gathering of the representatives of the congregations"[16] to plan a national Jewish union. Like Isaac Leeser's institutional dreams, the organizational vision of Wise had a specific Protestant referent. Its model was not the "High Church" Episcopalianism that appealed to Leeser; rather it was that of liberal Unitarianism.

Rabbi Wise's first pulpit was in Albany, New York, nestled within the cultural ambience of the Boston-based Unitarian church. Unitarianism was the most extreme version of tolerant, liberal Christianity within antebellum American culture. Its adherents were high-status and upper-class individuals who had cast aside ritual as well as Christian theological dogmas. They relied upon the ethical and social justice imperatives of biblical prophets for inspiration. The spread of Unitarianism in New England encouraged Rabbi Wise's hopes for the growth of Reform Judaism in the United States. In the mid-nineteenth century, "Reform Judaism and Unitarianism shared much in common. . . . a growing number of Reform Jewish and Unitarian intellectuals acknowledged each other's thinking and activities, resulting in . . . religious communication and social interaction between them."[17] In his *Reminiscences*, Isaac M. Wise recalled his memorable encounter with a kindred spirit, the liberal civic leader Daniel Webster:

I referred to Theodore Parker's conception of Unitarianism, and set over against this my conception of Judaism. This forced me to the conclusion that there was no essential difference in the matter of doctrine, but in historical development, which, however, did not enter into the question of doctrine. "It is well," said Webster . . . "You are indeed my co-religionist."[18]

Rabbi Wise's affinity to Unitarians can be traced to their public endorsements of his written rebuttals to Christian conversionists.[19] A further indication of this bond of collegiality was noted in Wise's letter to Isaac Leeser in August 1852. The Albany rabbi informed his Philadelphia colleague that since Isaac Leeser had refused to offer financial support for Wise's proposed weekly Jewish newspaper, Rabbi Wise planned "to make contact with a Mr. Bendurzne, who is a known publisher and a Unitarian and therefore willing to assist my enterprise." In the same letter, Rabbi Wise indicated that he was "promised 300 to 400 subscribers in Boston and the vicinity among [lay] Unitarians and the learned [Unitarian] clergy, which encourages me to run the risk." Significant to Wise's subsequent career, on 7 May 1852, his Unitarian friends on the East Coast organized their first Annual Conference of Western Unitarian Churches. This gathering advocated outreach to the unchurched, producing religious tracts, promoting Sunday school education, and establishing denominational colleges. The site chosen for this "opening up" of America's hinterland to their message was the "Queen City" of America's West, Cincinnati, to which Rabbi Wise would soon be beckoned.[20]

Given Rabbi Wise's close ties to the Unitarians, he rejected Leeser's two-tier version of unity based on the Episcopalian model of an ecclesiastical body plus a national congregation union. Rabbi Wise, like his liberal Protestant allies, wanted to eliminate ecclesiastical bodies composed solely of clergy. He advocated governance by an Annual Convention that would combine lay and ministerial congregational delegates. Isaac Mayer Wise sought to assign interim decisions to officers and a governing board.

Wise joined forces with Leeser in the quest to create a national Jewish union because of the convergence of one key element of Unitarian and Episcopal organizational strategy. Like the other American Protestant denominations, the national bodies governing both the Episcopalians and the Unitarians agreed to avoid doctrinal disputes among their own local affiliated churches. They did so in the interest of working in tandem to create denominational colleges, religious tracts, Bible translations, Sunday school materials, and other practical projects. So too, the neo-Orthodox Leeser and Reform Wise set aside ideological differences and worked together as advocates of a national religious union for the Jews in America.

The Wise-Leeser alliance nearly succeeded in its quest for union by calling for a conference in Cleveland during October 1855 for "the ministers and [lay] delegates of Israelitisch congregations." It failed, however, as a result of both ideological and sectional opposition. During the months immediately preceeding the conference, for example, neo-Othodox factions pressured three of the nine endorsing Jewish clergy to absent themselves from the proceedings. These traditionalists hoped to halt the spread of liberal Judaism in American life. The creation of German-style Reform *vereinen* (societies) within Baltimore's Har Sinai, New York City's Emanu-El, and other American synagogues had resulted in lingering feuds. Yet, even more disastrous to the Cleveland Conference's objectives was the sectional rivalry pitting Western rabbis such as Wise against East Coast religious leaders, notably the Reform-minded David Einhorn. "It depressed and discouraged me completely," wrote Rabbi Wise, "for without union among the reformers, who were the minority, no progressive measures could be hoped for."[21]

Rabbi David Einhorn had arrived in America only a brief period of time prior to the Cleveland Conference. He was born in rural Bavaria in Central Europe. Einhorn was a German-trained rabbi who also received German university tutelage in Würzburg and Munich. Einhorn was in every way deeply imbued with Germany and German culture.[22] He was a systematic reformer of Judaism, insisting upon harmonizing Jewish religion with modern scholarship and rational discourse. Furthermore, active participation in the well-publicized German Rabbinical Conferences of 1845 (Frankfurt) and 1846 (Breslau) shaped Einhorn's views regarding national Jewish gatherings.

In contrast to Wise and Leeser, the Germanophile David Einhorn opposed lay participation in nationwide Jewish conclaves. "Only men competent by their education, learning and knowledge can have a voice (in such lofty proceedings)." Rabbi Einhorn's opposition to lay involvement was a direct consequence of his disinterest in practical projects such as promoting membership among the unchurched. Within German Jewish life, deep-rooted communities possessed historic ties among their resident families. Unlike in the United States, nonaffiliation was not a major issue. For David Einhorn, the sole objectives worthy of assembling Jewish leadership were ideology, liturgy, and doctrine. In a clash with the pluralistic vision of American religious life, Einhorn insisted upon uniformity in belief and in practice. "In matters of religion, in things that concern the relations between man and his Creator, compromise [on theology or ritual] is out of the question."[23]

In addition, Einhorn rejected the Wise/Leeser aspiration for an American-style college. Einhorn insisted that the language and philosophical moorings of Reform Judaism had to be German. For David Einhorn and his allies, to be a rabbi meant to receive a combination of classic Jewish training plus philosophical instruction within the German university system. To Rabbi Einhorn, less than adequate tutelage in the application of scientific method to the religious treasures of Judaism meant primitive and unacceptable credentials. Such a view contrasted sharply with the vision of both Wise and Leeser. As Leeser wrote in 1844, American Jewry did not need German rabbis who "value the title of Doctor of Philosophy. They are Jewish philosophers, and we fear, not sufficiently embued with the true spirit to be safe guides to Israelites."[24]

Einhorn's relentless criticism of the American model of religious life reflected his scorn for the American culture from which it emanated. He derided the notions of persuasion, catering to popular appeal, prioritizing evangelism over creed, and emphasizing emotions over intellect. He criticized American church membership requirements that stipulated not adherence to a clear doctrine but a personal experience, a "conversion" through revivalism.[25] Moreover, Einhorn sensed that rigorous German culture, not American laxity, was intellectually more conducive to the long-term survival of commitment to religious reform. Einhorn surmised,

It takes little familiarity with the condition of American Jewish religious life to recognize that the English [Anglo-American] element under present circumstances, is a brake to Reform strivings. . . . [In contrast] German research and science are the heart of the Jewish Reform idea, and German Jewry has the mission to bring life and recognition to this thought on American soil.[26]

First in Baltimore, then Philadelphia, and ultimately Manhattan, Einhorn remained an implacable foe for Leeser and Wise and obstructed their efforts at union. David Einhorn's undermining of the Cleveland Conference embittered Isaac M. Wise. Wise lamented that "either all the little big-men must be sent to Salt Lake, and their schemes thrown overboard or there will, in a few years, be no more miserable place for Judaism than New York City."[27]

Following the sabotaging of the Cleveland-based effort at union, the next national venue for addressing the needs of American synagogues was the Board of Delegates of American Israelites, founded in 1859. The Board's founder was Rev. Samuel Isaacs, who was born in 1804 in Holland, where he remained until 1814 when the Isaacs family moved to England. During the next twenty-five years, the vibrant Jewish community of

London served as Samuel Isaacs's home and the formative environment for his ideology. Like Isaac Leeser and Isaac Mayer Wise, and in contrast to David Einhorn, Rev. Isaacs did not receive formal rabbinic training or certification. Nevertheless, in 1839 Isaacs accepted the call of New York City's oldest Ashkenazic congregation, B'nai Jeshurun, to become its "Preacher and Reader." Like Leeser's Mikveh Israel, B'nai Jeshurun had a tradition of domination by British Jews, and of turning to London for religious guidance. Isaacs later served as the rabbi of Manhattan's Shaaray Tefila, another British-oriented synagogue.

In response to the anti-Semitism accompanying the infamous Mortara Affair, the kidnapping and baptizing of a Jewish child in Bologna, Anglophile Samuel Isaacs emulated the British Board of Deputies in dispatching a letter to American President Buchanan requesting U.S. intervention. Disappointed by the White House's refusal to intervene, Rev. Isaacs and the board of trustees of Shaaray Tefila called for a meeting on 16 June 1859 to create an American version of the British defense organization. At this planning session, eight participating "moderate, traditional congregations" issued a general invitation to America's other synagogues to send representatives to a founding convention set for 27–29 November. The absence of liberal congregations reflected the difficulty of framing a "union" binding together diverse ideological elements. Although more reform-minded synagogues chose not to affiliate, the founding convention consciously selected a title and method of organization similar to the broad-based Board of Deputies of British Jews.[28]

The American Board of Delegates organized itself on the basis of congregational lay and rabbinic representation. With the survival of the Board of Delegates beyond the resolution of the Mortara crisis, Rev. Isaacs and other leaders sought to retain the loyalty of affiliated East Coast synagogues. To do so, they expanded the Board's functions, providing religious and educational support for local houses of worship. By the late 1860s, for example, the Board of Delegates succeeded in founding and maintaining a Jewish school of higher learning, Maimonides College. In addition, the Board launched an American Jewish publication society to produce tracts equivalent to those made available by Protestant groups.[29] Appreciative of these practical endeavors, more than fifty associations and congregations became members of the American Board.

Rev. Samuel Isaacs continued to champion the organizational approach represented by the Board of Delegates of American Israelites, an agency devoted to defending Jewish rights. Rabbi David Einhorn maintained his advocacy of a German-style rabbinic "Conference" as a solution for American Jewish doctrine and priorities. Following the death of Isaac Leeser in 1868, Rabbi Isaac M. Wise remained the primary advocate of an

American Protestant "union" strategy for Jewish life in the United States. Given three available and competing rabbi-inspired models for Jewish institutional activity offered by Wise, Einhorn, and Isaacs, influential lay leaders became impatient. Nevertheless, in 1871 a committee of rabbis using Wise's *Minhag America* approved a resolution to create a national congregational union. Aware of the futility of earlier unity ventures, in October 1872 pivotal members of Isaac M. Wise's KKBY, led by its President Moritz Loth, decided to add their support to this latest union initiative.

The forty-year-old German-born Loth was not only a successful businessman but also an intellectual and the author of novels. He was a founder of the Cincinnati Board of Trade that originated the Cincinnati Southern Railroad. He was a member of the Queen City's Committee on Transportation that raised funds to rebuild the Cincinnati Union Bethel Building.[30] In reflecting widespread approval for lay initiatives late in 1873 by Loth and his allies for a national Jewish congregational union, the 20 June 1873 edition of *The American Israelite* gloated:

Until now American Judaism has not been able to get over the effects of "great men's" [rabbis'] disputes and quarrels. . . . Are we [the laity] or are we not able to take care of our affairs without the lead of "great men"? If we are, let us do so in God's name. Let us shelve a few dozen of the "great men" till our affairs get settled, and then let them call again. In order to get over them, ambitious lay leaders . . . [must] act on their own.[31]

To avoid a confrontation with the like-minded Board of Delegates, Mr. Loth and his associates limited their geographical sights, seeking to attract only Southern and Midwestern congregations. Emulating prevailing trends within American Protestantism, the founders of the Union of American Hebrew Congregations (UAHC) determined to avoid local doctrinal disputes. The second and third "articles" of the UAHC Constitution stipulated that

[the UAHC] provide, sustain and manage such "practical" institutions which the common welfare and progress of Judaism shall require—*without however, interfering in any manner whatsoever with the affairs and management of any congregation* [emphasis added]. . . . (Article II)

Any [whether Reform or Orthodox] Hebrew congregation in the United States, lawfully organized, may become a member of the Union. (Article III)[32]

In Cincinnati, on 8 July 1873, Moritz Loth and his associates assembled lay and rabbinic delegates representing twenty-eight congregations as the constitutional convention of the Union of American Hebrew Congregations. The word "Union" implied a rejection of the Germanic approach espoused by Einhorn. Union was a neutral term in place of the definably Christian word "denomination." Union indicated an American national body of congregational clergy and lay representatives. Union meant setting aside differences in ritual or theology in order to unify all Jewish congregations in practical projects. Such projects would help the synagogues as voluntary associations to persuade unaffiliated Jews to become members.

Emulating Episcopalian, Unitarian, Methodist, and other American Protestant national religious unions implied creating a "union" college. Union also entailed providing aid for Sabbath schools, connecting more rabbis with isolated congregations in need, and creating a collective sense of being part of a nationwide religious entity. The word "American" in the title (Union of American Hebrew Congregations) symbolized the desire of constituent congregations and their members to be accepted as full-fledged Americans. "Hebrew" was the nineteenth century's most flattering parlance for referring to Jews. As Jonathan D. Sarna has observed, early American Jewish leaders, "hoped that modern 'Yahwists' . . . 'Hebrews,' or 'Israelites,' could be distinguished from (negatively regarded) premodern 'Jews,' and that stereotypes connected with the latter would not be applied to the former."[33]

The UAHC chose an Executive Board of twenty lay leaders. Four officers (President, Vice President, Treasurer, and Secretary) offered continuity between Board meetings. At the grass roots level, the supreme governing body of the Union was to be the "General Council," just as Methodists had their "General Conference," Episcopalians their "General Convention," and Presbyterians their "General Assembly." As with these Protestant national bodies, representation at annual UAHC Council sessions was determined on a basis similar to that of the two houses of the U.S. Congress. As in the United States Senate, each affiliated synagogue would automatically receive one delegate, just as each state sends two senators to Washington, D.C. In addition, the Union incorporated the proportional representation system of the House of Representatives. Congregations added another delegate for every twenty-five contributing members above an initial twenty-five.

The immediate success of the UAHC in capturing the loyalty of dozens of the new Midwestern and Southern congregations gained the attention of the Board of Delegates, an organization based along the Eastern seaboard. Due to the closing of Maimonides College and of several of its other educational projects, the Board's momentum had shifted from growth in affiliates to decline. In a last-ditch effort to reverse its deterioration, in 1875 a Committee on Reorganization considered a series of "practical" programs for recapturing its turf:

The Board shall, as soon as practicable, devise and carry out *a comprehensive and rational plan for the primary religious education of the Israelites on this continent* . . .

The Board shall, as soon as practicable, devise and carry out *a comprehensive and rational plan for the advanced religious education of the Israelites on this continent* [that is, a denominational college]. . . .

The Board shall, as soon as practicable, devise and carry out a just liberal method of supervising persons who are or may be desirous of becoming *Jewish ministers, to the end that only such as are competent intellectually, morally, and religiously, may be recognized as such.* . . .

The Board shall *publish* such of its proceedings as may be deemed advisable, and *also such matters, literary and religious, as may tend to promote the objects of its organization* [emphases added—A.S.].[34]

This reorganization plan failed to receive adequate support. Lacking other efforts to revive the vigor of the Board of Delegates of American Israelites, the organization continued its decline. By 1876, both the Board and the UAHC began to discuss a possible merger. As a first step, the Union agreed to collaborate with the Board of Delegates in the collecting and publication of all available statistics concerning the Jews of the United States. By the year's end, each organization appointed a delegation to attend a meeting in New York City designed to explore prospects for consolidation.[35] On 11 February 1877, the Manhattan meeting yielded a proposal calling for:

1. The Board of Delegates to cease its functions once the UAHC Constitution is changed to assume the defense of rights abroad and at home.
2. Three New York City-Philadelphia members be placed on the Executive Board of the UAHC.
3. Once enough Eastern congregations join the Union, to establish a New York based preparatory department of the Hebrew Union College [created in 1875 by the UAHC].[36]

By the time of the upcoming UAHC annual Council on 11 July 1877, these initial proposals had been refined, adding:

1. The UAHC Executive Board to consist of 30 members, 15 shall be from New England, New York, New Jersey, Delaware, Pennsylvania, Maryland, District of Columbia, Virginia and North Carolina.
2. The Executive Board shall be given all executive and administrative power . . . [with the annual] Council reduced to being merely legislative.
3. [All this] to be enacted as soon as [Eastern] congregations representing 2000 members and seat holders shall be obtained [as UAHC members].[37]

In 1878, the preconditions were carried out. A merger occurred between East and West. After nearly forty years of proposals, abortive efforts, and rabbinic rivalries, the UAHC achieved a nationwide union The lay leaders of the Union and the Board at last fulfilled the hopes of local synagogues across the land.

UAHC's Affiliated Membership

Even the more than 300 percent increase in the number of UAHC congregations, from 34 (1873) to 104 (1879) congregations encompassing the entire continent, does not tell the full extent of the growing influence of the UAHC. During those seven years of expansion, many other congregations affiliated for only a portion of the period. In total, some 120 Jewish houses of worship at one time or another affiliated with the Union during the 1870s. Also quite substantial was the growth in the number of members (families) paying dues represented by the affiliated temples in this initial era of UAHC membership growth.

Year	Currently affiliated congregations	Number of members
1874	56	—
1875	72	3,401
1876	81	3,776
1877	83	3,709
1878	86	3,870
1879	104	6,235

From 3,401 members paying dues associated with the Union in 1875, the number grew to 6,235 in 1870, and possibly as many as 7,500 for the entire group of 120 congregations involved at various times.[38] Because this was an era of substantial family size, it may be assumed that the 7,500 families represented close to 45,000 persons. This equals 20 percent of the estimated 230,000 Jews in the United States at that time.[39] In an era in which most Americans were not affiliated with either churches or synagogues, such as 20 percent figure at the national level represents a staggering achievement. It was a true American Jewish nationwide union for East, Midwest, South, and far West alike.

According to the data from the Board of Delegates' survey in 1877, 278 Jewish congregations existed throughout the United States. Of these, 52 (18 percent) were in New York State, 67 (24.1 percent) in other Eastern states, 69 (24.8 percent) in the Midwest, 74 (26.6 percent) in the South, and 16 (12 in California) equaling 5.8 percent in the far West.[40] A survey of each region indicates the remarkable inroads of the early UAHC. An example of impressive unanimity was that 50 of the 69 (72.5 percent) Midwestern Jewish congregations in existence in 1877 affiliated with the Union at some point in the nineteenth century. This was particularly true in Illinois (8 of 10), Iowa (all 3), Minnesota (the only one), Missouri (all 5), Nebraska (the sole congregation), and Ohio (17 of 24).

Equally extensive was the UAHC's success in the South. At one time or another during the last quarter of the nineteenth century, 50 of the 74 (67 percent) Dixie congregations extant in 1877 became members. Noteworthy achievements were in Alabama (6 of 8), Arkansas (all 4), Georgia (5 of 7), Kentucky (all 4), Mississippi (7 of 8), and West Virginia (both synagogues). In the far West, the sole Colorado and Nevada synagogues registered in the 1877 survey joined the UAHC at some point in this period, as did one of two Oregon Jewish congregations. One exception to this high percentage of affiliation among Jewish houses of worship with the fledgling Union occurred in isolated California, with 1 affiliate among 12 congregations. The other area of noninvolvement was the populous and ideologically fractious Northeast Coast. There, only 32 out of 119 (26.9 percent) recorded synagogues in 1877 ever became members of the Midwestern-initiated and controlled UAHC. The East's most noteworthy clusters of nonaffiliates included Massachusetts (1 affiliate out of 9), New Jersey (1 affiliate out of 8), New York (11 affiliates out of 52), and Maryland (3 affiliates out of 14).[41]

The Agenda of the UAHC

Goals of the UAHC

At the constitutional convention of 1873, the delegates made the focus of the Union practical goals, including the plan "to establish, sustain and govern a seat of learning for Jewish religion and literature; to provide for and advance the standards of Sabbath Schools; and to aid and encourage young congregations." At the first annual session of the General Council of delegates held in Cleveland, Ohio on 14 July 1874 President Loth sought to implement these aspirations. He created the Union's basic functional structure, assigning his Executive Board colleagues to several five-man standing committees: Theological Institute, Publications, Finance, Correspondence, and Reports of the Congregations. In addition, the President appointed two special committees, one on Sabbath schools and the other on circuit preaching. Loth charged the Sabbath School Committee with entering "upon correspondence with prominent teachers and directors" to collect information about current educational practices. The objective was the "improvement and unification" of America's Jewish Sabbath schools, in the same fashion as Protestant nationwide groups.[42]

The Special Committee on Circuit Preaching hoped to emulate the successes that the Methodists had displayed in their early, pioneering years as a national body. Like the Methodists, the Union arranged and financed circuit rabbis for isolated congregations, "attending to their religious needs as well as speaking to them about joining the UAHC and sending financial aid to the Theological Institute's 'Sinking Fund.'"[43] President Loth supplemented these initial seven committees at several points in the 1870s during annual Council gatherings. Additional committees arose for the Hebrew Union College (HUC) founded in 1875, the HUC Board of Governors, HUC Curriculum Committee, HUC Examiners, and a Committee on College Buildings and Grounds. Two committees also emerged that were not present within American Protestant institutional structures for reasons that will be discussed later in this chapter. These two unique groups were the Committee for Agricultural Pursuits and the Committee on Civil and Religious Rights, which took up the original task of the Board of Delegates. The priorities of the UAHC in its formative years can be appreciated through an examination of the roles of the following committees: Circuit Preaching, Sabbath Schools, Agricultural Pursuits, Civil and Religious Rights, and the Hebrew Union College.

Circuit Preaching

As early as 1871, discussions commenced regarding Jewish circuit preaching. Among the goals stated at the UAHC's founding 1873 convention was to "aid and encourage young congregations," most directly with circuit rabbis. This tactic was reintroduced on the American religious scene in the 1860s on many fronts. It appeared in the form of Church Extension Societies of Methodists, Baptists, and Congregationalists in the Midwestern and Southern frontiers,[44] and was also addressed by Moritz Loth and his colleagues. In its earlier formulation, "circuit riders" were the primary vehicle for the meteoric rise of American Methodism from a fledgling denomination in the 1780s to America's largest Protestant religious movement by the 1850s.

[early American Methodism] was equipped with a highly mobile ministry of traveling preachers who covered a vast territory instead of being rooted in a single locality. The more intimate nurture of the flocks they gathered was provided by local lay preachers and class leaders. No system could have been more admirably designed for moving quickly into new territory . . .[45]

A Committee on Circuit Preaching was one of only two special (project) committees created by the first annual UAHC Council in 1874. Such haste demonstrated the sense of urgency in adopting this Methodist idea. President Loth charged the Committee on Circuit Preaching with "attending to the spiritual wants of those scattered co-religionists and small congregations located all over the broad land, who by reason of isolation or want of means are deprived of religious encouragement; through properly qualified ministers." To carry out this ambitious charge, the five UAHC Executive Board members who comprised the Committee adopted a three-pronged strategy:

1. Frequent appeals should be directed to every Israelite in the land, particularly to such as live away from the influence of congregations, trying to arouse them to the importance of forming or joining Jewish societies or congregations, and as such, join and contribute to the Union, and by that enable it to work on behalf of the cause.

2. Empower the Executive Board to engage competent ministers to [volunteer to] give sermons [only reimbursing traveling expenses] and that such [ministers] also speak on behalf of Union and procure subscriptions to aid a Theological Seminary.

3. Encourage small congregations to band together and hire one rabbi for an area under auspices of Union [if a congregation cannot afford even this limited funding, the Union should subsidize].[46]

These general plans remained dormant, however, until 25 May 1877. At that time, the Committee on Circuit Preaching submitted a complete list of guidelines and received formal acceptance of these initiatives at the July annual council. The delegates incorporated the guidelines as official "Bylaws on Circuit Preaching," appended to the UAHC Constitution.[47]

Despite carefully articulated objectives and the subsequent call to isolated American Jews to respond, hinterland Jewish communities were unresponsive. President Loth had the unpleasant task of informing both the fifth and sixth annual Councils (1878 and 1879) that not a single Jewish community had issued a request for circuit preaching. Consequently, at the 1879 gathering, the Executive Board "deemed the establishment of circuits and employment of circuit preachers inopportune at the present time."[48] Undaunted by this pessimistic conclusion, the Special Committee on Circuit Preaching urged the General Council to exercise its authority to override the Executive Board's recommendation.

The Circuit Committee advocated the continuation of efforts to implement the program. To bolster their argument, members cited the related success of rabbis like Rabbi Messing (San Francisco) and Rabbi Blum (Galveston) in "arousing the dormant religious sentiment of contiguous communities." Furthermore, they pointed out that twenty-three rabbis had already agreed to serve in this project. To revive this struggling system, the Circuit Committee advocated that a maximum of $1,000 annually be allocated for circuit work by rabbis and teachers. They pleaded for servicing regions neglected by volunteers via a rabbi hired by the

Union to "visit communities . . . organize religious schools, stimulate the formation of congregations and secure their cooperation with the Union."[49] The plenum accepted the appeal of the Circuit Committee.

The vision of circuit preaching and outreach to congregations remained a practical goal of the Union. Nevertheless, viability was impeded by dramatic differences between the early Methodist circuit riders and the reality of the late-nineteenth-century American rabbinate. During its heyday, the cadre of circuit riders committed to Methodism included primarily "young men, unmarried, hardy, unshackled." They neither expected nor were promised any formal "salary." They packed and departed to their destination within minutes. They willingly ventured into areas totally devoid of organized Methodist religious life. Moreover, they did not require extensive formal training in sacred texts in order to be credentialed as a preacher, and thus were available in large numbers.[50]

In contrast, rabbis, like Protestant pulpit ministers of the 1870s, usually were married men with complex family responsibilities and an elaborate array of personal belongings. A sudden transfer to a new location required time and considerable effort. In addition, rabbis feared entry into hinterland communities devoid of synagogues. They agonized over possible anti-Semitism and despaired the absence of a critical mass of local Jews. Furthermore, rabbinic certification involved elaborate mastery of Hebraic literature. Thus, American rabbis were few in number, most frequently engaged by well-established synagogues, and unlikely to embark upon the itinerant life of the circuit rider.

Sabbath Schools

Perhaps the most universally accepted goal of all mid-nineteenth-century efforts to form Christian or Jewish national religious unions was the improvement of the quality of children's Sabbath schools. The religious education of children had been a prime focus of Jewish life for centuries. At the constitutional convention of the UAHC in 1873, the delegates dedicated themselves "to provide for and advance the standards of Sabbath Schools." The organizational model that paralleled religious school initiatives by the nascent Hebrew Union was the Protestant transdenominational American Sunday School Union (ASSU), launched in 1824, "to publish moral and religious works for children."[51] Similar to the American Bible Society and American Tract Society organized during that same decade, the ASSU was

initially founded as a confederation or consolidation of local, state and regional denominational efforts. . . . [It] devoted a good deal of energy to coordinating activities. . . . [Its leadership derived] from an alliance of well-to-do land-owners and businessmen, politicians and statesmen . . . reknowned clerics, upwardly mobile young men of affairs, and energetic women who found in the societies an alternative or complement to domesticity and schoolteaching.[52]

The ASSU concentrated on the publication of suitable materials, such as textbooks. It established networks of local women's Sabbath school auxiliaries to visit homes, sell subscriptions, collect funds, and serve as direct representatives to the general public.

In 1830, the American Sunday School Union resolved to "within two years, establish a Sunday School in every destitute place where it is practicable, throughout the valley (Midwest and South) of the (entire) Mississippi." Included in this ambitious vision was "a full-fledged program of teacher training to create a nation-wide Sunday School system literally ex nihilo." ASSU leaders were tireless. Men such as Stephen Paxton personally started over a thousand ASSU-sponsored Sunday schools. These leaders "vividly displayed every aspect of boosterism in education, [with] their interests and efforts spilling into every manner of organizational and instructional activity." By 1830, the ASSU had issued over six million copies of school books deemed worthy for the religious education of the young. Like the American Tract Society (ATS), the American Sunday School Union's publications were designed as systems of reading instruction. The ATS and the ASSU issued primers and other publications graded in linguistic and substantive difficulty like the popular McGuffey series of public education. The goals of these materials were to build "character" and "faith" for the youngsters involved, and to create "wholesome" Sunday school library collections throughout the localities of America.[53] During the next five decades, the profound achievements of the ASSU became well known to Christians and Jews alike.

With such a "practical" model for success in mind, the founders of the UAHC embarked upon a similar program. Along with the Committee on Circuit Preaching, at the very first Annual Council of the Union, President Loth appointed a Special Committee on Sabbath Schools in 1874. The initial task assigned to this five-man committee (Rabbis S. Wolfenstein, H. Mack, M. Halle, I. Reinthal, and M. Hirschberg) consisted of contacting teachers and religious school superintendents throughout the country. They were to deliver their findings to the Council. Their report was to assess the viability of a union approach (such as the ASSU) for America's synagogue schools. In this questionnaire, the Sabbath School Committee sought to ascertain:

1. The studies to be introduced in each Sabbath School
2. The time to be devoted weekly to each respective study in each class.

3. The existing English [language] text-books for these studies and their lowest price for the use of schools.

4. Where the necessity of text-books exists and how to be obtained best and cheapest.[54]

At this first Council session, the Sabbath School Committee also tried to generate added enthusiasm for their effort. They offered a prize of $100 for the best textbook to be written in biblical through post-biblical history and in "catechism."[55]

The following year, at the second Annual Council in 1875, the Sabbath School Committee made public the results of its survey of seventy religious schools of affiliated congregations. From among the twenty-six responding superintendents and/or head teachers, a clear curricular preference emerged:

1. Hebrew in all classes from the first elements of reading to the translating of portions of the Bible, and of Hebrew prayers, connected with instruction in Hebrew grammar.

2. Biblical history in all the lower grades.

3. Post-Biblical history in all the higher grades.

4. Catechism in all the classes preparing for confirmation and in confirmation class.

5. Singing, especially of religious songs.[56]

Based upon this survey, the Committee's report concluded that "the greater part of the time should be dedicated to Hebrew and the remainder equally divided among the other studies." The Sabbath School Committee also took note of the wide variation and poor quality of textbooks. History texts were almost unavailable. "Catechism" and Hebrew books abounded, but with no uniformity of use. "Most common were Dr. Szold's *Catechism* (30 cents), Dr. Szold's *Urim Vetumim* (40 cents), and Dr. Wise's *Judaism* ($4.50 per dozen). As for Hebrew texts, most schools used Mannheimer's *Mefalles Nossif* (60 cents) and Dr. Felsenthal's *Grammar* (50 cents)."[57]

In 1876, at the third Annual Council of the UAHC, the Sabbath School Committee took its first affirmative step beyond the collecting of data via the survey. They awarded prizes to Rabbi S. Deutch's (Hartford, CT) *Biblical History* and Rabbi Cassel's *Post-Biblical History* (in German). They hoped that the two books would become the standard educational tools for teaching these school subjects. Committee member Rabbi Sonneschein of St. Louis recommended that all Union-affiliated schools utilize the Mannheimer Hebrew text. This recommendation had the dual purpose of uniformity and of preparing some Sabbath school graduates ultimately to enter the Hebrew Union College. The UAHC also made available inexpensive editions of the Leeser English-language Jewish translation of

the Bible. Nevertheless, more dramatic progress by the Sabbath School
Committee was stymied during the following seven years of general
American economic chaos. Finally, in 1883, the Union of American
Hebrew Congregations granted permission to create a full-fledged He-
brew Sabbath School Union to emulate the successes of the Protestant
ASSU.[58]

Agricultural Pursuits

Being an American national religious union meant not only pursuing
broad practical goals that every group held in common; it also mandated
addressing the unique needs of one's own constituents. One of two
uniquely Jewish goals of the UAHC (the other being defense against
anti-Semitism) was addressed when President Loth appointed a Committee on Agricultural Pursuits. Several background factors motivated this
unique Jewish interest in working on the farms. As far back as the 1780s,
the debate in both Germany and France regarding the validity of granting
citizenship to Jewish residents centered upon Jewish work patterns.
Friends and foes alike, advocates of Jewish "Emancipation" like Christian
Dohm in Germany or anti-Semites like Voltaire in France, pointed to the
seemingly "age-old addiction [of Jews] to trade and other occupations
depending on the investment of money—especially usury."[59] In both
Central/Western and Eastern Europe, many Jewish leaders internalized
this critique. They acknowledged the necessity of moving coreligionists
out of merchandising and hoped to disperse young Jewish men and women
throughout the economic sectors of their host societies. Joining the liberal
advocates of Emancipation, Jewish spokesmen claimed that these goals
could be achieved by granting citizenship to the Jews. They assumed that
civic equality would make it more comfortable for Jews to live and work
among the Christian majority and to abandon Jewish residential ghettos
and Jewish occupational habits.

As the Emancipation debate intensified, by the 1820s "enlightened"
Jewish intellectuals (*maskilim*) actively sought to expose the European
Jewish masses to a world beyond "the 'heder' and the marketstall." *Maskil*
educators hoped that modern approaches to training the young could help
the next generation to abandon "unwholesome" activities such as peddling
and liquor dealing, and move into large-scale commerce, manual (produc-
tive) labor, and perhaps even into agriculture. As Isaac Baer Levinsohn
proclaimed, the Jew needs "a program of practical improvements for
Jewish life: secular education and a 'wholesome' vocational diversification
in manual labor and agriculture."[60]

In particular, there was concern for the negative image created by impoverished Jews clustering in second-hand merchandising, living off the meager profits of bartering the goods and produce created by others. This distress intensified with the movement of European Jews into Central and Western Europe, a battleground in the struggles for Jewish political equality. In the 1840s, for example, when German and Polish Jews moved with ever greater frequency into England, the resident Jewish population feared that low-status, foreign-looking coreligionists might jeopardize hard-fought civic rights victories. Consequently, "a Circular Letter issued in 1849, by Anglo-Jewish leaders asked the German Jews to restrict their immigration to England. . . . British [Jewish] philanthropic agencies sought to steer as many clients [who did arrive] as possible toward America."[61]

American Jewish leaders experienced similar social pressures. They too feared that the undesirable image associated with Russian and Polish Jewish newcomers would reflect negatively upon them. Since American Jews could not steer new arrivals on to other countries, they searched for alternative solutions. Like the Anglo-Jewish communal spokesmen, the Board of Delegates of American Israelites privately sought to stem the flood of Jewish immigration. In 1878, the Board sent delegates to an international Jewish conference in Paris and sounded a warning against indiscriminate Jewish migrations. Already in the late 1840s, Anglophile Jewish leaders in the United States, like Isaac Leeser, borrowed from British Jews the idea of dispersing their brethren into Jewish agricultural colonies. In the 1860s and 1870s, tensions mounted between settled German Jews and arriving Eastern European Jewish immigrants. To move impoverished newcomers out of their crowded urban points of entry, teeming with vice, cramped housing, and exploitation, seemed a praiseworthy goal.[62] Agriculture was a hotly debated topic among Jewish leaders at this time. Many of them believed that steering Jewish immigrants into farming would yield a more normal distribution of occupations and thereby demonstrate Eastern European Jewish suitability for America.

The Board of Delegates of American Israelites, along with B'nai Brith and the New York branch of the French-based Alliance Israelite Universelle, initiated related discussions in the early 1870s. At the UAHC's second Annual Council in 1875, President Loth launched a similar proposal. Moritz Loth sought to "call upon [poor, Eastern European Jewish] parents to direct their children into mechanical trades or into agriculture, rather than merchandising." Loth deemed these occupations to be too "hazardous" for Jews. Accordingly, he appointed the Union's third Special Committee to deal with "Agricultural Pursuits." Several years of investigation and private negotiations with the Board of Delegates resulted in the 1878–1879 merger agreement. A blended Committee reported its statement of purpose to the 1879 Annual Council. "We assert that true emancipation of the Jews consists in the greater infusion of the spirit of manhood and self-definition, which can best be done by encouraging the large masses of Israelites dwelling in Eastern and Southern Europe to become farmers, agriculturalists and mechanics."[63]

President Loth called upon the new Special Committee on Agricultural Pursuits to "take into consideration the feasibility and practicability of an active cooperation with sister societies in Europe . . . to encourage agriculture among Jews and the settlement in this country of such as are willing and able to devote themselves to that pursuit on the lands of the [American] West and the South, and to try to acquire land for such purpose."[64] In 1881, for instance, the Committee on Agricultural Pursuits worked in tandem with the Manhattan branch of the Alliance Israelite Universelle. They jointly contacted the Governor of Louisiana to obtain 160 acres of fertile ground for 173 Russian Jews interested in the offer. However, a series of calamities sabotaged this venture: the weather was excessively hot; a malaria epidemic ensued; the Mississippi River flooded the land; and the Jewish farmers longed for their wives and families. The effort ended in failure. Nonetheless, agricultural projects remained a goal of the UAHC and leaders like Rabbi Wise.[65]

Civil and Religious Rights

Part of the merger agreement of the UAHC and the Board of Delegates of American Israelites included the willingness of the Union to continue to pursue the Board's role as a Jewish "defense agency." The leadership fulfilled this promise via a new UAHC Committee on Civil and Religious Rights. This work had originated on the East Coast in proximity to the nation's capital, the center of the American political process. Consequently, the Committee on Civil and Religious Rights retained an East Coast profile in its membership. Of the fifty-four men who served as committee members from 1879 through 1898, twelve were from New York, the site of the defunct Board of Delegates. Of the others, fourteen hailed from nearby Eastern states, in particular, Pennsylvania (six) and Washington, DC (four). Most (eighteen) of the remaining twenty-eight individuals came from the Midwest, with only a token representation accorded to the South (eight) and the Pacific Coast region (two).[66] The Committee's mandate was:

to keep a watchful eye on occurrences at home and abroad, concerning the civil and religious rights of Israelites, and to call attention of the proper authorities to the fact, should any violation of such rights occur, and to keep up communication with similar central Israelite bodies throughout the globe [Board of Deputies of

British Israelites, the French Alliance Israelite Universelle and the German Deutsch-Israelitischer Gemeindebund].[67]

The dramatic outpouring of American Jewish concern during the anti-Semitic 1840 Damascus Affair and in response to the 1858 Mortara Case created important precedents. The former inspired Isaac Leeser's first call for union, and the latter brought into being the Board of Delegates of American Israelites. Even after the merger of the Board and the Union in 1877 and 1878, concern for anti-Semitism in the United States and in foreign countries remained paramount to American Jews. This concern created an ongoing desire for collective representation of grievances to American officials in Washington, DC.[68]

At this time, Jewish defense agencies (that is, British, French, German, or American) primarily worried about the threat to Jewish rights posed by persecution of the Jews within czarist Russia. With an office based in the District of Columbia, the Union's Committee on Civil and Religious Rights year after year urged the State Department of the United States to act. The Committee wanted the United States to apply pressure upon the oppressive czarist regime. Specifically, the Committee warned that continued anti-Semitic violence might damage trade and diplomatic relations between the two countries. The Committee also called the attention of the American government to the severe restrictions placed upon U.S. Jewish businessmen and tourists traveling inside Russia.

Other countries whose persecution of Jewish populations drew the constant scrutiny of the Committee included Morocco and Romania. In Tangiers, Fez, and neighboring cities, riots and oppressive legislation constantly aroused Jewish anxiety. In Bucharest, Jews protested Romania's refusal to honor its commitment to grant naturalized citizenship to its Jewish residents, as stipulated in the 1878 Treaty of Berlin. With regard to both Morocco and Romania, the Committee on Civil and Religious Rights remained in continual contact with the American Secretary of State and the U.S. Consuls in Tangiers and Bucharest. The Committee advocated the application of American diplomatic pressure to reduce anti-Jewish problems inside these nations.[69]

Within American society, the Committee on Civil and Religious Rights pursued domestic grievances, as did the British Board of Deputies, the French Alliance Israelite Universelle, and the German Gemeindebund for their own domains. The UAHC's Committee, for instance, battled against so-called American "Blue Laws" (Sunday compulsory work-stoppage regulations) and attempts to establish Christian religious dogma as part of the U.S. Constitution. Moreover, the Committee sought to aid the arrival, absorption, and settlement throughout the United States of Eastern European Jewish immigrants.[70]

Recognizing the advanced strategies of British and French Jewish agencies in this regard, the UAHC's Committee on Civil and Religious Rights established local fund-raising societies that contributed dollars to the growing costs of elaborate defense of Jewish rights efforts by the Anglo-American Jewish Association and the French Alliance Israelite Universelle.[71] The UAHC's role as a defense agency remained significant to the wider needs of American Jewish life. Yet this commitment reflected a necessary concession to the former Board of Delegates more than it did a true UAHC priority. It represented a clear departure from the pattern of services provided by American Protestant national bodies. The subsequent lack of adequate funding, however, as well as the growth of social anti-Semitism (for example, the aftermath of the Seligman-Hilton affair) frustrated the UAHC's defense efforts.

The Hebrew Union College

Hebrew Union College

The founding of a college for American Jews must be viewed in the context of similar efforts among European Jews and of American Protestant efforts in self-preservation through higher education. The successes of each of the early-nineteenth-century Protestant denominations in the United States depended on their creation of dozens of colleges throughout the country. Denominational colleges trained ministers, religious educators, and doctrinally knowledgeable laity. On the American Jewish scene, Isaac Leeser's efforts at union from 1841 to 1845 had centered on his desire to establish a Jewish school of higher learning. Similarly, within two years of his arrival in the United States in 1846, Isaac Mayer Wise began to agitate for an "educational establishment of a higher order to train up men who will be able to defend our cause, to expound our law, to inspire our friends, to silence our enemies, and to convert our opponents."[72] In 1854, from his new home in Cincinnati, Rabbi Wise articulated his plan for a Jewish college. First, Wise established Zion College Associations (to raise funds and support) in Cincinnati, Louisville, Cleveland, Baltimore, Philadelphia, and Manhattan. He then founded Zion College the following year in Cincinnati, in tandem with preparation for the Cleveland Rabbinical Conference of 1855.

The Zion College experiment revealed another strong cultural influence upon I. M. Wise at this early juncture of his career in America, that of the German university system. Wise's concept of a Zion College related to his awareness of the German states' development of a civil bureaucracy, their adaptation of Roman law, and their need for a corps of officials armed with university training. Middle-class and even well-to-do Germans contemplated a university education for their offspring. The rise to prominence of Hegel, Kant, and other intellectual giants of university-based German philosophy and *Wissenschaft* (intense, scientific quest for objectivity and evidence in scholarship) fostered a dramatic impression upon the clergy.[73] Many prominent ministers and rabbis graduated from these university programs.

In the early 1850s, Germany's first modern Rabbinical Seminary created by Zecharias Frankel tried to emulate the university-related German training of contemporary Protestant ministers. With German university and German Rabbinical Seminary models in mind, Rabbi Wise sought to create a hybrid. He wanted an American Jewish college emulating the successes of American Protestants. He planned to structure this college, however, "on the pattern of German universities . . . with a theological seminary [for rabbis-to-be] and a seminary for teachers" as well as the capacity to train an educated laity. He envisioned four distinct faculties ("classical, scientific, practical, and the arts") within this comprehensive "Jewish university" environment, providing Judaica as well as high-quality secular studies.[74] However, the rancor that followed the Cleveland Conference and Wise's subsequent inability to find adequate funding to survive the economic downturn of 1857 doomed Zion College.

Most subsequent initiatives to create an American Jewish school of higher learning would be based upon the Protestant "union" college model then paramount in mid-nineteenth-century U.S. collegiate education. By the time of the Civil War, for example, approximately two hundred "union" (denominational) colleges existed in a society that had contained only nine institutions of higher learning in 1769. Inspired by a second period of religious awakening and revivalism in the second quarter of the 1800s, Presbyterians, Methodists, Baptists, Congregationalists, and other Christian groups established outposts in America's growing frontiers. In the decades from 1830 to 1860, in Wise's Ohio alone, the following impressive list of colleges associated with specific Protestant groups survived the frantic pace of institutional boosterism:

Franklin (Presbyterian); Western Reserve (Congregational); Kenyon (Episcopal); Denison (Baptist); Oberlin (Congregational); Marietta (Congregational); Muskingum (United Presbyterian); Ohio Wesleyan (Methodist); Mount Union (Methodist); Baldwin (Methodist); Wittenberg (Lutheran); St. Xavier (Roman Catholic); Otterbein (United Brethren); Heidelberg (Reformed); Urbana (Swedenborgian); Antioch (Christian); Hiram (Disciples).[75]

As late as 1855, a sample of some forty thousand graduates of denominational college indicated that 25 percent had become ministers. Many others initially had entered college with the intention of pursuing the ministerial vocation. Even America's most prestigious and earliest college, Harvard, revealed similar goals in its initial period. Harvard's original logo, for instance, included the phrase "to advance learning and perpetuate it to posterity, dreading to leave an illiterate minister to the churches when our present [European trained] ministers shall die in the Dust."[76]

Some German Reform leaders, following the ideology of David Einhorn and his allies, tried to go against the tide. They advocated a German-style Jewish school. They established the ill-fated Manhattan-based Emanu-El Theological Seminary Association in 1865. The Association received the blessing of America's largest synagogue, the German Reform Temple Emanu-El in New York City. Nevertheless, the narrow base of support for the Association led to its decline and doom within several years, along with its fledgling Seminary.[77]

Parallel to this abortive Germanic effort was the Anglo-American experiment launched by the Board of Delegates of American Israelites and labeled Maimonides College. Maimonides College benefited by appealing to all ideological sectors of American Jewry. It extended its influence beyond New York City, creating an endowment fund and gaining the support of the substantial group of congregations that comprised the Board of Delegates. Unlike Zion College's grandiose emulation of the comprehensive German university system, Maimonides College limited its destiny to being a college "dedicated to the cause of Judaism and truth." It compared itself, not to the universities of Munich or Berlin, but to "the early days of Yale and Harvard, [which] struggled on from humble beginnings." As a locale, Maimonides College's founder chose Philadelphia in order to gain the devoted leadership of Maimonides College's first President, Isaac Leeser. The City of Brotherly Love also had the advantage of a large and supportive Jewish population, which combined with "convenient access to excellent libraries [and the facilities for attending the undergraduate courses of the University of Pennsylvania]."[78]

At first, this well-conceived project appealed to the pragmatic Isaac Mayer Wise. However, Maimonides College failed to gain adequate congregational support, in terms of both funds and students. By 1869, Rabbi Wise again turned attention toward creating his own institution. He imitated the limited successes of Maimonides College, and tried to avoid the pitfalls experienced by it and by Zion College and the Emanu-El Theological Seminary Association. Wise sought to establish an endowment fund and congregational fiscal support (via a union) in advance. Wise strove to retain pragmatic and simple American Union college goals rather than multifaceted German university aspirations. His goal was a "union" college that accommodated the full range of ideological and geographical sectors within U.S. Jewry.

At the U.S. Rabbinical Conferences of 1869 through 1872, Rabbi Isaac Mayer Wise remained steadfast in his advocacy of an American Jewish college. The pragmatic breakthrough in making possible this dream was the offer by one of Wise's members, Henry Adler of Lawrenceberg, Indiana, in 1870 to give $10,000 in trust to his rabbi for the establishment and support of a rabbinical college. "A sense of urgency was not created until Adler spelled out his terms in February of 1873, including the proviso that if the seminary should not be established within three years, then the gift would revert to the donor."[79] With such an incentive, the constitutional convention of the UAHC in 1873 listed as their "primary object," the charge "to establish, sustain and govern a seat of learning for Jewish religion and literature."[80]

The proposed college was not to be launched until at least $60,000 accrued in the "Sinking Fund." By the 1875 second Annual UAHC Council, fear of losing the Adler gift forced the hand of the delegates. Although barely $5,000 had been collected beyond Adler's contribution, the UAHC decided to proceed. The Union's leadership assumed that excitement accompanying the opening of a rabbinical school would motivate philanthropic individuals to contribute the remainder of the funds. This optimistic strategy proved accurate. Within months of the opening exercises in the Fall of 1875, generous donations from the Jews of Cincinnati and other areas of the country brought the "Sinking Fund" to $64,000.[81] The UAHC had established a "Hebrew Union College." Like other colleges of that era that were sponsored by a national religious body, the HUC would remain

under the close supervision of its parent organization; it was not even incorporated as a separate institution. . . . The Councils of the Union elected the entire [HUC] Board of Governors, which was obliged to present reports and proposed budgets to the Union for approval. Fund-raising and investment of assets were entirely the function of the Union, which was also the owner of the College property.[82]

As a location for HUC, Wise selected his home city of Cincinnati. The Queen City of the West was at the crossroads of the traditional trade flowing through the Mississippi and Ohio River valleys. Cincinnati's dominance in the Midwest would soon be challenged by rising "Lake Cities," notably, Chicago, with its emerging massive railroad and industrial connections. Nonetheless, in the mid-1870s, the Queen City still dominated the region. Wise's home city possessed the educational resources for a college. It had a fine public school system. It had its own nonsectarian University of Cincinnati, established in 1873.[83] Ready and willing academic resources would be crucial for a small, struggling Jewish college aspiring to train rabbis in accord with contemporary standards.

Moreover, Cincinnati was the home of the officers and primary financial supporters of the UAHC and its HUC. This group included HUC's Board of Governors' long-term President Bernhard Bettmann (from 1875 to 1910) and Vice-President Julius Freiberg (from 1875 to 1905). Mr. Bettman was a successful clothier and an active member of Wise's KKBY. Mr. Freiberg was a wealthy distiller and a member of sister congregation KKBI, also of Cincinnati. Both men had established distinguished reputations in philanthropic circles. They fulfilled the responsibilities implied by the so-called "stewardship of wealth," supporting the general and Jewish charitable agencies of the Queen City. Cincinnati congregations, first the Mound Street Temple (1875–1877) and then KKBY (1878–1881), were eager to serve as host locations for the school until a permanent site was found (1881). Finally, and most decisively, Cincinnati was the home of Isaac Meyer Wise, qualified and anxious to serve as College President.[84]

Presidents of religious colleges were pivotal to the successes of antebellum Protestant institutions of higher learning. In the pre-Civil War period, when Rabbi Wise gained his introduction into American life and culture, Clergymen served as presidents of almost every college in the United States. Even in the post-Civil War era, this pattern continued in direct contrast to the practice at newly emerging universities, such as Cornell (1864), Clark, and Johns Hopkins. In those cases, the trustees hired a new breed of professional administrators, for example, Andrew D. White, G. Stanley Hall, and Daniel C. Gilman. In the old-style college, "the president . . . was . . . the dominating influence . . . the greatest single force in college life."[85]

In a similar fashion, HUC President I. M. Wise acted as fund-raiser, faculty member, superintendent, but most of all overseer of the moral welfare of the predominantly indigent students under his charge.[86] The president of a college sponsored by a nationwide religious body occupied a "paternal" role. He was a symbolic "father to an entire student body." It was like "a large family, sleeping, eating, studying and worshiping together." In addition, "each student from outside the city had one member of the board [of governors] who was declared his legal guardian during his stay at the College. The faculty, the president and especially the board exercised a parental role toward the students." Rabbi James G. Heller later recollected that "every year his [President Wise's] 'boys' gathered about him, celebrated his birthday with him, and regarded him as a 'venerable sage, a wise counselor, a kind father.' His home and table were always open to them."[87]

The role of the president in shaping the moral character of his charges led to responsibility for discipline, both within the college and the university settings. As President Martin B. Anderson of the University of Rochester remarked in 1868, "no class passes through my hands that does not contain more or less young men who are on the eve of ruin from wayward natures, bad habits or hereditary tendencies to evil. These men must be watched, born with, and if possible saved to the world and to their families."[88] A major share of President Wise's duties included the imposition of strict rules of behavior upon the classes of entering students. Wise issued reprimands and dismissals for unexcused absenteeism, tardiness, misconduct, and any evidence of defacing the college's educational materials or physical facilities.[89] For potential rabbis and teachers who could be role models to America's new Jewish citizens, outlandish behavior had no place.

Similar to other college presidents, some of Wise's other requisite administrative tasks included the teaching of at least one upper-level class each semester. He also convened and chaired faculty meetings, invited guest lecturers to address the student body and provided assurance to the HUC lay Board of Governors (under UAHC auspices) regarding the implementation of the College's curriculum and regulations. In addition, President Wise's informal duties involved constant journeys on behalf of the college. He tried to increase subscriptions to the various endowment funds and sought prospective students and suitable, although affordable, faculty. For such purposes, Wise used personal appearances, correspondence, editorials in his weekly, the *American Israelite*, and advertisements in other Jewish newspapers throughout both America and Europe. Isaac Mayer Wise also assumed the official role of the director of student job placement. He tried to match candidates with congregations, keeping in mind the overall needs of the growing UAHC.[90] Even a long-standing rival, Rabbi Bernard Felsenthal, acknowledged that by 1883 Wise was the undisputed leader of the American Jewish national religious union:

Dr. Wise is now the head of the College not only, but of all Israel in the United States. It is he who educates the rabbis for America. It is he who defines the course in which Judaism in this country has to run. It is he who gives shape and color and character to our Jewish affairs. He is the central sun, around which the planets . . . are moving, some near to him, some more distant.[91]

As for other faculty, the initial staff of HUC was composed of dedicated clergymen, like most old-time colleges. They accepted the meager compensation allotted to them by Boards of Governors, constrained by severely limited financial resources. In this era, most colleges, did not have major benefactors, endowments, or bequests. They relied upon "Christian expressions of charity" and on broad-based campaigns for modest-level "subscribers" or supporters. Such an approach by the UAHC and its member congregations initially yielded barely enough capital to finance the minimum requirements for survival.

Through 1878, the entire faculty of the Hebrew Union College consisted of unsalaried Rabbis Wise of KKBY and Max Lilienthal of KKBI, plus one full-time salaried instructor, Solomon Eppinger. The first true scholar to join the teaching staff of the College was Dr. Moses Mielziner in 1879. The ability to hire a scholar reflected the growth of the size of financial base of the UAHC/HUC following the 1877–1878 merger with the Board of Delegates. Similar to the early years of religiously sponsored colleges of that time, HUC opened its doors with a meager library, "only 276 volumes . . . [and even these were] mostly prayer books." President Wise appealed, through *The American Israelite*, for the donation of additional volumes.[92] Only with the allocation of significant funds in the late 1870s and into the 1880s and 1890s did a library capable of attracting prestigious faculty begin to accrue.

The "College Way of Life"

The Hebrew Union College also emulated the "College Way of Life." For example, colleges sponsored by other religious groups offered literary and/or debate societies as an extracurricular outlet. From the outset of his College, Rabbi Wise fostered an Atzile Bene Yisrael (Noble Sons of Israel) literary society providing weekly debates, music, and drama. American colleges required students to attend morning and evening daily prayers, as well as weekly Sunday sermons.[93] Similarly, at HUC,

religious services took a very large share of the time that students had left over from their studies—and of course attendance was required. It was assumed that a prospective rabbi would want to devote himself regularly to prayer . . . Aside from daily worship . . . the student was expected to participate in worship each Saturday morning at one of the local congregations.[94]

The Protestant college placed its students in dormitories or in boarding houses under strict scrutiny "with unmarried professors and tutors living in . . . [and] serving as spies, policemen and judges . . . [with] a rigid, minute and often trivial code of laws." Similarly, at the Hebrew Union College, "explicit rules and regulations closely governed the life of the student in his boarding house."[95]

Nineteenth-century American colleges had difficulty attracting students. Middle- and upper-class parents, unlike those of later years, were not convinced of any economic benefit to their offspring through a college degree. Largely, only the lower classes aspired to the ministry. Persons of impoverished backgrounds viewed the educational opportunities offered as a means of improving their status. Thus, "as the number of colleges increased, they found themselves bidding [through scholarships] even more highly for students." As Francis Wayland, President of the prestigious and nonsectarian Brown College lamented in 1842, "we cannot induce men to pursue a collegiate course unless we offer it vastly below its cost, if we do not give it away altogether."[96] In like fashion at HUC, enrollment was a precarious problem. There were only fourteen students in the initial program, of whom only Israel Aaron, Henry Berkowitz, David Philipson, and Joseph Krauskopf finished the course in 1883. The survivors among the second entering class included Louis Grossman, Max Heller, Joseph Stolz, and Joseph Silverman.

These serious candidates for the rabbinate were joined at times by several graduates of Wise's KKBY's Talmud Yelodim Institute, "sons of his very good friends in Cincinnati who never had any genuine intention of going into the rabbinate, but who would surely not be harmed by being subjected to a little Hebrew education."[97] In contrast to the children of KKBY members, the entering youngsters who seriously considered the rabbinate generally came from impoverished families in Cincinnati, from the Cleveland Orphan Asylum, or from similar backgrounds in other parts of the country.

[Students] came from poor families of German origin in the Midwest and South or were the wards of Jewish orphanages. Well-to-do Jewish parents would not hear of their sons entering a profession which was for the most part poorly paid and lacking in prestige. . . . Wise was forced to turn to those families for whom the tuition-free education offered by the Hebrew Union College in conjunction with high school and university studies provided an opportunity they could not otherwise afford.[98]

Rabbi Wise's curriculum planned to produce American-trained Jewish gentlemen by providing the equivalent of high school, college, and rabbinical training. They were to be model contemporary citizens, who comfortably could delve into Judaic or secular sources of knowledge to preach and write eloquent renditions of Judaism. As Wise proclaimed during the dedication ceremony for HUC's first permanent facility, his goals was to create an atmosphere in which Judaism

shall have a fair hearing and thorough examination, where reason and faith, religion and philosophy, shall meet face-to-face, to be harmonized and re-wedded before the altar of truth . . . [and that such a synthesis of] Jewish literature [shall contain] for us the means of self-defense [by which] Judaism can preserve itself as a separate system of faith especially in an age of criticism and free discussion.[99]

In contrast to David Einhorn's German-style quest to train university scholars and theologians, Isaac Mayer Wise hoped to produce rabbis embued not just with book knowledge but more importantly with "zeal" and "enthusiasm" to market Judaism. As President Wise wrote, "if they lack religious zeal and enthusiasm . . . they will never be honest rabbis. . . . If you do not possess this excellent quality, you must cultivate it assiduously . . . [that is,] you must be conscientious in your religious practices as in your studies."[100]

American goals for training ministers in the mid-nineteenth century were in harmony with the following words uttered by Isaac Leeser as early as 1844. Leeser urged that American Jewry did not need modern German rabbis who "value the title of Doctor of Philosophy. They are Jewish philosophers, and we fear not sufficiently embued with the true spirit to be safe guides to Israelites."[101] President Wise borrowed from the American college scene of his day a sense of pluralism, a critical ingredient of the American "union" philosophy. Concentration upon Bible and Talmud and other sacred texts, "enabled Wise [like other college Presidents] to elude the often posed question whether the Hebrew Union College was orthodox or reformist in approach by replying simply that there was little in the curriculum to make it one or the other: the classical sources of Judaism were the common possession of all Jews."[102]

In addition to Bible and Talmud, the rabbinical portion of the course of study at HUC initially included Codes, Medieval Jewish Philosophical Texts, Jewish History, Ancient Languages (Syriac, Arabic, Hebrew, and Aramaic), and Medieval Hebrew Poetry, with a limited Introduction to Theology (taught by Wise) and two hours of Homiletics in the senior year alone. As with Protestant-sponsored colleges in the United States, pluralism was assured by appointing diverse boards of examiners annually, to give each college a stamp of approval. Similarly, President Wise invited a broad range of prominent rabbis to fulfill this assignment. "This was to prove a master-stroke. Many of those who had been his bitter enemies accepted his invitation (as examiners), came, and were won over." Among HUC's early "examiners" were not only previous opponents among German radical reformers, but also traditionalists within the reluctant neo-Orthodox camp.[103]

Through a pluralist ("union") strategy within the HUC, the College achieved a wide base of support. The Hebrew Union College became a source of pride and enhanced self-esteem for all sectors of American Jewry.

The logic to which circumstances had forced him was: first an alliance of congregations; then a college. But this was not the sole end of the Union; for it was to work toward the solidarity of the Jews of the United States, to arouse their self-respect, to help them defend themselves, and to raise them in the esteem of the American people.[104]

Conclusions

By 1879, lay leaders like Moritz Loth and Bernard Bettman and their rabbinic allies such as Isaac Mayer Wise achieved the goals that eluded Isaac Leeser and other seekers of a national religious "union" structure for all American Jews. They assisted synagogues such as the four sample temples described in chapter 1 to gain affiliates in the American "free marketplace of souls." Congregations wanted better religious schools, greater access to suitable rabbis, and a wider sense of belonging to a national Jewish collectivity. Parallel to American Protestants, Loth, Bettman, Wise, and other American Jewish dignitaries established a nationwide congregational union, a "union" college, a newspaper (*The American Israelite*), and one identifiable leader for the movement (Isaac Mayer Wise). Furthermore, these visionaries produced a national Sabbath school program, circuit rabbis, inexpensive English-language Bibles, religious school textbooks, and adult tracts. They also promoted the defense of Jewish civil rights at home and abroad, and the pursuit of agricultural options for Jewish immigrants.

American Jewry headed into the 1880s with an unprecedented sense of religious institutional unity. Individual Jewish congregations that affiliated with the UAHC were better suited than ever before to market membership among the unaffiliated. The UAHC/HUC network of institutions trained rabbis capable of preaching effectively in the English language. The Union forged a sense of belonging, of identification with a national religious body. When it eventually occurred, national unity had not come solely in response to the writings or advocacy of prominent rabbis or national lay leadership. A critical force that generated this institutional success was the pressure of the laity from within local congregations. Their needs combined with the plans of UAHC leaders to give birth to a nationwide response. Local social realities had contributed to the emergence of an American Jewish religious union.

Significantly, the cultural models implemented by a generation of German Jews in America did not emanate from Central Europe. The very nature of German society mitigated against national union. "The idea of cleavage permeated German political disunity, cultural cleavages and class cleavages." Religiously, Germany found itself almost equally split between Protestant and Roman Catholic camps. Ethnically, the independent German states formed a composite of Goths, Vandals, Franks, Burgundians, Anglo-Saxons, and Slavs. Politically, as late as 1800 the area consisted of 314 states and 1,475 estates, with a total of 1,779 independent sovereign powers. Whereas all of the larger nations of Europe achieved their unity in early modern times, Germany waited until 1870, and even then bitter divisions lingered.[105]

German Jewry did not produce a single permanent organization of regional, national, or international scope until 1870 when American Jewish plans for union already were well underway. The only significant religious "union" to be formed in Germany that might have served as a model for American Jews was that attempted by King Frederick William III of Prussia in 1817 (the tricentennial of the Protestant Revolution). This edict called upon German Lutheran and Reformed churches to join into an "Evangelical Church," the Church of the Prussian Union. The Prussian Union, however, did not possess any "practical" goals. Projects on behalf of religious schools, denominational colleges, religious tracts and newspapers, or even the dispersing of missionaries were absent from the Union's agenda. Unlike in American religious life, the focus of the Prussian Union was unity in doctrine and liturgy, an organic union, including a common prayerbook, communion service, and other unified doctrines. Even more incompatible with American Jewish mores, the Prussian Union attracted Friedrich Schleiermacher and anti-Semitic elements within German "Romanticism," who castigated Judaism as an arbitrary, antiquated collection of empty observances and prohibitions, lacking in inwardness and spirituality.[106] Thus, German models of "union" held no appeal for mid-nineteenth-century American Jewish leaders.

Instead, Jews of German descent in the United States turned to national religious unions, the dominant model of Protestant organization in both England and in the United States. With its "federative" approach to unity and its tolerance for diversity, the institutional techniques held in common by American Protestant groups were reflective of the strategies advocated by Leeser and Wise and adopted by the UAHC. Protestant-sponsored colleges, circuit preaching, Sunday school projects, religious tracts, Bible translations, religious newspapers, and a wide array of related efforts became the framework for parallel UAHC institutional innovation. As historian Jay Dolan noted in his assessment of American Catholic revivalism's resemblance to Protestant revivalism: "It should be emphasized . . . that Catholics were not imitating American Protestants . . . [but rather] they were adopting a [religious] . . . form of the pastoral ministry that fitted very well with the American environment."[107] So too, it should be stressed that nineteenth-century parallels between American Jewish and Protestant institutions reflected similar efforts at acculturation rather than conscious borrowing by the UAHC from Christian organizational models.

The premise upon which UAHC based its new institutional synthesis assumed ethnic and religious relative homogeneity within American Jewry. Union leaders hoped to forge a single American Jewish structure for all Jews in the United States, tolerating local doctrinal differences while collaborating in "practical" projects (for example, religious schools and publications). This ambitious goal seemed achievable. Until 1880, the majority of U.S. Jews either personally had emigrated from Germany or were the children of German immigrants. In addition, many synagogues in the United States were instituting similar reforms in ideology and religious practice. American Jewish religious life experienced a slow, steady drift toward liberalism. By 1880, America's Orthodox congregations, which had numbered 13 in 1840 and had grown to some 200 by 1860 when liturgical liberalism had just begun to gain mass popularity, were reduced to a mere handful of the some 275 synagogues.[108]

The Union's short-lived uniformity was undermined, however, by the subsequent decline of liberal religion in the United States, and by the arrival of large numbers of Eastern European Jews fleeing Russia in the 1880s. The entry, "of tens of thousands of refugees from Czarist pogroms and legislation, multiplied by ten- to twentyfold the number of [Jewish] congregations in this country."[109] The comprehensive unity initially achieved by the UAHC was splintered into small fragments pitting synagogues of Germans against those of Eastern Europeans, setting institutions of Jews from Galicia apart from those of Lithuanian Jews, and a vast array of other subdivisions. During the final two decades of the nineteenth century, reactions to this ethnic divisiveness proved decisive for directions taken at both the local and national levels of the Union.

PART TWO

❖

1880–1900

German Influences

❖ 3 ❖

Expanded Roles for the Local Temple

National origin and ethnicity have played powerful roles in the history of American religious groups. Among early nineteenth-century Protestants, immigrants from the British Isles dominated local churches until the 1840s. They comprised the majority of Episcopalians, Presbyterians, Methodists, and Baptists in the United States. By mid-century increasing numbers of German-speaking immigrants began to relocate to the United States, creating a cultural challenge for Protestantism. Whereas fewer than 7,000 Germans arrived in the 1820s, during the 1840s the pace of arrival increased enabling more than 434,000 German emigres to come to these shores. This challenge to existing religious groups was met in what was to become typical American fashion: subdivision into further denominations along the lines of national origin. For example, as their numbers grew, German immigrants founded German Lutheran and German Reformed churches. In the post-Civil War era, denominational patterns among American Protestants were tested further by the arrival of a large Scandinavian population. From 1860 to 1890 more than one million Scandinavians arrived. They too created houses of worship based upon the national origin of their membership, distinctive churches within an existing denomination, the Lutheran church.[1]

Among Roman Catholics, similar divisions based upon national origin surfaced as early as the 1840s with a growing immigration from Ireland. In that decade, over 780,000 Irish immigrants settled in the United States. In response, in the ten-year period from 1841 to 1850, both Irish and German Catholics created "national parishes," a Catholic variant of the "nation of origin" Protestant church. This pattern of religious separatism based on distinctive cultural enclaves characterized the behavior of subsequent American Catholics as well. During the final decades of the nineteenth century, for example, Italian Catholics pursued related institutional strategies. "Each group wanted to worship and pray in its own language and according to the tradition and custom of the Old World. . . . The national parish became the principal institution the immigrants established in their attempt to preserve the religious life of the old country."[2] In the era of America's mass immigration, the nation-of-origin church became a standard building block of religious life.

As demonstrated in Part One, the remarkable success of the Union of American Hebrew Congregations in the 1870s was based upon a certain degree of Central European homogeneity among America's estimated 250,000 Jews. These bonds of national descent among German-speaking Jews, however, were soon tested during the last twenty years of the nineteenth century. The arrival of 550,000 Eastern European Jews from 1880 to 1900 permanently altered demographic realities within American Jewish life. Polish and Russian Jewish cultural norms threatened to redefine the parameters of Judaism in the United States.

American Jews of Germanic descent had disdain for Eastern European Judaism, which they decried as "Orientalism," "Talmudism," "Rabbinism," "Kabbalism," and as "rigid, unbending, intolerant legalism." For example, Rabbi Joseph Krauskopf (KI of Philadelphia) remarked: "Though far away from Oriental cities and environments, he [the Eastern European Jew] still repeats prayer that had a meaning [only] there."[3] Nineteenth-century UAHC rabbis stereotyped the Russian Jews as the purveyors of a non-language, a "jargon": Yiddish. Rabbi Jacob Voorsanger of San Francisco's Emanu-El regarded "no greater drawback to the progress of the Jew in England and America than clinging to the almost unintelligible . . . [Yiddish] tongue." Expressing the anxieties of his peers, Voorsanger lamented this "invasion from the East" that threatened to "undo the work [of achieving social acceptance by America-at-large] of two generations of American Jews." He attributed the growth of anti-Semitism to the Eastern Jews' "tendency to congregate in large numbers in eastern cities."[4]

In addition to the challenge posed to American Jewish unity by the flood of Russian and Polish Jewish immigrants, the leaders of temples experienced growing estrangement from Reform Judaism among their own offspring. Although Jews of Central European heritage remained prominent in the leadership circles of U.S. Jewry, their Americanized offspring were less loyal to Old World traditions. Facing a similar frustration, the immigrant generation of American Christians of German background intensified efforts to retain the loyalties of their young adults, by "inventing" a German-American ethnic identity, including ethnic churches.[5]

German Jews in America of the 1880s emulated this innovation by forging ethnic German temples, the logical successors of national-origin synagogues. During the previous half century, German Jewish immigrants to the United States often had subdivided into congregations whose members had emigrated from Bavaria, Bohemia, Prussia, and Posen, (these were breakoffs from Westphalia, Hanover, and Hesse groups).[6] In the post-Civil War period, Jews whose parentage stemmed from these diverse areas among the former Germanic states gradually redefined themselves in America ethnically as "German" Jews. As Americans, they "linked to other members of their ethnic group by new attributes that the original immigrants would never have recognized as identifying their group." To the extent that many late-nineteenth-century Reform temples recast themselves into ethnic institutions led by American Jews of German descent,[7] ethnic considerations came to affect the goals of these local congregations, the roles of their rabbis, and the composition of their laity.

The Laity

Ethnic Segregation

As noted in chapter 1, during the early years of our four sample congregations, a core of German Jews had existed side by side with a smaller contingent of non-Central European coreligionists. This pattern of diversity in national origin was also true of other Reform temples whose founders included German as well as English, French, Dutch, or Polish Jews. The composition of individual congregations reflected the national-origin makeup of Jewish life in each locality.

The fluidity and diversity of local temples was reflected as well by their liturgical practices. Reform temples in the second half of the nineteenth century both in Germany and the United States displayed a variety of ritual patterns, notably *Minhag Ashkenaz* (the "German Rite" used in the congregations of Southern Germany) and *Minhag Polen* (the "Polish Rite" used in Prussian-Posen German congregations). Diverse nationalities and *minhagim* (customs) of distinctive European origins survived within Reform Jewish communities in America throughout the nineteenth century. Pluralism also was indicated in the adherence by some Reform temples to traditionalist observances such as celebrating the second day of Jewish festivals, and by the multiplicity of late-nineteenth-century non-Orthodox prayerbooks. In 1890, for example, Rabbi Isaac Mayer Wise still referred to the proliferation of "books of worship" at local temples as a source of "disunion and dissension."[8]

The arrival of large numbers of Russian and Polish Jews into American urban areas by 1900 threatened to overturn these pre-existing congregational patterns. In the midst of an emerging Eastern European ambience, the distinctiveness of UAHC temples was exhibited in part by attracting increasing percentages of Jews of Central (or Western) European descent. The results of this demographic shift are reflected in the changing membership composition exhibited by each of the four sample congregations.[9] For example, of 154 members of Cincinnati's KKBY located in the 1900 census records, 89 were born in Germany, and 8 were born in other central or Western European countries. Of the 56 American-born members, 54 had at least 1 German-born parent. Only 1 member, Bernard Goodman, was a Polish Jew.

A similar central European pattern was evidenced in the other sample institutions. Of the 154 members of San Francisco's Emanu-El located in the census data of 1900, 96 were of German birth. Of the 13 non-German, foreign-born members, 6 came from France, 4 from Bohemia, and 1 each from Austria, Hungary, Holland, England, and Canada. Only 1 member out of 154 in the sample was born in Russia and only 1 other member had a Russian-born parent. In New Orleans' Temple Sinai, 65 of the 139 members located in the 1900 census were German (59) or French (6). Of the 74 American-born members, 69 had at least 1 parent whose place of birth was either Germany (33), France (7) or England (2). No members of the temple were natives of Russia or Poland, and only Isidore Grossman had a parent (his father) of Polish descent.[10]

The largest and most impressive example of a congregation's Central European ethnicity can be found in the 1900 membership of Philadelphia's Keneseth Israel congregation.[11] Among the 266 male members for whom data were located, 123 were German born. Of the others, 88 were the American-born children of German parents and 9 were American-born offspring of 1 German-born parent and 1 American parent. Ten Austrian-born men continued the Central European pattern, as did 2 Hungarian-born men and 1 American-born man with 1 German-born and 1 English-born parent. Collectively, these Central European figures totaled 233 (89 percent) of the 266 sampled at KI.

Of the remaining 33 cases, the largest portion consisted of 9 third-generation Americans (children of American-born mothers and fathers). The U.S.-born Jewish parents were quite likely to have been of German descent and children of the earlier block of Central European Jewish immigrants (1820–1880). Most of the 24 other KI male members surveyed were of Western or Northern European background. There were 7 American-born sons of English parents, 4 native Englishmen, 3 American-born men with Dutch parents, 1 American-born man with 1

Dutch and 1 French parent, 1 Frenchman, 1 American-born man with French parents, and 2 natives of the British West Indies (Barbados and Jamaica).

Quite striking is the dramatic absence of Eastern European Jews in this sample. Out of 266 males members surveyed, only 4 had any trace of Eastern European ethnicity (2 are listed as Russians, 1 was a Romanian Jew, and the last member was American born of 1 German and 1 Eastern European parent. Notably, all 4 married women of German or other Central European backgrounds, probably women from the social circles of KI. These women made possible the entry into membership of their Eastern European spouses. This ethnic gap between German and Eastern European Jews is particularly remarkable given the large and growing Eastern European Jewish population in Philadelphia at the turn of the century. The UAHC and some of its member congregations increasingly had become the domain solely of German Jews and were off limits for most coreligionists of Polish and Russian background.[12] At the same time, the Eastern Europeans reciprocally felt estranged from the *Yahudim* (German Jews). In such an environment, maintaining a comprehensive religious union of all American Jews became impossible.

Age Factors

Differences in age distribution also acted to separate the Russian and German Jews. As indicated in chapter 1, the founding generation of the four sample temples (1840–1870) consisted overwhelmingly of men and women in their twenties and early thirties and their young children. Youthfulness was characteristic of pre-Civil War America, which was dominated demographically by immigrant populations. Though some older Europeans immigrated, the decision to uproot from Europe and to travel by boat to the United States was an adventure primarily for the young. As a result, prior to 1860 three-quarters of the U.S. population were under forty and two-thirds were under thirty. In the final years of the nineteenth century, this youthful pattern was repeated within the eastern European immigration. Most of the new arrivals were men and women in their early adult years or young children and teenagers. In contrast, the German Jewish temple membership was growing older, and most affiliates were middle-aged. People in their twenties and early thirties became scarce within the life of many UAHC congregations.

The aging of the temple populations is readily apparent in an examination of the census data. By the year 1900, the newest of the four sample congregations, Temple Sinai in New Orleans (established in 1870), retained the youngest population. Nevertheless, its membership too was

TABLE 3.1
Age of Temple Sinai Members, *1900*

20–29	10
30–39	39
40–49	39
50–59	35
60–69	17
70–79	12

Average age = 46 years old

This chart as well as the several that follow are composed of data that I compiled in gathering membership lists from our sample temples and searching for these Jewish families within the U.S. census returns of 1900.

TABLE 3.2
Age of Temple Sinai Wives, *1900*

20–29	31
30–39	31
40–49	39
50–59	18
60–69	3
70–79	1

Average age = 39 years old

significantly older than it was in the generation of immigrant founders. In 1870, most of Sinai's members were men in their twenties and thirties, while by the turn of century, the membership divided equally among males ages thirty to thirty-nine, and forty to forty-nine, and fifty to fifty-nine. The wives of members were somewhat younger, and their offspring were young adults. Tables 3.1 and 3.2 summarize the data.

K.K. B'nai Yeshurun in Cincinnati and Emanu-El of San Francisco, established in the 1840s and 1850s, respectively, reveal an even greater aging pattern. In both congregations, the founders were young men in their twenties and early thirties. By 1900, the average age of male members had climbed to fifty years, with wives several years their junior. Most significant is the virtual absence of men aged twenty to twenty-nine, the chronological peers of most Eastern European immigrants. Tables 3.3 through 3.6 clarify these findings.

By the turn of the century, the age range of the membership of UAHC temples was no longer that of the young families who had been the generation of the founders. Seat holders in their twenties and early thirties were quite rare. A middle-aged population emerged, and temple needs changed accordingly from primary education to programs for teenagers and young adults, the grown sons and daughters of middle-aged members. In contrast, the Eastern European Jewish immigrant population was composed primarily of young parents with small children.[13]

TABLE 3.3
Age of K.K. B'nai Yeshurun Members, 1900

20–29	0
30–39	19
40–49	50
50–59	35
60–69	28
70–79	13
80–89	3

Average Age = 48 years old

TABLE 3.4
Age of Emanu-El Members, 1900

20–29	1
30–39	22
40–49	38
50–59	52
60–69	26
70–79	11

Average age = 53 years old

TABLE 3.5
Age of K.K. B'nai Yeshurun Wives, 1900

20–29	10
30–39	45
40–49	35
50–59	31
60–69	13
70–79	5

Average age = 45 years old

TABLE 3.6
Age of Emanu-El Wives, 1900

20–29	12
30–39	42
40–49	58
50–59	22
60–69	6
70–79	3

Average age = 42 years old

Status Conflict

Differences in socioeconomic status also separated Russian and German Jews. The temples of the 1850s and 1860s had included all strata (though the preponderance of numbers were in the merchant class). By the 1880s within American religious life at large, a class differential was in place. "'Go into an ordinary church on Sunday morning,' declared a Protestant clergyman in 1887, 'and you will see lawyers, physicians, merchants, and businessmen with their families . . . but the workingman and his household are not there'"[14] A similar division had emerged which separated the established Central European synagogues in the United States from the largely Eastern European shuls. By the last quarter of the nineteenth century, most German Jewish immigrants and their offspring had risen to middle- or upper-middle-class status. In contrast, the Polish and Russian newcomers were regarded as lower class.

This is evident in a rating of occupations from this era provided by historian Peter Decker. Decker lists high status jobs as professionals, major proprietors—managers and officials (both merchants and nonmerchants), as well as general merchants (retailers). As lower status means of a livelihood, Decker includes clerks and salesmen, agents (insurance), bookkeeper, petty proprietor (bar/saloon keeper), petty merchant (peddler, grocer), skilled or semi-skilled laborers, and finally manual, unskilled workers.[15] At the turn of the century, many Eastern European Jews worked as skilled, semi-skilled, or unskilled workers in the garment industry. Frequently, others worked as urban push cart peddlers, or as petty proprietors in a host of stores ranging from butcher shops and candy stores to groceries and related goods.

In contrast to the lower class *Ostjuden*, the German Jews and their offspring were of significantly higher status. This pattern of material success was already evident in the census of 1890. "One-fifth consisted of accountants, book-keepers, clerks, collectors, agents. One-tenth worked as salesmen, one-twentieth served in the professions. One out of 8 occupied positions as skilled workers. Perhaps [only] one-half of 1 percent were laborers, and one out of a 100, peddlers."[16]

The membership of our sample congregations in 1900 exhibited a high degree of affluence, characteristic of prestigious temples such as San Francisco's Emanu-El. In Emanu-El, our sample of 154 heads of households does not include a single laborer, peddler, or even "petty proprietor." The only exceptions to the middle-and upper-middle-class rule are 2 retirees, 1 a former "teamster," and the other a former "policeman." Apart from 5 members involved in San Francisco's emerging banking industry (listed as "Banker," [two] "Capitalist," "Stock and Bond Broker," "Money Broker"), a "Publisher," a "Dentist," a "Lawyer," 3 insurance personnel and a "Miner," the rest were involved in merchandising ventures. These businesses included the wholesale or retail sales of hides and leathers, garments, meats, jewelry, tobacco, furs, shoes, liquor, crockery, and related items.

In Cincinnati's KKBY membership in 1900, a similar pattern prevailed. The only lower status occupations were three "Book-keepers," two "Peddlers in vegetables," two "tailors," a "Painter," a "Saloon Keeper" and a "Traveling Salesman." The remainder of the 154 heads of households located in the census data of 1900 were in prominent merchandising positions, ranging from "Manufacturers" of cigars, paper, umbrellas, woolen goods, trunks, carriages, and clothing, to "Merchants" of dry goods, metal goods, liquor, tobacco, shoes, notions and similar items. The exceptions were a "Judge in Common Pleas Court," seven "Life Insurance" agents, a "Publisher" and a "Printer."

New Orleans's Temple Sinai was even more homogeneous in high status occupations than the well-to-do San Francisco Emanu-El population. Among the 137 members located in the census data of 1900, we find 22 business owners in "dry goods" or related apparel, 17 "General Merchants," 16 "Cotton Merchants," 10 "Liquor Merchants," 8 "Manufacturers," 5 "Notions Merchants," 4 "Commercial Travelers," 4 "Commission Merchants," and 4 "Moneybrokers." The only lower status positions are 3 "Clerks," and 2 "Bookkeepers." Even in Philadelphia's KI at the turn of century, in the midst of America's second largest population of impoverished Eastern European Jews, very few of over 200 members in our sample worked in low-status occupations. These less desirable jobs included 1 "Book-keeper," 1 "Secretary," 1 "Clerk," 2 "Tailors," 1 "Machinist," 1 "Wine Worker," 1 "Dance Master," 2 "Butchers," and 2 "Grocers." Everyone else was self-employed in a business of a merchandising nature (170 out of 234 total), manufacturing (42), professionals (5) or Financiers (5) in a pattern similar to the other three congregations.[17]

Clearly, by 1900 Jews of Central European ancestry in UAHC temples were middle-aged persons of high socioeconomic status. Their age, ethnicity, and affluence made the lesser status Eastern Europeans feel uncomfortable. This stratified pattern was accentuated by residential trends. By this time, neighborhoods separated by class had developed. The wealthy and the American-born middle class began to abandon the inner city and relocate to new "suburban" areas, such as Cincinnati's Walnut Hills section that became identified as a distinctively Jewish neighborhood. While the German Jews moved "uptown" the less affluent Russian and Polish Jews stayed "downtown." For all these demographic reasons,

UAHC temples became German ethnic congregations, inhospitable to Russian and Polish Jews. Temple members expressed open disdain for the Eastern Europeans as potential affiliates.[18] With the pace of German Jewish immigration to the United States declining to fewer than 14,000 from 1880 to 1900, the future replenishing of the Union temples depended almost completely on courting the sons and daughters of members.

The Younger Generation

Among the lay leaders of Union-affiliated temples in the 1880s, there was a common perception that their youthful offspring felt alienated. "Reading the histories of local congregations, one is struck by the fact that at the end of the last century the individual [UAHC] congregations reached their lowest ebbs. . . . the children were rejecting perhaps not only their immigrant fathers but their . . . religion."[19] Retaining the loyalties of adult sons and daughters became a critical concern. Attention centered upon the dissatisfaction with Reform expressed by the young followers of Felix Adler's Ethical Culture Society and also by other alienated sons and daughters of temple members. Their complaints ranged widely. They expressed distaste for Reform liturgical services, dominated by scholarly but dry sermonic discourses on the weekly Torah portion. They accused affluent Reform temples of indifference to the social ills in America's bustling industrial and urban centers. Secular alternatives such as the Young Men's Hebrew Association (YMHA) offered desirable alternatives for young men. At the YMHA, a person could engage in cultural and social activities without feeling encumbered by religious sentiments with which he might be ambivalent or uncomfortable.[20] Furthermore, the daughters and wives of the founders resented their exclusion from formal temple membership. They sought congregational roles geared specifically to women.

In addition, attention should be given to what historian Marcus Lee Hansen described as the "uncomfortable position" of the children reared by nineteenth-century German immigrants. According to Hansen's evaluation, schoolmates had taunted these youths for exhibiting foreign cultural mores. Yet similarly, familial elders had chided them for being too American. A refusal to conform either to the cultural messages of the general society or to the religious and linguistic habits of their parents resulted in constant childhood torment. Consequently, upon reaching adulthood the second generation generally "wanted to forget everything, the foreign language that left a trace in . . . English speech, the religion that continually recalled childhood struggles . . . in an environment so different, so American, that all associates naturally assumed that . . . [they were] as American as they."[21]

Hansen admitted that this picture had been deliberately overdrawn. It did outline, however, some generational tensions that faced the children of the founders of these German American temples. The sons and daughters did not want their peers to be aware of the usage of the German language in many of the sermons in their parents' synagogues, in temple liturgy, religious schools, and meetings. Yet, in each of our four sample congregations, the residue of German speech and writing was still apparent.[22] In addition, may of these young people, notably those who attended Felix Adler's Sunday lectures at Manhattan's Ethical Culture Society, were thirsting for intelligent discussions of the burning social issues of their day. They rejected Temple sermons limited to the Bible and rabbinic literature. They felt a cultural gap between themselves and their contemporaries and the aging, German-accented rabbis.

To attract the younger generation, the local Reform temple of the late 1880s and throughout the 1890s introduced new programs. The roles of the temple, the religious school, the rabbi, and the cantor changed. As we have seen with the four sample congregations, at the time of their founding as voluntary associations, of like-minded, young Central European immigrants, temples assumed limited functions. They offered a cemetery, a Sabbath school, and rabbinic officiation at life-cycle ceremonies and in public sermons and prayer. Even as congregational membership expanded, as late as the early 1880s temples maintained a narrow domain. This was evident within the design of the impressive buildings occupied by urban Reform temples. Whereas the sanctuaries were enormous, the facilities provided very few vestry or meeting rooms for supplementary activity.[23]

Concentration on the worship and sermonic aspect of congregational life in Reform temples harmonized with Jewish religious needs in the 1860s. Within two decades, however, this narrow focus of activities became a source of intergenerational strife. As younger American Jews of German descent disaffiliated, Reform temples needed to lure them back to membership. Temple leaders recognized the threat to Jewish continuity posed by the impact of Americanization and of upward social mobility upon the second generation. To retain their sons and daughters, in a fashion which paralleled the experience of American Protestant churches, many Jewish congregations "adopted the style of the [multifaceted] organizational church; . . . they developed activities [intended] . . . to hold the second and third generation."[24]

UAHC temple leaders sought to attract their offspring by redefining what it meant to be a temple member. Young persons were questioning the validity of theological presuppositions. They found prayer and sermons uninspiring. To meet these objections, temples recast synagogue affiliation into a much broader mold. The German American "temple" widened its parameters to become the all-encompassing "temple center." The "Center" offered educational, recreational, and charitable activities differentiated along age, sex, and socioeconomic lines. Youth activities, sisterhoods, adult education, outreach to the poor, and other ventures became part of temple affairs. The role of the Reform rabbi expanded to include the supervision of these innovations. New facilities were constructed to accommodate the expanded spheres of activity, as evidenced by Keneseth Israel's building project of 1892. Like other turn-of-the-century newly constructed Reform Temples, the KI temple facility added a second floor suitable to "temple center" work. The Temple housed a large entertainment room, with a four-hundred-person dining capacity, including sliding partitions to host smaller affairs and meetings; six classrooms; a first-floor library; and a basement for social and educational events.[25]

The Temple's Role Expands

Young Adult Activities

At the midpoint of the nineteenth century, young men in their late teens and early twenties were regarded as fully functioning adults. By the 1880s and 1890s, however, among the upper middle class a protected status of "adolescence and young adulthood" emerged. It was precisely this group that was of concern to church and synagogue planners. Throughout the 1880s and 1890s, religious institutions responded aggressively. The first arena of response surfaced in the realm of public education. "Prior to the 1890s, very few educators thought of the high school as even potentially a mass institution. Most high school students . . . were female. Boys who attended high school at all were usually withdrawn after a year or two and placed in a trade [or business]." The situation changed in the 1890s: the sudden desirability of completing high school related to the credentials needed for new, white collar professions. These careers required not only a high school diploma, but also a college degree as prerequisites for a graduate professional education. Upper- and middle-class persons began to look positively upon the college experience as a necessary route to high-status jobs and an incentive for "ideals and higher ambition."[26] In harmony with these changes, the scope of both the Protestant Sunday and Jewish Sabbath schools expanded beyond the ages of thirteen or fourteen and into a full range of teen study.

Prolonged periods of formal learning enabled Reform temples and Protestant churches to lengthen the target years of their religious schools. Among our sample congregations, for example, already in 1895 KI in Philadelphia introduced a "post-Confirmation" class, and soon after that an Alumni Association. As KI's chronicler Howard Fineshriber recorded: "The idea was to pay dividends in the interest in congregational life which was built up and the fact that for those who took advantage of the opportunity it bridged the gap from Confirmation to active participation in the affairs of the Congregation." Beyond the extension of education into late teen as well as young adult years, a second arena for attracting the alienated young was recreational activity. By the mid-1880s, the YMCA had demonstrated the successful appeal of recreation to young adults. The ideas of Luther Gulick and the YMCA movement impacted upon both church and synagogue circles. Gulick taught that team sports and gym activities had spiritual as well as health value. To Gulick, "team sports encouraged 'heroic subordination of self to the group,' a quality which he viewed as essentially religious . . . Christ was not meek or gentle but forceful and dynamic, the first muscular Christian."[27]

Though uninterested in emulating a muscular Jesus, many Reform Jews could sense the value of athletics, especially for their younger members. Borrowing this successful urban strategy, in the 1890s numerous enlarged church buildings, as well as some Reform temple centers included a gymnasium within their facility and program goals. As the 1902 Central Conference of American Rabbis (CCAR) *Yearbook* reflected on events of the previous ten years:

the gymnasium . . . has latterly been introduced in a few temples . . . a self-defense measure, since the gymnasium of the Young Men's Christian Association—the only one available to our boys and young men—has become a menace to our cause [for example] in the city of Detroit, taking our children from us on the Sabbath morning, and inculcating, with their gymnastic instruction, also the elements of Christianity.[28]

The existence of temple centers already in the 1890s discounts the claim of many historians that Mordecai Kaplan invented the "synagogue center" twenty years later.[29]

The temple center trend in part was influenced by the Institutional Church Movement of the 1890 to 1915 era. "Institutional" implied expanding church functions to cover the secular needs of men, whether in the gymnasium or in cultural and social spheres. In describing this conscious church response to the allure of secular leisure-time activities, Institutional Church theorist Charles Stelzle wrote:

the open and institutional church aims to save all men and of the man by all means, abolishing, so far as possible, the distinction between the religious and the secular, and sanctifying all days and all means to the great end of saving the world for Christ.

The institutional church [notably St. Bartholomew in Manhattan] . . . succeeds because it adapts itself to changed conditions. . . . It sees that people have little or no healthful social life; it accordingly *opens* attractive social rooms, and organizes clubs for men, women, boys and girls. . . . In their homes people have few books and papers, in the Church they find a free reading-room and library. The homes afford no opportunity for intellectual cultivation; the Church *opens* evening schools and provides lecture courses [emphasis added].[30]

Advocacy of similar techniques appears in the same 1902 CCAR *Yearbook* article cited above regarding gymnasiums within temples. The author recommended the full gamut of "institutional" programs for temples:

I would place in the temple, a library and a reading-room, and fill its shelves with the best literature available, and I would invite my boys and girls to come there and feel at home. I would open my place of worship to lecturers on Jewish and humanitarian themes. I would encourage good musical entertainments there. I would give my young people every opportunity to assemble there for literary meetings and for discussions on topics, in which they are most interested . . . Bible classes, Young People's Temple Societies . . . Junior Choirs, Alumni Associations. . . .[31]

The expansion of the domain of the temple, in order to engage young affiliates, was not without its detractors within the UAHC. As early as 1897, at the CCAR Annual Convention, Rabbi Joseph Krauskopf of Philadelphia's KI, in an address entitled, "How We Can enlist Our Young Men In The Service of the Congregation," took note that

to be sure, there are churches—chief among them the institutional churches— that trumpet loudly their wonderful hold on young people. Careful observation, however reveals that, for the most part, it is not religion that attracts. . . . The only thing about some of these churches that points to heaven is the steeple.[32]

Similarly, in the pages of the *American Israelite* in late 1902 and into early 1903, Rabbi Max Heller of Temple Sinai in New Orleans criticized Rabbi Moses Gries's ten years of "Institutionalism" in his Cleveland temple as "secularism" and "materialism." In the words of Rabbi Heller:

we feel ourselves constrained to believe that these . . . exertions are not pursuing the proper road . . . [these exertions] exalt the perishable above the eternal . . . [that is, it does] not mean principally worship, but anything and everything which will bring people together, from the Sabbath worship down to the sociable, nay to the funny lecture . . . [Rabbi Gries] invites his people to amuse themselves in a course of entertainments in the very body of his temple, which becomes an everyday auditorium . . . but in our understanding, this is not Judaism.[33]

In his own defense, Rabbi Gries responded three weeks later in the very same pages of the *American Israelite*. He indicated that the "record of ten years of such activities is indeed a record of which we may be proud," with a rapidly growing membership and religious school. "I rejoice that ours is 'the Open Temple.' Its gates should stand ever open to all who would worship with us, to all who seek religious instruction and moral improvement. It must be to all of us a source of pride that our Temple has become the natural center of our Jewish activities." In direct challenge to Heller, Gries emphatically wrote:

I accept the thought [that] . . . temple going is not the all-important thing in Judaism. . . . See the truth so plain. Neither orthodox synagogues nor reform temples are reaching our men and women and children . . . [therefore the Temple] must be devoted to the study of life and of all its interests. . . . Judaism is concerned with the whole of life. It makes no false distinctions between the sacred and the secular. . . . All the interests of life are interests of religion. Therefore the activities of the temple should be larger than worship and religious school, as life is larger than Sabbath and Sunday. I believe in the Open Temple serving seven days in the week—"Thy gates shall stand open continually day and night. They shall not be closed."[34]

The impact of these institutional techniques was so overwhelming that even those who held it suspect, such as Rabbi Krauskopf's Philadelphia Keneseth Israel, did implement it to a degree. Although refusing to construct a gymnasium, KI created additional nonritual options for young adult activity. These innovations were facilitated "by adding [in its new building] lecture rooms for literary societies . . . [and] classes for the study of other than religious subjects." Already in 1892, KI's Rabbi Joseph Krauskopf founded the "Knowledge Seekers," an organization for young adults intending to further the "knowledge of Judaism among themselves and within the Congregation." Within a few months, this ambitious group "brought into being" within KI's facility a "Free Library," yet another focal point of the Institutional Church Movement. Less than twelve months later, the momentum of success generated by the "Knowledge Seekers" helped in the founding of the nationwide Jewish Publication Society. In late 1894, the "Knowledge Seekers" became a permanent dimension of KI's life, being renamed the "Lyceum," a term made popular by the American Lyceum (young adult education) Movement. The KI Lyceum of young adults organized frequent lectures on Jewish and contemporary subjects and printed a weekly educational publication as well.[35] Thus, a modified "Institutional" program of activities had arisen at Keneseth Israel.

Social Justice

Another related realm of UAHC temple activity intended to appeal to alienated young adults was social justice. To rebut the critique of temple life fostered by Ethical Culture, lay and rabbinic leaders sought to demonstrate that Reform Judaism practiced ethics and justice in a "hands on" fashion. Tangible efforts were critical because many Reform temples—like most well-established Protestant churches—had become the realm solely of the affluent. Once again, parallel models for best comprehending UAHC temple initiatives were available within the domain of America's Protestant churches; the specific referent was the Social Gospel Movement of the 1880s and 1890s, the heyday for liberal religion in the United States.

Major spokespersons of the Social Gospel were Reverends Walter Rauschenbusch, Josiah Strong, and Russell Conwell. Rauschenbusch was among those innovative American ministers of the 1880s who received his higher education in Germany. He implemented Social Gospel ideas during his service as the pastor of a German Baptist congregation near New York City's "Hell's Kitchen" slums. Reverend Strong began to advocate church involvement in social justice in the mid-1880s as well. He served first as the Minister of the Central Congregational Church in Cincinnati (1885–1887), then within Manhattan's urban ghettos. Russell Conwell inspired similar and simultaneous efforts at the Grace Baptist Church in Philadelphia.[36]

For the next several years, these urban reform trends within American Protestantism continued to evolve. In 1892, Rauschenbusch convened a fellowship of New York City and Philadelphia Baptist preachers to systematically address the goals of the social gospel. At a subsequent retreat in August 1893, this "Brotherhood" proclaimed:

every member shall lay stress on the social aims of Christianity, and shall endeavor to make Christ's teaching concerning wealth operative in the church . . . [and] each member shall take pains to keep in contact with the common people, and to infuse the religious spirit into the efforts for social amelioration.[37]

The commitment of individual East Coast Protestant congregational leadership in Manhattan and Philadelphia to launch social justice activities affected KI (Philadelphia) before the other sample temples and before the Reform movement at large. With the notable exceptions of Rabbi Emil Hirsch of Chicago and Rabbi Stephen Wise of New York City, UAHC rabbis did not issue social justice pronouncements until 1918. Yet in contrast to this delay, already on 6 May 1887, the Annual Presidential Address of Philadelphia's Keneseth Israel responded to the call for social justice. KI's president indicated that "the active sphere of a reform congregation is not alone assigned to its interior work; its duties and activity must extend themselves also outside of its fold . . . [to] the different charitable organizations of this city.[38]

President Klein could proudly point to his temple's pattern of community involvements. KI already had displayed leadership in Philadelphia's United Hebrew Charities, the Jewish Hospital and Home, the Jewish Immigrant Aid Society, the Jewish Foster Home and Orphan Asylum, as well as in the Orphans Guardians, initiated by KI's former Rabbi Hirsch. The President also mentioned the commitment of KI's women to assist the Jewish Hospital Association, the Hebrew Relief Society, the Ladies Society for the Sick Poor, the Ladies Sewing Society, and Mrs. Rosa Sachs's Industry Training School.[39]

In 1892, KI's new rabbi, Joseph Krauskopf, decided to build upon this rich legacy of Jewish activism. Inspired by Social Gospel church work in New York and Philadelphia, and anxious to attract young women of German descent, Krauskopf created the KI Sewing Circle. "Week after week, this group of devoted women . . . met at the Temple and produced garments for charity." With similar goals in mind, Rabbi Krauskopf began a series of initiatives aimed at alleviating hardships within urban slums. The rabbi launched a "Model Dwellings Association" to replace tenements with suitable housing; a Sterilized Milk and Ice Society to lobby for mandatory pasteurization of milk; and a "Personal Interest Society" to "help the poor to help themselves, by taking a personal interest in their lot, by seeking and finding employment for them and by encouraging cleanliness thrift and economy;" and a "model kitchen" program to teach poor persons how to prepare nutritious food in an economical fashion and to supply nourishment to those unable to feed themselves. In 1895, KI even helped to establish "The Home of Delight" for Philadelphia's less fortunate residents. The "Home" was "an early Community Center, having a library, game rooms, and organized clubs."[40] The commitment to social justice became a unique and distinguishing feature of other UAHC congregations as well.

Sisterhoods

A related effort both to combat the temple's alleged indifference to urban poverty and to establish meaningful roles for its women was the creation of the Sisterhoods of Personal Service in New York City in the late 1880s. Increasing leisure-time opportunities were arising for middle- and upper-class ladies throughout the United States. The availability of inexpensive live-in immigrant or American-born domestics continued throughout the nineteenth century. By 1900, almost all of the families in our four sample populations employed at least one household helper (domestics, cooks, nurses, and sometimes gardeners, coachmen, watchmen). These workers helped provide the woman of the home with additional free time.

Also, as formal school instruction expanded to encompass both elementary and teenage years, leisure hours for mothers whose youngest child reached five years of age were increased. Moreover, as affluent families, the German Reform households obtained up-to-date technological advances in food preparation and ready-made garments.[41]

Nevertheless, societal pressures limited the choices available to middle- and upper-class women for their newfound free hours. To accept a job for financial remuneration was a public embarrassment. It implied a middle-class husband's inability to support the family on a single income. As late as 1900, not even one wife of a temple member in the sample congregations was employed. Paid positions ranging from teacher, musician, artist, to saleslady, stenographer, and bookkeeper were reserved for single women of the household (daughters, sisters, cousins, nieces). As an alternative, prosperous married ladies occupied themselves with "literary societies," "garden clubs," and other forms of self-improvement.[42]

By the 1880s, strident critiques of upper-class insensitivity to the urban poor created interest in the plight of the slums and immigrant ghettos. Well-to-do ladies in America sought to exercise their "humanitarian, nurturing and compassionate qualities" to the social betterment of society. As a result, Jewish and Christian women in U.S. cities of the late 1880s became the first "friendly visitors," volunteer social workers. They implemented "personal service" through a broad range of activities." Such "service" attended to the individual needs of impoverished people. Its implementation was systematic, guided by the standards of the "scientific" Charity Organization Society movement.[43]

Although this friendly visitor phenomenon arose initially among affluent women engaged in secular organizations, the church and synagogue worlds also were affected. It was in this context that in the late 1880s individual church "sisterhoods" were created as auxiliary societies parallel to the male-dominated congregations. The sisterhoods established homes for working girls in the country as well as urban "settlement houses." Clergy took notice of the mounting interest in religious affairs exhibited by the wives of church and synagogue members. Thus, Rabbi Kaufman Kohler's Pittsburgh Conference keynote address of 1885 advocated the expansion of the synagogue role of Jewish women: "They do the work of charity everywhere . . . none of the . . . time-absorbing tasks of Con-gregational life is discharged with the same self-denying devotion and enthusiastic zeal by our men . . . as it would be done by ladies." Kohler advocated women's "full admission into the membership of the Jewish Congregation" or an official auxiliary role.[44]

Temples gradually had implemented changes in policies toward women. By the 1880s congregations permitted widows within the sample temples to retain the "seats" and membership rights of their deceased husbands. In the late 1880s and into the 1890s, single women, generally the unmarried adult daughters of members gained the right to acquire a "seat" and to become a "member." Women also began to serve the temple as volunteer teachers in the religious school. At KI, women acted as volunteer editors for the congregational weekly bulletin initiated on 2 February 1896. Moreover, women worked as paid faculty for specialized educational innovations such as Keneseth Israel's "Kindergarten."[45]

The most direct nineteenth-century expansion of women's roles within the temple was the creation of sisterhoods. Auxiliary women's societies for temples arose parallel to similar Protestant groups, such as the Methodist Society of King's Daughters in New York City, established in 1886. Volunteer activities for temple women first appeared at Temple Emanu-El of New York City in 1887 at the initiative of Rabbi Gustav Gottheil. The Emanu-El Sisterhood of Personal Service provided

personal relief, the support of religious schools, industrial and cooking schools, day nurseries, kindergartens, employment bureaus, workrooms for the teaching of trades to unskilled women, evening clubs and classes for young women employed during the day, and afternoon clubs and classes for children including classes for musical instruments . . . [and] assistance in the problem of juvenile delinquency.[46]

As with church women's groups arising in Manhattan in the 1890s, the synagogue ladies established a "Federation" of Sisterhoods in 1896. The Federation sought the "interchange of information regarding the work of the Sisterhoods as well as for the discussion of new methods of work." It hoped to avoid duplication by "dividing the city into districts and assigning every Sisterhood to a separate district."[47]

Following the example of the German temples of Manhattan, sisterhoods spread around the country. At Emanu-El of San Francisco for example, Rabbi Jacob Voorsanger initiated his own Emanu-El Sisterhood in 1894. Some founding members of Emanu-El ladies club were relatives of New Yorkers and were well aware of the New York City precedent. "The records [in San Francisco] for the year 1895 reveal that the Relief Committee of the Sisterhood aided 1,350 applicants; the Employment Bureau found jobs for a third of the 234 seeking work." In conscious emulation of their East Coast coreligionists, several years later "the Sisterhood opened a building . . . to provide classrooms for Russian immigrants, a kindergarten, a gymnasium."[48] Gradually, similar women's auxiliaries arose within other UAHC synagogues, eventually including each of the other sample congregations.

Temple Religious Schools

The decision to replace German-speaking and aging Rabbi Samuel Hirsch with the youthful, English-speaking Rabbi Joseph Krauskopf was part of Philadelphia's Keneseth Israel's effort to attract the younger generation of American Jews of German descent. As the President's Address in the KI Minute Books of 4 April 1880 reflected: "It is a sad story that young married men, sons and sons-in-law, do not have a seat in our Temple and are waiting till perhaps the growing children are in need of religious school."[49] Rabbi Krauskopf began his institutional overhaul with the religious school, the very arena that most directly affected young Jewish parents.

Educators imbued with the pedagogic ideas taught within the German University system had begun to apply systematic management techniques to the public school. Districts, standards, attendance, a graded curriculum, teacher certification, and other issues became popular. In the years following the Civil War, most American urban school systems gradually became *bureaucracies*, though educators did not use that term. "They developed elaborate rules to govern the behavior of members of the organization. . . . They created hierarchies of appointed offices, each with careful allocation of power and specified duties. John Vincent and other Protestant Sunday School reformers sought to transmit these "bureaucratic" notions to church schools.[50] Rabbi Krauskopf and other innovative pulpit rabbis strove to bring their temples' informal religious schools into harmony with these public and church school standards. In the early 1890s, Krauskopf created a formal list of "rules governing the Religious School of the Reform Congregation Keneseth Israel."

I. Pupils to be admitted must be over 8 years old, and be able to read ordinary English.

II. Pupils coming to school must at once repair to their respective classes. Playing in hall or street is strictly prohibited. The Class Rooms remain closed till thirty minutes before beginning of school session. Tardy pupils are not permitted to enter their respective classes till the next change of bells.

III. A record of each pupil's progress and decorum is kept by the teacher and sent to Parents or Guardians once a month, to be inspected by them and to be returned with their signature.

IV. A monthly average from 85 to 95 entitles the pupil to a Meritorious Note; a Distinguished Note is given for an average from 95 to 100. At the end of the school term the pupil that has the highest average of the class for the whole year, receives a Gold Medal; to the next highest average a silver medal is awarded. Yearly average from 90 to average receiving the Silver Medal are rewarded with the First Prize; yearly averages from 85 to 90 are rewarded with the Second Prize. An average of 70 is required for promotion.

V. Misdemeanors are punished with Demerits. The pupil receiving 25 Demerits within one month must report to the Superintendent. When the same pupil has received 25 Demerits a second time, the Superintendent is required to notify the Parents or Guardians. If a third time, the pupil is suspended for one month, the Parents or Guardians being notified thereof. A fourth similar offense is followed by expulsion.

VI. A pupil absent from the class is marked zero for all studies missed. When absence has been unavoidable an opportunity for hearing the lesson missed is afforded the pupil. Parent's or Guardian's written excuse for absence is required before pupil can be readmitted to class.

VII. All complaints respecting discipline or other matters pertaining to the school must be made to the Chairman of the School Board.[51]

In addition to supplying systematic rules to govern the affairs of the KI religious school, Superintendent Joseph Krauskopf also applied "bureaucratic" principles of organization. He subdivided the program into three distinct departments. There was a "Primary Department" for youngsters ages six through eight, a "Regular Department" for eight to fourteen, a "Confirmation Department" for pupils from fourteen to sixteen, plus supplementary post-Confirmation and Alumni Association departments beyond the scope of the religious school. Furthermore, the reorganized religious school program included "Normal School" teacher training opportunities in Jewish History, Literature, and Religious Ideology. The idea of formal training and certification for educators was in sync with the emergence of a professionally trained corps of teachers in public and church educational circles. Krauskopf's goal was to retrain public school faculty or other potentially qualified personnel. He needed Americanized staff suitable for educating more than four hundred fifty boys and girls in KI's expanding religious school of the mid-1890s. In tandem with enhanced standards of education, the religious school's capability was enlarged by the creation of a KI library and reading room on 19 November 1890. The library had "rationalized" categories of adult, juvenile, and elementary-age Judaica and general literature. It operated according to disciplined library rules and regulations.[52]

Similar "rationalized" changes are noted in the Minute Books of K.K. B'nai Yeshurun's Talmud Yelodim Institute. They were codified at the national level by the "Plan of Instruction in the Jewish Sabbath School" adopted by the seventh annual Convention of the CCAR in 1896.[53] As Rabbi Harry Mayer indicated to the 1902 CCAR Convention, in an evaluation of the previous ten years entitled "The Jewish Religious School."

The Jewish Sunday School in America [that is, a one day per week program] is an offshoot of the system that is in vogue in Germany. The Christian Sunday School in this country is virtually a "children church" with the same lesson in all classes, as assigned by the International Sunday School Board, and using the Bible as a storehouse of ethical and religious passages. The Jewish Sunday School on the other hand, like its German prototype, has a *graded system of classes* in which the Bible is taught as history, philosophy, ethics, literature and law [emphasis added].[54]

Changes in the Roles of Religious Leaders

The Rabbinate

Cincinnati's K.K. B'nai Yeshurun was served by Rabbi I.M. Wise for the unusually lengthy period of 1854 through 1900. Wise's tenure encompassed two "generations" of this study. The other three senior rabbis in the sample temples at the end of the nineteenth century were Jacob Voorsanger (who assumed the pulpit of Emanu-El of San Francisco in 1889), Joseph Krauskopf (who became the rabbi of Philadelphia's Keneseth Israel in 1887), and Maximilian Heller (appointed by Temple Sinai of New Orleans in 1887). Rabbi Wise and his peers of the "first generation" had been born between the years 1809 and 1820. The second generation of rabbinic leaders had dates of birth that ranged from 1852 (for Voorsanger) to 1858 (for Krauskopf) and 1860 (for Heller). Part of the effort to attract younger members in the 1880s was the hiring of youthful rabbis. Thus, the second generation in our study became senior rabbis of major congregations at relatively youthful ages (thirty-seven for Voorsanger, twenty-nine for Krauskopf, and twenty-seven for Heller).

The decade of the 1880s was a time of heightened Central and Western European identification by the UAHC temples. Each of the sample congregations selected a rabbi of national descent similar to their laity. Voorsanger was of German parentage and had been born in culturally allied Holland. Krauskopf's place of birth was inside Germany. Heller had been a native of Central European, German-speaking Bohemia like I. M. Wise. Reflecting the gradual impact of professional values, two of the three rabbis had been trained at the new Hebrew Union College (HUC) in Cincinnati. Krauskopf and Heller were graduates of the first and second classes, respectively, of the HUC. This pattern contrasted with the privately ordained or self-taught approach of Voorsanger[55] and of Rabbi Wise's earlier experience of informal tutelage.

In spite of their youth, these rabbinic candidates already had proven to be capable pulpit leaders. Rabbi Voorsanger had served with distinction in Providence, Rhode Island, in 1878, and in Houston, Texas, from 1879 to 1885. Rabbi Krauskopf ably conducted the affairs of B'nai Yehudah of Kansas City, Missouri, from 1883 to 1887. Max Heller had been an effective Associate Rabbi in Chicago's Zion Congregation (1884–1886) and then Voorsanger's competent successor in Houston from 1886 to 1887. Their youth and vigor, their ethnic characteristics, and their admirable professional experiences made these candidates highly desirable to prospective employers.

The critical link between many rabbinic candidacies and temple employment was Isaac Mayer Wise. Rabbi Wise had emerged as the "dean" of the late-nineteenth-century German American rabbinate. Isaac M. Wise was founder and President of the Hebrew Union College, a member of its faculty, and a constant traveler to congregations throughout the country. He was well suited to evaluate the abilities, performance, and current employment prospects of potential rabbinic applicants. The HUC graduates in particular felt themselves bound by his decisions. In his reminiscences of his first pulpit assignment, Rabbi David Philipson, one of the four graduates in the College's first class, reflected upon this perception.

Dr. Wise asked me to come to his office, as he had a very important matter to present to me. I had scarcely entered the room when he, without any ado, said, "You are going to Baltimore." I was startled and asked for an explanation of this sudden announcement. It then appeared that he had received a letter from the Har Sinai congregation, which was vacant. As I was the only graduate who was unplaced in a pulpit, it was Hobson's choice. "But," said I to him, "Doctor, you know that I do not want to take a position this year. I have refused four positions that were offered." "Ah!" replied he, "but this is different. This is the first offer from an Eastern congregation. And besides it is the Einhorn congregation. It is a great triumph for us that they ask for one of our graduates." He was really exultant. In vain I pleaded that I would rather remain and teach. But he was adamant. His will was law for me.[56]

Rabbi Wise had a powerful personality and growing influence with the new American rabbinate, increasingly composed of the graduates of HUC. Wise accurately boasted that for central European-oriented synagogues seeking a rabbi, his intervention was crucial. The "only proper way of making this declaration [that a pulpit is vacant and seeks candidates]" to the Jewish and general public was through Wise's *American Israelite*, and his personal network of relationships.[57] As Rabbi Wise indicated to his readers in the Spring of 1896:

as the confirmation usually takes place on this date [Shavuot], it may be considered as closing the year's work for the Rabbi. Congregations who have no incumbent for their pulpits or who are desirous of making a change will find it to their advantage to make their desires known now. Rabbis as a rule will not make application for election unless invited to do so, by advertisement of vacancies or otherwise. Congregations therefore should announce vacancies present or prospective, in these columns at once.[58]

Beyond the initial entree provided by Rabbi Wise for the most desirable of younger candidates, each temple proceeded with its own search process. An example of this technique was KI's recruitment of Joseph Krauskopf. In April 1885, the search committee of Keneseth Israel contacted Krauskopf about a position as associate rabbi and heir apparent to the aging Rabbi Samuel Hirsch. Krauskopf refused; however, KI recontacted him several months later when Hirsch decided to retire. This time the Kansas City rabbi expressed interest, although he refused to submit to the test of a trial sermon. This refusal may have been a matter of principle or a delaying tactic. Krauskopf simultaneously was pursuing a possible appointment as the associate rabbi to Gustav Gottheil at Manhattan's Temple Emanu-El, America's most prestigious and largest congregation.

By early 1886, Rabbi Krauskopf's chances for the New York City post had been dashed. Nevertheless, again he turned down the opportunity for a trial sermon at KI. Krauskopf professed that he was quite content to stay in Kansas City. Rabbi Krauskopf's continuing reluctance may have stemmed from the active interest in the KI position shown by his friend and colleague Max Heller. Meanwhile, the Philadelphia temple invited Rabbi Solomon Schindler of Boston to address the congregation. This invitation was an obvious indication that Rabbi Heller was an unlikely first choice. Although keen interest remained in recruiting Rabbi Schindler, the continued desire to recruit Joseph Krauskopf forced KI to alter its approach. The Philadelphia temple sent Arnold Kohn of the "Special Committee for Obtaining a Rabbi" to Kansas City to listen to Krauskopf's preaching and "if sufficiently impressed, to offer a $6,000 salary and a five year contract . . . [and if unsatisfactory] to go also to Louisville to hear Rev. Mr. [Adolph] Moses." Rabbi Joseph Krauskopf proved to be Kohn's choice, and the rabbi accepted the KI offer. At the very same time, after considering several candidacies of rabbis offering similar qualifications, Temple Sinai of New Orleans also chose Krauskopf to be their preferred successor to the recently deceased Rabbi James K. Gutheim. When Rabbi Krauskopf definitively rejected this offer, Temple Sinai turned to Max Heller. Rabbi Heller presented a successful trial sermon in New Orleans and then was "elected to office."[59]

Given the desirability and scarcity of attractive young rabbis, Krauskopf's B'nai Jehudah congregation in Kansas City decided to do battle with KI and Krauskopf to retain the rabbi's services. On the 25 September 1887, the President of Keneseth Israel received the following two telegrams.

Our congregation, our citizens and surrounding country insist that Rabbi Krauskopf remain among us. A delegation will be with you in a few days.

Louis Hammerslough

Great excitement prevails, the Congregation will not let me go and they bring the weight of the whole city to bear upon me, though sold out and packed up, I am asked to await the result of a conference between you and a delegation from here.

Jos. Krauskopf

Despite the lobbying effort by the Kansas City laity, KI's successful recruitment of Krauskopf prevailed.

With rabbis in great demand, the issue of breaking an existing employment arrangement with one's congregation was a growing source of national concern. In November of 1894, for example, Temple Sinai had to tender a $600 raise to Max Heller to ward off a recruitment bid by a prominent New York City congregation. This problem had been occurring for decades. The 21 June 1878 edition of the *American Israelite*, for example, offered the following lament: "[once a candidate] is elected, he enters upon his duties, but you find him again as a candidate as soon as the next place is advertised." In 1889 at the first national convention of the CCAR, Rabbi Hahn delivered a paper about occupational ethics. The paper stressed "the necessity of honoring contractual obligations," as well as "the professional ethics" involved in colleagues "competing for positions." Several years later, a Committee on Ethics recommended a formal code to end this source of chaos in synagogue-rabbi relations.[61]

The recruitment of this second generation of rabbis was sometimes part of a search for a second or "associate rabbi" to meet the needs of expanding temple institutions. The associate rabbi provided an additional preacher capable of delivering English sermons or lectures in rotation with the German sermons of the "senior rabbi." The associate's role involved interacting with younger, English-speaking members and prospective members. An example of this approach was the hiring of Rabbi James K. Gutheim in the late 1860s as an associate for Rabbi Gustav Gottheil of Temple Emanu-El in New York. However, some of Gottheil's contemporaries resisted this approach. For example, KI's German-speaking and aging Rabbi Samuel Hirsch indicated in February of 1881 that "two rabbis in a congregation cannot work harmoniously together . . . [and that] it is his right [as senior rabbi], as long as he is the rabbi to have the pulpit on Saturdays and holidays for himself, and not let someone else take over."[62]

By the mid-1880s, Samuel Hirsch and his generation of UAHC rabbis began to approach or exceed seventy years of age. Pressure mounted for the hiring of a younger rabbi to meet the needs of expanding congregational size and function, and to attract more young adults. In 1885, even Rabbi Hirsch acceded to these goals. Subsequently, his temple KI sought an associate rabbi, a search eliminated only because of Hirsch's sudden decision to retire. Similarly, in San Francisco's Emanu-El, aging Rabbi

Elkan Cohn agreed to the appointment of Associate Rabbi Abraham Illch in 1885. Illch tragically died of illness after only six months of service. Illch's successor in 1886 was Associate Rabbi Jacob Voorsanger. Voorsanger became the rare associate to be promoted ultimately to senior rabbi, in 1889, following the death of Elkan Cohn.

In 1889, Cincinnati's K.K. B'nai Yeshurun followed this pattern by providing a second rabbi to assist their elderly Senior Rabbi I. M. Wise.[63] To fill his new position, KKBY chose Rabbi Charles Levi, an 1889 HUC graduate. The bylaws of KKBY were changed to read:

> The assistant rabbi shall attend divine services regularly, read the prayers under the direction of the Board, preach from time to time, as shall be arranged between the Rabbi, himself and the Board; attend all funerals of members of this congregation and of any of their families and preach funeral services whenever requested to do so; perform the marriage ceremony whenever called upon in the absence, and with the consent of the Rabbi perform such duties as teacher of the Talmud Yelodim Institute [KKBY Religious School] as may be imposed upon him by the Board of such institution consistent with the dignity of his office; and in general to perform such duties of the rabbinical office as he may be called upon.[64]

By the mid-1890s, a second full-time rabbi was an accepted aspect of large UAHC temples, regardless of the age of the senior rabbi. The presence of associate rabbis enabled the congregations to serve a proliferation of needs among the laity. In 1893 at KI in Philadelphia, for example, Rabbi J. Leonard Levy (age twenty-eight and a graduate of Jews' College in London) was hired as the associate rabbi for the young and energetic senior rabbi, Joseph Krauskopf (age thirty-five). Lay leadership recognized the enormous increase in the temple's base of activities (for example, social justice projects, young adult activities, adult education, and religious school expansion). Thus, Keneseth Israel's president sought to introduce a "division of labor" into the five hundred plus member temple, also its "school and [auxiliary] societies . . . [since] it is our duty to see that the Doctor [Krauskopf] does not overwork himself."[65]

The role of the senior rabbi had not been altered dramatically since the founding generation of rabbis (discussed in Chapter One). Unlike the premodern rabbi who had served either a local *bet din* (rabbinic court with coercive authority) or *yeshivah*, the temple rabbi's domain was that of a single congregation. He preached at the Sabbath and holiday services that he arranged and conducted. When called upon, he officiated at weddings, funerals, and other life-cycle occasions. The rabbi communicated a modern approach to Judaism for the next generation. He supervised the affairs of the temple's religious school and taught the oldest children in their Confirmation studies. In addition, he was the liaison to the general community in ecumenical Thanksgiving and other civic celebrations and in contact with the larger Christian community.

Two major arenas of expanded rabbinic roles differentiated between the first and second generation of rabbis in the sample temples. These enlarged domains were concerned with his administrative and pastoral roles. The growing volume of auxiliary educational, cultural, and social action programs intended to attract the younger generation created a substantial administrative challenge. In terms of proliferating managerial tasks, one needs only to recall the innovations of KI's Rabbi Krauskopf. He instituted not just a departmentalized religious school, a post-Confirmation class, an Alumni Association, a "Knowledge Seekers" club, a library, and a Jewish Publication Society for young adults, but also social justice initiatives such as the Model Dwelling Association, the Sterilized Milk and Ice Society, the KI Sewing Circle, the National Farm School project, and the "Home of Delight" settlement house, all in addition to Sunday Rabbinic public lectures and classes. One might also call attention to Jacob Voorsanger's comprehensive social welfare initiatives launched by the Emanu-El Sisterhood for Personal Service, serving the educational, employment, and service needs of the Russian and Polish immigrants. In a parallel fashion, Protestant clergy experienced similar administrative challenges. "[The] minister presided over the multifarious activities of the institutional church. Success in this position required real administrative ability. The staff under his authority might include associate ministers . . . numerous lay volunteer workers, secretarial and custodial help."[66]

In addition to administration, a new expectation of "home visitations," a "pastoral role" at times of illness or distress, vastly expanded the role of the clergyperson. Pastoral work involved a substantial time commitment when dealing with hundreds of families.

Pastoral service is meant that the rabbi should be in close and frequent contact with the homes of the members of his congregation, should visit them in their illnesses, to comfort them and sustain their spirits, give them solace in their hours of grief and bereavement, as well as to be with his people in their homes on occasions of joy and happiness.[67]

The emergence of this extensive pastoral responsibility can be traced to American Protestantism's discomfort with urbanization and the impersonal nature of the city. In the 1870s, books abounded describing the minister not only as "physician of the soul" but also as "social director." Popular titles included Stephen Tyng's *Office and Duty of a Christian Pastor* (1874), William Plumer's *Helps and Hints in Pastoral Theology* (1874), James Hoppin's *Pastoral Theology* (1885), and G. B. Wilcox's *The Pastor Amidst His*

Flock (1890).[68] Pastoral efforts within urban areas sought to "strengthen the inner fellowship of the local church, to bring about a genuine community in which each individual has a sense of being a member of one body."[69]

Initially, this "pastoral" dimension of the rabbinate was not added formally to the bylaws of K.K. B'nai Yeshurun and the other temples in question. Seldom was it discussed by boards of trustees. Some rabbis of major Reform temples and their supporters even resisted this expansion of their role. As one of Rabbi Emil Hirsch's ardent supporters boasted, "[Hirsch] was spared the petty annoyances of latter day communal activities, such as pastoral calls, personal visitation on insignificant as well as noteworthy events among the members of his congregation." Yet as I. M. Wise took note in his 11 May 1893 *American Israelite* editorial about the changing pulpit rabbinate, the pastoral dimension had begun to be an expected part of the rabbinic agenda.[70] In a report on trends during the past decade written in 1902, the American Reform rabbinate was informed that with regard to

pastoral visiting of the rabbi . . . though here and there we find one [rabbi] to number it [disparagingly] among "chukat hagoy [imitation of non-Jewish practices]" and though very few rabbis, especially in the larger cities, find time or inclination to visit their people in their homes except on occasions of great joy or great sorrow, yet the practically unanimous opinion is that such visits do tend to help the work of the rabbi among the people.[71]

Pastoral responsibilities rapidly proliferated. Slightly more than a decade later, CCAR member Rabbi William Rosenau of Baltimore indicated that in the past twelve months alone he had made 637 pastoral visits accompanied by his wife and 1,122 by himself.[72]

The scope of the pulpit rabbi's involvements also increased with pressures to offer rabbinic speeches at times other than the Sabbath. Rabbinic lectures became necessary to respond to the courting of young people by secular orators like Felix Adler. Young men and women demanded rabbinic sermons and lectures that departed from the themes and proof texts of the weekly Torah reading. Some rabbis opposed this change. Throughout his lifetime, Rabbi Isaac Mayer Wise advised, "never preach a sermon without a text from the Bible, a text containing the theme that you can elaborate. The text is the best proof in support of your argument. A sermon without a text is an argument without a proof."[73]

Wise used the Torah portion as a springboard to address general ethical concerns. Wise's approach to homiletics had not changed during his half century of life in the United States. As an immigrant on the boat traveling to America, "one of his shipmates, a Boston schoolteacher, recommended that Wise obtain a copy of Hugh Blair's *Lectures on Rhetoric and Belles Lettres*. Wise followed that advice, calling his purchases of Blair's *Lectures* and Joseph Addison's *Spectator* his first 'important purchases in the United States.'" In 1888, as an instructor in homiletics at HUC, Rabbi Wise was still assigning "Blair's lectures on rhetoric," as a basic sermonic model.[74]

The new generation of rabbis was not content with this limited approach. Classical sermons in the vernacular had excited a pious, church- and synagogue-attending generation of the 1860s. The 1880s demanded a willingness to speak about contemporary issues as well, even during the worship service. The preaching of Jacob Voorsanger, representative of the second group of rabbis in our study, differed markedly from the preceding generation of German Jewish preachers in America. Voorsanger did not

"shy away from political and other controversial issues." He attacked with frenzy, in his sermons . . . Zionism, open immigration, Orthodoxy, ritual, the Philippine War, imperialism, legalism, socialism, materialism, Edward Bellamy, Rabbi Emil G. Hirsch, the Democratic Party, and his local Orthodox colleagues.[75]

Similar topics were among the themes of Joseph Krauskopf's sermons and lectures on the Sabbath as well as weekly Sunday services that he conducted as of 1887 at Philadelphia's KI. Krauskopf's topics included "Judaism and Unitarianism, Their agreements and disagreements"; "Judaism and the Ethical Culture Society"; "Who is Responsible, the Church or the State"; "Intermarriage"; "Jesus in the Synagogue"; "Is This A Christian Nation"; "Model Dwellings for the Poor"; "Anti-semitism: Its Cause and Cure." As Rabbi Gustav Gottheil of Manhattan's flagship Temple Emanu-El observed: "The Reformed Rabbi of today is a public teacher; he instructs at all services; the Temple is his academy. . . . [Preaching] does not confine itself to religious topics, strictly speaking, but draws into the sphere of its discussions every vital topic that occupies the public mind."[76]

Timely presentations excited the younger generation of American Jews of Central European descent. Nonetheless, a novel approach to preaching was not without its critics. As Isaac Mayer Wise claimed in the pages of the *American Israelite* of 5 December 1897:

one of the reasons that rabbis deliver lectures instead of sermons from their pulpits is because it is easier to do so. Any man with a university training can take a book, review it, well or indifferently, and by liberal quotations make the discourse more or less interesting. . . . It is a sign of weakness, or of mental poverty or of laziness for a Rabbi to offer such a substitute for his sermons when the work in question has solid value.[77]

Yet whether sermon or lecture, the pressure to produce twice or more each week major public statements regarding the great issues of the day represented a substantial increase in the preparation and self-study demands placed on pulpit preachers.

Besides growing responsibilities in administration, pastoral visits and sermon/lecture preparation, Rabbis Wise, Voorsanger, and Heller devoted time to Jewish newspapers as a medium of communication. Wise was the editor of the *American Israelite*. Voorsanger edited San Francisco's *Jewish Progress* from 1893 to 1895 when it was succeeded by his *Emanu-El* weekly edition. Heller edited the New Orleans *Jewish Ledger* in 1896 and 1897.[78]

As the time demands placed on the pulpit rabbi continued to multiply, personal scholarship suffered. Unlike I.M. Wise, this second generation of rabbinic leaders, teachers, preachers, pastors and administrators was unable to produce scholarly works. In *Isaac Mayer Wise: His Life, Work and Thought*, James G. Heller provides six full pages of Rabbi Wise's impressive list of publications. Noteworthy were his *History of the Israelitish Nation* (560 pages), *The History of the Hebrews' Second Commonwealth* (386 pages), *The Cosmic God* (a full-length theology), and *Minhag America* (a prayerbook). In contrast, only the most scholarly of the trio of Voorsanger, Krauskopf, and Heller was able to leave a scholarly legacy. Voorsanger produced manuscripts for translations of Obadiah, Jonah, and Psalms for the Jewish Publication Society (JPS). However, only the Book of Psalms material ultimately was published by JPS.[79] As I. M. Wise lamented in his 11 May 1893 editorial section of the *American Israelite*:

[the current pulpit rabbi] must preach or lecture twice a week; conduct the sabbath school properly; prepare annually the confirmation class and attend the post-confirmation class; officiate at weddings, funerals and such other occasions; do pastoral duty with the sick, mourners, and in other domestic cases; and have some time left for study and self-culture, or for literary employment . . . yet the fashionable world expects of him quite a number of social performances which a man of work cannot possibly accomplish, certainly not in a large congregation, without sacrificing the time which should be devoted to duty . . . this is the cause that with a few honorable exceptions we have no Rabbi scholars in this country and very little hope to produce any.[80]

The decline in the scholarly productivity of the pulpit rabbi was reflected also in the diminished frequency of rabbinic doctorates. In a sample of UAHC temple rabbis from 1880, 55 percent (14 of 26) possessed a Central European university Ph.D. (see Appendix Table A). By contrast, in 1900 the percentage of rabbis holding Ph.D. degrees had plummeted. Out of 72 HUC graduates between 1883 and 1900, the only advanced degrees were the following: 7 of the 8 initial HUC ordained rabbis (1883–1884) completed the College's D.D. program (however, almost no other Hebrew Union College graduates throughout the next 16 years pursued this D.D. path); two rabbis, Adolf Guttmacher and William Rosenau, both

German-born HUC ordainees, each received a Ph.D. at Johns Hopkins University. In addition, among the CCAR's membership of more than 150 rabbis in 1900, there were still quite a few European-trained rabbis (2 at the JTS of Breslau, 2 at Geiger's Hochschule, 1 at Jews' College, and 16 privately ordained), as well as 2 American-trained rabbis (graduates of the New York Emanu-El Theological Seminary) whose credentials did include a Ph.D. (see Appendix Table B). The future for the UAHC rabbinate was being molded by nonacademic trends within the HUC and local rabbinic experience. A shift of emphasis occurred in the direction of professionalized (practical) rather than scholarly (research and publication-directed) endeavor.

Reform "Cantorate" and Liturgy

A related feature of the UAHC temple at the turn of the century was its creation of a role for cantors. The appearance of Reform cantors represented a departure from the norms of the mid-nineteenth-century Reform service in America.

With its abbreviated Hebrew texts, its introduction of prayers and hymns in English, and its use of the organ . . . [the mid-nineteenth-century Reform service in America] caused a great technical difficulty in the musical rendition of the service. The historical interpretor of the synagogue song, the chazzan, could not suffice. . . . First, most . . . were not trained in modern music and in singing with organ accompaniment. Secondly, the song of the chazzan itself, the traditional chant in unrhythmical modes, no longer appealed to the occidentalized American Reform congregations. And finally . . . the American Reform congregations, like those in Germany, preferred a mixed choir, after the model of the Protestant Church.[81]

Rabbis in Germany during the first half of the nineteenth century liberally borrowed from the preaching style of the German Protestant church. The same type of indebtedness applied to mid-nineteenth-century American and German synagogue liturgy. Non-Jewish models had to be utilized to supply music for the Reform temple. Church organists were engaged in the temple and commissioned to hire the church choristers as well. Tunes for hymns often were adopted from the church, or, following the procedure of the Hamburg Temple, composed by Christian musicians in the Church style. Anthems and solos, a new item introduced into the Reform service according to the model of the Protestant church, also were taken from Christian sacred music.[82]

Given this cultural bias toward the liturgical standards of the Protestant churches, no *chazzan* tradition emerged within the American Reform temple until the latter part of the nineteenth century. During his early years as a rabbi in America, Isaac Mayer Wise's lamented about the old-time *chazzan*. "He was sui generis, half priest, half beggar, half oracle, half fool, as the occasion demanded. Among all the *chazzanim* who [sic] I learned to know at that time, there was not one who had a common-school education or possessed any Hebrew learning."[83] Old-style *chazzanim* had served during the antebellum years in congregations such as Wise's K.K. B'nai Yeshurun. However, a shortened service combined with the centrality accorded to the rabbinic sermon and to choir and organ made the *chazzan*'s involvement unnecessary.

The creation of the Society of American Cantors as a partner in composing the UAHC *Hymnal* in 1897 was related to the emergence of a modern American Reform "cantorate." In 1894, Temple Sinai of New Orleans hired the Hungarian-born Cantor Julius Braunfeld. In the early months of 1898, Cincinnati's K.K. B'nai Yeshurun, which had abolished the traditional office of "Reader" on 27 September 1889, decided to reverse itself by seeking to employ not an old-style *chazzan* but a contemporary Reform style cantor. Jewish periodicals took note of the restoration of the cantor's role in many German Reform temples. The very term "cantor," meaning "chanter" or "singer" in German rather than *chazzan*, first was used by a Jewish prayer leader, Cantor Salomon Sulzer (1804 to 1890 in Vienna). Sulzer revolutionized the Reform notion of the cantorate. His Austrian, Hungarian, and German disciples within the American Reform ambience created a distinctive niche for the temple cantor. Late-nineteenth-century Reform congregations still were able to get along without a *chazzan*, "but if a musical leader [cantor] came along who knew how to reshape and revitalize the service [along the lines which Sulzer had created], the laity might be swayed by his personality."[84]

Cantor Edward Stark was a disciple of Sulzer. Stark served San Francisco's Emanu-El from 1893 through the following two decades. Stark's father, Cantor Joseph Stark, trained in Vienna with Sulzer. Joseph Stark transmitted this legacy personally to his son. In the genre of the Sabbath and holiday service that the new-style Cantor would compose or implement, many works performed were his own. Frequently, he also included the compositions of Salomon Sulzer. A number of different (Central and Western European) composers and styles made up the remainder of his selections. They were adaptations of works of Haydn, Gounod, Auber, Flotow, and Reinecke as well as a few compositions by Schubert and Mendelssohn.[85]

Under the influence of Sulzer, talented and inspirational men like Cantor Edward Stark created yet another unique feature for Reform Judaism within the American Jewish scene.

Music was given a prominent position in the service. It consisted of the cantor's solo work, choral numbers, and congregational singing reinforced by the choir. Much of the music, including all large choral works and most of the congregational singing, was sung in English. The traditional congregational responses were sung in hebrew. The character of the service was very dignified.[86]

Cantor Edward Stark also fulfilled a variety of roles beyond composing and arranging Reform religious services. Although he was not intended to be the *kol bo*, the "jack of all trades" that Isaac M. Wise had disdained decades earlier, neither was he to limit his efforts to liturgy alone. The "Bylaws of the Congregation Emanu-El" listed the following description of the role of the cantor:

Article II. Duties of the Cantor. Section 1. The Cantor shall be present on all occasions of Divine service at the proper time. Section 2. He shall attend all funerals and read the service at the house of mourning at the request of the family. Section 3. He shall be assigned a class in the Religious School as teacher, by the Superintendent and School Committee. Section 4. He shall be director of the choir and perform such other duties as the Board of Directors may prescribe.[87]

In the fulfillment of these ample tasks, Edward Stark achieved a high status among his laity worthy of the handsome salary of $4,500 per year. Stark reached this plateau by the middle years of the first decade of the twentieth century. As Choirmaster, Cantor Stark worked diligently with organists Louis Schmidt (through 1896) and W. A. Sabin (1896 and thereafter). He hired the best singers in the Bay area available in local theaters, opera houses, and church choirs and rehearsed them according to a rigorous schedule. Stark was also a prolific composer whose creations were performed in the San Francisco community at large. As an educator, Stark collaborated with Rabbi Voorsanger in the publication of the temple's *Services for Children*. He wrote and directed drama productions at the religious school and taught and led singing within the Sabbath School's weekly sessions. At the pastoral level, Cantor Stark "conducted many, if not all, of the congregation's weddings, funerals and unveilings," during the hiatus of rabbinic service created for eighteen months by the sudden death of Voorsanger.[88]

The institution of a cantorial role in the last quarter of the nineteenth century was accompanied by wide-ranging changes in liturgy, responding to the malaise among younger prospective members. One accommodation to alienation already had been implemented by the first generation of rabbis in our study. They offered Sabbath services late on Friday evening, at a time more suitable to the average American work schedule.[89] This format had become almost universal in the Reform temples by the 1880s. In 1882, Rabbi Wise editorialized in the pages of the *American Israelite* that the reformed Friday evening service with lecture has proved most beneficial to our Congregations. . . . [I]t secures a good attendance in the house of worship at least once a week, and has in many localities fostered religious feelings and an attachment to the congregation, where absence from religious exercises has led to frigid indifference.[90]

A related experiment in this regard was the controversial innovation of a Sunday morning service akin to Felix Adler's Sunday Lectures. Basing this change upon German Rabbi Samuel Holdheim's proclamation four decades earlier at the Breslau Conference that "the religious purpose of the Sabbath can be realized on some other day . . . to save the Sabbath for Judaism," Kaufman Kohler introduced Sunday services to the American Jewish scene in his Chicago temple (Sinai), nine years after the Civil War. By the early 1880s, this experiment was implemented at Philadelphia's Keneseth Israel occasionally and continued at Chicago's Sinai Temple by Rabbi Emil Hirsch with regularity and great fanfare. In the pages of the Philadelphia *Jewish Exponent* of 9 December 1887, Hirsch claimed:

The Sunday services in Chicago were a necessity; they filled a want, and in consequence they are a decided success. Our Temple is almost filled every Sunday. . . . [T]he decline of [Saturday] Sabbath observance was the cause and the effect of our Sunday services. . . . Let anyone attend our services and he will not be long in doubt that he is in a Jewish house of worship and not a Christian one.

This specific accommodation to the "spirit of the times" was rejected by Isaac M. Wise and most other Reform rabbis as a "surrender to Christianity." On 3 October 1886, Wise's Temple KKBY forbade rabbis supporting "the transference of the Hebrew Sabbath from Saturday to any other day" from being guest preachers.[91]

Among the advocates of Sunday services was Rabbi Joseph Krauskopf of our sample congregation Keneseth Israel in Philadelphia. In his first full year at KI in 1887, Joseph Krauskopf substituted a weekly Sunday service for the Friday evening ritual. In defense of his program, Krauskopf proclaimed:

instead of surrendering to Christianity, because of the Sunday services, we may reasonably hope to gain by means of them many a Christian to our way of thinking and believing. His leisure on Sunday will enable him to attend our services. . . . [Moreover] the Friday evening substitute is dishonest. I saw them [congregants] rush from their stores to the Temple, and again to them after the conclusion of the services, and this one and one half hour they called "observing the Sabbath . . ." [whereas] Sunday . . . is an honest rest and recreation for twenty-four hours, from sunrise to sunrise.[92]

In 1888, the president of the temple acknowledged that Krauskopf's sermons are "bringing so many attentive hearers to the Saturday as well as

Sunday services . . . [that we] hope that present seat holders will soon become members by buying seats and that our young men and women will take renewed interest in Jewish matters."[93] The 1897 *KI Annual* reported:

President Lewin told in a brief but forceful address of the influence the Sunday Services had on the growth of the Congregation, and Max Herzberg, Esq. one of the young men of the Congregation, in most eloquent terms told of the influence for good the Sunday Services have had on the young people of Keneseth Israel.[94]

Another response to the perceived needs of the young was the UAHC's adoption in 1892 of the *Union Prayer Book*, to provide a basic unity to America's Reform temples, and a brief but clearly stated liturgy. As KI's chronicler Howard Fineschriber observed: "Members of the congregation would feel at home in the service when visiting other congregations and would have a greater sense of belonging to the family of Reform Jews." The composition of the *Union Prayer Book* was an example of how German "ethnic church" styles were intended to gradually replace the diversity of *minhagim* (local customs) of individual UAHC temples. The *Prayer Book* was an English-language version not of I. M. Wise's earlier *Minhag America*, but rather of Germanophile David Einhorn's *Olat Tamid*. On 29 January 1893, as an act of loyalty to the "uniformity" of the UAHC, Isaac Wise's K.K. B'nai Yeshurun consented to its rabbi's wishes and voted to replace his *Minhag America* with the new *Union Prayer Book*. On 27 October 1895, a similar experience occurred at New Orleans' Temple Sinai. Within ten years, the *Union Prayer Book* and its Friday night service dominated American Reform liturgy. Over sixty-two thousand copies of the *Union Prayer Book* were in circulation among 183 congregations.[95]

In addition, a participatory role was sought for the laity. This too was part of the effort to attract young adults. Congregational singing was intended to distinguish the temple service both from the *davening* (individually-paced) prayer services of Eastern European traditionalists as well as from the liturgical passivity of the previous generation of American Jews of German extraction. The effort to legislate greater participation in prayer built upon related efforts in temple religious schools. As early as 23 March 1877, for example, the board of directors of KKBY (Cincinnati) instructed Rabbi Wise to require attendance at religious services for the students of the Talmud Yelodim Institute (temple religious school). This requirement integrated participation in prayer with training youngsters in proper chanting and reading. By 30 September 1883, Philadelphia's Keneseth Israel introduced a series of hymns designed for congregational participation. KI also instituted a children's choir to further effect such goals.[96]

Reform Rabbi Joseph Leucht reflected the national surge of interest in this quest during his address to the East Coast Jewish Ministers' Association in 1887. Leucht lamented that "in eradicating the crying evil of disorderly participation . . . reform has trained the congregation into a lethargic state of indifferent listening to all that is taking place." The congregation's participatory role in prayer, "already restricted to docile, decorous hymn-singing in early German modernism, was cut back so far that by 1892 the CCAR began to worry that the spirit was going out of congregational worship by comparison to Christian practice." Like other UAHC rabbis in the 1890s, Isaac Mayer Wise was forced to acknowledge that "music is the language . . . of humanity and we have as yet been . . . too intellectual and too little emotional. . . . We need not become Methodists . . . but we should touch the soul, make people do what they seldom do in our synagogues, cry."[97]

Consequently, by 1896 temples like KKBY began to "introduce Congregational Singing," long absent from their highly formal and passive liturgy. Philadelphia's KI added similar practices that very same year, as did San Francisco's Emanu-El soon thereafter, and Temple Sinai during the subsequent decade.[98] Like Rabbi Krauskopf in Philadelphia and Rabbi Voorsanger in San Francisco, Rabbi Wise turned to the practice of increased choral singing by the laity and by religious school children. For this express purpose he created the Plum Street Temple Choral Society, "to become familiar with the traditional Jewish melodies, to assist the regular choir of the Temple."[99] To encourage this process, the CCAR issued a *Union Hymnal* in 1897, composed in tandem with the newly formed Society of American (German style) Cantors. The *Hymnal* consisted "mostly of English [language] hymns on universal themes, a few 'lifted bodily' from the hymnal of the Episcopalians." Each Reform temple gradually acquired and utilized the *Hymnal*, offering weekly classes and "rehearsals" to familiarize interested laity.[100]

To achieve active involvement in the prayer experience by the laity, several liturgical changes were introduced. The length of the Torah Reading was reduced. It was shortened from a triennial cycle to a seven-year cycle. In some temples, the Torah Reading was eliminated altogether, as at KI. Moreover, problems of passivity and boredom were addressed by limiting the Saturday morning format to one hour. The service was "stripped to its bare essentials." Hebrew sections were curtailed. "Service Manuals" were printed by most congregations, for example KKBY's *Manual* on 20 August 1888,[101] as well as KI's *Service manual* in 1888. The KI *Manual* included thirty different Sunday morning liturgies . . . [it was] entirely in English, except for one Hebrew sentence in each service to give it a "distinctively Jewish tone," and [included] . . . not only universal hymns by James Russell Lowell, John Greenleaf Whittier, and Joseph Krauskopf, but original prayers addressed to "Father of all" and filled with words that avoid sectarianism and exalt the religion of humanity.[102]

To appeal to American-born sons and daughters of members, Rabbi Krauskopf (KI) and his peers eliminated German sermons, German readings, and the use of German in conducting the liturgy. On 10 April 1881, for example, KI's president noted that "the sermon in the German language is unfruitful for the growing up generation."[103] Isaac M. Wise editorialized on the matter on 25 June 1882 in the *American Israelite*:

We protest against germanizing the synagogue. Our children are Americans. A great proportion of immigrating Israelites are not germans. . . . We have a national language [English] and it is the immigrants' duty to acquire it. . . . [Our children] must be taught and instructed in their native [English] language.[104]

The elimination of German had begun in Temple Sinai (New Orleans) and K. K. B'nai Yeshurun (Cincinnati) in the "first generation" of Reform rabbis. Both Rabbi I. M. Wise and Rabbi James K. Gutheim were able to alternate German and English sermons. In contrast, at Emanu-El (San Francisco) and Keneseth Israel (Philadelphia), neither Rabbi Elkan Cohn nor Rabbi Samuel Hirsch was sufficiently fluent in English. English sermons had to await the hiring of their successors, Jacob Voorsanger and Joseph Krauskopf in the late 1880s.[105]

Yet another concession to their courting of young adult offspring of temple members was devotion to church-like decorum. To create an ambience attractive to American-born Jews, elaborate rules of behavior were instituted. This represented an additional rejection of the informality of the synagogue life of Eastern European Jewry.[106] For example, KI's "Rules of Decorum" for 1891 to 1892 included the following stipulations:

1. A congregation's decorum in its House of Worship is an index of its Culture.
2. He that cannot honor God with a reverential behavior in His sanctuary dishonors himself.
3. A House of Worship is consecrated to Devotion, Instruction and Meditation, not to conversation and noisy behavior. . . .
5. Disturb not your neighbors' devotions by a noisy entrance after Service has begun, or by walking up the aisles during silent or standing devotion.
6. A congregation ever honors itself by honoring its minister with punctual attendance, with mannerly behavior and courteous attention.
7. The proper time for putting on wraps and coats is not till the Benediction has been given, and the minister has left the platform. . . .
10. Children that are too young to understand and to participate in the service will escape annoying you and your neighbors by being left at home.[107]

These aesthetic changes occurred within a global context. The history of modern Jewish religion has been characterized as a "civil war" between the norms of the Western synagogue and those of the Russian/Polish *shul*. An emphasis upon "order" and "decorum" had been imported into American Judaism from both Reform and neo-Orthodox Judaism of nineteenth-century Germany.[108] Additional influences in this direction came from English and American sources: Already in the 1840s Anglophiles such as Isaac Leeser and Isaac M. Wise afforded serious attention to western aesthetic concerns prominent among Episcopalian and other Anglo-American Protestant groups. In this fashion, many liberal as well as traditionalist American synagogues of the 1880s and beyond promoted Western cultural norms in conscious contrast to the ambience of Eastern European Jewry.

Just as institutional union was desired by both the Reform rabbinate and its laity, so were liturgical changes. Yet here again, in spite of similar goals, it was the tension between these two parties and their interactions that resulted in a unique configuration of liturgical innovations in the late nineteenth century. Rabbis were motivated to institute changes in response to the needs and demands of the laity, and the laity were influenced by the sage advice of its rabbis. But in the case of liturgical reform, the Reform laity often held the trump card. For instance, the decision whether or not to acquire the *Union Prayer Book* or *Hymnal* was determined by the Ritual Committee and the board of trustees, the ultimate ritual authorities within temple life. As the K.K. B'nai Yeshurun leadership reminded its rabbi on 25 February 1900, "no change shall be made in the ritual without the consent of the [Ritual] Committee."[109] On the one hand, the rabbi was present and actively participated in Temple Ritual Committee deliberations regarding a change in prayerbook, or the engagement of a cantor. On the other hand, the Ritual Committee members alone voted on these policies, and the board of trustees reserved the authority to veto the recommendations of the Ritual Committee.

Examples of the veto occurred when Temple Sinai's Board in 1893 forbade the adoption of the *Union Prayer Book* until further study, and when K.K. B'nai Yeshurun's Board in 1898 vetoed the use of the *Union Mahzor*. Veto power was all the more devastating for the rabbi or the cantor since both were excluded from attending board of trustee meetings, except for rare occasions when a special invitation would be tendered. Lay leadership closely guarded this separation of authority, as was evident by the opposition aroused when newly-appointed Rabbi Max Heller conducted an "unscheduled visit" to the Temple Sinai Board. A reprimand was issued warning against any repetition of this "infraction." Board members feared that "such a precedent would ultimately prove dangerous to the interests of the congregation." Contact for Heller and the other rabbis with the board of trustees was limited to written communication.[110] In this fashion, Reform lay leaders retained the upper hand in any power struggles with the pulpit rabbinate.

Conclusion

The innovations exhibited by local temples in the 1880s and 1890s primarily reflected a response to the secularization of American society and its impact upon second-generation German Jews. Secondarily, the changes indicated a group tension between an ethnically German Judaism and a flood of Jewish arrivals from Eastern Europe. In *The Sacred Canopy*, sociologist Peter Berger defines secularization as "the process by which sectors of society and culture are removed from the domination of religious institutions and symbols." The increase in leisure-time options in late-nineteenth-century America created intense rivalries for synagogues or churches seeking affiliates. "The vigorous tempo of American life . . . tended to crowd out the other-worldliness often associated with the life of the churches [and synagogues]." Sunday, the once unchallenged "Lord's Day," became to many Americans a day for visiting summer resorts, going to the theater, or attending sports events. The publishing of Sunday newspapers, the substantial increase in the use of railroads and street cars on Sunday, and the prevalence of a seven-day work week in numerous industries all indicated the use of Sunday for purposes other than churchgoing. Americans were also lured by the vitality of secular men's clubs and fraternal orders, ladies' benevolent societies and literary circles, recreational options such as the YMCA, and ethnic societies linking members to the language and customs of the Old World.[111]

In addition to facing stiff competition on the secular front, religious life within individual congregations stagnated. It reflected an antiquated vision of its mid-nineteenth-century founders. Neither recent immigrants nor the offspring of the founders were inspired by outdated aesthetic styles. Thus, the final years of the nineteenth century witnessed a crisis in churchgoing America. Many Jews and Christians alike became "alienated by long, dull sermons [no longer a novelty] and by the failure of some churches to present a service of spiritual vitality and inspiration." *Harper's Weekly* lamented that church liturgy was ill equipped to inspire the next generation. "Have not some of the poor children who, after being exhausted in Sunday School, are placed, without being permitted to sleep . . . up in those hard-seated galleries for long hours, been brought to dread the name of a church?" One alternative arena of urban religious vitality, the revivalism of Charles G. Finney and Dwight L. Moody with its fundamentalism and clearly missionizing intent, proved unappealing to American Jews, Catholics, and liberal Protestants.[112]

In response to the challenges of secularization, religious stagnation, and revivalism's missionizing, the UAHC adopted a marketing strategy that redefined the nature of synagogue life and synagogue membership. Temple leaders did not directly confront secularization; they refrained from challenging the unchurched to become more pious, more accepting of theology and prayer, and more willing to go against the tide. Instead Union affiliates—like Christian churches around them—co-opted secular activities within the programmatic agenda of the congregation. Rather than condemning cultural activities or philanthropic social service, houses of worship expanded their domain to incorporate these functions. To be a temple member came to mean involvement with any number of synagogue programs, such as prayer services, a religious school with departments for both elementary and teenage children, public lectures, women's social work projects, and temple center recreational activity. This enlarged framework catered to the consumers of religious life and made it easier to market synagogues to prospective members. By co-opting secular activities and gaining affiliates on that basis, temples deferred the core challenge represented by secularization to later generations.

It was also a strategy that addressed the challenge posed by increasing Jewish immigration from Eastern Europe in transforming UAHC congregations into narrowly ethnic churches. They confined their marketing efforts to Jews of similar ethnic background and socioeconomic status, focusing on their own children as the target population toward which additional reforms were aimed. Moreover, the interim success of local "institutional churches" and their expanded cultural offerings was limited for both Jews and Christians by bickering and by competition among neighboring institutions. To make the most of their initiatives, churches and synagogues pressured their denominational bodies to provide coordination. Adaptations by national Christian groups as well as by the UAHC during the final twenty years of the nineteenth century measurably aided this process.

❖ 4 ❖

The UAHC:
From Comprehensive Religious Union
to Distinctively Reform Movement

Although the majority of Jews in antibellum America were of
Germanic descent, for most of them German culture did not serve
as a primary frame of reference. The majority of these newcomers
were *Dorfjuden*, village "peddlers from Bavaria and tailors from Posen,
who had acquired minimal education in Europe and spoke little or no
German." This pattern was reflective of the experience of many German
Christian immigrants as well. Such Jewish and Christian immigrants often
entered the United States prepared to accept Anglo-American, in lieu of
Germanic, norms. Thus, they "proved singularly ineffective as a bridge
between their old and adopted countries."[1]

Moreover, the lack of available English translations of the major works
of German writers impeded cultural adaptation. In the pre-Civil war era,
the U.S. reading public was deprived of most English-language editions of
the works of Hegel and other German luminaries.[2] Without access to
German writings and ideas, Americans reacted with discomfort to overtly
Germanic notions offered indirectly by isolated university-trained central
European immigrants. As a result, Germanophiles like Rabbi David
Einhorn remained out of touch with American values and sensitivities.

Cultural historian Walter Metzger has concluded that: "[The] belated
recognition of Germany's real glory points up the factor of cultural
selection. Cultural goods can only be imported into friendly markets."
The 1860s was a momentous decade in the history of both the United
States and Germany. Both nations suffered major upheavals: the Civil War
in America and the wars of unification in Germany. The completion of a
transatlantic cable in 1867 sped transmission of news from Europe, so that
Americans learned early of the Prussian statesman Bismarck's diplomacy.
Bismarck maneuvered Austria and France into wars in 1866 and 1870,

respectively, and forged a united German empire in January 1871. With these stirring events being recorded for Americans, the image of Germany was enhanced within the United States. The 1870s "experienced a noticeable shift in America's attitude toward Germany from a feeling of somewhat condescending benevolence to one of respect and even admiration. . . . Both countries faced many of the same problems, stepped-up industrialization, rapid population growth, increased urbanization."[3]

The German university system provided a critical linkage between Central European and U.S. institutions. The founding of Johns Hopkins University four years prior to 1880 marked the first concentration of a large contingent of German-trained professors within one American campus. Nearly all of Johns Hopkins's 53 faculty members had studied in German university programs, including 13 German-sponsored Ph.D.'s. Inspired by the example of Johns Hopkins, over the next quarter of a century fifteen prominent graduate schools or departments were created. Whereas antebellum American colleges had not granted doctoral degrees, by the 1890s nearly three thousand postgraduate students pursued higher education in the United States.[4]

Aspiring historians, physicians, attorneys, clergy, jurists, writers, artists, scientists, educators, and social planners were affected by the German university system. They came to study in Central Europe or were influenced by German-schooled professors at emerging American graduate professional schools. To name a few, the following examples of subsequent molders of American life can be cited: journalist Lincoln Steffens, psychologist G. Stanley Hall, educator and philosopher John Dewey, anthropologist Franz Boaz, economist Richard Ely, theologian Walter Rauschenbusch, university innovator Andrew D. White, and philosopher William James. Symphony orchestras, operas, kindergartens, Bible scholarship, sociology, and virtually every other facet of American life was transformed by this process.[5] German culture became central to the late-nineteenth-century American frame of mind for Christians and Jews alike.

The Impact of German Culture

German Influences On American Jewish Life

The post-Civil War years were ripe for renewed American Jewish interest in developments within Central European Judaism. Throughout 1869, Reform Jewish leadership inside Germany achieved numerous successes.

Local and regional activity mounted, culminating in the widely publicized Leipzig rabbinical synod. Like-minded rabbis from Germany, Belgium, England, Austria-Hungary, and the United States attended the synod. As Philadelphia KI's Rabbi Samuel Hirsch proclaimed in 1871 at a German peace festival, there were "striking similarities between Germans and Jews . . . both were cosmopolitan, viewing the whole world as their home . . . both thought of liberty in terms of duty and responsibility to oneself and to God." American Jews admired German coreligionists for contributing richly both to general culture and to Jewish culture as well. In the decade and a half proceeding the 1880s, Jewish scholars in the United States translated into English the writings of luminaries of German Judaism, such as Geiger, Frankel, Zunz, Rapoport, Luzzato, Krochmal, and Holdheim.[6] German Jews in the United States took new pride in their central European roots and in Germany's mounting imperial prestige.

In addition, the growing number of German-born and German-trained rabbis arriving in the United States affected the American Jewish community. Only two years prior to mid-century, Isaac Leeser, I. M. Wise, Max Lilienthal, James Gutheim, Abraham Rice, and Leo Merzbacher were the sole German pulpit rabbis in America. But by 1880, this number had grown considerably, as evidenced by the following examples: Isadore Kalisch; Henry Hocheimer; Elkan Cohn; Liebman Adler; Bernhard Felsenthal, Samuel Adler; Benjamin Szold; Moses Mielziner; Marcus Jastrow; Samuel Hirsch; Adolph Huebsch; Kaufman Kohler; Adolph Moses; Isak Moses; Max Landsberg; and Gustav Gottheil.[7]

These men were not simply German by birth, but by training as well. Many received academic degrees within the German university system. Among German-schooled Ph.D.'s serving as the rabbis of UAHC congregations in 1880 were M. Samfield (Würzburg), M. Lilienthal (Munich), I. Schwab (Jena), S. Hirsch (Bonn), M. Jastrow (Halle), F. De Sola Mendes (Jena), S. H. Sonneschein (Jena), K. Kohler (Munich), G. Gottheil (Halle), A. Huebsch (Prague), M. Schlesinger (Prague), M. Landsberg (Halle), B. Felsenthal (Munich), and L. Wintner (Vienna). While the self-taught rabbis of antebellum America (such as I. M. Wise, Samuel Isaacs, and Isaac Leeser) modeled themselves after Protestant ministers, the German-trained U.S. rabbis of the 1880s were schooled and shaped by modern rabbinical seminaries. Central European rabbinical seminary graduates included F. De Sola Mendes (Breslau); B. Drachman (Breslau); A. Kohut (Breslau); M. Jastrow (Breslau); B. Szold (Breslau); S. Morais (Breslau); F. Adler (Geiger's Hochschule); E. Hirsch (Geiger's Hochschule); S. Sale (Geiger's Hochschule); S. Schulman (Geiger's Hochschule); and H. W. Schneeberger (Hildeshimer's Seminary).[8]

At the German rabbinical schools, native-born as well as Eastern European and American students were thoroughly Germanized. This was part of the effort to produce "cultured and sophisticated rabbis fit to represent German Jewry." Central European-trained rabbis found a receptive American environment in the 1880s. The general U.S. openness to Germanic trends during this era harmonized with an inbred tendency among the American Jewish laity to regard their liberal Judaism as Germanic. As immigrants, "they had been confirmed by liberal German rabbis; they were accustomed to a [German] reformed liturgy, to the newer German synagogue melodies, and the Reform ideas expounded from the liberal German pulpits. . . . They chose to preserve German in the home.[9] Admittedly, neither Central European concepts nor Reform Judaism gained total control within American Jewish life. Even in Cincinnati, the UAHC's home base, a monopoly was never achieved. Nevertheless, the time was ripe for Reform Jews to incorporate German organizational influences into their synagogues in the United States while still remaining in harmony with American cultural trends.

German Influences on the UAHC

The Pittsburgh Platform

A first example of the German influences on the UAHC was the replacement of the theological diversity of the Anglo-American union with the type of Central European ideological consistency previously advocated by David Einhorn. American Jews were not alone in facing a process of self-definition. American Christians too felt pressure to address challenges posed by Bible criticism, by Darwinian evolution, and by modern science and academic research emanating from Central and Western Europe. Aspiring clergy and social scientists returned from study within the German university system and challenged traditional religious assumptions. During "that seething decade 1883–93 . . . all the doctrines of Christianity were put in the crucible."[10]

In response, liberal Protestant and liberal Catholic thinkers in the United States attempted to harmonize age-old religion with modern ideas forging an approach known as "Modernism." Moreover, as a minority faith group in America, Catholic leaders articulated not only theological but also institutional responses to these challenges during the Third Baltimore Council convened in 1884. This national gathering became known as the "Magna Carta of American Catholic Church life." It established patterns of change in structure and belief that would resonate among American Catholics for decades to come.[11]

The mantel of mounting a similarly potent response by Reform Judaism fell to David Einhorn's son-in-law, Rabbi Kaufman Kohler, a Germanophile who convened a "synod" for Reform rabbis in Pittsburgh in 1885. Kaufman Kohler spent the first twenty-six years of his life in Germany. He remained very much a Central European. Rabbi Kohler came to the United States four years after the Civil War. He served briefly as the rabbi of Temple Beth El in Detroit, and then as the spiritual leader of Chicago's Temple Sinai. When his revered father-in-law passed away, Kaufman Kohler was named as Rabbi Einhorn's successor at Temple Beth El of New York City (1879). In 1884 and 1885, the liberal-minded Dr. Kohler publicly debated Rabbi Alexander Kohut, an impressive German Jewish scholar of traditionalist leanings, in well-publicized encounters pitting German Reform against its detractors. The tensions symbolized by these strident debates motivated Rabbi Joseph Krauskopf of Kansas City to write to Kaufman Kohler, urging him to convene rabbinic allies in defining a distinctive path for American Reform.[12]

Rabbi Kaufman Kohler's 1885 invitation to the Pittsburgh Conference was extended to "all such American rabbis as advocate reform and progress and are in favor of united action in all matters pertaining to the welfare of American Judaism."[13] In a manner reminiscent of German rabbinical conferences in Europe and of Einhorn's Philadelphia Rabbinic Conference, lay leaders as well as traditionalist rabbis were excluded from the deliberations. At Pittsburgh, true to the legacy of his deceased Germanophile father-in-law, Kohler advocated a clear and forceful ideological plank of commitments, an American Jewish version of Christian "Modernism." To gain support for this task, Rabbi Kohler invited the leading rabbis of the Union, including the first four graduates of the HUC.

Kaufman Kohler had an agenda that extended beyond ideology. His keynote address outlined a series of challenges, with programmatic goals including harmonizing Jewish religion with "modern research," conducting meaningful outreach to the "children" of "poor Russian or Polish Jews," the revision of the "too aristocratic" nature of Reform temples, greater involvement of Jewish women in the affairs of the Jewish community, transforming Reform worship services into an experience "more attractive" to the "younger element," combatting the "appalling ignorance" of the Reform laity, and providing Jewish Sabbath school materials and Religious Tracts.[14] The keynote address provided a ten-point challenge:

1. Adoption of a platform that would "declare to the world what Judaism is and what Reform means and aims at."
2. Organization of a Jewish mission to work with the entire Jewish population and particularly with Jewish laborers by means of Sunday services and other educational measures.
3. Creation of a well-organized literature and press to carry the Jewish message to every Jewish household throughout the land.
4. Creation of a plan for effective religious instruction for Jewish children.
5. Improving the mode of worship by means of a uniform ritual, especially for weddings and funerals.
6. Revision of the readings from the Law and the Prophets for the Sabbath and the Holy Days, omitting all such passages that might, when translated, give offense to the congregation.
7. Revision or new translation of the Bible together with the Apocryphal books.
8. Popularization of Jewish literature among the people.
9. Redefinition of the position of Judaism in relation to the Gentile world, toward proselytism, circumcision, and intermarriage.
10. Reintroduction of worship and religious observance into Jewish homes.[15]

The Pittsburgh Conference concentrated upon the first "point," the creation of an ideological platform. Nevertheless, the other items were not lost on the prominent Reform rabbis present. The remaining nine "points" served as the subsequent basis for a distinctive Reform movement in American Judaism.

The Conference's Pittsburgh Platform consisted of eight proclamations of Reform principles. In contrast to the avoidance of ideological self-definition within Anglo-American union, the Pittsburgh conferences articulated a German-style creed for religiously liberal American Jews. They sought a distinctive program of belief and practice for "progressive Jews individually or as represented in congregations":

["progressive"] people only see that we have broken away from the old landmarks, but they fail to discern a common platform. . . . most of our so-called enlightened Jews welcomed the watchword of Reform as long as it meant emancipation from the old yoke of Law, but when it demanded positive work, the upbuilding of the new in place of the torn-down structure, they exhibited laxity and indifference. . . . It is high time to rally our forces, to consolidate, to build.[16]

The principles articulated within the Pittsburgh Platform distanced the UAHC from the Eastern European Jews on the Right, as well as from the Ethical Culturalists on the Left. To achieve the goal of separation from Old World Orthodoxy, the Platform dismissed traditional patterns of observance and theology:

We recognize in the Mosaic legislation a system of training the Jewish people for its mission during its national life in Palestine, and today we accept as binding only the moral laws and maintain only such ceremonies as elevate and sanctify our lives, but reject all such as are not adapted to the views and habits of modern civilization. . . . We hold that all such Mosaic and Rabbinical laws as regulate diet, priestly purity and dress originated in ages and under the influence of ideas altogether foreign to our present mental and spiritual state. They fail to impress the modern Jews with as spirit of priestly holiness; their observance in our day is apt rather to obstruct than to further modern spiritual elevation.

[while] we reassert the doctrine of Judaism that the soul of man is immortal . . . we reject as ideas not rooted in Judaism the belief in bodily resurrection and in Gehenna and Eden (hell and paradise), as abodes for everlasting punishment or reward.

Rabbi Jacob Voorsanger of San Francisco's Emanu-El, Rabbis Wise, Philipson, Krauskopf, Kohler, Hirsch, and other contemporaries disdained Eastern European ritual as "Orientalism," "Talmudism," "Rabbinism," and "Kabbalism." Russian and Polish practices were denounced as inconsistent with modern learning and aesthetics. As Keneseth Israel's Joseph Krauskopf later proclaimed:

It [would be] . . . a miracle indeed were we to hear any other sound other than the wail of decline arising from out of their churches. We cannot expect different results from churches [or synagogues] in which doctrines that are preached one day as revealed gospel truth are proven absurd the next day in school and colleges, in which fable is turned into history.[17]

The Pittsburgh conferees also wished to oppose American Jewish sympathy for Eastern European Zionism. The German Reformers viewed Zionism as the misguided anguish of persecuted Russian and Polish Jews in response to the Russian pogroms of 1881. In 1882, Dr. Joseph Isaac Bluestone, an Orthodox Jew from Lithuania, called for the establishment of an American version of the *Hoveve Zion* (Lovers of Zion). His appeal to American Jews was not only that Zionism would produce a refuge for the persecuted in Europe, but also that it would serve as a bulwark against assimilation in hospitable environments like America. By 1884, Bluestone created the first American Jewish "Lovers of Zion Society" in New York City.[18]

The frequent Jewish newspaper attention accorded to Zionism was disturbing to the Reformers. In the mid-1880s, the new Zionist presence "was felt well beyond its organized framework. The Zionist causes with which some identified themselves fully were also occasional concerns of other, similar societies or family circles. The new Hebrew and Yiddish press that arose to serve the immigrant ghetto [also] reported items of Zionist interest."[19] The Pittsburgh conferees wished to respond forcefully to this threat. Thus, the Pittsburgh Platform proclaimed: "We consider ourselves no longer a nation but a religious community, and therefore expect neither a return to Palestine, nor a sacrificial worship under the administration of the sons of Aaron, nor the restoration of any of the laws concerning the Jewish state."

The rabbis assembled at Pittsburgh also defined themselves in opposition to the appeal of secularism and Ethical Culture to the offspring of their congregants. Consequently, the Pittsburgh Platform confronted Ethical Culture's social justice critique of Reform temples. As Kaufman Kohler noted in his keynote address: "It must be stated to the credit of the Ethical Culture Society at New York, that it has rendered it a matter of the highest ambition of the wealthiest young ladies and gentlemen to have so many poor families placed under the special care and guardianship of each." Rabbi Kohler faulted "[UAHC Reform] congregations . . . [as] too aristocratic. The pews and school-benches are monopolized by the wealthy who can afford to pay, whereas the poor remain uncared for."[20]

As evidenced by the four sample temples, conspicuous affluence adorned congregational buildings. A public display of Jewish wealth and style previously had been desirable in the United States. In the 1860s, architectural splendor had represented a proclamation that America's Jews were accepted by American society. By the 1880s, however, ostentatious wealth implied indifference to urban poverty, at least in the eyes of Felix Adler and his peers. Parallel American Protestant voices also were heard. The social gospel of Josiah Strong already had begun to influence U.S. religious life. The Inter-Denominational Congress held in Cincinnati in 1885, in combination with the Protestant Evangelical Alliance, resolved "to become an instrument for rousing the churches to their social mission" within urban settings.[21] In response, the Pittsburgh Platform proclaimed:

in full accordance with the spirit of Mosaic legislation which strives to regulate the relation between rich and poor, we deem it our duty to participate in the great task of modern times, to solve on the basis of justice and righteousness the problems presented by the contrasts and evils of the present organization of society.

The convening of a rabbinic conference to resolve a distinctive theological path for American Jewry eluded David Einhorn during his professional life in the United States (1855–1879). However, less than a decade after Einhorn's death, his son-in-law, Kaufman Kohler, garnered this very achievement. At the national level, the Pittsburgh Platform validated what was happening "in the pews." Just as Union temples were becoming enclaves solely for German Jews, German Reform's systematic ideology placed its imprimatur upon the UAHC. The national body gradually discarded its pluralistic "union" trappings, instead becoming a distinctively Reform movement.

Organizational Style

Besides adopting Central European ideological consistency, the UAHC emulated its local temples' organizational innovations. The Union too utilized American management techniques of German origin such as "rationalization" and "bureaucracy." By "rationalization," social scientists such as the German scholar Max Weber did not mean "reasonableness." Instead, they meant the substitution of explicit rules and procedures in place of reliance upon sentiment and the "rule of thumb." The popularity of "rationalization" began with German urbanized and industrial society. It moved on to English life and to the United States. Social and business planners began to deal with the vastly increased size of schools, civil agencies, and factories by rational methods. They created hierarchies of authority and achievement (bureaucracies), governed by specific goals, tasks, and rewards. Moreover, urbanization and industrialization led to specialization, a quest for greater efficiency, plus the pursuit of profit via an "economy of scale." In an increasingly competitive leisure time market, "the pressure to achieve 'results' . . . [led to] a *rationalization of the socio-religious structures*. . . . Such structural rationalization [expressed] . . . itself primarily in the phenomenon of *bureaucracy* [emphasis added].[22]

As noted in Chapter Three, in the last quarter of the nineteenth century, school systems began to develop uniform graded curricula, textbook assignments, teacher certification and training standards, as well as similar vehicles for replacing the haphazard practices of the past. These techniques applied as well to a wide range of other fields of endeavor. They stemmed from the profitable bureaucratic innovations of post-Civil War big business.[23]

As at the congregational level, the adaptations of the UAHC's national efforts were parallel to changes among American Protestants. In the post-Civil War era, amid rapid social and cultural change, Methodist and other denominations exhibited "increasing dissatisfaction with older . . . modes . . . and a search for new patterns of religious self-perception and commitment." Protestant denominations, responding to pressures from affiliated local churches, instituted a more rationalized structure. To attract increasingly disaffected young adults, the national bodies encouraged church-based recreational and cultural activities for men, women, and youth. Among the Methodists, such innovation in the late nineteenth century came to mean the Chautauqua Societies for men, the Deaconess movement for women, and the Epworth League for youth. In terms of education, this process included the harnessing of the American Sunday School Union in promoting a uniform and systematic curriculum for religious schools in church settings, as well as forging "Normal School" teacher training programs. This new synthesis included conscious attempts to elevate the status of the pulpit ministry by recasting the "vocation" of clergyman into a "profession."[24]

The UAHC did not hesitate to follow similar patterns of institutional response. The first arena in which the UAHC applied rationalization was to remedy the plight of Jewish Sabbath schools. As mentioned in Chapter Two, the Sabbath School Committee conducted a survey in the 1870s to ascertain existing curricula, text books, and personnel issues within the schools of affiliated congregations. After assessing these results, the UAHC decided in 1883 to form a Hebrew Sabbath School Union (HSSU).

This HSSU was an imitation of the Protestant transdenominational American Sunday School Union (ASSU) formed in 1824. By the 1880s, the ASSU had adopted rationalized curricular and management techniques. The proposed Hebrew Sabbath School Union's objective was the "maintenance and perfection of a common system, method and discipline of all the Sabbath schools in the United States," just as the Protestant ASSU sought to achieve for all Protestant religious schools. After formulating its committee structure and its goals, the UAHC's Sabbath School Committee issued a call in 1885 to all interested Jewish schools to attend a founding convention. One delegate was to represent each group of fifty students. Cautiously, I. M. Wise adopted an approach used during early attempts to establish a congregational union. The President of the UAHC was empowered to call for the Sabbath School Union's founding convention once twenty affirmative responses arrived from interested religious schools. Within several months, the requisite number was achieved and a date was set for a 3 May 1886 educators' gathering under the auspices of the Union.[25]

This ambitious plan was part of a general offensive in 1885 and 1886 by the UAHC and its leaders. They hoped to remedy the crisis of morale among the sons and daughters of member temples through educational reforms. Returning from the Pittsburgh Conference of November 1885, Isaac Mayer Wise lauded the conferees' clarification of the ideological stance of American Reform Judaism. Wise connected this new stance to a mandate for the HSSU. As Wise reflected in his *American Israelite*:

Now a Sabbath School Union has been rendered possible and practicable. For that Union must provide the schools with text-books and reading matter. . . . We cannot afford to teach the young precepts in which we do not believe. . . . This [series of beliefs] was hitherto undefined. . . . This uncertainty being overcome by the "Declaration of Principles." . . . A solid foundation for a Sabbath-School Union is now established.[26]

During the remaining years of the nineteenth century, the fledgling Hebrew Sabbath School Union achieved several important goals. First, it replaced the incomplete survey of the UAHC Sabbath School Committee with a systematic accounting of the size of local religious schools, the nature of their administration, their curricula, and their hours of instruction. The comprehensive survey enabled the HSSU to emulate rationalized public and Protestant school systems. This meant the drafting of uniform curricula, graded textbooks, suitable pamphlets and educational materials, as well as appropriate teacher standards and opportunities for training. These systematic goals reached fruition with the publication of a formal "Plan of Instruction for Sabbath Schools" in 1896. In tandem with the curriculum was a new series of "Union" graded school books and pamphlets. In addition, professional skills papers were published. The topics of the papers included the development of normal schools for teacher training, the idea of post-confirmation classes for late teens and young adults, and the creation of Sabbath School libraries.[27]

Another major domain in which the UAHC implemented contemporary organizational techniques was "agricultural pursuits." As pointed out in chapter 2, the plan to train and place young Jews in farms and in manual trades was part of a worldwide Jewish concern for "normalizing" Jewish occupational life. The Eastern European *maskilim* (modernizers), as well as Jewish philanthropists and communal leaders in Western and Central Europe, aspired to achieve this goal. So too did UAHC leaders, including Isaac Mayer Wise. As his biographer James G. Heller has pointed out, Rabbi Wise

deplored the fact that very few [of the impoverished Eastern European Jews] who came to America went upon the land, but had tended to form "new ghettos," especially in New York and Chicago. What the exiles from Russia needed was "physical and moral redemption which a long and intelligent toiling and tilling of the soil, steady association with nature, can only effect."[28]

As early as the second Annual Council of the UAHC, Union President Moritz Loth called "upon [poor, Eastern European Jewish] parents to direct their children into mechanical trades or into agriculture, rather than merchandising." For this purpose, Loth appointed a Committee on Agricultural Pursuits. After several years of deliberations, the Committee resolved in 1879 that "true emancipation of the Jews consists in the greater infusion of the spirit of manhood and self-definition, which can best be done by encouraging the large masses of Israelites dwelling in Eastern and Southern Europe to become farmers, agriculturalists and mechanics."[29] Accordingly, President Loth assigned the UAHC Committee on Civil and Religious Rights to take into consideration the feasibility and practicability of an active cooperation with sister societies in Europe for the purpose of encouraging agriculture among Jews and the settlement in this country of such as are willing and able to devote themselves to that pursuit of the lands of the West and the South, and to try to acquire land for such purposes.[30]

The findings of the Committee on Civil and Religious Rights brought to the fore the fiscal difficulties of farming and vocational training ventures. In 1883 the UAHC empowered its Committee on Agricultural Pursuits to establish an Agricultural Aid Fund under the financial umbrella of the UAHC treasury. By 1885, the Fund had achieved modest successes. Consequently, President Loth recommended the forming of an agricultural bond as a "bank" to use the Fund to assist potential Jewish farmers in the purchase of arable land.[31] Next, the UAHC conducted a thorough survey in 1885 of the whereabouts of Jewish agriculturalists in the United States.

Subsequently, the Union called for a founding convention of a national American Hebrew Farmers' Association, convened in January of 1886. The new association joined with another related agency, the Hebrew Union Agricultural Society (established in 1883) in a series of systematic (rationalized) projects designed to scatter young Eastern European Jews throughout America's hinterland. Committees were established, funds were raised and criteria for purchases were formulated. Accordingly, land was acquired in Kansas, Louisiana, Colorado, New Jersey, and the Dakotas. The Hebrew Union Agricultural Society subdivided estates into eighty-acre freeholds for ten families, free from the payment of rent for the first seven years. In the late 1890s, these efforts were fortified by the creation of the National Farm School in Pennsylvania by Rabbi Joseph Krauskopf (from Philadelphia's Keneseth Israel) and by the growing influence of the Baron de Hirsch Fund.[32]

The third arena in which the UAHC applied systematic management techniques was in its Committee on Circuit Preaching. As noted in chapter 2, the first decade of circuit preaching initiatives by the UAHC was not successful. This was true in spite of the tangible achievements of American Methodist "circuit riders" throughout the century and the applied successes of "church extension" techniques.[33] The Union was waiting for local, isolated synagogues to apply for assistance, but applications did not arrive. President Loth sought to place circuit preaching under film organizational management, as had already been done with Sabbath schools and with agricultural pursuits.

At the urging of a planning committee of Rabbis J. Voorsanger, G. Gottheil, M. Samfield, J. Wechsler, and their lay colleagues Isaac Cantrowitz, the UAHC agreed to eliminate the prerequisite of awaiting local congregational requests. In 1881, national headquarters of the UAHC began to send uninvited rabbis into unserviced areas of America's hinterland. Circuit preachers organized local synagogues and religious schools and advanced the cause of the Union. As a result, the Annual Report of the UAHC indicated in 1882 that "some effect is being made by small congregations that have no minister to avail themselves of the facilities of the Union." After initial progress, the program declined. To rescue this nascent effort, at the Council of 1883 a committee of three rabbis, J. Voorsanger, F. De Sola Mendes, and E. Schreiber offered an alternative strategy. They advocated a systematic dispersion of salaried "district rabbis" to care for isolated regions on a full-time basis.[34] With funding and support unavailable, this suggestion was not implemented. Lacking a stable base of management, effective circuit preaching within the UAHC came to a halt.

The UAHC revived this effort, however, in the mid-1890s. These initiatives were in response to a crisis in affiliation. Antagonized by the Pittsburgh Platform, traditionalist German rabbis and congregations became less enamored with the Union.[35] Moreover, the increasing identification of the Union with Central European Reform Judaism made affiliation by Eastern European shuls an impossibility. Consequently, by 1894, circuit preaching was launched anew in order to bring additional congregations into membership with the Union. The UAHC assumed that frontier areas were fertile grounds for cultivating affiliation with the Reform movement. American Jews of the South and West were far removed from the Orthodox Judaism of Europe and of America's East Coast. At the Annual Council gathering in New Orleans in 1894, Southern delegations welcomed this initiative and pressed the urgency of circuit preaching for their region. President Loth responded by upgrading the composition of the Committee on Circuit Preaching. He appointed HUC Board of Governors President Bernhard Bettman as chairman, and selected the managerially skilled Rabbi Edward Calisch as secretary.

Rabbi Calisch immediately sent letters to rabbis throughout the country. He urged them to submit lists of small Jewish communities within their region that included ten or more families of coreligionists. Calisch requested the name of at least one contact person, in addition to any rabbis in that vicinity. Edward Calisch implored his rabbinical colleagues to visit these communities once every eight to ten weeks. He beseeched them to conduct religious services and to attend to the functioning of the local Sabbath schools. Rabbi Calisch offered to supply printed pamphlets of the Union's recently published weekly service. Although 90 of the 130 letters were returned to Rabbi Calisch with 87 affirmative answers, only 15 provided the desired information. Undaunted by this grassroots inefficiency, Secretary Calisch tediously scanned the Bradstreet reports of the United States. He looked up "each town and city whose population seemed to justify [sic] and to locate this in reference to the nearest permanent rabbi," so as to assign specific visitations. As a result of Calisch's managerial stamina and conscientiousness, in 1895 and 1896 19 rabbis made 154 reported visits in 19 states and 53 towns. In addition, circuit rabbis organized three Sabbath correspondence schools and distributed four hundred copies of the Union's Evening Service pamphlet. The sparse Jewish population of the South was most receptive to this new, systematic program. The ideologically fractious East Coast offered the greatest resistance. Many Eastern Jews still expressed "prejudice against rabbis of the reform school."[36]

Buoyed by his successes, Edward Calisch expanded his well-organized program of circuit preaching through notices in local Jewish papers. He educated small-town Jews about this new option, and encouraged recent HUC graduates to devote the "enthusiasm of their youth" to this quest.[37] The effort continued to experience modest successes during the next twelve months. In his 1897 report to the UAHC Council, however, Calisch acknowledged circuit rabbis' assessments of "the indifference of the country Jews." He reported of the "coldness of the receptions that are accorded to the rabbis' overtures." Nevertheless, this upbeat circuit preacher organizer counseled that apathy was "to be expected" and that the task is to "arouse them from their lethargy."

With renewed zeal inspired by the annual council gathering, Rabbi Calisch returned to his mission. One year later he reported 122 visits to 47 towns in 17 states by 20 rabbis. Six new congregations joined as members of the UAHC. Circuit rabbis had organized seven Sabbath schools. Moreover, they founded two new congregations. Four synagogues reported regular visits at frequent intervals (Woodland, California, twice a month; New Castle, Pennsylvania, every week; Walden, New York, thirty-seven visits; Lincoln, Nebraska, every two weeks). Furthermore, Calisch reported many circuit lectures and sermons given to noncongregational audiences of Jews and Christians throughout the country. In response to this remarkable series of achievements, the 1898 General Council increased the Circuit Committee's paltry budget. The Council also agreed to sponsor the publication of holiday sermons for circuit preaching. In addition, the UAHC considered hiring full-time "field secretaries to prosecute the work."[38] In circuit preaching, as in agricultural pursuits and Sabbath school endeavors, "rationalized" management had yielded tangible results for the UAHC.

German Influence On Rabbinic Practice and Training

The Rabbinate

Another example of the accommodation of the Union to American trends of German origin was the professionalization of the UAHC rabbinate. The Union of American Hebrew Congregations sought to bolster the status of pulpit rabbis by elevating the vocation or "calling" of the rabbinate to a "profession." Profession was a concept that came to America via Victorian England. It was refined by the German university system with its graduate professional school approach to occupational training and certification. In the 1880s, however, America's clergy were not regarded as professionals. Instead, they suffered a general decline of status. As attendance at religious services declined, so did interest in sermons. As Richard Hofstader has noted in *The Age of Reform*, his classic study of status decline in this era:

the clergy were probably the most conspicuous losers from the status revolution. They not only lost ground in . . . outward ways, as most middle class elements did, but were also hit hard in their capacity as moral and intellectual leaders by the considerable secularization that took place in American society and intellectual life in the last three decades of the nineteenth century.[39]

As a response to this malaise, Reform rabbis, like Protestant ministers, sought to transform their vocation into a profession. One fundamental aspect of this transformation was the emergence of the professional association. Social scientists have characterized collegial associations as follows: First, they engage in research related to their work, to help expand the base of knowledge and expertise required for mastery within training programs. Second, they concern themselves with the promotion of a spirit of collegiality among their members. Third, societies devise codes of professional ethics and ways of standardizing behavior and techniques. Finally, the practitioners of each profession applies the growing base of technical expertise to "practical" benefit within the wider community.[40]

Americans of the mid-1880s proved receptive to this approach. The entire decade was part of an extended period during which American life was overtaken by what has been labeled as "the culture of professionalism." The rise of the professions represented an effort by "the middle class [to] . . . pursue its primary goals of earning a good living, elevating both the moral and intellectual tone of society, and emulating the status of those above one on the social ladder."[41]

Professionalization involved raising salary levels, formalizing educational credential requirements, and enhancing the social status associated with various occupations. In the late nineteenth century, professional associations arose for virtually every conceivable field of nonmanual, salaried endeavor. From the conclusion of the Civil War through 1880, such societies included the American Ophthalmological Society, American Neurological Association, American Chemical Society, and American Society of Chemical Engineers. During the ensuing decade, the pace of professionalization accelerated, with the creation of the American Forestry Association (1882), American Ornithologists Union (1883), American Society of Naturalists (1883), American Climatological Society (1884), American Institute of Electrical Engineers (1885), Geological Society of America (1888), National Statistical Association (1888), American Mathematical Society (1888), and the American Physical Society (1889). The 1880s also saw the development of associations for historians (1884), church historians (1888), economists (1885), political scientists (1889), modern language scholars and teachers (1883), and folklorists (1888).[42]

To meet this challenge, Christian denominations sought to elevate their ministries to the level of emerging professions by forging literary and other professional groups for clergy colleagiality and in recasting modes of training. Greater emphasis was placed on the professional character of the ministry. Vigorous attempts were made to upgrade the standards of ministerial training. Seminary education became "more professionalized—by emphasizing more specialized and practical training."[43] This same quest for professional associations and professionlized education became goals of UAHC rabbis as well.

The Emergence of the CCAR

Inspired by the convening of Kohler's Pittsburgh Conference, the year 1885 witnessed the launching of regional attempts to convene the rabbis of America. In the South, the Conference of Rabbis of Southern Congregations was created. In the East, the Jewish Ministers Association was established. The Conference of Rabbis of Southern Congregations (CRSC) conducted its organizational meeting on 14 April 1885, several months prior to Kaufman Kohler's Pittsburgh gathering. The Presidential address of James Gutheim of New Orleans's Temple Sinai outlined the CRSC's professional objectives. These aims were to expand the body of knowledge relating to the professional field of rabbinic service, to promote collegiality, and to enable religious schools and other "practical" projects to benefit from these endeavors. Rabbi Gutheim called for the following:

1. the interchange of opinions and views on all subjects appertaining to the functions of the Rabbinical office.

2. to promote and foster literary work appertaining to Judaism, its literature and history.

3. the promotion of fraternal feelings among the members of the conference.

4. the organization and government of congregational religious schools in accordance with approved methods.[44]

In addition, the CRSC empowered its Executive Committee with the following responsibilities, among others:

to answer all questions that may be propounded to them by members of the Conference in relation to objects for which the same has been founded.

to exercise their good offices for arbitration in any emergency that may arise involving the interests of congregations and ministers.

to assign [research] papers to members [on subjects within the scope of the Conference].[45]

To explain the motivation for establishing the Conference on a purely regional basis, Gutheim's presidential address maintained that the CRSC was "not designed as a sectional institution . . . it involves no schismatic objects [with regard to the national scope of the UAHC]. It has been organized solely for the sake of convenience, to facilitate the periodical reunions of its members." He assured the UAHC that the CRSC is "alive to the desirability of an unbroken union in American Judaism." Accordingly, this Southern Conference maintained cordial and "fraternal" contact with a Conference of Jewish Ministers on the East Coast. Moreover, the CRSC affirmed its support for the UAHC and the HUC and even endorsed the Pittsburgh Platform.

In this regard, we should point out the sectional nature of the Pittsburgh Conference. Except for Kaufman Kohler and David Philipson of Baltimore, the Conference did not include rabbis from East Coast urban centers and Southern communities. Those present were Midwesterners and rabbis of synagogues adjacent to the Midwest region. Rabbis I. Aaron (Fort Wayne), M. Bloch (Youngstown, Ohio), J. Krauskopf (Kansas City), L. Mayer (Pittsburgh), S. Sale (Chicago), E. Hirsch (Chicago), S. H. Sonneschein (St. Louis), and I. M. Wise (Cincinnati) all served pulpits in the Midwest. A. Guttman (Syracuse), S. Weil (Bradford, Pennsylvania), M. Schlesinger (Albany), A. Moses (Louisville), and M. Sessler (Wheeling, West Virginia) were rabbis in Eastern and Southern communities on the fringe of the Midwest region.

The Conference of Rabbis of Southern Congregations maintained fraternal contact with the East Coast Jewish Ministers Association and with the Midwestern Pittsburgh Conference. To carry out its mandate, the CRSC's founding convention appointed committees charged with "(a) the ceremony of marriage; (b) the rite of confirmation; (c) the burial of the dead; (d) the sabbath school; (e) normal school classes for teachers; (f) scholarly activities for rabbis." Within the first year of its existence, twenty-one rabbis of the deep South affiliated with this nascent professional association.[46]

The northeastern counterpart of the Southern Conference was the Jewish Ministers Association (JMA), also established in 1885. The "Prelude" to the JMA's initial *Proceedings* included a description of the origins of this East Coast effort:

Towards the close of the year 1884, six of the Jewish ministers of New York City, who had been accustomed for several years to meet regularly for social intercourse and for mutual cooperation [clearly professional association goals] . . . conceived the idea of broadening both the *social* and *useful* elements of their *association*, by inviting such of their colleagues as resided within comparatively easy distance of New York to join their number, to the end that conventions should be held at stated intervals throughout the year [emphasis added].[47]

Accordingly, they formed a Jewish Ministers Association for New York City and vicinity. Twenty-two rabbis from Albany to Philadelphia assembled on 19 January 1885 for the founding convention. They formulated the following professional goals:

[to promote] brotherly feeling and harmony among its members, to be mutually helpful by friendly counsels without fettering individual opinions, and to strive by friendly union and cooperation to advance and promote unity [of Reform and Traditional] in Judaism without interference in the congregational autonomy.[48]

The JMA held conferences semi-annually to discuss and act upon "matters of literary or practical interest," such as "original essays" and the needs of Sabbath schools. The Jewish Ministers Association, for example, was influential in originating the aforementioned Hebrew Sabbath School Union (HSSU). In 1886, due to JMA influence, the HSSU took over the functions of the UAHC's Sabbath School Committee. This change facilitated the Sabbath School Committee's subsequent successes. Besides school projects and scholarly essays, the JMA resembled the Southern Conference in its committee agendas: "(a) [to create standards and uniformity of rabbinic practice with regard to] marriages; (b) home prayer books; (c) Jewish funeral practices; (d) to introduce more congregational singing into the synagogue service; (e) to investigate and report on the credentials of applicants for the ministerial office in this country, whenever solicited by such candidates or congregations."[49]

Unlike the Southern Conference, which spoke apologetically of its sectional character, the JMA was proud of its regional approach. Jewish Ministers Association President Gustav Gottheil of Temple Emanu-El of New York City boasted about ". . . providing a uniquely successful [regional approach to the] assemblage of Jewish ministers at stated periods, either for the discussion of theoretical questions or the inaugu-ration and fostering of united work."[50] Gottheil called attention to forty years of failure of previous rabbinical organizational efforts in both Europe and America. He surmised that the sweeping national "synodical character given to their assemblies, proved fatal to them." In contrast, Rabbi Gottheil spoke optimistically about the future of the Jewish Ministers Association, with a membership limited to the Northeastern states. Gottheil had vivid memories of the loss of Northeastern Jewish autonomy with the demise of the Board of Delegates of American Israelites, and of the abortive plan for an Eman-El (NYC) Theological Seminary. Therefore, Gottheil refrained from mirroring the Southern Conference President James Gutheim's statements of allegiance to the national UAHC and HUC. Although a staunch Reformer, Rabbi Gottheil even expressed sectional pride about efforts by traditionalists to establish a non-UAHC Jewish Theological Seminary in New York City in 1885 and 1886.

The continued existence of the Eastern JMA and the Southern CRSC, along with the inability of the Pittsburgh (Midwest) Conference to reconvene, left unserviced the rabbis of the central region of the United States. The rabbis in the Midwest sought their own professional associa-tion to parallel the JMA and the CRSC. To assure adequate attendance at a contemplated "Central [Midwestern] Conference," Rabbi Wise patiently waited until the Hebrew Union College had ordained more than twenty rabbis (1889). Wise wanted others to display their support for a new venture in advance. A few weeks before the UAHC Annual Council of 1889, Wise wrote in the *American Israelite* about his concern:

"Will you call a conference [on your initiative alone]?" said one of our friends in a sort of admonishing tone. We will not [on our own], is our reply, although we are willing at any time to call the continuation of the Pittsburgh conference, if the majority of its members authorize us to convene it, or if, in July next at Detroit at the [upcoming] meeting of the council of the Union of American Hebrew Congregations the rabbis present want it so, or, [they want] to establish some new rabbinical connection. . . . [I]f you want a change that is, a new initiative], you must do [initiate] it, [otherwise] we are tied down to [awaiting the reconvening of] the Pittsburgh Conference.[51]

At Wise's prodding at the UAHC Annual Council of 1889, the thirty primarily Midwestern rabbis in attendance in Detroit convened a Central Conference of American Rabbis. The choice of the name "CCAR" was significant. "Central," as Wise stated several years later, implied Midwestern. At the CCAR Conference of 1894, he recollected:

the reason for calling it the Central Conference was this; there existed then two similar organizations, one in the South [CRSC] and another in the East [JMA] of the country. Therefore this body was called "Central" as a geographical distinction. It was supposed that its members would come, aside from the alumni and faculty of the HUC, from the Central states, Ohio and Mississippi Valleys.[52]

The term "American Rabbis" rather than "Rabbis Serving American Congregations" was an effort to include not just pulpit rabbis, but also rabbinic scholars and writers. The working paper devised by the committee of CCAR founders designated by the 1889 UAHC Council was even more liberal in membership eligibility.

Any rabbi in a congregation might join . . . all possessors of a Doctorate of Philosophy or Philosogy who also have a rabbinical degree . . . "all autodidactic preachers and teachers of religion who have been for at least three successive years discharging those duties in any one congregation"; all authors of eminent books on any subject appertaining to Jewish theology or literature; and "all who have rendered important practical help to the cause of Judaism."[53]

Although non-rabbis never joined, by the time of the CCAR's second annual gathering, in conjunction with the UAHC Council meeting in Cleveland in July of 1890, the Central Conference's rabbinic membership had grown considerably. To the surprise of Conference President Isaac M. Wise and the founders, dozens of Reform colleagues affiliated with the CCAR, not just from the Midwest, but from all over the country. With nearly one hundred affiliates, the Central Conference quickly became the largest body of rabbis in America or in Western Europe. The Southern Conference effectively disbanded, true to its public stance of seeking to affiliate with whatever oganizations the UAHC endorsed. Much more stubborn was the sectionally proud Eastern Jewish Ministers Association, which exhibited open hostility to the CCAR. As Isaac Mayer Wise remarked bitterly in his CCAR Presidential Address of 1890, the Conference should only consist of "men of national conceptions; without local prejudices, without sectionalism; also without selfish ambition or private interests." The breakthrough in regard to the JMA came about in 1892. Joseph Silverman, a graduate of HUC, invited the CCAR to conduct its annual Conference at his Temple Emanu-El of New York City, the focal point of Eastern Reform opposition to the Central Conference. Although Gustav Gottheil boycotted the meeting, most of the other prominent East Coast Reform rabbis—notably Rabbis Kohler, Leucht, and Benjamin— joined with this growing association of Reform rabbis.[54] The Jewish

Ministers' Association ceased to exist. The CCAR now was truly a nationwide professional association.

Functions of the CCAR

In terms of its functions, the CCAR built upon the foundations established by the Conference of Rabbis of Southern Congregations and the Jewish Ministers Association. Among the Central Conference's initial professional aims were a fraternal goal of fostering "a feeling of association and brotherhood among the Rabbis and other Jewish scholars of America"; a scholarly goal to "advance the cause of Jewish learning, to encourage all efforts toward the propagation of the teachings of Judaism"; and a collegial goal of making "provision for such worthy colleagues, as owing to advanced age or other cause, are prevented from following their calling." The CCAR carried out the last of these three purposes by the creation of a Relief Fund. This Fund was maintained by setting aside half of each CCAR member's $5 annual dues payment, "to relieve unfortunate colleagues or his family from becoming humiliated as the objects of charity."[55]

Increasing the pool of knowledge needed to enter the profession was achieved through a wide array of papers presented at the annual CCAR Conference and published in its *Yearbook*. Examples of papers on topics of use to practitioners of the rabbinate included: "Confirmation in the Synagogue," and "The Relation of the Rabbi to the Congregation" (Volume I); "Cremation from the Jewish Standpoint" (II); "Judaism and the Public School System of America" (III); "The Duties of the Rabbi in the Present Time" (IV); "The Philosophy of the Reform Movement in American Judaism," "Missionary Efforts in Judaism," "Formula for the Reception of Proselytes" and "A Jewish Summer School and Assembly" (V); "Method in the Pulpit" (VI); "The Rabbi as a Public Man" and "Funeral Agenda" (VII); "The Rabbi and Charities," "How Can We Enlist Our Young Men in the Service of the Congregation," "Why I am not a Zionist" and "The Justification of Zionism" (VIII).

The Central Conference also exhibited the "fraternal" need to bind rabbis together and defend the validity of their profession. In 1897, the CCAR issues standards of "professional ethics" to regulate a pulpit rabbi's availability to a call from another congregation, to limit competition among rabbis for pulpit positions, and to set standards for rabbinic contracts.[56] The CCAR sought to deal professionally with those disputes between a congregation and its rabbi that required discreet arbitration. At the 1898 Conference, for example, the leadership affirmed that, as certain abuses have appeared in the relations between rabbis and congregations, and between the rabbis themselves, we, the CCAR, favor the adoption of some regulations looking to a remedy for these abuses, and which the members of the Conference pledge themselves to live up to and enforce as far as it lies in their power to do so, and that a committee be appointed to draft these regulations. We recommend that all members of the Conference be requested to send to the Executive Board of the Conference complete accounts of such abuses, differences, or controversies, as may arise between congregation and minister, or rabbi and rabbis.[57]

In addition, the Conference adopted careful guidelines for entry into membership in the profession. The CCAR rectified the chaos of the past where "a large number of preachers in the synagogues and temples, whose titles were high sounding enough, such as reverend, doctor, rabbi and the like, and none could tell with any degree of certainty, whether those titles were assumed or conferred upon their bearers by proper authorities." In contrast, for the CCAR, the Admissions Committee screened a candidate's relevant professional and personal background. Only then were acceptable applicants presented to the general membership for ratification at the annual convention. The Central Conference stressed that it "protects the moral character of the American rabbinate, by refusing to admit to its ranks, anyone whose antecedents bear not the closest scrutiny or whose oral conduct is subject to criticism." The CCAR formulated constitutional provisions for expulsion of a colleague in the sad event of "public or private conduct . . . unworthy of membership," lest dishonor be brought upon the profession.[58]

The CCAR fulfilled its mandate as a professional association by applying an expanding pool of practical rabbinic knowledge to congregations at large when it produced "a rabbinical Guide or Hand Book" in 1894. It was a manual with recommended texts for rabbinic officiation at weddings, funerals, and other public ceremonies. The CCAR also standardized public worship within Union temples. The Conference issues a *Union Prayerbook* in 1892 and a *Union Hymnal* in 1897.[59] The Conference applied its professional expertise in assisting the Hebrew Sabbath School Union's formulation of a UAHC religious school cirriculum. Furthermore, the CCAR conducted related educational projects, offering teachers' training in a normal school, and publishing tracts for acquainting the laity with the Reform approach to customs and beliefs. By the conclusion of its first decade of service, the CCAR had become an indispensable third partner in a tripartite Reform institutional family of the UAHC, the HUC, and the CCAR.

The Hebrew Union College

The trend toward professional associations was linked to the growing impact of German graduate professional study, an innovation in job

TABLE 4.1
Training Schools

	1851–1875	1876–1900
Theology	72	47
Law	24	50
Medicine	33	86
Dentistry	7	47
Pharmacy	8	38
Veterinary	2	15
Total	146	283[60]

TABLE 4.2
The Number of College Graduates

1860s	928
1870s	1155
1880s	1437
1890s	2529[61]

TABLE 4.3
Colleges and Faculty

	NUMBER OF SCHOOLS	NUMBER OF FACULTY
1870	563	5,553
1880	811	11,552
1890	998	15,809
1900	977	23,868[62]

training that engulfed the American scene. America entered its "Age of the University," from 1876 to 1900. There was a proliferation of programs of German-style formal study to provide certification for an expanding middle class of professionals. Table 4.1 gives an indication of the change. As graduate professional school education became more desirable, the number of university undergraduates increased substantially. Table 4.2 presents a list of the average total of annual graduates within a list of "37 leading colleges and universities." The number of schools and population of university faculty expanded at a dramatic pace as well, as is shown in Table 4.3.

Protestant seminaries responded to these trends by altering their mode of training ministers. The goal shifted from being a denominational college aiding a clergyman in entering his "vocation" or "calling" into a graduate professional school offering instruction and certification to a modern-style minister. At Union Theological Seminary, for example, new faculty appointments included a cadre of German-trained professors committed to this shift in emphasis. Increased instruction was provided in practical theology, homilectics, and other areas of direct service to the needs of the laity. The study of classical religious literature alone no longer would suffice. "The academic life of Union [Theological Seminary] . . . evoked . . . new trends in theological education and . . . the ideal of a seminary as a theological university."[63]

This was the setting in which professionalization occurred at the Hebrew Union College. The graduates of the Hebrew Union College became more concerned with the expanding administrative and pastoral demands inside congregational life. In addition, the HUC graduates became ever more identified with the Reform movement. Consequently, pressure mounted for serious curricular change in the training of its students both as Reform rabbis and as professionals.

As Richard Hofstadter and C. DeWitt Hardy have noted in their study, *The Development and Scope of Higher Education in the United States*, "the curriculum (of a College or graduate professional school) is a barometer by which we measure the cultural pressures that operate upon the school."[64] HUC, like other schools, acceded to pressures for professional skills training. In the mid-1880s, the Hebrew Union College hired Rabbi David Philipson as its first full-time faculty member concentrating upon the practical skill of homiletics (preaching sermons). Later the College provided optional assistance in elocution. Seasoned pulpit rabbis like Isaac M. Wise joined in this educational process. They provided careful scrutiny to the public-speaking styles of the students during senior sermons at HUC's Saturday afternoon services. With increasing frequency, the College granted permission to upperclassmen to serve in weekend pulpits or within Cincinnati's Jewish Sabbath school programs. High Holy Day and often monthly or bimonthly weekend student pulpits provided the added benefit of securing small congregations for the UAHC and the Reform movement.

In spite of these moves toward professionalization, the trajectory of progress was limited by the preferences of the HUC administration. College President Isaac Mayer Wise remained uncomfortable with a departure from the sacred text focus of the denominational college curriculum, and so no dramatic changes were implemented until after his death in 1900. Under the presidency of Wise's successor, Kaufman Kohler, a major shift occurred. The organizational model of the HUC changed from a denominational college to a graduate professional school in keeping with general American trends in job training. As early as 1893, John Hopkins had established the first graduate professionalized medical school, combining German research with "professional" collegiality and practicality. The first graduate professional school of social work was the New York School of Philanthropy, created in 1898 to train people for occupations within emerging social agencies. The New York College for the Training of Teachers (later renamed Teachers College) in 1877 became the pioneer graduate program for preparing professional educators. A decade earlier, Harvard Law School already had introduced the very first effort of this type, a graduate professional approach to the training of attorneys. Even Christian schools of divinity, once exclusively sacred-text oriented, like I. M. Wise's original HUC, began to include professional skill "courses and supervision in missions, sociology, ethics and 'sacred oratory' . . . [In contrast, they increasingly de-emphasized] exegetical theology."[65]

Even before he took office as president of HUC, Rabbi Kaufman Kohler indicated to the board of governors that I. M. Wise's rabbinical curriculum was unacceptable to him. "He would not allow a new catalogue to go out bearing his name as responsible for the College until certain 'essential changes' had been made." To professionalize the College, President Kohler's first over-arching goal was "converting it [HUC] gradually [from a denominational college] into a *postgraduate* institution [emphasis added],"[66] similar to graduate professional schools in law, medicine, social work, teaching, and divinity. Second, Kohler replaced the study of random selections of Hebrew literature of ages past with the mastery of those sections of Jewish exegetical literature ("Midrash") he deemed most useful for preaching in the pulpit. Third, training in "elocution" became a regular curricular offering, as did "liturgy," the knowledge necessary to orchestrate public prayer services, and "pedagogics," the skill needed to conduct an effective Sabbath school. Fourth, in an era in which Reform Judaism (like mainstream Protestantism) became committed to social justice, training in "sociology" as well as "ethics" became mandatory. In Kohler's words, the professionalized curriculum added:

Practical Theology . . . The first and foremost part consists of *Jewish Homiletics* as the sermon constitutes an integral part of the divine service, it must, both as to its tenor and its choice of text and subject, bear the stamp and reflect the view and atmosphere of synagogue life by showing its continuity with the past. It is therefore studied in connection with the Midrash and the Homiletical literature of the past as well as modern times.

Comparative Religion . . . and especially of the sources of Christianity and Islamism to form the scientific basis for Jewish Apologetics.

Philosophical Literature of the medieval Jew is still indispensable to the modern rabbi as offering him the aid and suggestions for solving the great problems in the light of modern principles of thought.

Jewish Ethics is studied as a special system of thought different from Christian ethics in principle and character, based upon genuinely Jewish sources while in harmony with the broad psychological and historical views of the day.

Pedagogics . . . Questions such as how to conduct a religious school, how to teach religion and ethics and particularly how to use the Bible as a source of inspiration and religious instruction for the child.

Applied Sociology or the *Science of Philanthropy* . . . since upon the modern rabbi devolves a large part of the charitable work in a Jewish community and he must know how to combine the new method with the ancient spirit of Judaism in the field of practical righteousness (Zedekah), and social service [emphasis added].[67]

As a training institution solely for Reform rabbis, Kohler's HUC no longer shared Wise's earlier compulsion to appease Orthodox critics. Kohler insisted that "halakha was of little consequence . . . [and the] study of Talmud possessed value only insofar as it was conducted from a historical perspective . . . and as a source for moral maxims."[68] As a rejection of Zionism, the Hebrew Union College eliminated instruction in modern Hebrew language. President Kohler proclaimed to his student body:

The College [HUC] should have a thoroughly American character. The students should endeavor to be imbued with the American spirit. . . . Neo-Hebraic literature may be a necessity for Russian Jews who have no genuine national literature from which to derive culture and idealism. For us the English literature is a source of culture and enlightenment; wherefore Neo-Hebraism will be abolished here.[69]

The Kohler curriculum "expressed his conception that the College was not the equivalent of the Semitics faculty of a university and likewise not a modern yeshiva. It was a theological institution for training future Reform rabbis in the principles of their faith and the *Techniques of their profession* [emphasis added]."[70] American norms for professional skill replaced Isaac M. Wise's Anglo-American denominational devotion to a classical, general education for the clergy. The UAHC witnessed the evolution of a higher status Reform rabbinate, professionally accredited by the HUC and sustained by the CCAR.

National Reform Rabbinate

As described in chapter 3, the modern Reform rabbi like the Protestant pulpit minister occupied a pivotal role in the expansion of local congregational functions. Indeed, "many a local church [or synagogue] since the Civil War . . . lived by its preacher [or rabbi]." The rabbi was crucial to the congregation's array of social justice projects, temple center recreation activities, upgraded religious school organization, as well as sisterhoods (and ultimately brotherhoods). These younger men, often American-born and trained in HUC's modern ambience, viewed their career more as a profession than as a calling. "Lacking either a sense of permanency or commitment to a single congregation, the ambitious young minister [or rabbi] now could express his concern with a rising salary." Scanning the annual *Proceedings* of the UAHC, the professional career pattern of the typical Reform rabbi was clear. Except for the first few classes (1883–1885), HUC graduating seniors were placed in small, Union-affiliated "first pulpit" positions in isolated Jewish communities within America's hinterland. Throughout their subsequent careers, these CCAR members sought to move to higher status temples in larger urban settings. They generally gravitated to the East or Midwest, even from comparable size positions in the South or Far West or isolated Midwestern outposts (such as Kansas City).[71] Desirable rabbinical candidates were in great demand and recruitment competition was sometimes bitter indeed.

Excitement greeted the first HUC graduates to serve each of the sample temples. Joseph Krauskopf was recruited from Kansas City's Bene Yehudah to Philadelphia's KI in 1887. Louis Grossman was installed as senior rabbi at KKBY in 1901. Martin Meyer achieved senior rabbi status at Emanu-El of San Francisco in 1910. Max Heller's became Temple Sinai's primary religious leader in 1896. Unlike the self-taught rabbis of I. M. Wise's generation, or the graduates of German seminaries (like Kaufman Kohler and his peers), HUC alumni were schooled in an increasingly professionalized graduate school of divinity. They were members of a professional association, the CCAR. They were conversant in English not only in sermons on biblical topics, but on lecture subjects covering a wide range of contemporary concerns.

The new genre of professionalized Reform rabbis reclaimed much of the status that had been eroded by secular trends.[72] The professional rabbi gained the respect of his congregants primarily for his service as spokesman to Christians in public sermons, lectures, and classes, as well as advocacy for social reform. In addition, rabbis provided creative administrators of large "institutional" temple centers, pastoral care to the personal needs and life-cycle events of growing memberships, superintendents of sizable religious schools and teachers of Confirmation and post-Confirmation classes. The Reform rabbi became a popular figure on the American scene.

Available socioeconomic data about these Reform rabbis demonstrates their changing status. Among 41 rabbis of UAHC affiliated congregations located in the 1880 national census data, Central, Northern and Western European lineage were overwhelmingly prominent. Twenty-eight (68 percent) of these 41 clergymen were born in various parts of Germany, notably Bavaria, Prussia, Posen, and Alsace-Lorraine. Seven of the non-Germans were Hungarians. One hailed from Bohemia, another from Holland. Two were Jamaicans (British West Indies). The only exceptions were 1 Eastern European (Polish-Russian) individual and 1 native-born American.

By 1900, this ethnic pattern changed considerably, as evidence by census data regarding 127 of the 165 members listed in the CCAR membership directory of that same year. Although the largest single group of foreign born was comprised of 40 men of German extraction, this percentage barely equaled 30 percent of the total. This figure was exceeded by 41 American-born rabbis (a dramatic increase from the nearly universal foreign birth pattern of twenty years earlier). Of the remaining 46 CCAR members, most hailed from other places in Central, Northern, or Western Europe, notably Hungary (18), England (9), Austria (6), Bohemia (3), Moravia (two), Luxembourg (1), Sweden (1) and Holland (1). Only 9 (7 percent of the 127) were Russian or Polish Jews, a striking contrast to the rabbinate of American Orthodox synagogues of the time.

The growing success of the Reform movement in attracting English-speaking and native-born American men into the pulpit rabbinate projected an image of successful acculturation among the laity. Most American-born HUC graduates hailed from Midwestern and Southern cities, within the primary orbit of influence of I. M. Wise and his College. Of the 41 U.S. natives in question, 19 came from the central region, most commonly the pivotal states of Ohio (10), Illinois (4), Indiana (3), and Michigan (2). Nine others were Southerners, including 3 natives of Louisiana, 2 each from Alabama and Virginia, and 1 apiece from Tennessee and Kentucky. Predictably, only 1 rabbi came from the sparsely settled Far West. Within the East Coast region, 7 of the 13 CCAR rabbis in question hailed from the margins of that region: Lancaster, Pittsburgh, and Allegheny (Pennsylvania); Syracuse, Rochester, and Greenport (New York); and East Attleboro in Massachusetts. Only 6 CCAR rabbis came from large Eastern European and Orthodox-dominated Jewish communities like Manhattan (4), Newark (1), and Boston (1).

The appeal of CCAR rabbis to American-born Jewish young adults—the age group the UAHC sought to reach—was attributable in part to the increasing youthfulness of the Conference's membership. In our sample of 41 Reform rabbis in UAHC congregations in 1880, the average age was 43.9. Twenty-eight of the 41 (68 percent) were of ages ranging in the 30s and 40, with 17 of the former and 11 of the latter. Only 2 of these rabbis were younger than age 30, and only 11 were older than age 49, with none exceeding 65 years of age. By 1900, the average age within the much larger and more diverse CCAR sample of 127 rabbis had dropped to 40.6. (It was actually as low as 39 when excluding 6 retired rabbis in their 70s and 80s.) The primary cause of this significant drop in the average age of America's practicing Reform rabbis was the appearance of 38 (34.2 percent of the total) men in their 20s, mostly American-born HUC graduates or graduates of the by then defunct Emanu-El Theological Seminary of Manhattan. The trend toward youth within the CCAR is evidenced also by the presence of an additional 36 CCAR members in the age range of 30 to 39. Thus, 74 (60 percent) of the 121 practicing Reform rabbis in our sample were under age 40.

The UAHC was able to entice attractive, young, and American-born candidates by raising the status of the Reform rabbinate to a "professional" category. This achievement meant that Reform rabbis commanded comparatively lucrative salaries. By 1900, in an era when U.S. census data indicates that common laborers earned less than $500 per year, farmers under $250, financiers (real estate and insurance brokers) barely $1,000, and Protestant ministers $731, by comparison Reform rabbis received enormous salaries. Among our sample congregations, as early as the 1860s and 1870s such a pattern was evident, paced by I. M. Wise (Cincinnati's KKBY), who was receiving $6,000 by 1873, and James Gutheim (Temple Sinai of New Orleans) being paid $6,000 in 1872 By 1888, the *American Israelite* reported that Emil Hirsch of Chicago's Sinai Temple received a "$12,000 salary plus a free dwelling and payment of a $10,000 life insurance policy. Add to this his additional income from other sources, and the sum at his command will not fall short of being the equivalent of $15,000 per annum, handsome income for any man."[73] See Appendix Table C for examples of rabbinic salaries culled from congregational histories, demonstrating the widespread nature of this pattern.

A letter signed by "L. W.," in the *American Israelite* edition of 3 February 1888 indicates the attitude of Jewish laity at that time:

A Rabbi is a member of one of the learned professions . . . he has a right to ask for the largest possible emolument to maintain his family and himself in comfort or even luxury during his working days and make due provision for old age and death. . . . We want our best and most talented men in our pulpits. If we need able attorneys and physicians, we can, if we prefer, seek them among those who do not profess Judaism, but we cannot very well invite Christians into our pulpits and Sabbath-Schools. . . . No profession which does not offer high honors and rewards to the most successful will ever attract the flower of our youth.[74]

By the end of the first decade of the twentieth century, as the New Orleans *Jewish Ledger* observed: "It is therefore not surprising that the [major] American Jewish pulpit attracts men of supreme ability. . . . Even middle-class and suburban [small] congregations, many of them burdened with a building debt, strain their resources in order to place their Rabbis in a position of comfort and independence."[75]

Conclusion

Responding to the changes instituted by local temples in the 1880 to 1900 era, the UAHC was transformed and in the process furthered the innovations of affiliated congregations. Reform synagogues became "ethnic churches" composed of American Jews of German descent and organized along American-style parameters of German origin such as rationalization and professionalization. The Union soon followed suit, proclaiming itself to be exclusively German Reform in ideology and structure. Paradoxically, as the Union found itself riding a wave of American openness to German cultural influences, it also limited itself to an identity that eventually became constraining.

When the Pittsburgh Platform abandoned the American model of pragmatic union and defined Reform Judaism ideologically, it effectively cut off the UAHC not only from Eastern European Jewish groups, but from future German traditionalist synagogues as well. By limiting its constituency to German Jews in Reform temples, the Union was swimming against the demographic tide. In an era when Jewish immigration from Germany had slowed to a trickle while Jews left Russia and Poland in droves, the Union lacked the cultural resources to appeal to its only potential new market. This rejection of growing sectors of American Jewry precipitated a decline in the Union's national percentages of affiliation. Between 1880 and 1900, the total number of UAHC congregations remained unchanged even as the total number of American Jewish houses of worship jumped by more than 100 percent to 589. Whereas 63 percent of Midwestern, 50 percent of Southern, 26 percent of Eastern, and 20 percent of Far Western Synagogues belonged to the Union in 1878, by 1900 these percentages had dipped to 22 percent, 31 percent, 8.5 percent, and 15 percent, respectively. By 1907, Rabbi David Philipson's partisan history of the Reform movement lamented: "The past fifteen years have witnessed remarkable changes in Jewish religious life in the United States. The reform group which at one time was in the majority has become a minority."[76]

In an effort to overcome this loss of control, the UAHC offered institutional innovations at the national level. Just as local houses of worship applied "bureaucratic" means to better manage their religious schools and to broaden their range of functions, so did the Union apply similar institutional methods imported from Germany. During the late 1880s and throughout the 1890s, the UAHC upgraded its services and "rationalized" its organization through systematic surveys, carefully designed administrative departments, and aggressively marketed affiliation with the Reform Union. The UAHC also yielded to American pressures of German origin seeking to change the nature of the rabbinate. The administrative and pastoral roles of the local pulpit rabbi expanded as they did for American Christian clergy. Changing rabbinic needs were met in a professional association, the CCAR, and by the metamorphosis of the Hebrew Union College into a postgraduate professional school for rabbis. Both manifestations of "professionalization" harmonized with nationwide occupational trends, derived from German graduate professional training. The vocation or "calling" of the Reform rabbi was transformed into a credentialed and monitored "profession" serving a Reform national movement and its affiliated temples.

What success remained for local synagogues and nationwide Reform institutions was premised upon the marketability of their German-style characteristics. As it happened, however, this marketability was not destined to last. German culture had been influential within late-nineteenth-century U.S. society. It enjoyed a high social standing among American opinion makers in the post-Civil War era. Nevertheless, the seeds of dissent against this European source of vitality were being planted in the late 1890s as a distinctively American nationalism came to the fore. American foreign policy triumphs and overseas trade successes yielded unprecedented American pride. American imperial expansion produced mounting enthusiasm for overseas missions by United States church groups. The United States began to export goods, ideas, religious zeal, and political fervor to the rest of the world.

In the aftermath of the American victories in the 1898 Spanish-American War, Senator Albert J. Beveridge stated: "We will not renounce our part in the mission of the race, trustee under God of the civilization of the world. . . . He has marked the American people as His chosen nation to finally lead in the regeneration of the world. This is the divine mission of America."[77] As the United States entered the "American [twentieth] Century," to be an "American" came to mean utilizing distinctively American approaches to institutional life. Identification with German-Jewish ethnicity became ever less suitable for a religious movement aspiring to recruit affiliates from among American-born Jews, let alone from among Eastern Europeans.

PART THREE

❖

1900–1930

American Corporate Culture

❖ 5 ❖

Further Americanization of the
Local Reform Temple

In the United States prior to 1880, denominationalism nationally and voluntarism locally predominated within religious communities. Reform Judaism proved to be no exception to this Anglo-American cultural trend. In the final two decades of the nineteenth century, however, the UAHC and its member congregations underwent a shift to organizational models of German origin such as professionalization and bureaucracy. This transition harmonized with a demographic tilt toward German ethnicity within UAHC temple membership. But in the early decades of the twentieth century, yet another transition was in store as Central European influence gave way to a distinctively American style of Reform Judaism premised on both U.S. economic successes and the increasing rate of Jewish immigration from Eastern Europe.

The advent of "Americanism" in the early years of twentieth century was shaped by national pride and by a growing U.S. economic role in the world scene. The Spanish-American War earned the United States a reputation as a formidable force in world events and gave rise to powerful currents of American nationalism. In a related fashion, after surviving continuing cycles of depression during the final quarter of the nineteenth century, the U.S. economy emerged with a newfound confidence. A consensus solution to business woes was the quest for markets abroad. Economic planners sought "increasing exports so that plants could dispose of their surplus goods and resume full productivity and regular employment." As such plans came to fruition, America was recast into an emerging global giant of multinational enterprise. Whereas in the past, ideas and goods flowed from Europe to the United States, American foreign trade achievements reversed the process. "The U.S. triumph abroad was one of ingenuity: new products, new methods of manufactur-

TABLE 5.1
Jewish Immigration to U.S.

	RUSSIA	AUSTRIA-HUNGARY	ROMANIA	GERMANY
1881–1890	135,003	44,619	6,967	5,354
1891–1900	279,811	83,720	12,789	8,827
1901–1910	704,245	152,811	47,301	6,273

See Samuel Joseph, *Jewish Immigration to the United States from 1881–1910* (New York, 1914).

ing, and new sales and advertising."[1] American military and business success overseas promoted a general quest of new frontiers, and the identification of new categories of persons to be served.

Meanwhile, UAHC expansion had leveled off by the turn of the century. Despite the aggressive programmatic initiatives of Reform temples, adult sons and daughters of temple members frequently remained uninvolved. Like the sluggish pre-1898 U.S. economy, Union-affiliated congregations needed new frontiers, new markets for their goods. An obvious opportunity presented itself as the numbers of Eastern European immigrants continued to rise through the turn of the century (see Table 5.1). This massive pool of newcomers and their sons and daughters represented the demographic future of American Jewry. In a time when U.S. corporations sought economic strength through the cultivation of new markets and American Christian religious movements targeted as yet untapped immigrant groups, the challenge facing the UAHC was clear: Future vitality would require the inclusion of the children of the *Ostjuden* of Russia, Romania, and other parts of Eastern Europe.

Shifting Patterns of Relations between Germans and Eastern Europeans

Legacy of Antagonism

Within American Christendom, the "old immigrants" from the British Isles, Germany, and Scandinavia had to adapt during the final decades of the nineteenth century to the "new immigrants" out of Russia, Poland, Italy, Greece, and numerous other countries as well. Social tensions existed between the middle- and upper-class American-born Protestants and Catholics and the often unskilled lower-class new arrivals.[2]

German Jewish leaders faced similar challenges when confronted by the arrival of hundreds of thousands of Eastern European Jews in the late nineteenth century. Mutual animosities marred the relationship between American Jews of Central and Eastern European heritage. So bitter was the encounter that Jacob Voorsanger and numerous other Reform rabbis throughout the late 1890s advocated immigration restriction. "I believe in restricting immigration," Voorsanger wrote, "[not because of the Russian Jews'] illiteracy, physique, criminality, immorality, speech and demeanor . . . [but because of their] naturally gregarious tendencies."[3] As late as 1909, Joseph Krauskopf informed his KI "Alumni" (young adult graduates of his Confirmation program) that

the vast masses of immigrants . . . [are] fast crowding Reform Judaism into the rear. Instead of shaking off their foreign soil, they wrap themselves all the more strongly in it . . . larger and larger grows their jargon press and literature. Louder and louder grows their clamor for Zionism, which to the American not infrequently means that the Jew is not identified with our country and its interests.[4]

Moreover, once Russian and Polish Jews entered the United States, the German Reformers wished to maintain a social distance from their low-status coreligionists. On 29 August 1895, Isaac Mayer Wise's *American Israelite* lead editorial disdainfully reported,

on the average, the President [Wise] of the HUC receives two petitions a week . . . from New York, from young students who wish to enter the HUC. Most of these applicants are Polish or Russians. . . . *It is strange that those applicants do not know that there exists an Orthodox theological seminary . . . in New York, or knowing it do not wish to go there* [emphasis added]. . . . Friends of education are politely requested to make known among these young people, that there is an Orthodox theological seminary in the city of New York.[5]

If the Reformers found the Eastern European Jews legalistic and traditional-bound, Eastern Europeans were equally suspicious of their acculturated German-American counterparts. A contemporary Russian Jewish source observed: "In the eyes of the Eastern Jew, the Western Jew is a cad. His education is superficial and flashy; his philanthropy ostentatious and insincere; his manners a cheap imitation of the Gentiles upon whom he fawns; His religion a miserable compromise in which appearances count for everything."[6]

Despite social barriers, the potential existed for building future bonds among Western and Eastern Jews. As social scientist Will Herberg has noted: "With the turn of the century, unitive forces and processes began to make themselves felt. As the newcomers advanced in Americanization, prospered, and improved their social status, the cultural divergence between the two [German and Eastern European] communities was narrowed and ethnic amalgamation encouraged through intermarriage of 'Germans' and 'Russians.'"[7] Common enterprises as well as the decline of German ethnicity helped to bridge the chasm.

The Decline of German Ethnicity

A foreshadowing of the decline of German ethnicity among American Jews of Central European descent was perceivable as early as the late nineteenth century. As the Jewish community grew larger and formed their own organizations, diminishing numbers of Jews participated in the activities of German cultural groups. Within UAHC temples, German influences also eroded. Already ten years prior to 1900, as part of outreach to the Americanized younger element of his temple's community, Rabbi Joseph Krauskopf advocated the elimination of German sermons. He noted that

the German [language] which, however necessary it may have been for our German born grandparents and parents, has ceased to be with us. . . . Has it [German] any greater merit before God than the language of our own blessed country? Why conduct all of Saturday and holiday services in that tongue, and preach a sermon in it every other Saturday?[8]

This changing sentiment also was linked to developments in Germany. Reform Jewish leaders in America increasingly identified German language with the anti-Jewish national chauvinism of Bismarck's Germany. In the words of Rabbi Jacob Voorsanger, "the language of the German anti-Semite Adolf Stocker has no place in the American synagogue."[9]

Moreover, Reform Judaism within Central Europe had entered into a period of stagnation. Central Europe was no longer the prime source of global vitality for Reformers. The 17 March 1898 edition of the *American Israelite* noted that the tide had turned, and German Jews were beginning to emulate American Jewish Reform practices, especially the late Friday evening service "with sermon and choral music." As long-time Germanophile Rabbi Kaufman Kohler acknowledged, "Judaism in the new world will reinvigorate Judaism in the old. American Jewry had learned from Germany, now it was ready to teach." The completion of the *Jewish Encyclopedia* (1901–1905) provided "sure evidence that the torch of Wissenschaft had passed from Germany to America."[10]

In addition, the number of German-language publications in the United States had begun to decline, as had German-language instruction to American Christian children. Interest waned for sending future American professionals to study at the universities of Germany. Ph.D.'s for aspiring scholars, such as Rabbi Stephen Wise or Dr. Cyrus Adler, now were acquired in institutions of higher learning inside the United States. Furthermore, America's influential business community increasingly portrayed Germany's behavior as "militarism [by] . . . aristocratic classes" and as an obstacle to the growth of American overseas trade.[11] To be a loyal American gradually came to mean distancing oneself from identification with Germany.

Any residual focus upon German identity was torn asunder by a World War that pitted the United States and its cultural allies against Germany. Summarizing the wartime anti-German feelings of the nation in its 4 July edition at the war's conclusion in 1918, the *American Israelite*'s front page reflected:

The use of German in print or in speech to convey information useful to the enemy or to keep up the strength of pro-German sentiment and even afford favorable medium for spy service. . . . [Use of German language creates] influences tending to separate what belongs together, divide German feelings from American feelings, and continue an alien solidarity which has long hindered the amalgamation of citizenship. . . . [Moreover] the study of German [in some quarters] has been promoted for purely racial reasons, to prevent detachment from the mother country among Germans of the second generation and to intensify German clannishness and national pride.[12]

The military clashes of World War I severed the already eroded American linkages to cultural and organizational life in Germany. Whereas before the Civil War American organizations enlisted English models of activity, and from the 1870s through 1900 German organizational strategies predominated, between 1900 and 1914 pressure mounted to create uniquely American institutions.

The xenophobia resulting from the military conflicts of 1914 to 1918 dramatically altered collective sentiments shared by most Americans toward the lands of their European heritage. In the aftermath of World War I, "the most popular organs of [American] public opinion depicted Europe as hopelessly decadent and deadbeat, with leanings toward bolshevism." This shift of attitude against European trends was particularly noteworthy with regard to Germany. "The fury that broke upon the German-Americans in 1915, represented the most spectacular reversal of judgment in the history of American nativism."[13]

With the German declaration of submarine warfare against Britain on 15 January 1915, American public opinion turned against persons labeled by President Wilson as "hyphenate Americans." Americans of German heritage "fell subject to the plain and simple accusation in which every type of xenophobia culminated: the charge of disloyalty, the gravest sin in the morality of nationalism." UAHC temples as well as local churches hastened to divest themselves of a Germanic appearance, wanting to be perceived as part of an American movement. As a graphic demonstration of their preference for U.S. citizenship over German ancestry, local temples and local Christian congregations moved rapidly to extend membership to coreligionists among the "new immigrants."[14] In particular, for UAHC synagogues this membership solicitation extended to second-generation American Jews of Eastern European background.

Initial Contacts with Eastern European Jews

Given the increasing volume of both Protestant and Catholic immigrants in the final two decades of the nineteenth century, the Christian tradition of missionizing among the unchurched mandated institutional responses.[15] As historian Winthrop S. Hudson has noted,

the Protestant approach to the newcomers . . . was motivated by a varying mixture of religious concerns, humanitarian sentiment, patriotic fervor. . . . Many were convinced . . . that the "safety and welfare and Christian civilization of our country depends in no small degree upon transforming" the immigrant "into a true American," and that "nothing but Christianity, as incarnated in American Protestantism," can accomplish this end.[16]

Mission work among the impoverished immigrant coreligionists crowding into urban slums included English-language instruction, child care, aiding adaptation to American ways of shopping and food preparation, and religious outreach.

Just as American churches responded with programs of social service to impoverished newcomers from Eastern and Southeastern Europe, so too did Reform temples. Each of the four sample congregations had exhibited dual-pronged efforts of excluding most Eastern European Jews from temple membership while at the same time aiding their coreligionists in their distress both abroad and in the United States. On 1 October 1881, for example, the trustees of K.K. B'nai Yeshurun in Cincinnati

called on all the congregations of the city to come together and to devise plans "for the relief of the Russian refugees, who are arriving in this country" . . . [and] at a general meeting of the congregation on October 11, the president and the trustees of the congregation were instructed "to devise a plan by which contributions of money and clothing could be obtained in liberal amounts to aid their brethren who are now arriving in the United States from Russia in a most destitute condition, as the Russian fanatics have destroyed their homes and robbed them of all their possessions."[17]

As a result of this plea, K.K. B'nai Yeshurun created an ongoing Committee on Russian Relief.

UAHC rabbis such as KI's Joseph Krauskopf also aided Russian and Polish Jews in the 1880s and 1890s by assuming leadership roles in American chapters of the *Alliance Israelite Universelle*, the French-based Jewish defense organization. Through this organization, German Reform leaders raised substantial sums of money for the overseas relief efforts. In addition, local congregational and rabbinic efforts were motivated by the nationwide call of the UAHC for financial contributions to help Eastern European coreligionists adjust to the United States. In 1891, for example, UAHC President Julius Freiberg urged UAHC members "to do everything possible to assist Jewish immigrants in becoming acquainted with the language and customs of America."[18] Similarly, Kaufman Kohler's keynote "Conference Paper" at the pivotal Pittsburgh Conference of 1885 noted that

even if the poor Russian or Polish Jew is, on account of his religious mistrust or fanaticism, inaccessible to our ministrations, his children are not. They are easily Americanized, and we ought to assist in, and direct the process of naturalization. We ought to cultivate and maintain friendly relations between them and the wealthier classes of Jews.[19]

An important variation of this theme was the aforementioned training of Russian and Polish Jews for distant farming communities. These efforts were encouraged by the Baron de Hirsch Fund of New York, the Jewish Colonization Association of Paris (ICA), and the UAHC Committee on Agricultural Pursuits. At the local level, Temple Sinai of New Orleans registered a modest success in this regard. Sinai boasted that it was "the first community in the country that attempted to solve the problem of the Russian Jewish mass immigration by establishing an agricultural colony," the "Sicily Island Colony" in Louisiana. In 1882, 173 people came, including 35 families from Kiev and 25 from Elizabethgrad. The financial support for this short-lived project was shared by the local temples and by the New York City-based American chapter of the French Alliance Israelite Universelle.[20]

Similarly short-lived was the involvement of Cincinnati's K.K. B'nai Yeshurun in a Jewish agricultural colony experiment in Kansas during 1884.[21] The first of the sample congregations that succeeded in sustaining this bold vision on a permanent basis was Philadelphia's Keneseth Israel in the mid-1890s, under the creative guidance of its Rabbi Joseph Krauskopf.

Through the assistance of U.S. Ambassador and President of Cornell Andrew D. White, the Rabbi received an invitation [in 1894] to visit Leo Tolstoy on his farm. Tolstoy told Krauskopf that he could do nothing for Russian Jews, but . . . [h]e advised Krauskopf to return home and help settle America's arable land with poor urban dwellers. That visit changed Krauskopf's entire career and in 1897 launched his National Farm School in Doylestown, Pennsylvania, "to train ghetto children to be farmers."

Krauskopf hoped that Jewish farming would contradict the stereotype of "Jewish exclusiveness, Jewish proneness for consorting only with their own, Jewish leaning toward trade."[22]

One final aspect of local temple activities on behalf of the Russian and Polish Jews involved providing "social work" services to the newcomers. Jacob Voorsanger and San Francisco's Emanu-El emulated the creation of New York City's Emanu-El of a Sisterhood of Personal Service in 1894. Voorsanger's Emanu-El Sisterhood of Personal Service assisted recent Jewish immigrants to the Bay area. The Sisterhood's activities paralleled "visiting" (social assistance) provided by Methodist Deaconess and other Christian Sisters' groups to needy coreligionists. In 1888, the Methodist General Conference defined "the duties of the deaconesses [as] . . . minister to the poor, care for the sick, provide for the orphan, comfort the sorrowing, seek the wandering."[23] In similar fashion, Emanu-El's Sisterhood reached out to Russian impoverished immigrants through relief efforts, job placement, settlement houses, and educational and recreational opportunities for their children.

Service to the Eastern Jews also was reported by the early Reform Temple Brotherhoods, in a fashion parallel to initiatives undertaken by Christian Brothers' groups. This was particularly true in New York City, the urban area most beset by Jewish immigrants requiring assistance. Organized in 1903, the first UAHC Brotherhood was formed by Temple Emanu-El in Manhattan. Initially, the Brotherhood intended to be a "religious" outreach effort to less fortunate immigrant Jews. Friday evening services were conducted in the northern section of the Lower East Side, targeted toward the young adult sons and daughters of the Eastern European newcomers. In 1904, the Emanu-El Brotherhood added to its agenda the creation of a Sunday school, plus the option of twice-weekly meetings of Hebrew classes.[24] By 1911, new quarters were acquired to accommodate "club" activities as well. The facilities included a library, a study room, a game room, model kitchen and an outdoor gym. An "Americanization program" offered English-language courses and instruction in civics and American history.

Several decades of philanthropic assistance to Russian and Polish Jews in foreign lands as well as in the United States impacted upon the attitudes of both the German temple members and their Eastern European clients. By 1908, the long-time critic of the Eastern European Jews, Rabbi Jacob Voorsanger, returned from a visit to Manhattan and expressed an attitudinal shift. He concluded that the long-awaited "processes of adaptation [which Kaufman Kohler had prophesied in 1885] are already underway. Anyone who compares the Jewish East End of New York of even a decade ago with that of today will discern amazing changes and the unmistakable growth of tendencies in the direction of wholesome and loyal Americanism." New receptivity manifested itself as the sons and daughters of

Eastern Jews began to participate in the programs of Reform temples. For example, the 1905 Annual Meetings of Cincinnati's K.K. B'nai Yeshurun Talmud Yelodim Institute reported that its downtown Temple School site (in contrast to its affluent suburban Hill School location) was populated overwhelmingly by the offspring of Russian and Polish newcomers. "In our Temple School the enrollment was 195, consisting of 190 non-members, and only 5 members' children . . . nearly 150 of the children down town were poorer families, many of them within the last few years, immigrants to this country."[25]

The Rise of an American Jewish Ethnicity

American Reform temples felt both internal and societal pressures to reduce their German influences flavor, and the welcome Russian and Polish Jews as part of their service population. Simultaneously, the high status offered by Reform Judaism attracted many Eastern European Jewish immigrants and their offspring. Trends at the national level in the second decade of twentieth century aided this process of mutual rapprochement. During World War I, U.S. Jewry experienced the rising influence of the Eastern Europeans within American Jewish institutional life. Between 1914 and 1918, the German Jews lost control of American Jewry. Through the Joint Distribution Committee, American Zionist circles, and the American Jewish Congress movement, the Russian Jews emerged as a formidable force on the American Jewish scene.

Other factors contributed to a postwar bonding of American Eastern and Western Jews. The expansion of public transportation, highways, and affordable automobiles facilitated the creation of new suburbs. This process placed the purchase of one's own home within the economic reach of America's middle class. This middle-income sector expanded dramatically in size due to the proliferation of white collar professionals, such as clerks, stenographers, and managers. English-speaking, upwardly mobile German and Russian Jews moved together into the arising suburbs. All were identified without distinction by their Gentile neighbors as "American" Jews, just as Catholics, Lutherans, and so forth, became regarded as part of "American" ethnic groups. Second-generation Jews often blurred previous "distinctions between Uptown and Downtown Jews, between wealthy American Jews of German descent and poor eastern European immigrants." A new American Jewish ethnicity was forged among the children of the immigrants by common job experiences and neighborhood living.[26]

These ethnic realities in American Jewish life, as well as postwar nativist pressures to Americanize Jewish immigrants,[27] were not lost on the Reform movement. Reform temples and affiliated national institutions became active recruiters of middle- and upper-class second-generation Eastern European Jews. This change occurred during a time of growing church affiliation in American society. Percentages of church membership mounted from 34 percent (1890) to 41 percent (1916) to 44 percent (1936). Reform Jewish leaders were able to tap simultaneously into a new market of potential members and a generalized openness to affiliation. The more acculturated among Eastern European Jews began to join Reform temples. Simultaneously, increasing percentages of admittees to HUC were of Eastern European extraction. Often these eastern Jewish laymen and rabbis brought a sympathy toward Zionism and toward some Jewish traditional practices. Given the influx of newcomers, it was no longer desirable for the German Reform rabbis or congregational leaders to disregard the sensitivities of Eastern European coreligionists.

Changing Roles of Local Temples

A Return of Traditional Practices

Part of the effort by Christian and Jewish congregations to attract the "new immigrants" included accommodating some of the Eastern and Southeastern European religious liturgical practices. These adaptations by churches and temples occurred in the context of the overall decline of liberal religion in America at the end of the nineteenth century, as well as the revival of evangelical (right-wing) American Protestantism. This shift in the religious life in the United States had been termed by some historians as "the Great Reversal."[28] It marked the gradual turning away from theologically rational sermons and a church service sanitized of much ritual in favor of more emotional, passionate, ceremonial religious expressions.

In the final decades of the nineteenth century, America's legacy of Protestant revivalism, with both missionizing and fundamentalism, began to be reenergized by Charles G. Finney and Dwight L. Moody. This genre of revivalism shifted its focus from the declining rural churches to the burgeoning cities. Moody, in particular, was "an innovator in the techniques and administration of urban revivalism. Moody's objectives were clear: to Christianize the city, the nation, and if possible, the world."[29] Reinvigorated Protestant mission and extension societies successfully targeted many of America's Christian and Jewish immigrants.

Eastern European Jews arrived in U.S. cities in this very period, as the objects of right-wing Protestant missionizing, and as bearers of Polish and Russian traditional Judaism. The "Great Reversal" within American Protestantism impacted upon the return to more traditional preaching and ritual practices by many liberal American churches and synagogues. Parallel to emerging efforts by established Reform congregations to recruit Eastern European Jews to Reform Judaism probably were their desires to keep pace with American religious trends back toward age-old rites. Thus, the immigration of Eastern Jewry may have heightened and helped to shape a return to Jewish ritual practices within America's Reform Judaism that might well have taken place in any case.[30]

In this regard, the reemergence of Jewish customs and ceremonies set into motion a process that gradually attracted some Jews of Eastern European descent into Reform temples. These liturgical trends may have been accelerated once the presence of Jews of Russian and Polish descent attracted others to affiliate as well. In 1904, Temple Sinai, not unlike other Reform congregations of its day, built a Sukkah for the first time. Sukkot became a major annual celebration. The CCAR Convention of 1905 indicated that "concern is no longer in liberalizing observances, but in retaining some at all." In 1907, the CCAR presented a full discussion entitled "The Reinstituting of Rituals by Temples." CCAR deliberations reflected that "the more general celebration of Purim, Hanukah and Succoth, and the reinstituting of the home ceremonies of our religion seem to have been a feature of the past year's activities . . . in a number of cities a Congregational Seder was instituted."[31]

In 1912, New Orleans's Temple Sinai reintroduced the study of Hebrew as an option within its religious school. At San Francisco's Emanu-El, from the time of his arrival in 1910 as Senior Rabbi, Martin A. Meyer "urged the choir to recruit a higher proportion of Jews; sought to restore a number of traditional practices, such as baby namings and praying for the ill—which had fallen into disuse decades earlier, and unlike his predecessor, Rabbi Voorsanger, he refused to sanctify intermarriages under any circumstances." Similarly, Joseph Krauskopf's successor at KI, Rabbi William Fineshriber, reestablished the option of Bar Mitzvah in 1924, restored the reading of a portion of the Torah at Sabbath services, and hired a traditionally oriented Cantor, Benjamin Grobani.[32] As Rabbi Fineshriber indicated to his rabbinic colleagues at the CCAR Convention of 1920:

We have Protestanized our service sufficiently. It is time now to follow the tradition and practice of *Catholic Israel* [the slogan of Solomon Schechter, president of JTS] in having at least one service daily in the synagogue. There is nothing incompatible in our reform theology with the reintroduction into our daily lives of prayers for all occasions of joy and sorrow, at meal times and whenever the need calls for it.[33]

TABLE 5.2
Ethnicity of HUC Students, 1904 to 1929

	U.S. BORN	GERMAN	EAST EUROPEAN
1904–1909	15.8%	10.5%	58.0%
1910–1914	9.1%	4.5%	77.2%
1915–1919	6.5%	3.2%	87.1%
1920–1924	11.5%	5.8%	69.1%
1925–1929	0.0%	0.0%	83.4%

Abraham Franzblau survey of HUC student body, "A Quarter Century of Rabbinic Training," 1933, available at AJA Archives in Cincinnati.

The 31 May 1929 edition of the *American Israelite* concluded, "Reform Judaism in America is undergoing remarkable changes. It has ceased to combat orthodoxy . . . signs of the Judaizing swing in Reform are legion." The return of ritual was championed in particular by UAHC leaders anxious to recruit their Eastern European coreligionists. In 1911, for example, San Francisco Emanu-El's Rabbi Martin Meyer remarked that "frankly, the future of the Jew in America will be in the hands of the Russian-descended contingent . . . because of the preponderance of numbers."[34]

The future predicted by Rabbi Meyer soon became the present. As a survey by D. Max Eichhorn revealed, already by the year 1900, 48 percent of the HUC students were the children of Russian or Polish parents. An additional 4 percent had one Eastern European parent married to a Central European. Significantly, 52 percent of the students identified their mothers and fathers as "Orthodox." As early as 1916, five of the eleven members of the HUC graduating class had been born in Russia.[35] By 1930, over 80 percent of the HUC students were of Eastern European ethnicity (see Table 5.2). In terms of the Reform laity, by the mid-1920s a survey in the UAHC journal, *The Jewish Layman*, indicated that nearly half the lower-echelon members of local temples traced their roots to Eastern Europe. As a 1930 UAHC national survey of the laity concluded, "the proportion of Jews of Eastern European origin or parentage who belong to Reform Temples is increasing rapidly, as compared with those of German origin or parentage."[36]

A Case Study: Emanu-El—San Francisco

As previously noted, by 1908 Rabbi Jacob Voorsanger of Emanu-El, formerly a harsh critic of the Eastern Jews, had developed a newfound admiration for them. Voorsanger's successor, Rabbi Martin A. Meyer, energetically furthered this rapprochement with the immigrants. Rabbi

Meyer expressed kinship with the Russian Jew "because he is conscious of his Jewish affiliations and anxious to perpetuate the traditions of his people." Reflecting on German-American kinship with Russian and Polish coreligionists, Meyer reminded his readers in the weekly San Francisco Jewish newspaper, *Emanu-El*, that "if we are not the children, we are certainly the grandchildren of that Orthodoxy." To reach out to the Eastern Europe Jews and their offspring, Rabbi Meyer recruited Cantor Reuben Rinder in 1913 to succeed the retiring Cantor Edward Stark. As mentioned previously, Cantor Stark was the epitome of Salomon Sulzer's Central European version of the Cantor. In contrast, Reuben Rinder was an Eastern European Jew, a Zionist, and a traditionalist. Rinder's goal was that "Hebrew prayers, as well as the vast body of traditional Jewish folk music (rather than church melodies) could be utilized in the modern synagogue service." The appearance of cantors such as Reuben Rinder, the reintroduction of traditional prayer melodies, and enhanced congregational singing were met with approval in many parts of the country.[37]

Besides liturgical accommodations, Rabbi Meyer catered to the Eastern European Jews in terms of their social needs. Meyer reached out to Yiddish-speaking Jews by actively encouraging their immigration to the Bay area; by helping to establish a San Francisco office of the Hebrew Immigrant Aid Society (HIAS); by launching the Esther Hellman Settlement House and an expanded YMHA; and by his own staunch advocacy of both the American Jewish Congress movement and of the cause of Zionism. Under Meyer's inspired leadership, in the early 1920s, Emanu-El approved the construction of a new temple building reminiscent of the "Institutional" or "Open" synagogue of prior decades. While the temple center of the early 1900s hoped to attract the secularized children of German Jewish immigrants back to the temple, the "Institutional" Temple of the 1920s aimed at welcoming the alienated adult offspring of Eastern European arrivals.[38]

In the course of thirty years of experimentation, the American Protestant community had refined the outreach efforts of the urban "Institutional Church." As the year 1900 approached, New York City, for example, had more than a dozen institutional churches. At very same time, prominent churchmen were able to identify 173 similar congregations in other urban settings. By 1908, nationally renowned Rev. Josiah Strong assessed "that there were few urban churches that had not in one form or another introduced activities that might be described as institutional." The Institutional Church supplemented its religious observances with a constant flow of recreational and cultural activities. In the early 1920s, in his study of a thousand churches throughout the United States, H. Paul

Douglass identified a vast array of church-based programs, including Women's Club, Boys Club, Orchestra Band, and Adult Classes.[39] In this context, Rabbi Meyer of Emanu-El insisted that

> community service is the word of the day, not only on the basis of the economic waste of a plant which is idle the greater part of the week and the year; but because we feel that any church or synagogue deaf to the possibility of social and community service is doomed . . . one thing is certain, that just a house-of-prayer idea for weekly services and religious school instruction is apt to be barren.[40]

Meyer's programmatic vision also called for altering the upper-middle-class homogeneity of Reform temples. Meyer sought to expand the agenda of the temple by enlarging its membership and its range of activities. Rabbi Meyer hoped that his "new Temple . . . might accommodate up to a thousand families, [including] a much broader cross-section of the community [that is, many more Eastern Europeans, and not just the wealthy]."[41] Due to the new facility and the Temple's growing programmatic base, membership mounted from only 342 in 1900 to 565 in 1924, 710 in 1925, 890 in 1926, and nearly 1,000 by 1930.

Similar expansion and diversification of membership (in terms of ethnicity as well as wealth) accompanied the construction of a temple center in New Orleans in 1928. This was true as well with the Isaac Mayer Wise Temple Center facility in Cincinnati of 1927. The Wise Temple Center was "so designed that gymnasium apparatus be removable, to the end that the hall can be used for dances and for dinners."[42] In this fashion, Reform temples succeeded in attracting many acculturated offspring of Eastern Jews. Membership growth reflected proof of the successes of these local congregations:

Emanu-El	342	(1900)	996	(1930)
KI (Philadelphia)	506	(1900)	1,443	(1930)
KKBY (Cincinnati)	350	(1900)	784	(1932)
Temple Sinai	321	(1900)	630	(1930)[43]

Auxiliaries for Men and Women of All Ages

In the late nineteenth century, Temple "Sisterhoods for Personal Service" had been philanthropic organizations solely devoted to serving the poor. They had served in a fashion parallel to Methodist Deaconesses, Catholic Sisters, and related church-based women's groups. In the early years of the twentieth century, the function of Temple Sisterhoods, like that of their Christian counterparts, shifted to serving the internal needs of the sponsoring congregation. This refocusing was partly tied to ethnic factors.

Now that American Jews of Russian and Polish descent were joined UAHC temples and immigrants were joining local churches as well, Jewish or Christian sisterhoods no longer needed to function as outreach to socially excluded newcomers. Servicing American Jews both of Central and Eastern European descent best could be accomplished by programming efforts within the internal life of the congregation. Moreover, the professionalization of social work "rendered obsolete the work of and the need for dedicated but untrained friendly visitors."[44]

Temple Sisterhoods turned to encouraging attendance at religious services, enhancing educational settings for all ages, assisting in congregation hospitality, providing food and beverages, as well as other similar arenas of service. In tandem with the women's suffrage movement, Sisterhood members sought formal admission to temples as "members" in their own right, not simply as adjuncts of their husbands.[45] Examples of this temple-centered focus were exhibited by Sisterhoods early in the century. In New Orleans, for example, on 15 May 1900 an inner-directed Temple Sinai Women's Guild took "charge of the [temple] furnishings and maintenance of the [temple] building." Over the next twenty years, the Guild's Committee structure expanded to include House, Choir, Sunday School, Entertainment, Decoration, Garden, Program, Library, Press, Purchasing, Hospitality, Membership, Uniongram, Museum, and Scholarship. Temple Sinai's Rabbi Max Heller credited his women's auxiliary with

introducing congregational singing at the end of the service in 1904, rehearsals for the Seder Family Service; introducing the practice of gathering annually the parents of confirmands to make sure of simplicity in dress and adornment; sees to the reservation of pews on Confirmation Day for use of parents who are non-members . . . brought about the use of white suits by boy confirmands . . . decorates the Sukkah . . . [created] in 1918 a scholarship in memory of Rabbi James K. Gutheim, as well as a variety of other accomplishments ranging from providing books and book cases for the library, to caring for the trees and shrubs around the Temple building, and dedicating white drapes for the Ark and Pulpit for the Holy Days.[46]

As the pace of female involvement within the temples accelerated, women gradually made up the majority of the worshippers at Reform religious services. In the words of a contemporary observer, "without them [women] . . . the spacious and luxurious temple would be almost empty." Virtually every UAHC-affiliated temple created its own Sisterhood. Emanu-El (San Francisco) and Temple Sinai (New Orleans) arranged to have their women's clubs join the National Federation of Temple Sisterhoods (NFTS), established by the Union in 1912. Later that year, at the behest of the NFTS, Philadelphia's Keneseth Israel formed an affiliated

Sisterhood. Similarly, on 3 December 1912 the trustees of Cincinnati's K.K. B'nai Yeshurun were informed by Rabbi Louis Grossman "that a letter had come from the Union requesting the congregation to call such a women's organization into existence."[47] Within twelve months, the KKBY Sisterhood had been chartered.

By the 1920s, the successes of the Sisterhoods as temple and church auxiliaries inspired the creation of Brotherhoods as well. In the Reform movement, the goal of Brotherhoods was to promote a more active role for men within the life of the temple. "Before there were Brotherhoods, Abba Hillel Silver noted in 1926, the 'essential work of the liberal synagogue was largely in the hands of women and ecclesiastics.' The men would simply attend services from time to time and a few manage the Temple's financial affairs." Prior to the 1920s, the role of temple Brotherhoods—like that of nineteenth-century temple Sisterhoods—had been limited to social service projects among the impoverished and unaffiliated Eastern Europeans akin to Christian Brothers' groups.[48] In 1914, the Emanu-El (New York City) Brotherhood celebrated the tenth anniversary of its crowning achievement, the social service program. At the Emanu-El Brotherhood's "religious settlement house" in Manhattan's Lower East Side, more than thirteen hundred people per month attended Friday evening services. A Hebrew school instructed some two thousand students. Moreover, the settlement house's program

also included a daily free kindergarten, a circulating library and an outdoor playground; sewing, millinery, typing, bookkeeping and music classes; sports activities and club and game rooms that were used by more than 800 young people each week. . . . [C]ourses in Judaism and general religious studies were offered for adults and were well attended.[49]

Like Sisterhoods, and like church-based Brotherhoods, temple Brotherhoods gradually shifted their attention to an internal temple agenda, seeking to serve each congregation's middle-income male members of both German and Eastern European descent. This expansion of internal temple activity was initially rejected by rabbis like Max Heller who opposed the "temple center" concept generally. In a section of his published debate with Rabbi Moses Gries regarding the "Open Synagogue" in the 22 January 1903 edition of the *American Israelite*, Max Heller noted, "Regarding the . . . theory . . . that a [men's] club shall serve as a 'feeder for the church,' that it shall get men interested in the church, etc., I merely have to declare that it fails."[50]

Despite such skepticism, fifteen years later the need to recruit members gave a sharpened focus to temple Brotherhoods seeking to serve temple members' personal interests. With this goal in mind, two of the Union's "cathedral" congregations acted as pacesetters for the rest of nation. In 1917, Manhattan's prominent lay leader Louis Marshall submitted a request for creating a Men's Club to his Temple Emanu-El board of trustees. Marshall's request resulted in the launching of a Temple Emanu-El Men's Club charged with meeting the social, recreational, cultural, and religious needs of Emanu-El male members.[51]

At Emanu-El's neighboring Temple Beth El, a similar Men's Club came into existence in 1918. This effort was inspired by the role played by Beth El's men toward meeting the urgencies emanating from World War I. In particular, they had used religious school classrooms as a canteen for sailors and soldiers. As the founders of the Beth El Men's Club observed, "the various men who gave of their time and energies to this beneficent [World War I] undertaking developed a spirit of comradeship so binding that, when the War ended, they decided that their dedication should be projected into a more permanent organization."[52] The objectives of the Beth El Men's Club were formalized in its constitution of 1920.

1. To unite the men of the congregation and to stimulate interest in congregational life.
2. To foster and promote social spirit among the members.
3. To engage in intellectual, spiritual and philanthropic work.
4. To foster and promote an interest in behalf of civic and social righteousness of a non-partisan and non-political nature.
5. To participate in such movements as may make for better citizenship and more devoted Americans.[53]

So effective was the pioneering work of the Beth El Men's Club, that its primary leader, Roger W. Strauss, was selected as the first President of the National Federation of Temple Brotherhoods. Strauss served in that post from the organization's inception in 1923 until 1931. Similar Men's Club programs gradually arose within each of the four sample congregations. San Francisco's Emanu-El created a club in 1920; Cincinnati's K.K. B'nai Yeshurun did so in 1921, as did Philadelphia's Keneseth Israel in 1923 and Temple Sinai of New Orleans in 1929. This pattern spread throughout the country. By the early 1920s, more than seventy-five Temple Brotherhoods existed within affiliated UAHC congregations. Nevertheless, the emergence of men's auxiliaries within Reform temples did not solve the problem that men remained more scarce than women within the religious life of these institutions. In their successes, the Brotherhoods "stressed sociability rather than piety. . . . Their emergence in the 1920s betokens an attempt to find new ways to strengthen institutional loyalty in the face of waning spiritual commitment."[54]

Youth Activities

Synagogue auxiliary groups also were formed for the young adults of Reform congregations. The "alumni" of local temple Confirmation programs became ever more active in the 1920s, inspired by the local Sisterhoods and trends in society at large. Jews and Christians alike began to be more concerned about the socialization of "youth" within their local communities.

> Youth suddenly became a social problem in the 1920s. Part myth, part reality, the youth [ages 18 through 28] problem was for contemporaries a symbol for the strains of a culture running headlong into the twentieth century. . . . In the journals of middle-class opinion like the *Atlantic Monthly*, the *Literary Digest*, and the *Ladies Home Journal*, and in volumes of social analysis by judges, poets and educators, the children not of the outsider [the immigrant, the poor], but of the insider, of the native, urban middle classes, were pressed to the center of attention and debate.[55]

Initiatives for urban temple outreach to young adults paralleled American Protestant programming. Already four years prior to 1900, for example, just as temple activities extended to young men and women, American Methodists boasted over sixteen thousand local chapters of its youth movement, the Epworth League. By 1912, these church and temple techniques were widely adopted by clergy, as was the case with America's most renowned Reform Rabbi, Dr. Emil Hirsch of Chicago's Sinai Temple. As the New Orleans' *Jewish Ledger* reported, at Rabbi Hirsch's new Temple Annex "there will be a social club. . . . [T]here will also be a gymnasium, swimming tank, locker accommodations, reading rooms, rooms for billiards, pool and bowling and general assembly halls."[56]

Cincinnati's K.K. B'nai Yeshurun launched a similar effort in 1907 to involve young Jewish people within suburban areas through social, literary, and philanthropic activities. These initiatives led to the transformation of the Temple's new suburban religious school building of 1915 into "the Wise Social Center." As the Cincinnati-based *American Israelite* observed in its 20 April 1916 evaluation of "congregational centers":

> the [congregational center] movement was somewhat late in reaching Cincinnati but when it came, it was with a rush. Wise Center . . . was in its inception an independent organization but it soon became affiliated with B'nai Yeshurun and was given the use of the Congregation's Sabbath School building in [suburban] Avondale for its meetings, lectures and social functions, in fact even dances. Wise Center's example was followed [almost immediately] by [neighboring Reform Temple] Bene Israel [Rabbi David Philipson] and Congregation Sherith Israel Ahabath Achim [Rabbi Joshua H. Kaplan], making three [Cincinnati congregation centers] where a few months ago there was one.[57]

A similar pattern of activity directed toward young adults emerged within San Francisco's Temple Emanu-El. Following the catastrophic San Francisco fire of 1906, in which the temple's building was destroyed, all activity was postponed. Nevertheless, with the completion of a religious school facility in 1911, Rabbi Martin Meyer gradually introduced an "Athletic League," a Boy Scout Troop, and a "Pathfinders" program for postconfirmands. In the early 1920s, Rabbi Meyer's successor, Rabbi Louis Newman, persuaded the board of trustees to construct "a four-story Temple House, including not only classrooms, offices and a library, but a gymnasium and theater as well." The relative nonresponsiveness of Rabbi Max Heller's Temple Sinai of New Orleans to temple center activities was related both to his ideological opposition and to woefully inadequate facilities. As late as 1922, Rabbi Heller lamented Sinai's "unattractive and uncomfortable school rooms," its "lack of modern conveniences," its "remoteness from the residences," and the basic need for a "modern Temple [building] in an uptown location."[58] The new Sinai Temple constructed in 1928 remedied these physical and conceptual limitations and launched the congregation into "center" programs.

By the late 1920s, young adult recreational activity existed in many urban Reform temples. Simultaneously, however, local YMHA's and Jewish Community Centers created impressive facilities that quickly dominated Jewish young adult recreation, superceding the temple centers. By 1933, Jacob D. Schwartz of the Union's Department of Synagogue and School Extension, in completing an extensive national survey, concluded:

the gymnasium is [no longer] found [but] in only a relatively small number of [UAHC] congregations, most of them in metropolitan [downtown] centers and is used regularly in still fewer. Games and sports under [Reform] synagogue auspices are likewise confined almost exclusively to a few metropolitan cities. Swimming pools and swimming activities in the synagogues are almost non-existent.[59]

Moreover, a decade of abortive efforts by the Reform movement to address the spiritual needs of Jewish students on America's campuses had failed, being replaced in 1923 by B'nai Brith Hillel.[60] Given limited financial resources, the national UAHC sought the less costly technique of young adult involvement within the existing religious and educational structures of local Reform temples. This effort was intensified due to the dire conclusions of the Union's parallel research, which lamented the erosion of attendance at worship services by the younger generation. Arthur L. Reinhart's 1928 NFTB study entitled *The Voice of the Laity: A Survey of the Jewish Layman's Religious Attitudes and Practices* revealed,

1. . . . . on comparing the answers from men under thirty years of age with those over forty, the replies from the younger men indicate *less*

2. desire for Saturday morning service
3. knowledge of Hebrew
4. affiliation with a congregation
5. regularity in attendance of services throughout the year
6. attendance at services on minor holidays
7. comfort with prayer
8. actual amount of praying
9. increase of need for prayer in time of joy
10. observance of Yahrzeit
11. desire for Hebrew in service
12. enjoyment in Congregational singing
13. desire for spiritual matters and biblical themes as sermon topics
14. reciting of grace at meals.
15. reading about Jewish life and religion [emphasis added][61]

To confront this challenge directly, by 1929 innovative temples such as Cincinnati's K.K. B'nai Yeshurun created "Youth Temple" programs. Their purpose "was to unite young men and women for religious worship, and for religious education." KKBY's "Youth Temple" immediately "proved to be a genuine success. It was widely used in the remainder of the country." Jacob D. Schwartz's aforementioned national UAHC survey of 1932/1933 also revealed widespread efforts by Reform temple youth organizations to sponsor "lectures, addresses, discussions or debates on Jewish or general current events and problems," as well as "classes in Judaica, workshops in Jewish drama, all seeking to constitute the connecting link between attendance in Religious School and adult membership in the congregation."[62]

Rabbinic Trends

Eastern Europeans Attracted to Zionist Advocates

More and more, Protestant clergy accommodated the diverse viewpoints of Christian immigrant and ethnic groups. Similarly, changing ideological views among UAHC religious leaders proved attractive to the offspring of Russian and Polish Jews. In the second decade of the twentieth century, Rabbi Max Heller (Temple Sinai) and Rabbi Martin Meyer (Emanu-El) joined with prominent CCAR members such as Rabbi Stephen S. Wise and later (1920s) Rabbi Abba Hillel Silver as well as other Reform rabbis as advocates of American Zionism. As early as 1912, Rabbi Max Heller served as a professor of Hebrew literature at Tulane, teaching the writings of modern Hebrew authors advocating a return to Zion. During the school year of September 1917 through June 1918, Heller renewed

Hebrew language instruction in the Temple Sinai religious school, simulating a "Trip to Palestine" on ships represented by the various classes. Rabbi Martin Meyer of Emanu-El in San Francisco chaired mass meetings for Zionism throughout World War I. At the national level, he battled staunchly against anti-Zionism within the CCAR.[63]

Rabbi Joseph Krauskopf of KI, formerly opposed to Zionism, was transformed into a defender of Zionism by his 1916 visit to agricultural settlements in Palestine. His "conversion" stemmed from the continued devastation of the Jewish communities within Europe and his growing interest in a Jewish return to till the land as represented by his National Farm School. Krauskopf was influenced also by Louis Brandeis' formulation of Zionism that did not demand *aliya* for American Jews. Instead, Brandeis advocated constructing a Jewish national home for persecuted Eastern European brethren based upon American Progressive ideals.

Of the four rabbis in the sample temples at the time of World War I, only Louis Grossman (K.K. B'nai Yeshurun, Cincinnati) remained opposed to Zionism. His opposition was an act of loyalty to his revered predecessor, Rabbi Isaac M. Wise. Nonetheless, Grossman's successor in the early 1920s, Rabbi James G. Heller (Max Heller's son), publicly endorsed the pursuit of a Jewish national home in Palestine. By 1930, UAHC surveys demonstrated the scope of this ideological shift. They determined that unlike in the past, "Zionists are present in one out of every five of our families" in affiliated Reform temples. Moreover, 69 percent of the rabbinical students at the Hebrew Union College expressed a "favorable" attitude toward Zionism. While many CCAR rabbis remained anti-Zionists, support for a Jewish national home in Palestine was but one example of the diverse adaptations crafted by the rabbinic leadership of Reform temples in order to accommodate Eastern European Jews.[64]

Changing Rabbinic Role

The continuing expansion of the size and scope of institutional church and temple activities to all ages and to American coreligionists of any national origin whatsoever changed the role of the pulpit clergyman yet again. By the year 1900 the Reform rabbi was a public speaker delivering sermons, lectures, and classes, an advocate for social justice concerns, a pastor to the personal needs and life-cycle events of his membership, superintendent of religious school departments, and a teacher of the confirmands and postconfirmands, and most important in the eyes of his laity, "an ambassador to the gentiles." In the early years of the twentieth century, mounting administrative responsibilities within the temple center further augmented the rabbi's plethora of tasks. By the 1930s, surveys of Rabbinic "time management" indicated that 14 percent of his week, the largest single allocation of congregational time outside of sermon preparation, was accorded to "administration." As Jacob D. Schwartz concluded on the basis of another national UAHC survey of 1932/1933:

> Of the time given by the Rabbi to the work in his own congregation, the average spent on rabbinical duties pertaining to divine services and to officiating at other religious ceremonies was 14 percent; preparation of sermons, 20 percent; religious education, 11 percent; leadership of synagogue groups and auxiliaries, 4 percent; pastoral work, 11 percent; *administration, 14 percent* [my emphasis]; scholarly work 11 percent; general cultural pursuits, 11 percent; miscellaneous activities, such as special addresses, weddings, and funerals for the unaffiliated and the like, 4 percent.[65]

In recognition of this substantive change in task, the Rabbi became an official part of the temple's administrative structure. In 1923, Cincinnati's K.K. B'nai Yeshurun pioneered in this direction by accepting their Rabbi James G. Heller as an ex officio member of the board of trustees. As a rationale, the KKBY leadership indicated:

> of course, in managing the financial and business affairs of the congregation, the assistance that can be rendered by the rabbi is usually negligible, but to present the needs of the Sabbath School, the time and arrangement of services and for special services upon occasions, his advice and suggestions must of necessity be valuable. Congregations should bear in mind that there are many things in which the judgment of the Rabbi is superior to their own, because he has given more careful thought and study to the matter. This step of KKBY is something of an innovation, but it is an example that might with advantage be followed by all congregations in the country.[66]

One major casualty of the expansion of the rabbinic administrative role was the further decline of scholarly productivity by pulpit rabbis. By the 1920s, editorials, such as the lead column in the *American Israelite* edition of 22 April 1926, lamented that the "American Rabbinate [is] . . . lowered to intellectual barrenness." By 22 November 1929, Mr. Arthur Meyerowitz, a prominent lay leader within the UAHC, remarked to the Jewish journalistic community just how "shocked" he was to realize that no pulpit rabbi "has produced a worth-while book" during the previous entire year. A similar critique appeared in the *Jewish Ledger* 4 July 1930 editorial page, disparagingly describing the Temple Rabbi as "social worker . . . fine mixer . . . good after-dinner speaker, but, as a rule, he lacks woefully in Jewish scholarship and often in religious fervor through which he might kindle the religious fervor of his congregants."[67]

Due to time constraints, many congregational rabbis relinquished communal leadership roles as well. As the Philadelphia *Jewish Exponent* of

4 June 1926 observed, "the [administrative] work within the congregation has increased so greatly that it engages all his [the Rabbi's] energy and attention to the exclusion of other activities."[68] Whereas the nineteenth-century American rabbi was expected to be a public leader, more and more the twentieth-century rabbi's "outside" involvements had to be "justified" to his membership. The 1929 "Annual Report of the President" of K.K. B'nai Yeshurun of Cincinnati reflected this apologetic tone:

> When Rabbi Heller was engaged by this congregation, it was with the distinct understanding that he was not to confine his efforts to congregational activities. He was engaged as much for the benefit he might be to the community as well as to our Temple itself. . . . If you mingled with people outside of the congregation you would understand more fully how valuable an agent and representative he is, to the credit of this organization. His fame as an orator has, in a few short years, not only become a by-word in Cincinnati, but has spread all over the country.[69]

Rabbi Heller's continuing efforts to justify his choices of time allocation are also painfully evident in the annual "Report of the Rabbi" issued in the KKBY *Yearbook* of 1929/1930. First, James Heller reminded the laity of his enormous responsibilities, such as "carrying on the pulpit work so that it attracts and interests the congregation; leading the religious school, improving its religious instruction, etc.; and acting as an emissary for the Jews of the city to the non-Jewish population. In addition to this some of us [as rabbis] are called upon to take more or less of a part in national Jewish activities, such as those of Zionism, Jewish education, and national Jewish governing bodies, such as the HUC, the CCAR, and the Hillel Foundation."[70] James Heller proceeded to place his "pastoral" role into a favorable context, noting that,

> for the Rabbi to do all of the preceding things, and to pay social calls on a large congregation, is a physical impossibility. [Nevertheless] I have always tried to visit those who are ill or who have suffered a loss, and those who have some anniversary or joyous occasion in the family. Even this is made difficult by the fact—which I notice is common to other congregations, that members expect the rabbi to know of these occasions without notifying him.[71]

Conclusion

During the early years of the twentieth century, the shape of religious identity and synagogue affiliation was broadened. The once-narrow parameters of the German-American temple widened into those of a fully developed temple center, directed both by the professionalized Reform rabbi and cantor and by a new genre of synagogue staff person, the temple executive secretary. In 1910, Manhattan's Beth El again pioneered in the management of congregational life by hiring Samuel Berliner as its administrator. Four years later, Chicago's Sinai Congregation engaged S. D. Schwartz in a similar position. These two able individuals innovated in applying the techniques and procedures of scientific administration to the distinctive realm of the Reform temple.[72]

These Reform initiatives represented a model example of institutionalized American religious life, imitated as well by middle-class Conservative and Orthodox synagogues in the years immediately following World War I. Prominent examples of such emulation were Manhattan's Orthodox synagogue Kehillath Jeshurun and the Brooklyn Jewish Center, a Conservative congregation. In the 1920s, Kehillat Jeshurun (KJ) not only instituted a Men's Club, a Sisterhood, youth activities, a congregational Hebrew school, social activities, and adult education, but also adopted many of the aesthetics accepted decades earlier by Reform temples. KJ established:

a uniform code of behavior within the sanctuary, a code of behavior governing everything from dress to devotion . . . all male congregants were obliged to wear a black silk kipah [no hats] and, of course, tie and jacket . . . a system of ushers [both male and female] to ensure the maintenance of proper behavior; the use of a uniform prayerbook and guidelines . . . for congregational singing, responsive reading and English interpolations.[73]

KJ's Rabbi Joseph Lookstein embodied the qualities of professional rabbi. Lookstein earned a B.A. from City College and an M.A. from Columbia University in sociology. He received his rabbinic education at Rabbi Isaac Elchanah Theological Seminary, reorganized in 1915 by Dr. Bernard Revel as a graduate professional school for the training of rabbis. Rabbi Lookstein's sermons were not "*droshes* in the traditional sense, rather, he used the sermon [in a professional fashion] to enhance religious behavior, to edify and uplift, to inform and to inspire" akin to the great Protestant church and Reform temple preachers of his day. Joseph Lookstein was "determined to have his synagogue stand as a peer with [Conservative] Park Avenue Synagogue and [Reform] Temple Emanu-El." In Lookstein's words, "The appearance, the conduct, the dignity [within KJ] should be what prevails in a Temple."[74]

A similar pattern emerged at the Brooklyn Jewish Center, a high-profile Conservative congregation established in the early 1920s. Here too, the synagogue created a Sisterhood, Men's Club, youth group, adult classes and lectures, with a professional staff comprised of a rabbi, cantor, Executive Director, and a large contingent of support personnel. Services were conducted "in fine decorum and a spirit of reverence."[75] The Center's Rabbi Israel Levinthal possessed professional qualifications similar to those of Joseph Lookstein and to well-known Reform rabbis of the 1920s. Levinthal was a master preacher and a brilliant strategist for maximizing the programmatic potentials of synagogue life.

In a fashion similar to the Reform temples of the post-World War I era, both Conservative congregations like the Brooklyn Jewish Center and Orthodox synagogues such as Kehillath Jeshurun welcomed all American Jews regardless of national descent. This new *American* Jewish vision for Orthodox, Conservative, and Reform congregations alike was articulated by rabbis and by lay leaders. A prime example was Julian Morgenstern, the President of the Hebrew Union College throughout the 1920s. With the restrictive immigration laws of 1921 and 1924 severely curtailing the arrival of additional Jews from Russian and Poland, a unified American Judaism began to emerge. It seemed possible to harmonize the tradition-alism of the East with the modern cultural standards of the West. Many upwardly-mobile Russian Jews accepted contemporary aesthetic stan-dards, while German Jews reincorporated some ritual, Hebraic, and peoplehood concerns.

Morgenstern's argument—which he repeated often—went like this. A period of American Jewish history has ended . . . [country of origin] differences among Jews would [now] disappear, revealing anew Isaac Mayer Wise's vision of a united American Judaism. The significance of their German origins would increasingly diminish among Reform Jews even as awareness of their east European back-ground declined among descendants of the newer immigrants . . . "If America represents a large melting pot," Morgenstern told his rabbinical colleagues, "then Jewry in America represents a smaller melting pot into which are cast Jews and Judaism from various lands."[76]

As a consequence of the institutional strategies pioneered by Reform temples and adopted by other synagogues as well, in the 1920s more local congregations joined all three movements, the UAHC, as well as the Orthodox Union (OU) and the (Conservative) United Synagogue. On the local scene, the decision by synagogues founded by second-generation Jews of Eastern European descent whether to be Reform, Conservative, or Orthodox often was accompanied by ideological controversy. "When a congregation found it impossible to alter religious practice with unanim-ity, the segment whose ideas were not accepted seceded and reconstituted itself as a separate group. . . . the national Jewish congregational orga-nizations attempted to give this localized process direction and cohe-sion."[77]

As many new synagogues aligned with one of the three Jewish religious movements, Reform, Conservative, and Orthodox national institutions increased in size. From barely 100 affiliated congregations in 1900, for example, the total of UAHC member temples jumped to 200 by 1917 and

285 thirteen years later. The number of affiliated families, just over 9,000 at the turn of the century, equaled 23,000 seventeen years later and over 60,000 by 1930. Nevertheless, this growth did not keep pace with the dramatic increase in the overall size of the American Jewish population. Hundreds of thousands of Russian and Polish Jewish immigrants had entered the United States in the years prior to World War I. Subsequently, the post-war period was dominated by the adult offspring of these Eastern Europeans. In the vicinity of New York City, middle-class, second generation Jews devoted their energies to establishing Conservative and sometimes Orthodox synagogue centers. "They rejected the institutional model offered by their German Jewish predecessors as decisively as had immigrant Jews."[78]

Due to these ethnic considerations pitting Eastern European Jews against coreligionists of Central European descent, in the post-war era the Orthodox Union gained the membership of dozens of New York area congregations as well as of some Orthodox synagogues in other industrial American cities. Although its national figure of 96 affiliated synagogues remained relatively constant from the time of its founding in 1898 until 1918 in the aftermath of World War I, the OU's ranks increased dramatically to more than 200 congregations by the end of the 1920s. Even more substantial was the post-1918 expansion of the (Conservative) United Synagogue at the grassroots level, growing from only 22 founding congregations in 1913 to over 150 in 1923 and to 229 affiliated *shuls* by the end of the decade. This achievement generated a modest "sense of triumph" within the burgeoning Conservative movement, at the expense of the Reform UAHC.[79]

The three national religious bodies continued to adjust their focus to service the needs articulated by upwardly mobile, increasingly secularized Jews. As had occurred one generation earlier, attracting second-generation Jewry to American synagogues required a redefinition of the religious congregation to incorporate associational, recreational, and educational functions. In the battle to attract the young, each movement borrowed from and in turn influenced the institutional initiatives of the others. This process of mutual interactions, and recruitment of members motivated by social and cultural concerns generated a period of numerical expansion that masked a spiritual crisis. As in church circles, American Jewish life experienced a decline in attendance at religious services, in personal religious observances, as well as in the quality of Jewish education of the young.[80]

Behind the malaise lay a profound change . . . that affected all religions. Church attendance was also declining . . . showing a "marked religious slump." After its

stridency at the beginning of the decade [1920s], Christian fundamentalism . . . had begun to lose moral authority. . . .
     "A religious depression," according to one historian, "preceded the economic
depression in the United States."[81]

Although the founding of new synagogues was a positive sign, it did not
occur at a pace equivalent to the dramatic growth in the American Jewish
population, bolstered by the Eastern European immigration. Instead, the
true institutional boom of the 1920s for America's Jews occurred among
the secular agencies, notably the Jewish Center movement. The Centers
recast the culturally oriented YMHA of the nineteenth century into a
social and recreational hub of early-twentieth-century Jewish communities. In 1900, the model new "Y" was completed at 92nd Street and
Lexington Avenue in Manhattan. Other localities quickly followed this
pattern. In 1913, the leaders of rapidly emerging local "Y" programs
attended a founding conference of the Council of Young Men's Hebrew
Associations and Kindred Associations. By 1929, the Centers claimed
100,000 members nationally, a figure that exceeded the membership
numbers of any of the three Jewish religious movements. "The persistent
question addressed by rabbis and laity in this period was therefore how to
stem the synagogue's continuing drift toward the periphery."[82] To assist in
this pursuit, local congregational leadership turned toward their growing
national organizations for a collective identity, suitable printed materials,
and trained professional staff. These proliferating challenges demanded
innovative management techniques from the UAHC, the Orthodox
Union, and the United Synagogue.

❖ 6 ❖

American Corporate Culture Prevails

Changes in local temple life from 1900 to 1930 created pressure for yet another national accommodation by the UAHC to its American environment. When the Union responded, its initiatives reflected the quest by individual congregations to reach out to the sons and daughters of Eastern European immigrants. Also, the desire to abandon identifiably German organizational techniques led to implementation of institutional approaches characteristic of the United States. The first quarter of the twentieth century in the United States has been characterized as an American age, an age of the "expert" and of "scientific management." New strategies yielded unprecedented successes for business and other organizations. The application of "bureaucratic means" to national religious bodies at the turn of the century created a uniquely American approach to religious organization. The launching of an American institutional style was related to the upsurge in U.S. nationalism in the final years of the nineteenth century.

Spurred on by the rapid growth of U.S. export trade in the late 1890s (which nearly doubled from $684 million in 1890 to $1.040 billion by 1900) and the spread of American spheres of global influence (to Cuba, the Philippines, Hawaii, China, Panama, and Latin America), the mood of American Protestants was one of great confidence. From 1890 to 1920, the churches exhibited "a vigorous and growing condition" that manifested itself in an expansion of "Foreign Missions," efforts to spread an American version of Christianity around the globe.[1] Political and economic nationalism reached a dramatic climax during the years of World War I, by which time *Americanism* became the dominant cultural bias of the United States.

The Shift in Emphasis of the Reform Movement in American Judaism

The Popularity of American Business Techniques

The application of business techniques by Christian and Jewish denominations in the early twentieth century created a distinctively American style of religion. Historian Ben Primer appropriately labeled this process "the bureaucratization of the church." The transformation meant a shift from simple denominations to more complex national religious movements. No longer were countrywide religious bodies committed solely to denominational colleges and other limited educational objectives. Instead, their province expanded dramatically, as they sought new clients through the provision of added services. Each emerging movement established a series of interrelated "departments" serving not only "education," but also aggressive outreach projects, entitled "Church and School Extension" or "Christian Endeavor." By the early years of the twentieth century, American Protestantism emulated the bureaucratic structures of rising corporations within American life. Their innovative organizational techniques were borrowed not from English models or from German cultural trends as was true in the past, but rather from initiatives within burgeoning American business.[2]

During the final four decades of the nineteenth century, the American corporation became "the dominant institution in the nations' life, determining what Americans would possess, controlling where and how they would work, and shaping almost every aspect of their lives from birth to death." Men like John D. Rockefeller, H. P. Morgan, and Andrew Carnegie were household names, held up as paragons of success.[3] Industrial growth enabled America to exert its power worldwide. The American factory and its "corporate culture" spread to every other part of the globe. American industrial and farm goods began to flood into the British Isles, Germany, and other former sources of consumer products and ideas. Books reflecting foreign concerns appeared, notably Fred A. McKenzie's *American Invaders* (1902) and Sir Christopher Furness's *American Invasion* (1902) in England, and Brooks Adams's *American Economic Supremacy* (1900) in the United States.

Between 1897 and 1902, Europeans pointed to "the American invasion of Europe"—an invasion of American manufactured goods. The phrase "American invasion" was first used by the Austrian minister of foreign affairs; it came to be frequently repeated . . . an Englishman, writing in 1901 [recorded that] . . . the invasion goes on unceasingly and without noise or show in five hundred industries at once. From shaving soap to electric motors, and from shirt waists to telephones, the American is clearing the field.[4]

Owing to the remarkable achievements of U.S. industry, corporate culture emerged as the prime referent for organizational planners within every sector of society. Its gospel spread via newspapers, journals, and books, as well as through speeches presented at organizational groups within the United States. Its influence was exerted by laymen, by professional journalists, by businessmen, or industrialists either individually or in groups such as the National Association of Manufacturers. The techniques of U.S. industry (hiring of professional managers, expansion of functions to seek "new economic frontiers," specialization, and departmentalization) surpassed British and German concepts as sources of American local and national institutional innovation.[5]

Social historians have defined this process as "cultural diffusion . . . [for example] a flow of ideas and values . . . from high status or power groups in a culture [in this case, American industry and corporate life] to those with less stature and power [religious organizations]." This society-wide process, observed with increasing frequency by American historians, has been described as "making America corporate." The parallel shift to corporate culture within American religious groups became evident in the first decades of the twentieth century. National denominational leadership began to discuss the problems of administration more frequently. Lay boards formed committees to study administrative efficiency.[6] Several key assumptions guided this process: equating growth with success; providing a larger range of services to clients; hiring professional managers; adopting systematic finance; and instituting a bureaucratic institutional structure.

Scientific Management

In the early years of the twentieth century, scientific management techniques already had emerged within organized American religious life. Each of the major American Protestant denominations expanded the role of its national structure by hiring professional administrators, effectively raising more funds, and constructing or purchasing larger buildings for central headquarters. During this transformation into corporate-style "religious movements," each denomination enlarged its focus. In the past, their primary objectives as denominations were fostering denominational colleges, conducting haphazard "circuit" missionizing, and producing Sunday school curricular materials. The new mandate as Christian religious movements was "Church and School Extension." Extension work meant marketing religious wares to unchurched urban immigrants as well as to isolated souls within the railroad-accessible U.S. hinterland.[7] This shift from denomination to religious movement required a change in emphasis, from support solely for national institutions to support for both national projects as well as for direct servicing of local needs.

In organizational terms, to achieve these more aggressive goals American religionists adopted what church administrator Shailer Matthews referred to in 1912 as "scientific management for the churches." Matthews and his peers consciously borrowed from Frederic W. Taylor's "scientific management" and "efficiency" techniques of early-twentieth-century business and industry. Harrington Emerson popularized the principles of "Taylorism" as including:

1. Develop a science for each element of man's work, which replaces the old rule-of-thumb method
6. Standard records
7. Planning
8. Standard conditions
9. Standardized operations
10. Standard instructions
11. Standard schedules
12. Efficiency reward[8]

Taylorism insisted that these principles be applied "to all social activities; to the management of our homes; the management of our farms; . . . of our churches, our philanthropic institutions, our universities, our governmental departments." This approach to organizational challenges gained unparalleled popularity due to the highly publicized hearings before the Interstate Commerce Commission of the U.S. Federal Government in the Fall of 1910. During the hearings, Louis Brandeis and his team of attorneys defended the demand for higher wages by railroad employees on the basis of projected cost-cutting measures through more "efficient" Taylor-like methods. By 1911, the full text of Frederic W. Taylor's *The Principles of Scientific Management* appeared. American society and the world at large were caught in a frenzy of responses. Translations of Taylor's volume appeared in French, German, Dutch, Swedish, Russian, Italian, Spanish, and Japanese. "In the flood of enthusiasm, an attempt was made to apply the principles of scientific management to many aspects of American life, including the army and navy, the legal profession, the home, the family, the household, the church, and . . . to education."[9]

The American church unquestionably was touched by what social scientist Ralph Henry Gabriel termed the "Age of Efficiency."[10] Books and articles on the subject rolled off the religious presses, among them: Shailer Matthews, *Scientific Management in the Churches*, 1912; George A. Andrews, *Efficient Religion*, 1912; Charles A. Barbour, *Making Religion Efficient*,

1912; and Henry F. Cope, *Efficiency in the Sunday School and the Efficient Layman*, 1911. The Efficiency Society, organized in New York City in 1912, heard addresses by Charles S. MacFarland, Secretary-General of the Federal Council of Churches, and by Charles Stelzle. Both men spoke on the need for "church efficiency." The Society organized a Church Efficiency Committee, which included Stelzle and MacFarland. In 1913, the Society's journal published three articles on efficiency in church work.

Just as these business methods surfaced within American Protestantism, so too did they appear among American Jewish secular and religious organizations. The institutions serving Jews in the United States adopted more systematic approaches to their fund-raising challenges. The emerging world of "Jewish social service," for example, exhibited an adherence to corporate "principles and methods." In particular, notable progress occurred in fund raising and allocations among emerging Federations of Jewish Social Agencies (established on a city-by-city basis), the National Conference of Jewish Charities (founded in 1899 by hundreds of Jewish charitable societies), and the Joint Distribution Committee (unification in 1914 of Jewish overseas welfare activities as a result of the suffering of European Jews during World War I). Jewish philanthropies acknowledged that the critical ingredient for success in acquiring and administering charitable contributions was "efficiency."

The problem of raising funds for philanthropic purposes, as expressed in the *modern term of efficiency* [emphasis added], is to secure the greatest amount of money with the least possible expense and effort—to provide a permanent income for the maintenance of existing activities, and to conserve the interest, as well as the resources, of the community. . . . The Federation plan fully meets these tests.[12]

The organizational arms of the Reform movement in American Judaism expressed similar concern for corporate "efficiency." As early as the spring of 1910, for example, the New Orleans *Jewish Ledger* featured coverage for the UAHC's national pursuit of "efficiency" for both synagogues and religious schools. By 1916, the President of the National Federation of Temple Sisterhoods Annual Address to the UAHC focused upon her goal of "organizational efficiency." Ultimately, the Union of American Hebrew Congregations established its own national "committee on Efficiency" to address this challenge.[13]

The UAHC Adopts Corporate Culture

The Realm of Finance

One of the practical achievements of the transformation of American church and synagogue management was the development of more efficient strategies for financing religion at the national level. The challenge of "straitened finances" perpetually confronted the nineteenth-century UAHC. In 1890, the UAHC national fund-raising efforts yielded only $6,760 in dues, $4,272 in annual contributions, $6,423 in donations and bequests, $1,785 toward the "[HUC students'] Stipendary Fund," $1,950 as "Donations and Bequests to the Endowment Fund," $1,174 in interest, and $8,005 for cashed in mortgages for a total of $30,369. The activities of the institutions and committees of the UAHC were severely restricted in the nineteenth century because of the Union's lack of funds. "Throughout the first thirty years of the Union its leaders endlessly lamented their financial woes."[14]

Given this ongoing quest for funding, UAHC leaders were acutely aware of the fund-raising achievement of the local Jewish Federations and the United Hebrew Charities (UHC), established from 1895 to 1901. Two of our sample communities, Cincinnati (1896) and Philadelphia (1901), were among the first five Jewish communities to be organized in this fashion. In Cincinnati, the home of the Hebrew Union College, where two of the primary lay leaders of the Reform Union (Bernhard Bettman and Louis Levi) served as President and Vice President of the United Hebrew Charities (consolidated in 1896), in its first year of operation the UHC raised $32,400 of annual income.[15]

Philanthropy was for many years the hallmark of Cincinnati Jewry, what set it apart from other Jewish communities across the United States. . . . [The well-respected] Boris Bogin . . . considered the city's Jewish community to be nothing less than "the exemplar of social service for the eyes of all other Jewries."[16]

In 1902, Philadelphia's Jewish Federation campaign reported $121,860.07 in total subscriptions.[17] The cumulative national totals among city-wide Jewish campaigns rose to the hundreds of thousands of dollars.

Sudden and dramatic Protestant fiscal successes also gained the attention of Reform Jewish circles. On 4 January 1901, the *American Israelite* reported that America's "Methodists expect to raise $20 million where of $8 million have already been obtained; Presbyterians, Episcopalians and others are raising great twentieth century funds for church work." The primary goal of denominational bodies became direct assistance to the practical needs of the local affiliated congregation, its children, its men and women, and notably its growing sector of middle-class businessmen and professionals. Getting "local churches excited about and involved in the [national fund raising] drive"[18] made possible the solicitation of a large potential pool of donors.

The slogan for each emerging religious "movement" was "to get our local people to comprehend our program." To achieve this goal, American

Protestants employed active public relations and an aggressive expansion of direct services to a growing local membership. Intensified concerns for individual church needs created a momentum of fiscal successes. Church and school extension efforts yielded not only more monetary contributions but also more members for affiliated neighborhood churches. Larger church membership rolls meant additional prospective donors to be solicited by the national denomination. Due to church extension efforts, dramatic increases in the number and size of member congregations created new sources of national funds.[19]

Creative fund-raising techniques, reminiscent of those employed by American businesses, facilitated this process. For example, Protestant movements offered the "station plan," by which a local church enabled a donor to designate the specific project to receive his or her contribution. Within this category, an $800 gift, for instance, sponsored a single missionary, while a $1,200 amount sufficed for a married couple. By the 1920s, the quest for aggressive techniques yielded a "systematic finance" approach. In systematic finance, the focus of activity was an "Every Member Canvass for a Contribution" dimension. "Tracts on 'systematic finance' were sent to all churches. . . . Books on technique proliferated. A six-month planning schedule was mapped out, including directions on when to publicize, when to order supplies, and when to train canvassers." Religious movements hired advertising firms to "engage in *scientific* propaganda work." "Efficient" measures for soliciting "pledges," for conducting "campaigns," for developing "endowment" funds and bequests benefited from the unprecedented levels of broad-based philanthropic giving during World War I."[20]

The 1920s saw the rise of professional fund-raising companies assisting institutions [colleges, churches, community chests]. . . . Spurred by the success of the war drives, the community chest movement . . . reflected the force of the "New Era." . . . It expanded the number of givers, increased the amount of money available for social work and ultimately released social agencies from dependence upon a few well-to-do givers.[21]

As more funds became available, congregations, like industry, began to measure their sense of attainment in relation to their monetary successes.[22] In the two decades from 1910 to 1929, with the dollars generated by fund-raising innovations, nineteenth-century American Protestant denominations were transformed into religious movements now capable of engaging in a wide range of additional functions. Simultaneously, they concentrated on meeting the needs and soliciting the gifts of local members.

The UAHC adopted the practice of "systematic finance" in toto. As an indication of the impact of business-style techniques upon Reform Judaism's fund raising, for the fiscal year ending 31 October 1912, the UAHC registered income exceeding $131,000 as compared to only $30,000 in 1890. As a result of these corporate-like strategies, by 1930 the annual receipts of the Union exceeded $612,000. As recorded in the 1916 edition of the CCAR *Yearbook*, the Reform movement attributed its fiscal success to the merging of "Philanthropy and Efficiency." As early as 1912, the HUC rabbinic curriculum launched by College President Kaufman Kohler added "Applied Sociology" and the "Science of Philanthropy" to the established course of study. Interest in these topics by the Reform movement also had been spurred by the millions of dollars being contributed to Joint Distribution Committee (created in 1914 to aid distressed Jews inside wartorn Europe) and by the continuing growth of philanthropic campaigns for city-wide Federations of Jewish Philanthropies.[23]

During and immediately after the war . . . the federations and welfare funds thoroughly canvassed the community. . . . The funds raised in federation drives supplemented the overseas [JDC] campaign . . . to support local health, education, cultural and community-relations organizations, and sustained national agencies. . . . Federations captured the imagination of businessmen. Modelling themselves on the most progressive business and organizational structures. . . . [24]

As a summary of the collective wisdom of American Jewish fund raising, in 1917 the Director of Cincinnati's United Jewish Charities, Boris Bogen, published *Jewish Philanthropy*, a guidebook for the management of Jewish Federations. The text reflected the techniques employed in capital campaigns among the charitable organizations within American Jewry. Bogen devoted an entire section to "Methods of Fund Raising for Jewish Philanthropic Agencies."

The constituent temples of the Union of American Hebrew Congregations benefited from their own increasingly effective, business-like pledges, solicitations, and campaigns. Consequently, they built larger and more luxurious temple buildings, as did each of the four sample congregations during the 1920. The pride of Cincinnati's K.K. B'nai Yeshurun in its financial success was indicated by the following assessment of KKBY's achievement of the full campaign goal needed to construct its Isaac Mayer Wise Temple Center in 1928:

It is a matter of intense gratification that the funds finally have been raised to pay for the entire cost of the structure. This Congregation may well be proud of its accomplishment. . . . In this period of less than six years we have collected in cash about three hundred and twenty thousand dollars . . . and we have on our books good pledges for over sixty-six thousand dollars. . . . The remarkable nature of this accomplishment may be seen from the fact that out of a regular membership of less than six hundred persons, approximately four hundred contributed an average of almost one thousand dollars apiece.[26]

KKBY of the 1920s offered another example of "efficient" methods of funding within an individual temple, such as larger dues payments by the wealthy. As early as 1898, the *American Israelite* speculated that "one of the reasons why so many congregations have so little money for their work is because the rich members pay, for equal advantages, no more than those of lesser means."[27] In 1928, KKBY abandoned a uniform membership dues program in favor of a "fair share" approach. As KKBY's *Year Book* recorded,

Just recently the congregation took a most important and idealistic step in abolishing the system of fixed dues. Henceforth, membership in the congregation will be open to all, without respect to wealth. Naturally this can be done only if each voluntarily gives in proportion to his means. . . . We hope to bring within the fold of our congregation thereby many who have been unable to join.[28]

Size Equals Success: The Pursuit of Additional Affiliates

Fund-raising success for the UAHC emerged in tandem with an upgrading of programmatic efforts. The Union of American Hebrew Congregations shifted from a singular focus on maintaining its rabbinical college (HUC) and HUC's related educational efforts toward a dual aim. The Union now supported the HUC and offered "hands on" service for the local needs of affiliated congregations. In 1902, for example, the Board of Governors of the Hebrew Union College adopted rules that reflected this dual objective. For the first time, the College identified itself not simply as an institution assisting American Jewry but one devoted to aiding the UAHC as a national organization responsible for servicing its own constituents:

1. No student of the College [during his student years] shall officiate in any congregation that is not a member of the UAHC except with the permission of the President of the College and the President of the Board of Governors. . . .

4. We recommend that no student of the graduating class shall apply for a permanent position in any congregation that is not a member of the UAHC. In the case a congregation, not a member, desires his services, we recommend that he make the effort to induce the congregation to enter the Union before he consents to accept the position.

5. We earnestly request all graduates of the College who are officiating in congregations not members of the Union, to use their every effort to have their congregations become affiliated with the Union, the foster mother of the College.[29]

In 1903, UAHC Vice President Samuel Woolner delivered an address to the Annual Convention entitled, "Enlarging the Work of the Union." He noted that whereas in the past, as with other nineteenth-century religious bodies, the work of the Union centered on the college,

now the time has come for broadening our work by extending our efforts to promote the congregational interests and the communal life of Israel which needs workers in Jewish communities, call them missionaries if you choose, whose duties shall be to arouse congregations to their obligation of joining the Union, and help to increase opportunities for usefulness which can be effected only if our revenues are ample. . . . We ought for this purpose to have at least three hundred congregations as members.[30]

Subsequent resolutions approved by that 1903 Annual Convention called "for a more efficient system of organizational local support for affiliation to the UAHC." The 1903 CCAR Convention also advanced the cause of being a national "movement" through the proposed issuance of an affiliated congregational "membership card." The card was to "serve as a means of introduction [when moving to another city and seeking another UAHC temple]" and entitling a member to "courtesy in other affiliated congregations . . . when away from home, especially on the High Holy Days."[31]

Imitating the systematic organizational models for efficiency made popular in business and industry and applied by Christian extension and endeavor in that era, further resolutions called for the following:

A. Strategies for Affiliation
    1. One central and important point shall be chosen in each state to be the center of a confederation [UAHC regional affiliate].
    2. Any community having ten adults may join the confederation.
    3. The affairs of the confederation shall be directed by a board composed of delegates from the various communities.
    7. [It shall be] the duty of [a] Rabbi of [a nearby] central [large] community to arrange that some Rabbi shall hold services at least once a month in every community belonging to the confederation and to also organize a Sabbath school there, whose workings he shall superintend on his monthly visit. He shall also provide that in the event of a death in any of the communities, a rabbi shall officiate without any charge to the family, his expenses to be defrayed from the treasury of the confederation.
B. Creation of a Handbook
    [Moreover] the Secretary of the Union, under the direction of the Executive Board, be authorized to collect from the congregations of this country all printed books, pamphlets and other matter issued by them and shall make, or have made, a digest of the methods in vogue for the organization, conduct and administration of Jewish congregations . . . information . . . be issued in concise form . . . and be circulated throughout the country. [And] *that the methods prevailing in other religious*

denominations for furthering the founding, maintenance and government of congregations be investigated, and be included in the said compilation [emphasis added].

C. Hiring of Staff

[And] that the Chairman of the Convention appoint a Committee of Five to raise immediately or as soon as possible $15,000 to pay the annual salary and expenses of one or more field secretaries, whose duty it shall be to endeavor to organize and maintain Jewish congregations in such places in the United States where it shall be deemed necessary and feasible.

D. Educational Outreach to Children

[Create strategies to meet] the immediate need of measures for reaching the children of the non-affiliated members of Jewish communities in small towns, and that we do urgently recommend that work of organizing Sabbath schools in small communities be undertaken by the UAHC by the appointment of a field secretary and the appropriation of a sum large enough to carry out the work.

E. Outreach to Young Single Jewish People [for example, Campuses]

[T]hat efforts to increase the affiliation of non-attached Jewish men [and women], particularly young men [and women], to congregations, be encouraged.[32]

These five categories of resolutions represented a blueprint for the transformation of the Reform movement in American Judaism, continuing its focus on the Hebrew Union College and other national projects but also attending to the needs of affiliated and potentially affiliated localities. Programmatic, publishing, and public relations efforts targeted the local needs of temples and schools for direct servicing. Over the next fifteen years, mirroring similar efforts among America's Protestants, the UAHC attempted to implement these goals, albeit with limited success.[33]

Professional Managers

The first critical step in the process of evolving American corporate culture was the hiring of full-time professional administrators. This rising class of salaried managers was the backbone of America's emerging corporate culture. Corporate goals were adopted and devised by an aspiring new salaried class that grew with the corporations. Talented Protestant organizers like Charles Stelzle, the Superintendent of the Presbyterian movement's Department of Church and Labor, made a forceful impact upon the American religious scene. Among the Protestant religious movements in the United States, "by the early years of the century, denominational executives were exhibiting an increasing degree of professional consciousness . . . [and] more frequent contact among themselves." Just as with the Methodist, the Episcopalians, the Baptists, other American Protestant bodies as well as local Jewish Federations and

United Hebrew Charities, the UAHC perceived the need for an executive staff.[34] Within a year of the adoption of the 1903 resolutions for changing the focus of the Union, the UAHC *Proceedings* reported two executive appointments. In 1904, they engaged the services of Rabbi George Zepin, as well as his assistant, Rabbi Alfred T. Godshaw, to expand the preexisting yet vague mandate of the "Circuit Work" Committee.

George Zepin was the first American Jew of Eastern European descent to occupy a decisive role in the future of the Reform movement in American Judaism. Zepin was born in Kiev, Russia in 1878. He arrived in the United States three years later, received his undergraduate degree at the University of Cincinnati at age eighteen, and was ordained as a rabbi by the Hebrew Union College in 1900, at twenty-two years old. During his three years (1900–1903) of pulpit experience in America's hinterland (in Kalamazoo, Michigan), Rabbi Zepin witnessed first-hand the local aggressiveness of Protestant organizational techniques. He did not marry until 1914, and consequently was available for considerable travel within the heartland of the Unites States.[35]

Acknowledging indebtedness to American Protestant religious trends, at the outset of his service to the UAHC George Zepin suggested that his department be changed from the "Committee on Circuit Work" to the "Board of Synagogue Extension." According to Zepin, the name indicated "more clearly what we are doing . . . [since] this is the name uniformly adopted by other church organizations to designate a similar kind of work." America's largest and most institutionally aggressive denomination, the Methodists, had created Church Extension Societies in most major American cities in the aftermath of the Civil War. Within fifteen years, church extension experienced significant successes. The societies specialized in "mission work," notably in the founding and funding of additional churches and the construction of new church buildings. "The Chicago Society scored the most brilliant record. . . . [After only fifteen years of activity] by 1900 the Society raised over a million dollars for a hundred churches which comprised at least a third of the Methodist membership of the city."[36]

Rabbi George Zepin specified that to emulate Protestant successes, a corporate-like organizational arrangement was mandated. The UAHC restructured itself bureaucratically into three departments. One was devoted to the Hebrew Union College, the Union's earliest aim. The second department was committed to the "defense" goals of the defunct Board of Delegates. The third department became a Board of Synagogue Extension. Over the next decade, the HUC continued to prosper without added UAHC attention and the work of the Board of Delegates (in existence until 1925) increasingly deferred to the American Jewish Committee formed in 1906.[37] Thus, the majority of the Union's initiatives related to Zepin's Department of Synagogue Extension, charged with the creation of an American religious movement.

During George Zepin's first year of service, he addressed the goal of gaining Union affiliates within America's hinterland. Like the Methodists, Rabbi George Zepin conducted personal visits into isolated communities. "In the pursuit of . . . [his] work in the states of Ohio, Indiana, Mississippi and Louisiana, . . . [Zepin] visited forty-five cities for the purpose of organizing congregations." In the process, he complied an investigative report entitled, "Jewish Religious Conditions in Scattered Communities," documenting the opportunities as well as the difficult challenges ahead. Educational outreach to unaffiliated Jewish children was Rabbi Zepin's second objective. In January 1905, Zepin's Board of Synagogue Extension assumed the role of the UAHC's Hebrew Sabbath School Union of America, for example, the "publication and distribution of Sabbath School literature." The Board of Synagogue Extension worked in tandem with a UAHC Committee on Religious Education in creating a comprehensive Sabbath school curriculum.[38] As a result of this expanded role, Zepin's department changed its title to the Department of Synagogue and School Extension.

As a third objective, beyond gaining affiliates for the Union and providing educational materials, Rabbis Zepin and Godshaw and their appropriate Committees sought to address the needs of small congregations in isolated locations devoid of rabbinic assistance. For example, they provided sermonic materials to be read from the pulpit by lay leaders. In addition, the department offered limited religious services to the growing number of Jews on America's college campuses. A priority within campus work was the recruitment of potential rabbinical students to study at HUC. Recruitment was necessary to staff the increasing number of rabbinic positions within the expanding UAHC framework.[39] Zepin and his colleagues also placed upon the Union's agenda extension work within the urban slums on behalf of Eastern European Jews and their children.

This burst of activity came to a halt with George Zepin's sudden decision to return in 1906 to the life of a pulpit rabbi and Rabbi Godshaw's subsequent departure in 1909. However, just as sudden and dramatic was the resurgence of activity upon the reengagement of Rabbi Zepin in 1910 as the Director of Synagogue and School Extension for the UAHC. This reappointment occurred precisely at the moment when America's churchmen collectively realized that "decision-making by national legislative [lay person] conventions [alone] was sluggish." Effectiveness required skillful, salaried, full-time national executive staff. Moreover, the upgrading of George Zepin's role coincided with the intensive burst of popularity for

"Taylorism," for "scientific management," for "efficiency," and for the "efficiency expert," who "in the fall of 1910," "made his grand entrance into American society." As the popular Protestant journal *The Churchman* argued in 1910, any religious movement lacking an executive head was "without that which in the common experience of humanity has proved essential to doing any business well."[40] The return of an invigorated George Zepin to the administrative helm of the UAHC marked a critical turning point.

Bureaucratic Implementation

In an initial comprehensive report to the UAHC, Rabbi Zepin outlined the plans that guided the noticeable growth of the Union during the next several years. First and foremost was Zepin's incorporation of scientific management procedures. In a national press release, Rabbi Zepin proclaimed his department's intention to "extend the number and increase the efficiency of synagogues and religious schools." In a corporate-like assessment of the Union's ambitious goals yet modest resources, Zepin indicated that "an ideal program carried out would necessitate the expenditure of considerable sums of money and we are sensible of the fact that we will be compelled to work only to the extent of our resources."[41] In a manner similar to the corporate management techniques of his Protestant church administration colleagues, George Zepin's department bureaucratically subdivided the nation into forty-six districts under the watchful eye of regional rabbinic supervisors of Circuit Work.

Let the Board of Managers [of Synagogue and School Extension of the UAHC, appoint in each populous district a Supervisor of Circuit Work. The Supervisor should not be one of the men who themselves engage in circuit preaching. His work should be distinctly that of supervision. Once a year, preferably at the opening of the season, the Supervisor should visit at our expense, the four or five circuit-cities in his neighborhood. His duty would be merely to encourage the several congregations to resume their usual activities including circuit preaching. The actual work of circuit preaching should be performed by some of the neighboring ministers. In order to give this plan a definite trial, I would suggest that during the first season, not more than ten Supervisors of Circuit Work be appointed, and that the expense of this work for this first season be limited to $500.00.[42]

Over the next half dozen years, scientific management proved somewhat successful in making possible synagogue and school extension work. Zepin's projects targeted various populations including rural Jewish communities, scattered Jewish groups inside cities of all sizes, Jews at summer resorts, Jewish college students, Jewish soldiers and sailors, Jewish delinquents, and handicapped individuals in institutions, as well as among isolated religious school teachers.[43]

In his Annual Report of December 1916, Zepin devoted 48 pages to detailed lists elaborating upon the UAHC's successes. He reported that "during the past year the Department has conducted some form of religious work in a number of metropolitan centers, in 49 colleges, in 1,492 rural communities, in 109 scattered Jewish groups located in small cities, in 11 institutions for defectives, in 47 institutions for delinquents, in 27 military encampments and forts, in 29 summer resorts and in connection with eight Jewish religious teachers' associations":[44]

The work is accomplished through a very unique organization consisting of District Supervisors, Deputy Supervisors, Congregations and Sisterhoods. Supervisors and Deputies, and individual members of Congregations and Sisterhoods have traveled to many cities; visited colleges, institutions and soldiers' camps; have organized services, schools and study circles, and have preached and taught the message of Judaism wherever they found a hearing . . . [they] have made Synagogue Extension possible. Many readers of this report will probably be surprised to learn that the Supervisors, Deputy Supervisors, Sisterhood representatives and Congregational representatives, and the Directors [George Zepin and his new Associate Jacob D. Schwartz] of Synagogue and School Extension have traveled 166,043 miles in pursuance of their work.[45]

To illustrate this elaborate synagogue and school extension effort, let us examine how the four senior rabbis of the sample congregations were involved in the building of a religious movement, (as were the rabbis of the other major UAHC temples):

1. Rabbi Joseph Krauskopf [KI in Philadelphia] was the Supervisor of District 6—Eastern Pennsylvania [one of forty-six Districts] for Synagogue and School Extension in Rural Communities. As such, he arranged holiday services in seven small rural communities, and he supervised correspondence work by the Department [national] Office for seventy-one other tiny locations. Dr. Krauskopf was also responsible for eleven scattered Jewish groups within small cities, for which he supervised the visits of rabbis from Wilkes Barre, Scranton and Allentown for organizing religious schools, conducting services and establishing study circles. In addition, Joseph Krauskopf supervised rabbinic visits to the campuses of Muhlenberg, Lafayette and Jewish contacts with out-of-town Jewish students at Philadelphia area campuses. Moreover, Krauskopf involved his Sisterhood in providing matzah to local penal institutions and the State Sanitorium, as well as in caring for the needy wives of Jewish inmates and patients.

2. Rabbi Maximilian Heller [Temple Sinai in New Orleans] was the District Supervisor of District No. 15 covering Southern Mississippi and

Eastern Louisiana. Accordingly, he arranged holiday services in six rural communities, and supervised correspondence work by the department [national] office for eight other similar locales. Moreover, Heller arranged for the Rabbi of Vicksburg, Mississippi, to conduct services and assist with the religious school in Port Gibson, Mississippi. Rabbi Heller also supervised rabbinic visits to Louisiana State University, to the Baton Rouge Parish Jail, and to the Louisiana State Penitentiary. Dr. Heller was also among those rabbis who assisted the Mississippi, Tennessee, and Louisiana Jewish Religious School Teachers Association.

3. Rabbi Louis Grossman [KKBY in Cincinnati] was the Supervisor of District 25, covering Southern Indiana. Accordingly, he arranged holiday services for nine rural communities, as well as correspondence work for two other towns. Rabbi Grossman also personally conducted services at the vacation locale of Lake Harbor, Michigan. Dr. Grossman also supervised the visits of the rabbi of Louisville, Kentucky, to the Indiana Reformatory, with materials supplied by George Zepin's office.

4. Rabbi Martin Meyer [Emanu-El in San Francisco] was the Supervisor of District No. 38 covering Northern California. In addition "to arranging correspondence work by the national office to five rural communities, under the supervision of Dr. Martin A. Meyer . . . the Extension Department of his congregation has given religious instruction through correspondence to many Jewish children scattered in [twenty-two] small communities in the State of California and in [seven towns in] neighboring states [Oregon, New Mexico, Idaho, Washington, and even Iowa and Kansas]. . . . Sixty children were instructed by this method." Dr. Meyer also personally supervised the religious school needs of nearby small Jewish communities in Berkeley, Napa, and Alameda, California. Furthermore, Rabbi Meyer personally kept in touch with the estimated 150 students at the University of California, Berkeley campus, as well as made monthly visits to Jewish inmates at Alcatraz Island, and to the State Prison at San Quentin. Similarly, he arranged for rabbinic visits to the State Prison in Folsom City, and to the Preston Industrial School for Boys in Watterman, California.[46]

Publications and Advertising

Rabbi George Zepin's department also launched a publications effort, characteristic of American business' and American Christianity's commitment to the printed word, to advertising and to public relations. During the fifteen years following the Civil War, the volume of advertising increased threefold. "By 1900 it stood at $95 million a year . . . a tenfold increase over . . . 1865. By 1919 it exceeded half a billion dollars, and by

1929 it reached $1.2 billion."[47] Protestantism witnessed an explosion of marketing publications, typified by *Advertising the Church: Suggestions by Church Advisors*, compiled and published in 1924 by Francis H. Case for Abingdon Press. By the 1930s, standard guidebooks for clergy, such as Robert Cashman's 1937 volume, *The Business Administration of a Church*, routinely would include sections concerning advertising and publicity.

Having assumed the portfolio of the UAHC's Hebrew Sabbath School Association of America, by 1905 Zepin's Department of Synagogue and School Extension generated textbooks, leaflets, and teachers' guides for the religious education of the young. Some of this ongoing material was published within the pages of the magazine entitled *Young Israel*. *Young Israel* was a publication "consisting of an 80 page monthly, devoted for the most part to Juvenile interests, and a 20 page weekly, consisting largely of Sabbath School material." Similarly, the monthly *Jewish Farmer*, initiated in 1910, provided Jewish educational materials to scattered rural districts. By 1913, a *Home Study Magazine* had been developed as well. In his Annual Report of 1916, Zepin noted that 7,206 reprints of the *Union Daily Prayerbook* and *Union Sabbath Prayerbook* in leaflet form were distributed within one year alone, in addition to hundreds of union Hymnals and other adult religious tracts. Furthermore, Zepin reported sending out 4,975 art calendars, 10,030 other educational pamphlets, plus 50,000 pieces of mail related to the correspondence work, with instructional lessons mailed to isolated religious school children. All of the above continually appeared in the full view of constituents in Zepin's *Union Bulletin*, initiated in 1912. This information was reprinted in weekly, affiliated-Temple bulletins, such as those created by KI (Philadelphia) in 1896, KKBY (Cincinnati) in 1921, and Emanu-El (San Francisco) in 1926.[48] The publications and "religious propaganda" generated by Rabbi Zepin's "Bureau of Publicity," as well as his general "Synagogue and School Extension," defined for America's Jews the activity of the Union.

Additional Functions of the UAHC

Expanded Scope: Serving the Eastern Europeans

George Zepin's department responded as well to the pressures generated by local temples to involve the sons and daughters of Eastern European Jews. By 1913, Zepin's colleague in synagogue extension work to the immigrants, Rabbi Max Reichler, concluded: "Reform Judaism must vindicate its claim that its principles and form of worship are adapted to present day conditions by gaining and holding the descendants of our immigrants from whatsoever countries they have come."[49]

In an interesting reversal of influence, the UAHC emulated the tactics initiated by the Union of Orthodox Jewish Congregations (OU) to meet the challenge of appealing to second-generation Eastern European Jews. This Orthodox Union, established in 1898, openly courted young men and women of Eastern European descent. Parallel to Christian Endeavor Society strategies, the OU created the Jewish Endeavor Society (JES) in 1901. The JES represented a cooperative venture of the Union of Orthodox Jewish Congregations and the Jewish Theological Seminary (JTS), the New York City-based rabbinical school supported by traditionalist Jews who were dissatisfied with the HUC. The Endeavorers "inaugurated their campaign to bring an 'indifferent generation back to ancestral faith.'" They organized "young people's synagogues" within the Lower East Side Jewish enclave in Manhattan, analogous to successful "young people's churches" within the nationally prominent United Society of Christian Endeavor.[50] Under the tutelage of Rabbi Bernard Drachman, affiliated with both the JTS and the OU, the "people's synagogues" created a ritually traditional yet aesthetically modern ambience. Without challenging Jewish theology or ritual norms, the Endeavorers introduced dignified Western services. They offered some English prayers for those Eastern European youngsters not fluent in Hebrew, providing a weekly sermon in English and creating an overall sense of decorum. As a result of subsequent successes, the Endeavorers, the Orthodox Union and the Seminary became influential within the Lower East Side.

Witnessing the effectiveness of these Jewish adaptations of Christian Endeavor techniques, Rabbi George Zepin targeted the offspring of Eastern European Jews in South Philadelphia for a UAHC experiment. Zepin chose Philadelphia because of both its large Russian and Polish Jewish population and its distance from the influence of the New York-based OU. In August 1904, in the city of Brotherly Love, Zepin launched an experimental "People's Synagogue." He enlisted the aid of local Reform temples such as Keneseth Israel in this emulation of Protestant "Young Peoples Churches" for the unchurched. The objective of George Zepin's People's Synagogue was "to provide a place of religious instruction for those men and women who no longer observed the Orthodox forms and whose lives showed no evidences at all of Jewish religious influences." Although the initial service of the "People's Reform Synagogue" drew a large attendance, initial curiosity waned and the venture failed. "Organ, choir, and a modernized liturgy could arouse the curiosity of the new immigrants but could not create a lasting attachment."[51] From this Philadelphia experience, Rabbi Zepin concluded:

This truth was made clear. There is a vast number of men and women of Jewish birth who are without any Jewish affiliations. Our experiment showed that these men and women can be attracted to our religion, if Judaism is properly presented to them. If we do not put forth an effort to bring these men and women back into our standard then Ethical Culture, Unitarianism, Socialism as a cult, Intermarriage—point the inevitable direction of their drifting. . . . To overcome this unnatural condition we must use extraordinary methods. I submit for your consideration the plan to start a Synagogue and School Extension Fund . . . to be used to help defray the expenses of organizing [such] congregations throughout the land. . . . This work to be most effective should be started in the city of New York where almost one half of the Jews of America reside.[52]

Zepin's commitment to recruiting the sons and daughters of formerly denigrated Russian and Polish Jews led to the formation of Sinai Congregation in the Bronx, "a (Reform) People's Synagogue, with many institutional features," under the guidance of Rabbi Max Reichler. With reference to this New York experiment, Zepin noted that it was

our object to demonstrate that a synagogue adopting modernized methods, such as family pews, choir and organ, an English speaking rabbi and a religious school [affixed to the congregation], would find a host of adherents in this section of the city that was considered exceedingly Orthodox in theory and hopelessly irreligious in practice. The congregation now had 300 members and seatholders, a very fine school with 400 pupils, crowded services . . . and points with satisfaction to the fact that its example has induced a number of congregations in the Bronx to adopt some of its methods.[53]

Slowly, the Reform movement began to make progress in its goal of attracting some of the children of Russian and Polish Jews into the UAHC religious movement. Reform publications such as the *Jewish Farmer* (launched in 1910) began to include Yiddish instructions to assist Eastern European Jews in the use of home study materials by their children. The CCAR Convention became conscious of this profound challenge. Papers regarding recruitment of the children of Russian Jews were presented in 1904 and 1905, and frequently cited at subsequent Reform gatherings.[54]

The achievements of UAHC temples in working with these young people became yet another barometer for measuring the movement's success. As the Reform-oriented New Orleans *Jewish Ledger* editorialized on 10 January 1913,

the second generation of immigrants who find themselves out of sympathy with the older form of Judaism are often allowed to drift away entirely. . . . It will be more and more the work of the future to attract this class of people back to the synagogue. Reform Judaism must vindicate its claim that its principles and form of worship are adapted to present day needs and conditions by gaining and holding the descendants of our immigrants from whatsoever countries they have come.[55]

Several decades of philanthropic assistance to Russian and Polish Jews by Reform temples and their Sisterhoods and Brotherhoods impacted upon the attitudes of both the German temple members and upon the Eastern European beneficiaries of this outreach. Moreover, intermarriage occurred with ever greater frequency between young Jews of German extraction and the sons and daughters of upwardly-mobile Russian and Polish Jews. Gradually the newcomers became receptive to American Reform Judaism, its social status and institutional prominence. In many middle-class neighborhoods, the Reform temple "was the single established institution that the Jew, aspiring for self-advancement and self-fulfillment, could embrace."[56]

Federations for Temple Auxiliaries

George Zepin's Department also created the National Federation of Temple Sisterhoods (NFTS) in January 1913 with forty-seven charter chapters and thirty-seven additional local societies affiliating during the first year of its existence. This federated body arose in the context of the spread of federations throughout American society. Such federations included the American Federation of Labor (1881), the Federation of Churches and Christian Workers (1895) and the Federal Council of Churches of Christ in America (1908). Federations of Jewish social agencies and welfare funds were founded around this time in virtually every substantial American Jewish community.[57]

Federation implied efficiently raising and disbursing charitable contributions. Its financial successes captured the imagination of businessmen "by promising efficient coordination and organization of the community welfare machinery, immunity from multiple solicitation, economical collection and distribution of funds, and the development of a broad base of support that would relieve the pressure on the small circle of large givers." The federated ideal also spread to nationwide organizations for serving Jewish women. The National Council of Jewish Women was formed seven years prior to 1900, Henrietta Szold's Hadassah in 1912, and subsequently women's auxiliary departments emerged within the national B'nai Brith and the American Jewish Congress. These organizational achievements by American Jewish women in part were inspired by the late-nineteenth-century membership successes of the Women's Christian Temperance Union (WCTU), which spread its influence around the globe. By 1911, the Temperance Union had enlisted 245,000 members and became the largest women's organization in the United States.[58]

The creation of a National Federation of Temple Sisterhoods in 1913 harnessed the enormous potential energies of the existing Temple Sisterhoods of Personal Service of local congregations. In an effort to further the Reform Union, the NFTS transformed its chapters from volunteer social workers into builders of the emerging Reform movement. In his Annual Presidential Message in 1913, the President of the UAHC affirmed:

With the building of synagogues and the increased congregational activities, many women's organizations known as Temple Sisterhoods and Women's Auxiliary Societies have been formed within the congregations. Acting upon a suggestion that these societies might be federated under the auspices of the Union, communications were sent to all the congregations, asking for statistical information. The replies when tabulated showed that a very large number of congregations have women's organizations engaged in more or less active work. Undoubtedly here is an energy that should be organized in the interest of the larger affairs of Judaism.[59]

Efforts by ladies to encourage "temple going" and affiliation with the temple, as well as to strengthen congregational programmatic life, were met with great enthusiasm by the UAHC hierarchy. At the Annual Meeting of the Union in January 1915, Mrs. Abram Simon, the President of the NFTS, addressed the Convention on behalf of "over one hundred [Sisterhood branches], embracing a membership of fifteen thousand women." In her paper entitled "Women's Influence in the Development of American Judaism," Mrs. Simon urged Sisterhood members to take a leadership role in "cultivating the habit of regular attendance in the Temple [worship service]," in aiding the congregation's religious school, as well as in "philanthropy" and "hospitality to strangers." The NFTS guided its constituent groups into involvement in synagogue and school extension work, in outreach to college students and to inmates of institutions and their spouses. The National Federation of Temple Sisterhoods also developed the UAHC's Jewish Arts Calendar, the "Union Museum for Jewish Ceremonial Objects," a "Directory of Temple Sisterhoods," and an "Exchange Bureau" as a "repository of plans whereby [individual] sisterhoods have raised money" and carried out other critical programs.[60]

By 1923, the achievement of the NFTS inspired the collective bonding of more than seventy-five local temple Brotherhoods into the UAHC's National Federation of Temple Brotherhoods (NFTB).[61] With this formidable initial constituency, the NFTB established the following "National Committees":

On [promoting] Synagogue Attendance
On Religious Propaganda
On Social Service
On [university] Student Welfare
On [seeking] Membership

On Cooperation [among local clubs]
On Open Forums [programs]

Through the NFTS and the NFTB, a new dimension of "Synagogue and School Extension" was achieved. In keeping with the techniques of American corporate culture, Rabbi George Zepin and the Union sought to attract more clients (affiliates) through these auxiliary activities. If a person was not interested in the religious life of the congregation, he or she could still join a UAHC temple based upon its women's or men's groups. Consistent with the ethos of this American epoch, a national federated structure to assist each local club provided maximum "efficiency" in the Union's quest to expand.

Education and Youth

Zepin's other major initiatives included setting the national foundations for educational leadership and for youth work. Rabbi Zepin remembered the UAHC experiences in the final years of the nineteenth century that suggested that prospective members often would be attracted by temple programs catering to their children. In 1910, at the outset of nationwide fascination with "Taylorism," the CCAR Convention included Isaac Landman's assessment of Philadelphia's Keneseth Israel religious school organization, utilizing the categories of scientific management. Landman evaluated the temple school according to the "efficiency" criteria of American public education as well as church Sunday schools. These standards included proper physical facilities, equipment, grading, curriculum, teacher training and certification, school governance, attendance requirements, and record keeping. Similar discussions occurred at the UAHC Annual Council of 1912, the CCAR Convention of 1914, and in related gatherings.[62]

The pedagogic response of the Union followed the trends not only of public and Protestant education but also of the Jewish educational world-at-large. In the ambitious experiment of the New York City Jewish Kehillah of 1907 to 1916, the "rule of thumb" *cheder* was replaced by the modernized Talmud Torah and Sunday school, under the direction of the Bureau (bureaucratization) of Jewish Education (BJE). In harmony with the American organizational trends of this era, the BJE created numerous departments following a pattern of departmentalization:

Finance Department
Textbook Department
Department of Investigation, Collection and Attendance, to investigate

the status of all new pupils, establish tuition collection routes, and monitor school attendance.

Department of Propaganda, to acquaint parents and the public at large with the problem of Jewish education

Department of Standardization

Department of New Schools

Department of Extension Work

Department of Preparatory Schools

Department of Teachers

Department of Out-of-Town Schools

Similar Bureaus of Jewish Education emerged in Boston (1918), Philadelphia (1920), Baltimore (1921), Chicago (1923), Cleveland (1924), Detroit, St. Louis, and Cincinnati (1926).[63]

The Bureaus instituted the educational balance sheet, cost accounting, fixed tuition, salary scales for faculty, routinized allocations of scholarships and time allotted to each subject, as well as standardizing the types of organizational techniques discussed at the CCAR Convention of 1910. The Bureaus conducted need assessments for local Jewish communities through scientific educational surveys. The surveys were administered by the first generation of American Jewish educational "experts" in these matters, including Dr. Samson Benderly (BJE Chairman) in 1911 and 1912, and Benderly's associates, Rabbi Mordecai Kaplan in 1909 and Dr. Alexander Dushkin in 1917 and 1918.

The Bureaus, led by Benderly's New York BJE, also pioneered in the professionalization of religious school educators and administrators. Beginning with Mordecai Kaplan's Teachers Institute of the Jewish Theological Seminary in 1909, under the influence of Columbia University's Teachers College, a series of Jewish educators programs emerged:

A Teachers Institute Department within HUC (1909)

Teachers Institute of Yeshiva University (1917)

Jewish Teachers Seminary and People's University [New York] (1918)

Baltimore Hebrew College and Teachers Training School (1919)

Hebrew Teachers' College [Boston] (1921)

Herzliah Hebrew Teachers Institute (New York) (1921)

Sol Rosenbloom Teachers Training School of the Hebrew Institute of Pittsburgh (1923)

College of Jewish Studies (Chicago) (1924)

Hebrew Teachers Seminary (Cleveland) (1926)

Hebrew Teachers Training School for Girls, maintained by the Women's Branch of the Union of Orthodox Jewish Congregations (New York) (1929)[64]

To implement American educational norms, in 1924 Rabbi Zepin recruited Dr. Emanuel Gamoran. Gamoran was an educator of Eastern European and pro-Zionist background. He was trained by Dr. Samson Benderly, Rabbi Mordecai Kaplan, Professor John Dewey, and the initial corps of professional American Jewish educators at JTS' Teachers Institute and Columbia's Teachers College in Manhattan. Astute UAHC leaders such as George Zepin were willing to overlook Gamoran's lack of previous involvement with the Reform movement in order to gain his administrative expertise in *American* pedagogy. American Protestant denominations had already proven successful in such endeavors.

In 1908 there were 3,429,915 teachers and pupils in the Sunday schools of the Methodist Episcopal church. . . . The [Methodist] Book Concern cooperated in the Graded Lesson Series which was being developed by several denominations together. This was a pioneer attempt to offer a complete system of religious instruction for everyone, from childhood to young manhood and womanhood. . . . Succeeding years brought further developments—the group graded and closely graded lessons that were designed to suit the individual needs of various age groups. Finally came the lessons for small schools without the resources or leadership of the larger schools in the strong city churches.[65]

Under Emanuel Gamoran's dynamic leadership, the Union's Commission on Jewish Education set out to achieve similarly ambitious goals. The Commission conducted a national educational survey of 125 Reform temple religious schools in 1925. This was a prerequisite to designing a plan for educational improvement. Graded text books, teachers' manuals, programs for teacher training, and an array of publications followed soon thereafter, establishing higher standards for the congregational school. Gamoran achieved for Reform education what Zepin had done for Reform's quest to upgrade congregational finance and membership solicitation.

Gamoran was tireless. He commissioned and edited new textbooks, worked out a religious school curriculum, and was co-author of a series of primers in modern Hebrew. He founded and edited a quarterly magazine called *The Jewish Teacher*; he traveled about the country visiting schools and trying to raise their level. . . . The UAHC published books for adults, written by Hebrew Union College professors, as well as for children. Illustrations, attractive typography, and good paper made religious school books no longer seem a generation behind their public school equivalents.[66]

Youth Activities

The success of Young People's Societies in churches and of (Conservative Judaism) United Synagogue's Young People's League as well as the growth of youth activities within local reform temples stimulated a UAHC response. In 1927, Isaac M. Wise's daughter, Mrs. Albert May, a leader within the NFTS, launched a campaign to pressure the UAHC into forming a national Federation of Young Folks' Temple League. As Mrs. May stated to the 18 January 1927 Annual NFTS Convention: "We seemed to have forgotten the youth of our country . . . taking it for granted that by some wizardry they would slip into our adult groups [NFTS, NFTB], without an idea of their purpose, or without a whit of training."[67] On 8 April 1927, Temple Emanu-El in New York City served as the locale for the initial meeting of the New York State Federation of Young Folks' Temple Leagues. The eleven chapters in attendance, spanning ages eighteen through twenty-eight, formulated a statement of purpose:

1. promote the Knowledge of Judaism and Jewish Values
2. promote the welfare of the Jewish people
3. stimulate cooperation between the groups
4. encourage sociability
5. cooperate with the NFTS and the UAHC[68]

Pressure continued for a nationwide framework for youth activities. On 1 November 1927, the UAHC agreed to fund the mimeographing and distribution of THE YOUTH LEADER, "a forum for the exchange of programs and ideas and . . . a source of training to prospective youth leaders.[69] Over the next several years, youth federations arose in Illinois, Ohio, and Pennsylvania. Support mounted within the NFTS, the NFTB, the CCAR, and the UAHC. By 1932, the Union's Department of Synagogue and School Extension hired Dr. Harry L. Comins as national Director of Youth Work. The groundwork was set for what ultimately became in 1939 the UAHC's National Federation of Temple Youth. This organization completed a full range of national "federations" for temple auxiliaries.

Conclusions

In part because of the Americanization of German Jews and the anti-German feeling associated with World War I, Reform temples of the postwar era courted upwardly-mobile American Jews of Russian and Polish descent. By 1930, nearly half of the lower echelon members in UAHC congregations were Jews of Eastern European extraction. Adult offspring of immigrants were impressed by the social status enjoyed by local Reform temples, by their expansive physical facilities, by the equal involvement in congregational life offered to Jewish women, by the Temples' unchallenged influence within local chapters of B'nai Brith and

the National Council of Jewish Women, by the moral tone of Reform
social action programs, and by the impressive English-language sermons
delivered by CCAR rabbis.[70]

The people that count, possessing power and prestige as well as the reins of
leadership, were Reform Jews. The Temple [was] . . . the visible embodiment of
what Jewry had achieved in America. The children of the immigrants, ambitious to
attain these goals, affiliated as soon as their means permitted or when they were
welcome.[71]

The success of the Reform movement in recruiting some of the sons
and daughters of Eastern Europeans threatened the future of rival
Orthodox and Conservative groups. Previously, these non-Reform movements had assumed that Reform outreach would be limited to Jews of
German descent alone. But once second-generation Russian and Polish
Jews began to opt for Reform temple membership, the leaders of
Conservative and Orthodox synagogues sought to emulate the techniques
refined by the Reformers at the national level as well as the decorum and
middle-class aethetics within the local Temple setting. In 1910, for
example, Rabbi Herman Rubenovitz, a graduate of the (Conservative)
Jewish Theological Seminary, reflected with horror upon the caliber of
Jewish religious life in Boston.

Assimilation [is] . . . rampant, and its leading exponent [is] . . . the Rabbi of the
Reform Temple Israel, the wealthiest and most prominent Jewish congregation in
New England . . . the traditional Sabbath had been made secondary to the
Sunday service. Even intermarriage between Jew and Gentile [is] . . . openly
advocated. But what [is] . . . even more menacing to the future of Judaism
hereabouts [is] . . . the fact that by far the greater part of the Sunday morning
congregation . . . [is] made up of the sons and daughters of orthodox [Eastern
European] Jewish parents.[72]

In response to growing concern about the sons and daughters of
Russian and Polish immigrants, rabbis of Conservative congregations
began to advocate the need for a "Conservative Union" to challenge the
organizational successes of the Reform Union on a national scale. At an
August 1909 gathering of the alumni of the (Conservative) Jewish
Theological Seminary (JTS), rabbis Herman Rubenovitz and Charles
Hoffman urged their fellow alumni to lead "in the establishment of a
union of conservative forces in America." They envisioned that this union
would seek "to print an inexpensive prayerbook; to prevent the isolated
men [the rabbi] from being swallowed up; to prevent the isolated
synagogue from being swallowed up; to see that our views are fairly
represented in the press; to have regular traveling representation; to have
a Sabbath observance department"; in other words, the simulate the

techniques of the Reform Union. The plan was delayed by the opposition of the JTS leadership to abandoning its self-definition as representing *klal yisrael* (the total Jewish community) and to creating a partisan union.[73]

The increased appeal of the UAHC's Extension programs to younger Eastern European Jews, combined with mounting financial woes, ultimately convinced the JTS' administration to relent. Solomon Schechter's decision to establish the United Synagogue was a result of his

conviction that Reform could not be long withstood on the American scene without adequately organizing traditionalist forces. The combination of inadequate immigrant-founded congregations, ubiquitous social climbing, the Reform Temple as the hub of the Jewish communal structure, . . . [was] causing the continuing attrition from traditionalist ranks to Reform.[74]

In 1913, a founding convention was convened. Initially the new organization was to be called "the Jewish Conservative Union" or "the Orthodox-Conservative Union," as conscious responses to the Reform Union and the Orthodox Union. The selection of the compromise title, the "United Synagogue of America," apparently was inspired by the presence at the convention of JTS' first graduate Rabbi Joseph Hertz, who had been elected during the previous week as the Chief Rabbi of the British Empire. In his inaugural address in 1913 as the United Synagogue's first President, Solomon Schechter proclaimed that "we [too] want Synagogue Extension, but this in the sense that our ancestors understood it."[75]

The subsequent success at the local level of Conservative congregations can be attributed partially to encouragement from its national organization. Shortly after its founding, the United Synagogue introduced new techniques to win and retain adherents. For example, several district offices were established to publicize United Synagogue activities and recruitment efforts. A newsletter advertised and coordinated the activities of affiliated synagogues. Furthermore, the United Synagogue's vague ideological parameters, seeking to accommodate all non-Reform synagogues, offered an appeal for tradition-minded congregations reminiscent of the successes of the early UAHC. In a fashion similar to nineteenth-century religious unions, the United Synagogue of America brought together congregations sharing the "practical" (institutional) goals of the movement, while consciously overlooking localized liturgical and/or doctrinal differences.

Of the twenty-four charter-member congregations in the United Synagogue [1913] . . . no more than two can be characterized as both Conservative in ritual—mixed seating, etc.—composed of East European Jews. . . . Some thirteen were nineteenth-century, formerly Orthodox or Conservative congregations composed of German Jews. Two others were headed by Seminary rabbis and attracted East European constituents, but . . . did not break ritually [as yet] from American styles of Orthodoxy.[76]

Even more important to Conservative Judaism's appeal than its national qualities, however, was its unique synthesis at the local level. It offered partial adherence to Orthodoxy's link to Eastern European traditions and immigrant experience (in areas of first and second settlement) as well as to Reform's adjustments to middle-class American life (in areas of third settlement). Thus, on the one hand, the Conservative synagogues implemented the American institutional techniques proven effective by Reform Judaism, while retaining a traditional (Orthodox) approach to theology and ritual practice.[77]

Despite severe financial limitations, the United Synagogue of America benefited from the triumphs of local Conservative synagogues, often replacing Reform temples as the congregation of choice for young American Jews moving into new residential areas. Second-generation synagogue leaders frequently chose to affiliate their congregations with the United Synagogue, regarding Conservative Judaism as the most comfortable compromise between Eastern European traditions and Americanization. Consequently, the Conservative United Synagogue blossomed into a 229 congregation movement by 1929.

Professional management was provided as of 1917 by Rabbi Samuel Cohen, a Conservative counterpart to George Zepin and Jacob D. Schwartz. Rabbi Cohen offered guidance to congregations that had no clear denominational allegiances in the hope of winning them to the Conservative cause. "Moreover, he approached lay leaders in communities where there was no Conservative presence and tried to convince them of the need to establish a congregation affiliated with the United Synagogue."[78] Programmatic vitality was provided the United Synagogue's women's auxiliary, the Women's League for Conservative Judaism, launched in 1918 and boasting 262 chapters by the end of its first decade of existence. In 1921, the United Synagogue also created a young People's League, with 119 affiliated groups by the close of the 1920s. Furthermore, in 1929, a men's auxiliary, the National Federation of Jewish Men's Clubs, brought together the more than fifty chapters already present within Conservative congregations.

In order to compete with the UAHC's outreach to Eastern European Jews and the zeal of the new United Synagogue of America, in the early years of the twentieth century the Orthodox Union adopted the same array of institutional techniques. As OU President Rabbi Henry Pereira Mendes urged in 1913, "The special sphere of duty and usefulness of the Union [OU] is to attempt to guide the hundreds of orthodox congregations . . . toward cultured orthodox ideas so that they can flourish in their American environment." By the 1920s, the OU became a "clearinghouse . . . a rallying point for issues of concern to the modernized Orthodox Jew . . . the public address of America's [modern] Orthodox community." Through the *Union Recorder* and pamphlets, publications, program guides, and national personnel, the Orthodox Union advocated the creation of Sisterhoods, Men's Clubs, youth groups, adult education, congregation-based Hebrew schools, and the full range of activities proven successful by Reform temples. As a result of its new assertiveness, the OU membership increased from 96 synagogues in 1898 (remaining relatively constant through 1915) to 180 in 1925 and over 200 by 1927. However, in contrast to the Reform Union's 280 temples, and the United Synagogue' 262 congregations, the Orthodox Union's membership was limited primarily to smaller shuls and remained vital by and large only in the areas close to New York City.[79]

Having successfully adapted the marketing techniques of American corporate culture, during the 1920s the Reform, Conservative, and Orthodox movements in American Judaism catapulted to new plateaus of organizational success. Upwardly mobile Eastern European Jews increasingly faced viable choices among middle-class Reform temples, Conservative Synagogue Centers, or Modern Orthodox congregations as a symbol of their new status. All three movements entered the 1920s as competitors for the loyalties of acculturated American Jews. As historian Jeffrey Gurock has written, "Denominational competition for the allegiances of affiliating second-generation [Eastern European] Jews began in earnest in the 1920s. The battlegrounds were the clean streets and the fresh meadows of the outer boroughs, city limits and early suburban neighborhoods of America's immigrant metropolises."[80] More and more, the UAHC and other American Jewish and Christian national bodies placed the needs of local congregations at the forefront of their agenda. In addition to maintaining support for their rabbinical training schools and other national institutions, the techniques of corporate culture were harnessed by American Jewish movements to create publications, programs, and public awareness suitable to directly inculcate loyalty among affiliated laity and their sons and daughters.

Conclusion

In the 1840s, the institutional life of American Judaism was impoverished. Congregations offered prayer services and cemeteries, without providing any activities for affiliated members. Rabbis were in short supply, self-taught, and imported from Europe. Religious education for Jewish children was meager and largely unavailable. Neither national nor regional bodies coordinated the efforts of individual synagogues with one another. Christian missionizing to the Jews posed a great threat.

By 1930, the agenda of individual houses of worship expanded to include Sisterhoods, Brotherhoods, youth activities, adult education, and Sabbath schools with departments for both elementary and teenage children of members. In addition, congregations offered frequent rabbinic sermons and public lectures, and religious services conducted with decorum and Western aesthetic standards. Reform, Conservative, and Orthodox movements came to include local congregations, professional rabbinic associations, and graduate professional schools for training rabbis, and national federations for assisting synagogue Sisterhoods, Brotherhoods, and youth groups. Religious school curricular material was printed and distributed, as were religious tracts suitable to each of these three Jewish denominations. This ninety-year saga offers themes for further consideration.

This study reflects the significance of social history, a "people's history," in the evolution of religious life. The theology and programmatic ideas of elites, of national leaders, were critical to the formation of the nationwide movement. Some ideas were transplanted from Germany, and others evolved within the American setting. Equally necessary, however, was the pressure exerted from below at the local level by the emerging needs of individual members of American synagogues. As historian Michael A. Meyer has written,

[Reform Judaism] was not merely a movement for doctrinal or liturgical reform unrelated to the realities of Jewish existence, and therefore its history cannot be adequately studied using only the tools of the history of ideas or the history of religions. . . . It is only by attention to the interplay of idea and social situation that the Reform movement becomes fully comprehensible.[1]

To gain a more complete understanding, congregational archives, minute books, and corresponding United States census data reflect diverse responses by individual temples to the changing roles of affiliated women, children, young men, and families. As voluntary associations within an American "free marketplace of souls," temples had to respond to the evolving needs of the "Jews in the pews," if they were to compete effectively.

Examples of this pattern of response to constituents' needs abounded. When mid-nineteenth-century young families were recruited, synagogue Sabbath schools were added. When a secular German-American second generation was the target for post-Civil War outreach, Sisterhoods, youth activities, social justice projects, and public lectures entered the array of congregational life. The role of the pulpit rabbi was expanded from preacher and educator to include pastor and administrator of creative programs.

When the children of Eastern European immigrants became desirable potential members in the early years of the twentieth century, temples responded again. They restored some traditional practices, engaged the services of more ritual-oriented staff and furthered the scope of temple center functions, proven suitable to second-generation needs twenty years earlier. National bodies such as the UAHC reacted to the needs articulated by the members of affiliated temples. In turn, subsequent Union committees and projects furthered the ability of local congregations to incorporate these needs.

Thus, social history demonstrates the critical importance of the congregational unit and of congregational histories for creating a comprehensive understanding of national religious movements. In recent years, the Lilly Foundation has inspired intensive studies of religious congregations in America. The historical study of local churches and synagogues can produce a more complete perspective with regard to the history of religion in America.[2] Social scientist Carl Dudley has observed:

The denomination sees the congregation as an outpost for denominational distribution. . . . [The denomination and its seminaries assume] we have the truth, the resources, the insights, which we will pass out to the people at these local

outposts. . . . [But congregational studies indicate] congregations are equal
partners as carriers of the faith. In congregations, faith is real, sometimes more
alive than in the denomination. Congregations are not just the reception and
distribution centers; they are also the producers of the faith.[3]

Examination of the congregation as an institution therefore can provide a
fresh perspective. Rabbi Bertram Korn suggested to me, during my
investigation of the archives of Keneseth Israel of Philadelphia in the late
1970s, "Historically, large temples often led the Reform movement, more
than vice versa."

Further research should examine this social history pattern within the
UAHC in greater detail. Subsequent studies might address: To what
degree did experiences within their own family's temple mold the policies
advocated by lay leaders of the UAHC at the national level? In what
fashion did affiliated congregations overtly or more subtly pressure the
Union into responding to local needs? Was the local synagogue the
primary source of institutional innovation, or did it generally implement
creative techniques emanating from the Reform movement's national staff
and leadership? How did the reality of temple life in smaller or rural
congregations differ from the prominent urban synagogues described in
this study? Although underrepresented in the national governance of the
UAHC, how did these other houses of worship pressure Reform movement leaders to meet their unique needs?

Furthermore, this study demonstrates the powerful impact upon the
Reform movement of cultural factors both from within the Jewish world
and from American society at large. Clearly, many of the institutional
innovations by local Reform temples and by the UAHC were motivated by
internal Jewish concerns: the need to ward off the advances of Protestant
missionaries; the desire to resettle some impoverished Eastern European
urban Jewish masses in agricultural areas; the necessity of defending
Jewish civil rights at home and abroad; the wide range of responses to
Zionism and to a resurgence of traditional rituals among U.S. Jews of
Russian and Polish descent; the ongoing tug-of-war between Reform and
neo-Orthodox Judaism in offering religious adjustments to the modern
world; and in the rising and ebbing of social and cultural tensions, pitting
settled American Jews of Central European background against Jewish
newcomers from Eastern European lands.

Nevertheless, numerous other factors from an all-encompassing American environment also influenced the shaping of the Reform Judaism's
organizational life.[4] As Gerson D. Cohen concluded in an assessment of
some major trends in Jewish history:

To a considerable degree, the Jews survived as a vital group and as a pulsating culture because they changed their names, their language, their clothing and with them some of their patterns of thought and expression. This ability to translate, to re-adapt and re-orient themselves to new situations, while retaining a basic inner core of continuity, was largely responsible, if not for their survival, at least for their vitality.[5]

The Reform movement in the United States developed in a fashion consistent with that historic pattern. The unique institutional style of the twentieth-century UAHC in part was a product of its accommodation to the cultural ambience of the United States.

In each of three periods of time, "megatrends" within American life served as a framework for both national and local institutional innovation by Reform Jews. In the antebellum period, British models dominated. This was evident in terms of abolitionism, the women's rights movement, support for universal free public education, reform of penal and welfare systems, as well as in terms of denominationalism for upgrading the effectiveness of Christian institutions. Accordingly, American Jewish leaders strove to create an American Jewish national religious union compatible with this Anglo-American model, finally reaching their goal in 1878. At that time, the Union of American Hebrew Congregations (UAHC) merged with the Board of Delegates of American Israelites into a single comprehensive UAHC.

In the last twenty years of the nineteenth century, earlier Anglo-American institutional influences were recast into a form consistent with new American institutional ideas emanating from the German university system. Prominent social planners, historians, philosophers, administrators, and religious leaders traveled to Germany to study. Subsequently, they returned to the United States intent upon implementing Central European concepts. The UAHC and its member temples once again accommodated their institutional lives to keep pace with American society at large. Ideological consistency, rationalization, and professionalization became guiding principles. Local Reform temples became "ethnic churches," primarily serving Jews of German descent and acting as part of a distinctively Reform movement within American Judaism.

This synthesis was challenged anew during the first three decades of the twentieth century. American corporate culture and American ethnic blending of citizens from countries of diverse origins contributed to yet another major accommodation by the Reform movement. This time the Union refocused upon "Synagogue and School Extension" efforts to meet the needs of lay persons and schools within its structure. Union temples also adapted by reaching out to second-generation Jews of Eastern European extraction.

In addition, as further evidence of accommodation, this study demonstrates the value of examining developments among American Protestant church movements as a context for assessing organizational trends adopted by America's Jews. Isaac Leeser and Isaac Mayer Wise were inspired by the successes of Episcopalians and Unitarians, respectively. In its early years, the UAHC sought acceptance within the contours of American religious life by borrowing some Protestant denominational terminology and goals, such as circuit preaching, aide to Sabbath schools, newspapers, Bible translations, and a college. An understanding of Reform movement initiatives in the late nineteenth century is amplified by examining ways in which temple activities paralleled the programmatic visions of the Institutional Church and the Social Gospel. Moreover, the inclusion of corporate culture within American synagogue life in the early years of the twentieth century evolved in a fashion similar to the prior incorporation of scientific management inside Protestant churches and national bodies.

Nonetheless, it should be emphasized that these comparisons and similarities do not imply that Reform leaders were constantly imitating American Protestants, but rather that both Christians and Jews in the United States adopted parallel techniques well suited to the American environment.[6] Subsequent research should examine to what extent the Protestant parallel initiatives, upon greater scrutiny, reveal characteristics at odds with UAHC efforts. Moreover, given the illuminating insights offered by the extensive comparisons described in this discussion, perhaps other nineteenth- and early-twentieth-century Jewish institutions (hospitals, community-sponsored religious schools, clubs, literary societies, etc.) could be better understood in comparison to parallel Protestant institutions.

Like American Protestant groups, Reform temples and Reform national leadership chose not to directly confront the lack of piety of each successive younger generation. Instead, they continually redefined the nature of temple life in order to incorporate the very secular activities that enticed the adult sons and daughters of temple founders. Sisterhoods, Brotherhoods, and youth groups, temple center activities and a host of recreational and cultural goals expanded the previously narrow confines of Reform houses of worship. In this fashion, the affiliation of the younger generation was achieved. Commitment to temple life became an ethnic loyalty, often an expression of Jewish identity or feeling rather than a statement of faith or of religious practice. By accommodating effectively to its U.S. environment, the UAHC became a model of acculturation for the Conservative and Orthodox sectors of the American Jewish religious community as well.

In the years immediately following World War I, the Conservative and Orthodox movements joined the Reform movement as significant factors within the American Jewish scene. In 1926, the tripartite reality of American Judaism was formalized in the creation of the Synagogue Council of America, joining all three groups to "expand the national influence of Judaism as a religion." At the local levels, the Orthodox Union (principally in the areas close to New York City), and the (Conservative) United Synagogue (in cities throughout the United States) effectively competed with the UAHC in seeking the membership of middle-class American Jews of Eastern European descent. As more and more U.S. Jews of Russian and Polish descent affiliated with these more tradition-oriented national groups, "proportionately [the Reform movement] . . . declined as Conservatism [in particular] made rapid gains [in many urban areas]."[7]

This stiff grassroots competition, combined with its own apparent "anemia [and] . . . indifference" in the final years of the 1920s, retarded the pace of growth by the Reform Union. "Even before the Wall Street crisis of 1929, the Reform movement had begun to stagnate. From 1927 until 1929, membership in the Union went up by only 264 souls while the number of congregations decreased by one." Nevertheless, in spite of intense local competition from its rival Jewish religious movements, the UAHC's financial supremacy and organizational centrality helped sustain Reform Judaism's institutional edge at the national level. Monetarily, by 1928 the total fund-raising of the Reform Union exceeded $600,000 in contrast to less than $45,000 by its nearest rival, the United Synagogue of America. As United Synagogue Executive Director, Rabbi Samuel M. Cohen, lamented in October 1928: "Despite its limited resources [the United Synagogue] . . . is rendering invaluable service to synagogues throughout the country. This work must be expanded. . . . To do so effectively, greater financial resources are necessary."[8]

Institutionally, from the time of its inception in 1873, Reform Judaism's primary focus had been its national congregational union (UAHC), governed by entrepreneurial businessmen. In contrast, the United Synagogue of America was dominated by a much more cautious and deliberative school of higher learning, the Jewish Theological Seminary (JTS). In particular, JTS' chancellors Solomon Schechter and Cyrus Adler served as the initial presidents of the United Synagogue, subsequently being succeeded by JTS faculty and rabbinic alumni. As Conservative Judaism's fountainhead institution, JTS even provided office space for the United Synagogue's national headquarters. In this underfunded and subordinate role, the United Synagogue of America remained "relatively weak." Thus, as late as 1941, in spite of continued growth by Conservative congregations at the local level, (Conservative) Rabbinical Assembly leader Rabbi Robert Gordis would conclude with envy that the national Reform movement is "incomparably [still] the finest *organized* group in Jewish religious life in America [emphasis added]."[9]

Though the American Jewish religious scene in the twentieth century remains a dynamic one still responsive to trends within American society at large, many basic contours of the current map of Jewish organizational life in the United States already had taken shape by the 1930s. In terms of institutional initiatives within synagogues, American Jews had followed pathways reflected as well within Protestant religious life, similarly responding to "megatrends" within society at large. For Jewry, these religious trends initially were laid out by the accommodation of the UAHC and its congregations to their American environment, and by the institutionalizing of Reform Judaism in the United States.

APPENDIX OF TABLES

TABLE A.

1880 Rabbis with Ph.D.s*

NAME	UNIVERSITY
Max Samfield	Wurzburg
Max Lilienthal	Munich
I. Schwab	Jena
Samuel Hirsch	Bonn
Marcus Jastrow	Halle
F. De Sola Mendes	Jena
S. H. Sonneschein	Jena
Kaufman Kohler	Munich
Gustave Gottheil	Halle
Adolph Huebsch	Prague
Max Schlesinger	Prague
Max Landsberg	Halle
A. Wise	Halle
Leopold Wintner	Vienna
Bernard Felsenthal	Munich

*Utilizing the list of UAHC-affiliated congregations in 1880 and searching for biographical information about their rabbis, these were the only Ph.D.s present among the 26 rabbis located.

TABLE B.
*1900 CCAR Ph.D.s**

NAME	UNIVERSITY
Gotthard Deutsch	Berlin
William Greenburg	Heidelberg
Adolph Guttman	Berlin
Maurice Harris	Columbia
Leon Harrison	Columbia
Emil Hirsch	Leipzig
Abram Isaacs	CCNY
Jacob Jacobsen	Germany
K. Kohler	Berlin
Isidore Lewinthal	Germany
M. Machol	Breslau
Julius Magil	Germany
H. Malter	Heidelberg
Jacob Mandel	CCNY
Max Margolis	Columbia
F. De Sola Mendes	Jena
Aaron Messinger	Germany
Moses Mielziner	Berlin
Samuel Sale	Berlin
Max Samfield	Wurzburg
Max Schlesinger	Prague
Emanuel Schreiber	Berlin
Solomon Sonneschein	Jena
Leopold Wintner	Vienna
Stephen Wise	Columbia

*These data were gathered by correlating the names within the CCAR membership list of 1900 with available biographical information, such as the *American Jewish Yearbook* of 1904.

TABLE C.
Rabbinic Salaries

Salary	Date	Congregation
$12,000	1888	Chicago (Sinai)
$10,000	1884–1885	Manhattan (Emanu-El)
$10,000	1900	Philadelphia (KI)[a]
$9,500	1899–1900	Manhattan (Emanu-El), for Emeritus
$8,000	1899–1900	Manhattan (Emanu-El), Senior Rabbi
$7,000	1900	Pittsburgh (Rodeph Shalom)
$6,000	1874–1900	Cincinnati (KKBY)
$6,000	1892	Cincinnati (KKBI)
$6,000	1872	New Orleans (Sinai), Rabbi Gutheim
$6,000	1898	New Orleans (Sinai)[b]
$6,000	1900	Chicago (KAM)
$5,600	1899	New Orleans (Sinai)
$5,500	1900	Denver (Emanu El)
$5,000	1867	Philadelphia (Rodelph Shalom)
$4,200	1896	Kansas City (Bene Jehudah)
$4,000	1899	Baltimore (Baltimore Hebrew Congregation)
$3,600	1900	Manhattan (Shaaray Tefila)
$3,500	1900	Atlanta (Hebrew Benevolent)
$3,500	1898	Peoria, Illinois (Anshai Emeth)
$3,000	1885	Galveston, Texas (Bnai Israel)
$3,000	1891	Detroit (Beth El)
$2,500	1899	St. Paul, Minnesota (Mount Zion)
$2,400	1893	Portland, Oregon (Beth Israel)
$2,100	1890	Little Rock, Arkansas
$1,800	1879	Charleston (Beth Elohim)
$1,500	1896	Akron, Ohio (Akron Hebrew)
$1,500	1894	Minneapolis
$1,500	1898	Macon, Georgia
$1,200	1881	Ft. Wayne, Indiana (Achdus Vesholom)
$1,200	1884	Omaha, Nebraska (Israel)
$1,000	1879	Paducah, Kentucky (Yeshurun)
$1,000	1890	Huntsville, Alabama (Bnai Sholem)
$900	1896	Grand Rapids, Michigan (Emanuel)
$800	1881	Easton, Pennsylvania
$650	1897	Portsmouth, Ohio (Bene Abraham)
$400	1889	Springfield, Ohio (Ohev Zedukah)

[a] Krauskopf, having increased from $5,000 in 1886, growing to $6,000 to $7,700 to $8,000 and then to $10,000.
[b] Rabbi Heller, having increased from his initial $4,000 in 1887.

Notes

Introduction

1. Egal Feldman, *Dual Destinies: The Jewish Encounter With Protestant America* (Chicago, 1990), pp. 81–82.

2. David Philipson, *The Reform Movement in Judaism* (New York, 1931), pp. 334–35; also see Beryl H. Levy, *Reform Judaism in America* (New York, 1933); Nathan Glazer, *American Judaism* (Chicago, 1957), pp. 32–33; Joseph L. Blau, *Judaism in America: From Curiosity to Third Faith* (Chicago, 1976), pp. 39–45; and more recently Abraham J. Karp, "Overview: The Synagogue in America—A Historical Typology," in Jack Wertheimer (ed.) *The American Synagogue: A Sanctuary Transformed* (New York, 1987), p. 10.

3. Leon A. Jick, "The Reform Synagogue," in Jack Wertheimer (ed.), *The American Synagogue: A Sanctuary Transformed* (New York, 1987), pp. 86, 89 as well as in a more lengthy fashion in Jick's *The Americanization of the Synagogue* (Hanover, N.H., 1976); also see Robert Liberles, "Conflict over Reform: The Case of Congregation Beth Elohim, Charleston, South Carolina," in Jack Wertheimer (ed.), especially pp. 292–93 (endnote 5); Jenna Weissman Joselit, "The Special Sphere of the Middle-Class American Jewish Woman: The Synagogue Sisterhood, 1890–1940," in Jack Wertheimer (ed.), especially pp. 225 (endnote 17), 226 (endnote 35); as well as Jonathan D. Sarna, "The Debate over Mixed Seating in the American Synagogue," in Jack Wertheimer (ed.) pp. 372–78.

4. Michael A. Meyer, *Response to Modernity: A History of the Reform Movement in Judaism* (New York, 1988), chaps. 1–7.

5. UAHC *Proceedings*, 1873–1900, as evident in the nature of Committee appointments; Although large congregations with membership exceeding 100 adult males comprised a small minority of UAHC affiliated temples, according to my calculations (based upon the UAHC *Proceedings* of 1873–1900) delegations from these larger synagogues comprised from 35 to 60 percent of the attendance at the General Council gatherings; UAHC *Proceedings*, 1873–1930; UAHC *Proceedings*, 1878–1898; UAHC *Proceedings*, 1873–1900 (with the sole exception being Samuel Woolner of Peoria, Ill., who held a symbolic Vice Presidency for one

two-year term; UAHC *Proceedings*, 1873–1879, 1881, 1883, 1885, 1887, 1889, 1891, 1893, 1895, 1897, 1899.

6. E. Brooks Holifield, "Review of Recent Studies of the American Synagogue," *Religious Studies Review*, Vol. 17, No. 3, July 1991, p. 203.

1. Local Synagogues as Voluntary Associations

1. Jacob Dorn, "Religion and the City," in Mohl and Richardson (eds.), *The Urban Experience* (Belmont, Mass., 1973), pp. 147 ff.

2. Donald M. Scott, *From Office to Profession: The New England Ministry, 1750–1850* (Philadelphia, 1978), p. 150.

3. James M. Gustafson, "The Voluntary Church: A Moral Appraisal," in D. B. Robertson (ed.), *Voluntary Associations: A Study of Groups in Free Societies* (Richmond, Va., 1966), p. 299; Alexis de Tocqueville, *Democracy in America* (New York, 1956), p. 198.

4. Marjorie Lambertie, *Jewish Activitism in Imperial Germany* (New Haven, 1978), pp. 1–5.

5. Donald M. Scott, p. 149.

6. Jay P. Dolan, *The Immigrant Church: New York's Irish and German Catholics, 1815–1865* (Baltimore, 1975), chaps. 2–4; Hasia R. Diner, *A Time For Gathering: The Second Migration 1820–1880* (Baltimore, 1992), pp. 50, 53.

7. Hasia R. Diner disputes the extent of this German majority, claiming a more substantial non-German minority than generally assumed; see Hasia R. Diner, pp. 49–54.

8. For the observations in this paragraph, I am indebted to the recommendations provided to me by Dr. Malcolm Stern.

9. Cited in Steven Hertzberg, *Strangers Within the City: The Jews of Atlanta, 1845–1915* (Philadelphia, 1978), pp. 14–15; See *Historical Statistics of the United States: Colonial Times to 1970* (United States Bureau of the Census, 1971), p. 106, for the basis for my calculations.

The presence of Jews from England, France, and Holland among the founders of early New York City congregations is indicated by the founding of B'nai Jeshurun (English Jews) in 1825, Anshe Chesed (Dutch, German, and Polish Jews) in 1828, and Shaaray Brocha (French Jews) in 1851, as indicated by Daniel J. Elazar, *The Organizational Dynamics of American Jewry* (Philadelphia, 1976), p. 152; Annual Report, U.S. Immigration and Naturalization Service, 1973, reprinted in Leonard Dinnerstein and David M. Reimers, *Ethnic Americans: A History of Immigration and Assimilation* (New York, 1975), pp. 162–63.

10. D. Sulzburger, "The Growth of the Jewish Population in the U.S.," *Publication of the American Jewish Historical Society*, No. 6, 1897; see *Historical Statistics of the United States: Colonial times to 1970* (United States Bureau of the Census, 1971), p. 106.

11. Hasia R. Diner, p. 51.

12. Data were collected from the following U.S. census records: Philadelphia (1850), Cincinnati (1850), San Francisco (1860), and New Orleans (1870). These data were correlated with the membership lists of the sample congregations found in their Minute Books during their founding years.

13. See note 9 above.

14. Glenda Riley, " 'Not Gainfully Employed': Women on the Iowa Frontier 1833–1870," in Jean E. Friedman and William G. Shade, *Our American Sisters:*

Women in American Life and Thought (Lexington, Mass., 1982), pp. 267 ff, especially pp. 267–68.

15. United States Census reports from the 1820 to 1860 period consistently report such findings; see citations in Burton J. Bledstein, *The Culture of Professionalism: The Middle Class and the Development of Higher Education in America* (New York, 1976), p. 206.

16. James G. Heller, *As Yesterday When It Is Past: A History of the Isaac M. Wise Temple K.K. B'nai Yeshurun, 1842–1942* (Cincinnati, 1942), chap. 2; also see Howard Fineshriber, *Reform Congregation Keneseth Israel: Its First Hundred Years, 1847–1947* (Philadelphia, 1950), chap. 1.

17. *Occident*, May, 1846, p. 61; consult *Occident*, December 1844, p. 415; also see Jonathan D. Sarna, "The American Jewish Response to Nineteenth-Century Christian Missions," *Journal of American History*, Vol. 68, 1981/1982, pp. 35–51.

18. Moshe Davis, *The Emergence of Conservative Judaism* (Philadelphia, 1963), pp. 40–41, for example, describes the indebtedness of Rebecca Gratz' Jewish Sunday school in the late 1830s to parallel Christian Sunday school programs.

19. For further information, see Peter Decker, "Jewish Merchants in San Francisco: Social Mobility on the Urban Frontier," *American Jewish History*, Vol. 67, June 1978, pp. 396 ff.

20. New Orleans City Business Directory, 1870; also see Elliot Ashkenazi, *The Business of Jews in Louisiana, 1840–1875* (Tuscaloosa, Ala., 1988).

21. See Steven M. Lowenstein, "The 1840's and the Creation of the German-Jewish Religious Reform Movement," in W. E. Mosse, A. Paucker, and R. Rurup, (eds.) *Revolution and Evolution: 1848 in German Jewish History* (Tubingen, 1981), pp. 255 ff, especially the charts regarding ritual reforms on pp. 286 ff, as well as the appendices listing and evaluating the Reform rabbinical attendees at the Reform rabbinical conferences of the 1840s.

22. Robert Liberels, *Religious Conflict in Social Context: The Resurgence of Orthodox Judaism in Frankfurt AM Main, 1838–1877* (Westport, Conn., 1985), pp. 43–52.

23. KKBY Minute Books; James G. Heller, pp. 80–118; also see Jonathan Sarna, "The Debate over Mixed Seating in the American Synagogue," in Jack Wertheimer (ed.), *The American Synagogue: A Sanctuary Transformed* (New York, 1987), pp. 363–90; Minutes of KI (Philadelphia), 21 March 1869.

24. Emanu-El (San Francisco) Minute Books; Fred Rosenbaum, *Architects of Reform: Congregational and Community Leadership, Emanu-El of San Francisco, 1849–1980* (Berkeley, Ca., 1980), chaps. 2–3; Fred Rosenbaum, chap. 2; the Minute Books of Temple Emanu-El (San Francisco), 1864, available at the Western Jewish History archives in Berkeley, Ca.

25. *American Israelite*, 3 September 1886.

26. Leon A. Jick, *The Americanization of the Synagogue, 1820–1870* (Hanover, N.H., 1976), pp. 179–80, notes that "in the 1860s there was hardly a (church or synagogue) congregation in America which did not build a large and sumptuous new edifice. . . . the new sumptuousness of the synagogue edifice was a sign of Israel's redemption in a transformed world. American Jews were moving from . . . ostracism to brotherhood, from darkness to light." Rachel Wischnitzer, *Synagogue Architecture in the United States: History and Interpretation* (Philadelphia, 1955), pp. 67–73.

27. James G. Heller, *As Yesterday When It Is Past: A History of the Isaac M. Wise Temple K.K. B'nai Yeshurun, 1842–1942* (Cincinnati, 1942), p. 108.

28. Michael A. Meyer, *Response to Modernity: A History of the Reform Movement in Judaism* (New York, 1988), p. 42.

29. For a prime example of the ideal of "the Temple" espoused by such synagogues, see Isaac Mayer Wise's sermon on the day of the dedication of his K.K. B'nai Yeshurun's new building in 1866 in James G. Heller, pp. 102–106; Harriet Kohn Stern, "Origins of Reform Judaism in New Orleans," M.A. thesis, University of New Orleans, 1977, pp. 56–57.

30. Leon A. Jick, "The Reform Synagogue," in Jack Wertheimer, *The American Synagogue: A Sanctuary Transformed* (New York, 1987), pp. 86–89; *Occident*, Vol. 6, December 1848, pp. 431–36.

31. Alexander Altmann, "The New Style of Preaching in Nineteenth Century German Jewry," in Alexander Altmann, *Essays in Jewish Intellectual History* (Waltham, Mass., 1981), pp. 191–200.

32. Israel Tabak, "Rabbi Abraham Rice of Baltimore," *Tradition*, 1965, pp. 100–20.

33. Bertram W. Korn, "American Jewry in 1849," in B. W. Korn, *Eventful Years and Experiences: Studies in Nineteenth Century American Jewish History* (Cincinnati, 1958), p. 39.

34. Donald M. Scott, p. 153 and pp. 43–46, assessing the reasons for the growing significance of individual local congregations within American religious life.

35. Francis P. Weisenburger, *Ordeal of Faith: The Crisis of Church-Going America, 1865–1900* (New York, 1959), describes in great detail the process of secularization within American society, and the need to "compete" in order to attract worshippers to church or synagogue; George Harris, *A Century's Change in Religion* (Boston, 1914), pp. 207–23, demonstrates religious laxity in contrast to the earlier strictness of "the Lord's Day" as shown on pp. 15 ff; Donald M. Scott, pp. 143–44. Similarly, the ability of an effective preacher to attract crowds within Germany's religious life is described within Michael A. Meyer, pp. 47–48, 55.

36. Robert S. Michaelsen, "The Protestant Minister in America: 1850 to the Present," in H. Richard Niebuhr and Daniel D. Williams (eds.), pp. 280–83.

37. *American Israelite*, 27 February 1896. Nathan Kaganoff, "The Traditional Jewish Sermon in the United States from its Beginnings to the First World War," unpublished Ph.D. dissertation, American University, 1960, claims that during the 1850s English became the dominant language of American synagogue sermons. This conclusion is disputed by Robert I. Kahm, "Liberalism as Reflected in Jewish Preaching in the English Language in the Mid-Nineteenth Century," unpublished Ph.D. dissertation, Hebrew Union College, 1949, who claims that the predominance of the English-language sermon within American synagogue life occurred in the 1860s.

38. Carl Borne, "Early American Preaching," *Historia Judaica*, Vol. 15, 1953; Isaac Mayer Wise, *Reminiscences* (Cincinnati, 1901), p. 41; also see Robert V. Friedenberg, pp. 65–75, who points out Wise's indebtedness to the preaching style techniques of Hugh Blair and Blair's books, notably *Lectures on Rhetoric and Belles Lettres*.

39. Bertram W. Korn, pp. 39–41. For the impact upon American religion caused by Christian "princes of the pulpit," also see Lawrence A. Cremin, *American Education: The National Experience, 1783–1876* (New York, 1980), pp. 381–88; Donald M. Scott, p. 113, shows that Raphall's salary equaled the highest compensation levels among Protestant ministers as well.

40. James G. Heller, *Isaac M. Wise: His Life, Work and Thought* (New York, 1965), p. 79.

41. Leon A. Jick, *The Americanization of the Synagogue, 1820–1870* (Hanover, N.H., 1976), pp. 184–85.

42. James G. Heller, *Isaac Mayer Wise: His Life, Work and Thought* (New York, 1965), p. 240.

43. Fred Rosenbaum, p. 8; also see Joshua Stampfer, *Pioneer Rabbi of the West: The Life and Times of Julius Eckman* (Portland, Ore., 1988), pp. 56–62.

44. James G. Heller, *Isaac Mayer Wise: His Life, Work and Thought*, pp. 237, 240–41.

45. Minutes of Temple Sinai (New Orleans), 25 April 1872. Concern on the part of rabbis for security within their pulpit positions was consistent with the fear among Protestant clergy of arbitrary dismissals, as recorded by Donald M. Scott, pp. 120–23.

46. James G. Heller, *As Yesterday When It Is Past* (Cincinnati, 1942), p. 91; pp. 115–18; Minute Books of KKBY for 1873, p. 115, available at the congregation's office. Information regarding salary levels for Protestant clergy in America of this era can be found in Donald M. Scott, p. 113.

47. Harriet Kohn Stern, "Origins of Reform Judaism in New Orleans," unpublished M.A. thesis, University of New Orleans, 1977; see 16 June 1868 excerpt.

48. James G. Heller, *As Yesterday When It Is Past*, pp. 115–18; Harriet Kohn Stern, chap. 3; Howard Fineshriber, *Reform Congregation Keneseth Israel: Its First Hundred Years, 1847–1947* (Philadelphia, 1950), pp. 16–17; Fred Rosenbaum, p. 7; *Historical Statistics of the United States: From Colonial Times to 1970*, Part I, U.S. Bureau of the Census, 1971; see the aforementioned congregational histories of each of the four sample temples.

49. *American Israelite*, 3 February 1888, p. 2.

50. *Occident*, October 1844, pp. 314, 316, 318–19.

51. C. Ellis Nelson, "Congregations' Educational Strategy," in Carl S. Dudley, Jackson W. Carroll, James P. Wind (eds.), *Carriers of Faith: Lessons from Congregational Studies* (Louisville, Ky., 1991), p. 159–60.

52. *Occident*, December 1843, p. 411, Isaac Leeser's article entitled "Jewish Children under Gentile Teachers."

53. This discussion is indebted to Yechiel Lander, "The Talmud Yelodim Day School," an unpublished essay within the collection of the American Jewish Archives, based exclusively upon the Talmud Yelodim Institute Minute Books; also see James G. Heller, *As Yesterday When It Is Past*, pp. 50–60.

54. Yechiel Lander, "The Talmud Yelodim Day School"; also see Lloyd P. Gartner, "Temples of Liberty Unpolluted: American Jews and Public Schools, 1840–1875," in Bertram W. Korn (ed.), *A Bicentennial Festschrift for Jacob Rader Marcus* (Cincinnati, 1976), pp. 164–73; and Nathan H. Winter, *Jewish Education in a Pluralist Society: Samson Benderly and Jewish Education in the United States* (New York, 1966), pp. 5–7.

55. Yechiel Lander, "The Talmud Yelodim Day School"; also see Lloyd P. Gartner, pp. 165–67.

56. Lloyd P. Gartner, pp. 157–82; also see Jonathan D. Sarna, "The American Jewish Response to Nineteenth-Century Christian Missions," *Journal of American History*, Vol. 68, 1981–1982, pp. 35–51; Yechiel Lander, "The Talmud Yelodim Day School"; KKBY (Cincinnati) Minutes, 20 October 1867.

57. Cited in Lloyd P. Gartner, p. 77.

58. William W. Sweet, *The Story of Religion in America* (New York, 1950), pp. 245–55; also see Robert W. Lynn and Elliot Wright, *The Big Little School: Sunday Child of American Protestantism* (New York, 1971), chaps. 1 and 2.

59. Cited in Leon A. Jick, p. 62; also see Joseph R. Rosenbloom, "Rebecca Gratz and the Jewish Sunday School Movement in Philadelphia," *PAJHS*, Vol. 48, December 1958, pp. 71–78.

60. Joseph Rosenbloom, "Some Conclusions About Rebecca Gratz," in Jacob R. Marcus (ed.) *Essays in American Jewish History* (New York, 1975), pp. 180–81; also see Moshe Davis, pp. 45–48, 404.

61. This description is taken from (San Francisco) Emanu-El's brochure of the early 1860s, available in the archives of the Western Jewish Historical Society, Berkeley, Ca.

62. Minutes of KI (Philadelphia), 10 November 1870.

63. This information is contained in the aforementioned Emanu-El brochure regarding its school.

64. Owen E. Pence, *The Y.M.C.A. and Social Need: A Study of Institutional Adaptation* (New York, 1939), Part I; also see Benjamin Rabinowitz, *The Young Men's Hebrew Association, 1854–1913* (New York, 1948); and Deborah Dash Moore, *B'nai Brith and the Challenge of Ethnic Leadership* (Albany, N.Y., 1981), p. 12.

65. Jonathan D. Sarna, "The Jewish Response to Nineteenth Century Christian Missions," pp. 38–39.

66. Naomi W. Cohen, *Encounters With Emancipation: The German Jews in the United States, 1830–1914* (Philadelphia, 1984), p. 45.

2. A National Religious Union

1. Cited in Russell E. Richey (ed.), *Denominationalism* (Nashville, 1977), p. 22.

2. Sidney Mead as cited in Russell Richey, p. 71.

3. Franklin H. Littell, *From State Church to Pluralism: A Protestant Intepretation of Religion in American History* (New York, 1962), p. 37.

4. *Occident*, 1848, p. 69.

5. Allan Tarshish, "Jew and Christian in a New Society: Some Aspects of Jewish-Christian Relationships in the United States, 1848–1881," in Bertram Wallace Korn (ed.), *A Bicentennial Festschrift for Jacob Rader Marcus* (New York, 1976), pp. 579–80.

6. Jonathan D. Sarna, "The American Jewish Response to Nineteenth-Century Christian Missions," *Journal of American History*, Vol. 68, June 1981, pp. 35–51; Lance Jonathan Sussman, "Isaac Leeser and the Protestantization of American Judaism," *American Jewish Archives*, April 1986, pp. 6–7; For insight into Leeser's hebraic capabilities, consult Lance Jonathan Sussman, "Another Look At Isaac Leeser and the First Jewish Translation of the Bible in the United States," *Modern Judaism*, Vol. 5, No. 2., May 1985, p. 174, and especially his endnote 104; Isaac M. Wise, *Reminiscences* (Cincinnati, 1901), p. 57, in which Wise attributes this comment to Leeser. Historian Lance Sussman regards Wise's characterization of Leeser's alleged ignorance as unfair; see Lance Jonathan Sussman, "Confidence in God: The Life and Preaching of Isaac Leeser (1806–1868)," Rabbinical thesis, Hebrew Union College, chap. 12, p. 200.

7. Lance Jonathan Sussman, "The Life and Career of Isaac Leeser, 1806–1868: A Study of American Judaism in its Formative Period," unpublished Ph.D.

dissertation, Hebrew Union College, 1987, provides a comprehensive study of Leeser.

8. Letter available at the Leeser Archives of Dropsie College in Philadelphia. The Leeser Collection at Dropsie College contains several other such items. The Leeser Collection at Mikvah Israel synagogue has not been made available for researchers in general. It probably includes similar materials.

9. See Daniel Walker Howe, "American Victorianism as a Culture," *American Quarterly*, December 1975; and his essay "Victorian Culture in America," in Daniel Walker Howe (ed.), *Victorian Americva* (Philadelphia, 1976); Frank Thistlethwaite, *The Anglo-American Connection in the Early Nineteenth Century* (Philadelphia, 1959) provides the most extensive discussion of this transatlantic process; also see Charles I. Foster, *An Errand of Mercy: The Evangelical United Front, 1790–1837* (Chapel Hill, N.C., 1960) for an assessment of the transmission of British denominationalism into the religious institutional life of the United States.

10. *Occident*, March 1845.

11. As early as 1844, Leeser published an essay entitled "The Jews and Their Religion," which appeared within I. Daniel Rupp's assessment of all religious denominations in the United States: *He Pasa Ekklesia. An Original History of the Religious Denominations at Present Existing in the United States Containing Authentic Accounts of Their Rise, Progress, Statistics and Doctrines Written Expressly for the Work by Eminent Theological Professors, Ministers, and Lay Members of the Respective Denominations* (Lancaster, Pa., 1844), pp. 350–69; Leeser was aware of hundreds of Christian journals in America, as well as of Jewish newspapers in Europe, for example, in Germany, the *Universal Jewish Gazette*, the *Israelite of the Nineteenth Century*, and the *Orient*; in France, the *Israelitish Archives of France*; and in England, the *Voice of Jacob*; for details see Lance Jonathan Sussman, "Confidence in God: The Life and Preaching of Isaac Leeser (1806–1868)," Rabbinic thesis, Hebrew Union College, 1980, pp. 156–57.

12. *Occident*, February 1844, "Demands of the Times." A similar term "federative" union was used by Rev. Samuel Schmucker and the Americanizing Lutherans of German descent in this era, to contrast their Anglo-American institutional goals with Germanic systems; see W. A. Wentz, *Samuel S. Schmucker* (Philadelphia, 1964); *Occident*, August 1845, p. 227.

13. Benny Kraut, "American Jewish Leaders: The Great, Greater and Greatest," *American Jewish History*, Vol. 78, No. 2, December 1988, pp. 208–17, discusses Leeser and Wise working in tandem as "culture brokers" and "culture creators."

14. Isaac M. Wise, p. 331.

15. Martin B. Ryback, "The East-West Conflict in American Reform Judaism," *American Jewish Archives*, January 1952, pp. 122–43; *Occident*, March 1848, pp. 431–35. A discussion of Reform "mission" theory is provided by Benny Kraut, *From Reform Judaism to Ethical Culture* (Cincinnati, 1979), pp. 25–26. Sefton Temkin, "Isaac Mayer Wise," Ph.D. disseretation, Hebrew Union College, 1970, p. 168.

16. Isaac M. Wise, pp. 78–87; also see *Occident*, Vol. 5, 1847, pp. 158 ff.

17. Benny Kraut, "Judaism Triumphant: Isaac Mayer Wise on Unitarianism and Liberal Christianity," *AJS Review*, Vols. 7 and 8, 1982–1983, pp. 179–80.

18. Isaac M. Wise, pp. 187–88.

19. Jonathan D. Sarna, "The American Jewish Response to Nineteenth-Century Christian Mission," *Journal of American History*, Vol. 68, June 1981, pp.

35–51, posits that much of institutional innovation within antebellum American Jewish came about in defensive response to Christian missions.

20. Benny Kraut, pp. 186–87; George Willis Cooke, *Unitarianism in America: A History of Its Origin and Development* (Boston, 1902), pp. 168–69.

21. Isaac M. Wise, *Reminiscences*, p. 313; also see Moshe Davis, pp. 130–35; Michael A. Meyer, pp. 243, 236–37; MARTIN B. RYBACK, "THE EAST-WEST CONFLICT IN AMERICAN REFORM JUDAISM," *American Jewish Archives*, January 1952, pp. 135–37; Isaac M. Wise, p. 318.

22. Bernhard N. Cohn, "Early German Preaching in American," *Historia Judaica*, Vol. 15, 1953, p. 105.

23. *The Jewish Times*, 4 June 1869, cited in Sefton Temkin, *The New World of Reform*, pp. 7–10.

24. For the context of this Germanic image of the rabbi, see Ismar Schorsch, "Emancipation and the Crisis of Religious Authority: The Emergence of the Modern Rabbinate," in W. E. Mosse, et al. (eds), *Revolution and Evolution: 1848 in German-Jewish History* (Tübingen, 1981), pp. 205–47; *Occident*, September 1844.

25. Michael A. Meyer, *Response to Modernity*, pp. 248–49; also see Sidney Mead's assessment that this era had "a need for a certain type of leaders— energetic, persuasive, popular, political (princes of the pulpit)—speaking a language to arouse emotions, rather than theologians," cited in Russell E. Richey (ed.), p. 82.

26. Nathan Glazer, pp. 39–40, see note 5.

27. *American Israelite*, 23 November 1855, p. 4; also see James G. Heller, p. 297.

28. Bertram W. Korn, *The American Reaction to the Mortara Case* (Cincinnati, 1957), chap. 3.

29. Jonathan D. Sarna, *JPS: The Americanization of Jewish Culture, 1888–1988* (Philadelphia, 1989), pp. 6–8.

30. Michael A. Meyer, p. 260; for further information regarding M. Loth, see Steven A. Fox, "On the Road to Unity: The Union of American Hebrew Congregations and American Jewry, 1873–1903," *AJA*, November 1980, pp. 148, 158; See "Moritz Loth" entry in "Biographical Sketches of Jewish Communal Workers in the United States," *American Jewish Year Book*, Vol. 7, 1905, p. 83; also see *The Biographical Encyclopedia of Ohio of the Nineteenth Century* (Cincinnati, 1876), pp. 73–74.

31. Cited in James G. Heller, pp. 409–10. A similar observation appeared in the New York Ckity–based *Jewish Messenger*, 29 May 1874, "What the clergy have failed to do, the laymen are striving very faithfully to begin and to advance."

32. See UAHC Constitution in UAHC *Proceedings*, Vol. 6, 1978, pp. 422–23.

33. Jonathan D. Sarna, "The 'Mythical Jew' and the 'Jew Next Door," in David A. Gerber (ed.), *Anti-Semitism in American History* (Chicago, 1986), p. 73.

34. Moshe Davis, pp. 381–85.

35. Board of Delegates of American Israelites, *Annual Session*, 1877, pp. 10–15, 18–22; also see UAHC *Proceedings*, Vol. 4, p. 245.

36. UAHC *Proceedings*, Vol. 5, 1877, pp. 346–47; also see *American Israelite*, 11 February 1877.

37. UAHC *Proceedings*, Vol. 6, 1878, pp. 381–82; also see *American Israelite*, 11 July 1877.

38. UAHC *Proceedings*, 1873–1879; the previously mentioned lists within each

volume of affiliated synagogues and their local number of members were the sources for these calculations.

39. Board of Delegates of American Israelites 1877–1878 demographic survey, available at the American Jewish Historical Society in Waltham, Mass.; also see David Sulzberger, "The Growth of Jewish Population in the United States," *Proceedings of the American Jewish Historical Society*, Vol. 6, 1897.

40. Data derived from the Board of Delegates 1877–1878 survey, plus calculations of regional and statewide totals available from the UAHC *Proceedings*, 1874–1900, membership charts.

41. Calculations based upon the 1877–1878 survey of congregations conducted by the Board of Delegates of American Israelites.

42. UAHC *Proceedings*, Vol. 1, 1873, pp. 22–23. These were the universal goals of both Protestant as well as Jewish denominational advocates within the mid-nineteenth-century world of American religion; UAHC *Proceedings*, Vol. 2 (reporting the data of 1874), p. 87.

43. UAHC *Proceedings*, Vol. 2, pp. 87 ff.

44. Halford E. Luccock and Paul Hutchinson, *The Story of Methodism* (New York, 1926), pp. 217–22, traces the origins of "circuit riders" to the earliest days of American Methodist organizational successes initiated by Francis Asbury.

45. Winthrop Hudson, *Religion in America: an Historical Account of the Development of American Religious Life* (New York, 1965), pp. 121–22.

46. UAHC *Proceedings*, Vol. 2, 1874, pp. 36, 93–94.

47. Article IV, Bylaws—Circuit Preaching, UAHC Constitution, 1877.

48. UAHC *Proceedings*, Vol. 7, 1879, p. 580.

49. UAHC *Proceedings*, Vol. 7, 1879, p. 580–81.

50. Halford E. Luccock and Paul Hutchinson, *The Story of Methodism* (New York, 1926), pp. 219–22.

51. UAHC *Proceedings*, Vol. 1, 1873, pp. 22–23; cited in Lawrence A. Cremin, *American Education: The National Period: 1783–1876* (New York, 1980), p. 58.

52. Lawrence A. Cremin, p. 59.

53. William W. Sweet, *The Story of Religion in America* (New York, 1950), pp. 254–55; Lawrence A. Cremin, p. 306.

54. UAHC *Proceedings*, Vol. 2, 1874, pp. 87–92.

55. UAHC *Proceedings*, Vol. 2, 1874, pp. 87–88. Such techniques were directly derived from the American Sunday School Union. For further information on this context, consult Edwin W. Rice, *The Sunday School Movement and the American Sunday School Union, 1780–1917* (Philadelphia, 1917).

56. UAHC *Proceedings*, Vol. 4, 1876, pp. 142–43.

57. UAHC *Proceedings*, Vol. 4, 1876, pp. 142–44.

58. UAHC *Proceedings*, Vol. 6, 1877, pp. 237–38; also see James G. Heller, p. 412; UAHC *Proceedings*, Vol. 13, 1884, see "Hebrew Sabbath School Union Report." For an evaluation of the economic impact of general monetary instability within American life from 1873 to 1879, see Arthur C. Bining and Thomas C. Cochran, *The Rise of American Economic Life* (New York, 1964), pp. 380, 391–395, 410–12.

59. Michael A. Meyer, *The Origins of the Modern Jew: Jewish Identity and European Culture in Germany, 1749–1824* (Detroit, 1967), pp. 46, 64–68, 137, on Dohm; see Arthur Hertzberg, *The French Enlightenment and the Jews* (New York, 1970), on Voltaire; the dire impact of the charge of usury upon nineteenth-century European Jews is examined in Michael Burns, "The Rural Exodus of Alsatian Jews,

1791–1848," in Jehuda Reinharz (ed.), *Living With Anti-Semitism: Modern Jewish Responses* (Hanover, N.H., 1987), pp. 19–41.

60. For additional context see Michael A. Meyer, *The Origins of the Modern Jew: Jewish Identity and European Culture in Germany, 1749–1824,* (Detroit, 1967), chap. 5; cited in Howard Morley Sachar, *The Course of Modern Jewish History* (New York, 1977), p. 205; also see Michael Stanislawski, *Tsar Nicholas I and the Jews: the Transformation of Jewish Society in Russia, 1825–1855* (Philadelphia, 1983), pp. 49–59.

61. Cited in Salo Baron, "The Modern Age," Leo Schwartz (ed.), *Great Ages and Ideas of the Jewish People* (New York, 1956), p. 400.

62. See Esther L. Panitz, "The Polarity of American Jewish Attitudes towards Immigration (1870–1891)," in Abraham J. Karp (ed.), *The Jewish Experience in America: Volume IV: The Era of Immigration* (New York, 1969), pp. 3–62; for tensions within the American scene between German Jews and the newly arriving Eastern Europeans see Naomi Cohen, *Encounter With Emancipation: The German Jews in the United States, 1830–1914* (Philadelphia, 1984), pp. 302–304, 324–44.

63. Allan Tarshish, "The Economic Life of the American Jew," in J. R. Marcus, *Essays in American Jewish History* (New York, 1975), pp. 289–90; UAHC *Proceedings,* Vol. 4, 1876, pp. 114 ff, "President (Loth's) Report," Vol. 8, 1879.

64. UAHC *Proceedings,* Vol. 7, 1879, "President (Loth's) Report."

65. James G. Heller, *Isaac M. Wise: His Life, Work and Thought,* pp. 438, 457, 584–89. Professor Russell Richey has suggested to me that parallel agricultural pursuits existed among American Protestants because of a concern for rural depopulation and nostalgia for America's agrarian past; see William Warren Sweet, *The Story of Religion in America* (New York, 1950), pp. 352–53, and Henry Nash Smith, *Virgin Land: The American West as Symbol and Myth* (Cambridge, Mass., 1978), chap. 11.

66. UAHC *Proceedings,* Vol. 8, 1880, pp. 676 ff ("Report on the Board of Delegates on Civil and Religious Rights"); calculations based upon the UAHC *Proceedings,* 1878–1898, with each volume providing a complete list of the leadership of the Board of Delegates, and of their hometowns as well.

67. UAHC *Proceedings,* Vol. 8, 1880, pp. 676 ff; also see UAHC *Proceedings,* Vol. 6, 1878, pp. 422, Article II, Section 2, of the UAHC Constitution. For parallel information regarding the Deutsch-Israelitischer Gemeindebund, consult Ismar Schorsch, *Jewish Reactions to German Anti-Semitism, 1870–1914,* (New York, 1972), chaps. 1 and 2, pp. 23–78. For information regarding the strategy of the Alliance Israelite Universelle, see Michael R. Marrus, *The Politics of Assimilation: A Study of the French Jewish Community at the Time of the Dreyfus Affair* (Oxford, 1971).

68. Cyrus Adler and Aaron M. Margalith, *With Firmness in the Right* (New York, 1946), detail the vigilance of Jewish political lobbyists of this late-nineteenth-century period, notably Simon Wolf and Max J. Kohler, in defense of Jewish rights at home and abroad. Also consult the annual reports of the Board of Delegates presented each year within the *Proceedings* of the UAHC: Vol. 7, 1880, p. 676 (protecting Jewish rights in Rumania); pp. 676–77 (Morocco); pp. 677–78 (Palestine); Vol. 8, 1881, pp. 895–96 (Russia); Vol. 11, 1884, pp. 1402–1403 (protection of U.S. Jews against negative impact of "Sunday Laws").

69. Ongoing information about these issues can be obtained from the annual reports provided in the UAHC *Proceedings* regarding the Board of Delegates: pp.

676, 894–95 (Romania); pp. 676–77, 896–98 (Morocco); pp. 677–78 (Palestine); pp. 895–96 (Russia).

70. UAHC *Proceedings*, 1879–1900, pp. 1402–1403 (Sunday Laws).

71. UAHC *Proceedings*, 1879–1900, pp. 678, 900–901, 1400–1401.

72. For information regarding the establishing of the Italian Instituto Rabbinico Lombardo-Veneto, Abraham Geiger's Hochschule in Germany, L'Ecole Rabbinique in France, and Jews College in England, see Michael A. Meyer, *The History of the HUC-JIR* (New York, 1976), pp. 8–10; Frederick Rudolph, *The American College and University: A History* (New York, 1962), chaps. 3–5; cited in Moshe Davis, pp. 56–57.

73. Walter Metzger, *Academic Freedom in the Age of the University* (New York, 1961), pp. 96–100, discusses the powerful influence of the German University system; Ismar Schorsch, "Wissenschaft and Values," in Ismar Schorsch, *Thoughts From 3080: Selected Addresses and Writings* (New York, 1988), pp. 30–31, indicates that for Jews, "Wissenschaft des Judentums" meant "a collective art of translation, a sustained effort to cast the history, literature, and institutions of Judaism in western categories."

74. Ismar Schorsch, "Emancipation and the Crisis of Religious Authority: The Emergence of the Modern Rabbinate," in W. E. Mosse, A. Paucker, and R. Rurup (eds.), pp. 205–47; also see Ismar Schorsch, "Zecharias Frankel and the European Origins of Conservative Judaism," *Judaism*, Vol. 30, 1981, pp. 343–54; James G. Heller, p. 273; Michael A. Meyer, *Hebrew Union College—Jewish Institute of Religion: At One Hundred Years* (Cincinnati, 1976), pp. 15–16, 35; James G. Heller, p. 279.

75. Frederick Rudolph, *The American College and University: A History* (New York, 1962), p. 54.

76. Frederick Rudolph, pp. 50–60.

77. Bertram W. Korn, "The Temple Emanu-El Theological Seminary of New York City," in Jacob Rader Marcus (ed.), *Essays in American Jewish History* (New York, 1975), pp. 359–71.

78. *Proceedings of the Board of Delegates of American Israelites*, 1867, p. 9; also see Bertram W. Korn, "The First American Jewish Theological Seminary: Maimonides College, 1867–1873," in Bertram W. Korn, *Eventful Years and Experiences* (Cincinnati, 1954), pp. 151–213; 1 August 1866 letter to Board of Delegates from the Executive Committee in the American Jewish Historical Society Archives, Waltham, Mass. An evaluation of the reasons for the failure of Maimonides College is offered by Bertram W. Korn, "The First American Jewish Theological Seminary: Maimonides College, 1867–1873," pp. 189–95.

79. Michael A. Meyer, *HUC-JIR*, p. 17; also see Michael A. Meyer, *Response to Modernity*, pp. 262–63.

80. UAHC *Proceedings*, Vol. 1, 1873, pp. 4, 22; also see Steven A. Fox, "On the Road to Unity: The Union of American Hebrew Congregations and American Jewry, 1873–1903," *American Jewish Archives*, November 1980, pp. 180–81.

81. UAHC *Proceedings*, Vol. 1, 1873, p. 18.

82. Michael A. Meyer, *HUC-JIR*, pp. 31–32; also see Steven A. Fox, pp. 180–82.

83. James G. Heller, pp. 415–16. For further details regarding the history of Cincinnati, see Clara Chambrun, *Cincinnati: Story of the Queen City* (New York, 1939).

84. Steven A. Fox, pp. 158–59 (regarding Julius Freiberg); also see Michael A.

Meyer, *HUC-JIR*, p. 35 (regarding Bernhard Bettmann). The rise of philanthropy needed to support America's emerging educational institutions and other nonprofit organizations is related to the emergence of the notion of the "gospel of wealth" and its philanthropic corollary the "stewardship of wealth." See Jesse B. Sears, *Philanthropy in the History of American Higher Education* (Washington, 1922); Michael A. Meyer, *HUC-JIR*, pp. 10–17.

85. Cited in Frederick Rudolph, p. 164. For a case study of the impact of college presidents upon a denominational college of this era, see Robert T. Handy, *A History of Union Theological Seminary in New York* (New York, 1987), chaps. 2 (1850–1870) and 3 (1870–1890), pp. 25–67.

86. Frederick Rudolph, p. 168; also see Michael A. Meyer, *HUC-JIR*, p. 28.

87. Frederick Rudolph, p. 87; also see Michael A. Meyer, *HUC-JIR*, p. 28; Rudolph, p. 88; Meyer, p. 28; James G. Heller, p. 420.

88. Frederick Rudolph, p. 168.

89. Michael A. Meyer, *HUC-JIR*, pp. 27–29.

90. Michael A. Meyer, *HUC-JIR*, pp. 36–37; David Philipson, *My Life As An American Jew* (Cincinnati, 1941), in which he recollects Rabbi Wise's role in placing him in his first pulpit.

91. Cited in Michael A. Meyer, *Response to Modernity: A History of the Reform Movement in Judaism*, p. 263.

92. James G. Heller, pp. 415–17, p. 420, explains Wise's means of reimbursement for expenses incurred. Efforts for denominational colleges of this era to carry out "subscription drives," etc., are detailed in Frederick Rudolph, pp. 179–90. James G. Heller, p. 442; Michael A. Meyer, *HUC-JIR*, pp. 23–24, indicates the origins of the HUC faculty and of its library; also see Frederick Rudolph, pp. 99, 122, who indicates the general problem of denominational college libraries being saddled with low budgets and inadequate holdings.

93. Frederick Rudolph, pp. 138–42; Michael A. Meyer, *HUC-JIR*, pp. 29–30; also see Charles Franklin Thwing, *A History of Higher Education in America* (New York, 1906), pp. 390–94; Frederick Rudolph, p. 75.

94. Michael A. Meyer, *HUC-JIR*, p. 30; also see Charles F. Thwing, pp. 380–83.

95. Frederick Rudolph, p. 75; also see Michael A. Meyer, *HUC-JIR*, pp. 104, 27.

96. Frederick Rudolph, p. 199; Charles F. Thwing, pp. 400–403; Rudolph, p. 198; Thwing, pp. 323–31.

97. James G. Heller, p. 418.

98. Michael A. Meyer, *HUC-JIR*, pp. 25–26.

99. 24 April 1881 speech at dedication of HUC's new building, *American Israelite*, 24 June 1881.

100. Cited in James G. Heller, p. 419.

101. *Occident*, September 1844.

102. Frederick Rudolph, chap. 6; Robert T. Handy, chaps. 2 and 3; Michael A. Meyer, *HUC-JIR*, pp. 21–22.

103. Courses are listed in Michael A. Meyer, *HUC-JIR*, pp. 21–22; also see a similar classics-focused curriculum at Union Theological Seminary, cited in Robert T. Handy, pp. 59–60. For this general pattern consult Charles F. Thwing, chap. 13 ("The Course of Study"); James G. Heller, p. 441.

Foremost among the examiners were: 1877, Sonneschein of St. Louis and Mayer of Pittsburgh; 1878, Morais of Philadelphia, Wolfenstein of Cleveland, and

Zirndorf of Detroit; 1879, Huebsch of New York, Felsenthal of Chicago, and Hahn of Cleveland; 1880, F. De Sola Mendes of New York, Adler of Chicago, and again Sonneschein of St. Louis (Michael A. Meyer, *HUC-JIR*, p. 20). For perspectives regarding the role of these examiners, see David Philipson, pp. 10–11. The actual list of "examiners" was taken from the annual reports of the HUC submitted to the "Union," see UAHC *Proceedings*, 1875–1884.

104. James G. Heller, p. 412.

105. Koppel Pinson, *Modern Germany: Its History and Civilization* (New York, 1966), pp. 3–11.

106. John T. McNeill, *Unitive Protestantism: A Study of One Religious Response* (Nashville, 1930), pp. 303–307; Jacob Katz, *Out of the Ghetto* (New York, 1978), pp. 119–21.

107. Jay P. Dolan, *Catholic Revivalism: The American Experience, 1830–1900* (South Bend, IN, 1978), p. 188).

108. Hasia R. Diner has challenged the claims of high percentages of Jews with actual German descent, claiming a much larger minority of non-Germans than previously assessed; see Hasia R. Diner, *A Time For Gathering: The Second Migration 1820–1880* (Baltimore, 1992), pp. 49–54; Jeffrey S. Gurock, "The Orthodox Synagogue," in Jack Wertheimer (ed.), *The American Synagogue: A Sanctuary Transformed* (New York, 1987), p. 43.

109. Martin E. Marty, *Righteous Empire: The Protestant Experience in America* (New York, 1970), pp. 177–87; Jeffrey S. Gurock, p. 51.

3. Expanded Roles for the Local Temple

1. Sydney E. Ahlstrom, *A Religious History of the American People* (New Haven, CT, 1972), pp. 388–471; *Annual Report*, U.S. Immigration and Naturalization Service, 1973, reprinted in Leonard Dinnerstein and David M. Reimers, *Ethnic Americans: A History of Immigration and Assimilation* (New York, 1977), p. 11; Abdel Ross Wentz, *A Basic History of Lutheranism in America* (Philadelphia, 1964), pp. 70–125; 191–95.

2. *Annual Report*, U.S. Immigration and Naturalization Service, 1973, reprinted in Leonard Dinnerstein and David M. Reimers, p. 11; Jay P. Dolan, *The American Catholic Experience: A History from Colonial Times to the Present* (New York, 1985), pp. 148–52, 162–63.

3. Cited in Stuart Rosenberg, "Some Sermons in the Spirit of the Pittsburgh Platform," *Historia Judaica*, Vol. 17, 1956, p. 61.

4. Marc Lee Raphael, "Rabbi Jacob Voorsanger of San Francisco on Jews and Judaism: The Implications of the Pittsburgh Platform," *AJHQ*, Vol. 63, No. 2, December 1973, pp. 192–94.

5. Kathleen Neils Conzen, "German-Americans and the Invention of Ethnicity," in Frank Trommler and Joseph McVeigh (eds.), *America and the Germans: An Assessment of a Three-Hundred Year History*, Vol. 1, pp. 133–34.

6. For this observation I am indebted to the observations provided to me by Dr. Malcolm Stern.

7. Nathan Glazer and Daniel Patrick Moynihan, *Beyond The Melting Pot* (Boston, 1963), p. 13; While this pattern of German predominance was evident in each of the four large, urban temples studied, subsequent research should be conducted into the social history of the smaller, isolated Reform congregation, serving as the sole synagogue for a diverse local Jewish population.

8. Jakob J. Petuchowski, *Prayerbook Reform in Europe: The Liturgy of European Liberal and Reform Judaism* (New York, 1968), pp. 35, 168–69. For example, the origins of KKBY (Cincinnati) are attributed to the desire of some Jewish immigrants in Cincinnati of the 1840s to practice *Minhag Ashkenaz* in lieu of Kehillat Kodesh B'nai Israel's use of Minhag Polen; see James G. Heller, *Isaac M. Wise: His Life, Work and Thought* (New York, 1965), pp. 102–103.

For further details regarding this American phenomenon consult Eric Lewis Friedland, "The Historical and Theological Development of the Non-Orthodox Prayerbooks in the United States," Ph.D. dissertation, Brandeis University, 1967. Rabbi Wise is cited in Lou H. Silberman, "The Union Prayer Book: A Study in Liturgical Development," in Bertram Wallace Korn (ed.), *Retrospect and Prospect: Essays in Commemoration of the Seventy-Fifth Anniversary of the Founding of the Central Conference of American Rabbis, 1889–1964* (New York, 1965), p. 46.

9. Admittedly these four temples had already exhibited a distinctively Central European pattern among their founders, not necessarily as evident in each and every local Reform congregation. Nevertheless, from the times of their establishment until the year 1900, the percentage of members with Central European descent had increased in all four cases despite the dramatic growth of the Russian and Polish Jewish populations of Cincinnati, Philadelphia, San Francisco, and New Orleans. Future social histories of other Reform temples will best determine the extent to which this trend was reflective of nationwide American Jewish developments among Reform congregations.

10. My calculations are based upon the sample of members whose data I was able to locate in the membership lists available in the archives of each sample congregation correlated to the census records of 1900.

11. Such unusual accessibility was made possible by KI's listing of its members and their addresses. The presence of addresses greatly facilitated the retrieval of information from the census archives.

12. Although these four sample temples admittedly displayed a central European profile from their earliest days, the pattern of increasing German Jewish dominance applied in varying degrees to other UAHC congregations throughout the country; see Michael A. Meyer, p. 292.

13. Charles S. Bernheimer, *The Russian Jews in the United States* (Philadelphia, 1905), pp. 51–52, shows that out of a population of 55,000 Eastern European Jews in Philadelphia in 1904–1905, 11,686 were elementary-age children. Therefore, many of the remaining 42,000 + Jewish residents were parents of these youngsters. This large group of young fathers and mothers of offspring ages five through fourteen was socially analogous neither to the young, single adult offspring of Reform temple members nor to the middle-aged members themselves.

14. Arthur Schlesinger, *The Rise of the City* (New York, 1933), p. 332.

15. Peter Decker, *Fortunes and Failures: White-Collar Mobility in Nineteenth Century San Francisco* (Cambridge, Mass., 1978), pp. 271–72.

16. Nathan Glazer, *American Judaism* (Chicago, 1957), p. 44.

17. My calculations are based on membership lists for each temple within their Archives correlated with the census of 1900.

18. Gibson Winter, *The Suburban Captivity of the Churches* (New York, 1962), pp. 43–66, evaluates this process of the flight to the suburbs of the growing middle-class congregations for both Christians and Jews.

A description of the anti-Eastern European rhetoric that in part motivated the framers of the Pittsburgh Platform of 1885 will be provided in chapter 4; also see the discussion in chapter 5 of similar antagonism at the local level.

19. Nathan Glazer, p. 52.

20. Benny Kraut, *From Reform Judaism to Ethical Culture: The Religious Evolution of Felix Adler* (Cincinnati, 1979), chap. 4 ("Creating a New Movement"); Naomi W. Cohen, *Encounter With Emancipation* (Philadelphia, 1984), pp. 53–55, in which a contrast is also provided between the YMHA and the YMCA.

21. Marcus L. Hansen, "The Third Generation Immigrant," in *Proceedings of the Massachusetts Historical Society*, 1939.

22. German-language sermons continued in all four temples until at least the final years of the 1880s. Moreover, German-language instruction remained as part of the curriculum of each temple religious school until the mid-1890s.

23. Deborah Dash Moore, *New York Jews* (New York, 1980), p. 9, describes a similar phenomenon as bringing about the programmatic innovations of Conservative synagogue centers in the 1920s, as an effort to attract the second generations.

Such was the case with KKBY's building in Cincinnati (constructed in 1866), KI's "temple" in Philadelphia (1864), and Emanu-El's facility in San Francisco (1866).

24. Gibson Winter, p. 110.

25. For a survey of such recently constructed temple facilities, see *CCAR Yearbook*, Vol. 12, 1902, pp. 210–15; Howard W. Fineshriber, *Reform Congregation Keneseth Israel: Its First Hundred Years, 1847–1947*, (Philadelphia, 1950), pp. 20–30.

26. Joseph Kett, "The History of Age Grouping in America," in Arlene Skolnick, *Rethinking Childhood* (Boston, 1976), p. 223; Joseph Kett, *Rites of Passage: Adolescence in America from 1790 to the Present* (New York, 1977), p. 181.

27. Howard W. Fineshriber, p. 27; Joseph Kett, *Rites of Passage*, p. 203.

28. *CCAR Yearbook*, Vol. 12, 1902, p. 213

29. Abraham Karp, "Overview: the Synagogue in America," in Jack Wertheimer (ed.), *The American Synagogue: A Sanctuary Transformed* (New York, 1987), p. 19; Nevertheless, Michael A. Meyer does call attention briefly to the Reform role in innovating the "temple center" in Michael A. Meyer, *Response to Modernity*, p. 304; also David Kaufman presented a paper at the 1991 Annual Conference of the Association of Jewish Studies elaborating upon this "temple center" precedent to later "synagogue center" efforts.

30. Charles Stelzle, "The Institutional Church, 1907," in Robert D. Cross (ed.), *The Church and the City* (New York, 1967), pp. 341–42.

31. *CCAR Yearbook*, Vol. 12, 1902, pp. 211–12.

32. *CCAR Yearbook*, Vol. 8, 1897–1898.

33. *American Israelite*, "The Philosophy of Institutionalism" 25 December 1902, p. 4; also see Gries's response in *American Israelite*, 15 January 1903, and Heller's counter-article in *American Israelite*, 22 January 1903.

34. *American Israelite*, 15 January 1903, p. 4.

35. *American Israelite*, 20 April 1916, p. 4, credits KI with being the "first to extend the temple's sphere of activities," in this fashion.

The aspiration to establish and maintain an American Jewish Publication Society had been articulated first by Isaac Leeser in the 1840s and continued to be expressed again and again for the next half century. Joseph Krauskopf's JPS was the third Jewish Pulbication Society to be launched; Howard W. Fineshriber, pp. 21–26.

36. DeWitte Holland, *Preaching in American History* (Nashville, Tenn., 1969), p. 231.

37. Cited in White, Hopkins, and Bennette, *The Social Gospel: Religion and Reform in Changing America* (Philadelphia, 1976), p. 73.

38. Naomi W. Cohen, pp. 194–202; also see Leonard Mervis, "The Social Justice Movement and the American Reform Rabbi, AJA, Vol. 7, June 1955; KI Minute Books, 6 May 1887, President David Klein's Address.

39. KI Minute Books, President's Addresses in 1887 and 1884, in KI Archives.

40. Howard W. Fineshriber, pp. 24; 27.

41. The data that I correlated from Temple membership lists against the census of 1900 revealed that virtually every family in all four temples had at least one, and sometimes two or several live-in domestics.

The growth of attendance of youngsters from middle-class homes at junior high and high school, thus expanding these years of childhood activity, are described in Lawrence A. Cremin, *American Education: The Metropolitan Experience, 1876–1980* (New York, 1988), pp. 546–47; Carl Degler, *At Odds: Women and the Family In America From the Revolution to the Present* (New York, 1980), chap. 13.

42. My data is gathered from correlating the temple membership lists with the records of the U.S. census of 1900. Ladies societies began to appear as early as the 1850s; see Charlotte Baum, Paula Hyman, and Sonya Michel, *The Jewish Woman in America* (New York, 1976), p. 46.

43. Roy Lubove, *The Professional Altruist: The Emergence of Social Work as a Career, 1880–1930* (New York, 1972), chap. 1.

44. Aaron I. Abell, *The Urban Impact upon American Protestantism, 1865–1900* (Hamden, Conn., 1970), pp. 194–222, details a wide variety of women's involvements in church-sponsored auxiliary functions of social service in this era.

Pittsburgh Conference of 1885, "Conference Paper," in Walter Jacob (ed.), *The Changing World of Reform Judaism: The Pittsburgh Platform in Retrospect* (Pittsburgh, 1985).

45. As noted in Chapter One, during the 1850s and 1860s family pews became standard practice. Confirmation ceremonies also replaced male-only *bar mitzvah* rituals; see Jonathan De. Sarna, "The Debate Over Mixed Seating in the Synagogue," in Jack Wertheimer (ed.), *The American Synagogue: A Sanctuary Transformed* pp. 363–94, especially p. 379; KI Minute Books, 2 February 1896 and 3 March 1901. By the early 1920s, with the granting of suffrage to women by American society at large, our sample temples changed their constitutions to permit full women's membership eligibility and even service within the Board of Trustees. For example, the KKBY Constitution was changed accordingly on 22 May 1922, the same year that similar changes were made at KI and the other two temples.

46. Israel Goldstein, *A Century of Judaism in New York: A History of B'nai Jeshurun* (New York, 1930), p. 194.

47. Israel Goldstein, pp. 194–95. The constitution read: "to develop and secure 'personal service" on the part of its members in all human enterprises and in elevating the moral standard of the people, improving the condition of their homes, teaching them self-reliance and self-respect, promoting their moral and mental education, and developing technical skill among the young of both sexes."

48. Fred Rosenbaum, *Architects of Reform: Congregational and Community Leadership, Emanu-El of San Francisco, 1849–1980* (Berkeley, Ca., 1980), pp. 51–52.

49. KI Minute Books, 4 April 1880.

50. David B. Tyack, *The One Best System* (Cambridge, MA, 1974), pp. 39–59, describes this process during the 1870s and 1880s within the public school system of America. David Tyack, "Bureaucracy and the Common School: The Example of Portland, Oregon, 1851–1913," in Michael Katz (ed.), *Education in American History* (New York, 1983), pp. 164–65. Robert W. Lynn and Elliot Wright, *The Little Big School: Two Hundred Years of the Sunday School* (New York, 1971), pp. 64–69.

51. *KI Annual*, 1888–1889.

52. *KI Annual*, 1888–1895; 1894–1895, pp. 10–11. The 450 pupils are listed in regard to an 27 April 1893, report of the School Committee. *KI Annual*, 1890–1894; also see Sidney H. Ditzion, *Arsenals of a Democratic Culture: The Library Movement, 1850–1900.*

53. TYI Minute Books are available at the KKBY Archives, and the *CCAR Yearbook*, 1896, pp. 3–8, includes the "Plan of Instruction"; on a more modest scale, Max Heller recommended similar changes regarding Temple Sinai's religious school on *22 September* 1889, as recorded in the Minute Books of the Temple.

54. *CCAR Yearbook*, Vol. 12, 1902, p. 188.

55. U. S. Census data: Philadelphia (1880), Cincinnati (1880), San Francisco (1880), and New Orleans (1880); Kenneth Zwerin and Norton B. Stern, "Jacob Voorsanger: From Cantor to Rabbi," *Western States Jewish Historical Quarterly*, April 1983, pp. 195–96, disputes other claims that Voorsanger had been formerly ordained at the Jewish Theological Seminary of Amsterdam.

56. David Philipson, *My Life As An American Jew* (Cincinnati, 1941), p. 27.

57. *American Israelite*, 24 May 1894.

58. *American Israelite*, 2 April 1896, p. 4; or similarly, see Temple Sinai Minute Books, for 10 November 1886, in which the President appointed a committee of three "to place themselves in communication with the leading rabbis of the U.S. in order to find some suitable person to fill our vacant pulpit."

59. KI Minute Books, 31 May 1887; Temple Sinai Minute Books, 31 October 1886, 10, November 1886, 10 February 1887.

60. KI Minute Books, 25 September 1887.

61. Temple Sinai Minute Books, 29 November 1895; *American Israelite*, 21 June 1878; *CCAR Yearbook*, 1889–1890, plus 1890–1900 volumes.

62. KI Minute Books, 27 February 1881.

63. KKBY Minute Books, 28 October 1888; also see James G. Heller, p. 138; this matter was approved by the congregation in June 1889.

64. James G. Heller, p. 158.

65. KI Minute Books, President's Report, 20 October 1892.

66. Robert S. Michaelsen, "The Protestant Ministry in America: 1850 to the Present," in H. R. Niebuhr (ed.), *The Ministry in Historical Perspective* (New York, 1956), p. 263.

67. Abraham Feldman, "The Changing Functions of the Synagogue and the Rabbi," in *Reform Judaism: Essays by H.U.C. Alumni*, (Cincinnati, 1949), p. 215.

68. E. Brooks Holifield, *A History of Pastoral Care in America* (Nashville, 1983), pp. 174–75.

69. Robert S. Michaelsen, p. 262.

70. Michael A. Meyer, *Response to Modernity*, p. 281; *American Israelite*, 11 May 1893.

71. *CCAR Yearbook*, Vol. 12, 1902, p. 212.

72. Isaac M. Fein, *The Making of an American Jewish Community: the History of Baltimore Jewry from 1723 to 1920* (Philadelphia, 1971), p. 185.

73. Robert V. Friedenberg, *Hear O Israel: The History of American Jewish Preaching, 1654–1970* (Tuscaloosa, Ala., 1989), p. 71.

74. Robert V. Friedenberg, p. 65.

75. Marc Lee Raphall, "Rabbi Jacob Voorsanger of San Francisco on Jews and Judaism: the Implications of the Pittsburgh Platform," *AJHQ*, Vol. 63, No. 2, December 1973, p. 187.

76. Michael A. Meyer, *Response to Modernity*, p. 281.

77. *American Israelite*, 9 December 1897, p. 4.

78. From 1902 through 1914, Heller subsequently served as a weekly columnist for the *American Israelite*. Rabbi Isaac M. Wise's successor, Rabbi Louis Grossman of KKBY, assumed some of the editorial responsibilities at the *American Israelite* following Wise's death in 1900.

79. This material was to be published in 1917; see Jonathan D. Sarna, *JPS: The Americanization of Jewish Culture, 1888–1988* (Philadelphia, 1989), chapt. 5.

80. *American Israelite*, 11 May 1893; also see a similar passage in *American Israelite*, 5 December 1889, p. 4:
It is no less a fact that the young rabbis in our country can do no scientific work as long as they must preach twice a week, conduct Sabbath schools, postgraduate classes, literary societies of dilletants, preach and preach agains at weddings, funerals and other occasions. It is evident that they must do a large amount of reading to keep themselves posted for their pastoral work, and that kind of reading gives no impetus to scientific research in any field. The rabbi has become a day laborer, always engaged in popular work.

81. A. Z. Idelsohn, *Jewish Music In Its Historical Development* (New York, 1929—original date of publication, reprinted 1956), pp. 320–21.

82. Alexander Altmann, "The New Style of Preaching in Nineteenth Century German Jewry," in A. Altmann, *Essays in Jewish Intellectual History* (Waltham, Mass., 1981), pp. 190–200, 321.

83. Mark Slobin, *Chosen Voices: The Story of the American Cantorate* (Urbana, Ill., 1989), p. 44.

84. James G. Heller, pp. 167–68; also see KKBY Minute Books in which the new associate rabbi (Charles Levi) was instructed to "perform the duties of Chasan and Reader," and six months notice was given to the previous *chazzan* for the purposes of his locating a new position elsewhere, 27 September 1889; *American Israelite*, 3 November 1892, p. 4; also see the *Jewish Ledger (New Orleans)*, 17 April 1903; Mark Slobin, p. 46.

85. Jeffrey Zucker, "Cantor Edward Stark at Congregation Emanu El," *Western States Jewish History*, April 1985, p. 243.

86. Jeffrey Zucker, p. 234.

87. *Constitution and By-Laws of Congregation Emanu El*, see Fred Rosenbaum, *Architects of Reform: Congregational and Community Leadership, Emanu El of San Francisco, 1849–1980*.

88. In 1905; see Jeffrey Zucker, p. 233; Jeffrey Zucker, "Cantor Edward Stark at Congregation Emanu El, Part II," *Western States Jewish History*, July 1985, p. 318.

89. As indicated in Chapter One, as early as 1862 at San Francisco's Emanu-El and 1866 at KKBY in Cincinnati, Rabbis Elkan Cohn and Isaac M. Wise, respectively, initiated a late Friday service ritual and sermon.

90. *American Israelite*, 2 June 1882, p. 4.

91. KKBY Minute Books, 3 October 1886.

92. Joseph Krauskopf, *Sunday Lecture Series I*, "The Saturday vs the Sunday Sabbath," 8 and 15 April 1888.

93. KI Minute Books, 6 April 1888, p. 41.

94. KI *Annual*, 1897, p. 9; also see *CCAR Yearbook*, Vol. 16, 1906, pp. 87–112, "The Influence of the Sunday Services"; as well as Kerry M. Olitzky, "The Sunday Sabbath Movement in American Reform Judaism, Strategy or Evolution?" *AJA*, April 1982, pp. 75 ff.

95. Howard W. Fineshriber, p. 40; Lawrence Hoffman, *Beyond The Text* (Bloomington, Ind., 1987), pp. 61–63.
   This decision shattered any hope of maintaining the flexibility necessary to develop a single liturgy for all [Western and Eastern European] Jews. American Reform was fast becoming a specific movement whose standard of liturgical propriety was that pioneered in Western Europe. American Reform was left with a radicalized version of German Reform in English translation.
   KKBY Minute Books, 29 January 1893; Temple Sinai Minute Books, 27 October 1895; Marc Lee Raphael, *Profiles in American Judaism: The Reform, Conservative, Orthodox and Reconstructionist Traditions in Historical Perspective* (San Francisco, 1984), pp. 37–38.

96. KKBY Minute Books, 23 March 1877; KI Minute Books, 30 September 1883.

97. Jewish Ministers Association, 1887 *Proceedings*, Paper on "Congregational Participation in Public Worship"; Mark Slobin, p. 45.

98. *KI Annual*, 1896; in 1904; see Jeffrey Zucker, "Edward Stark and Emanu El," *Western Jewish History*, April 1985, pp. 232 ff; *Jewish Ledger (New Orleans)*, 11 November 1904, p. 3, also see 25 November 1904 describing its successes.

99. "History of the Plum Street Choral Society," available in the KKBY Collection at the AJA; at KI on 28 June 1897 parents were notified to encourage their children to learn the congregational singing.

100. Michael A. Meyer, p. 280; Jeffrey Zucker, "Cantor Edward Stark at Congregation Emanu El," *Western States Jewish History*, 1985 April p. 235; also see 15 May 1905 KI Minute Books describing rehearsals in order to train congregants in the use of the *Union* Hymnal; a more complete discussion of this trend is provided in the CCAR *Yearbook*, Vol. 22, 1912, pp. 333 ff.

101. Temple Sinai Minute Books, 25 November 1900; Howard Fineshriber, pp. 22–26, including Krauskopf's creation of a Service Manual, as well as the 1888 modern version of service adopted at KKBY in Cincinnati as described in James G. Heller, p. 136.

102. Marc Lee Raphael, p. 36.

103. KI Minute Books, 10 April 1881, p. 109.

104. *American Israelite*, 25 June 1882, p. 4.

105. Fred Rosenbaum, chap. 3; Howard Fineshriber, pp. 20–30; relative to the problem of phasing out German, see Leon Jick, *The Americanization of the Synagogue, 1820–1870*, (Hanover, N.H., 1976), pp. 143–46.

106. Decorum also played a role in the Sephardic tradition, as evident in the early constitutions of Manhattan's Shearith Israel, see David and Tamar De Sola Pool, *An Old Faith In The New World: Portrait of Shearith Israel, 1654–1954* (New York, 1955), pp. 258–64.

107. KI Annual, 1891–1892, pp. 15–16; the fetish for decorum extended to

congregational meetings as well, as is described for KKBY by James G. Heller, pp. 161–64.; also see the KKBY Minute Books for the work of the Committee on Decorum, 20 August 1888.

108. Ismar Schorsch addressed the 1990 Convention of the Rabbinical Assembly on this topic, see the 1990 RA *Proceedings;* Jakob Petuchowski, *Prayerbook Reform In Europe: The Liturgy of European Liberal and Reform Judaism* (New York, 1968), chap. 6: "Order and Decorum."

109. KKBY Minute Books, 25 February 1900.

110. These events are described in the Minute Books of the two congregations; Temple Sinai Minute Books, 23 October 1887; KKBY Minute Books, 10 May 1886.

111. Peter Berger, *The Sacred Canopy: Elements of a Sociological Theory of Religion* (New York, 1967), p. 107; Francis P. Weisenburger, *Ordeal of Faith,* pp. 46–47; George Harris, *A Century's Change in Religion* (New York, 1967), pp. 207–23.

112. Francis P. Weisenburger, p. 39; also see the remainder of the chapter entitled "Why Some Church Pews Were Empty," pp. 39–45. Marion L. Bell, *Crusade in the City: Revivalism in Nineteenth-Century Philadelphia* (Lewisburg, PA, 1977), pp. 232–39.

4. The UAHC

1. Hasia R. Diner, *A Time For Gathering: The Second Migration, 1820–1880* (Baltimore, 1992), p. 163. Diner does acknowledge, however, that when equivalent Jewish institutions were unavailable at the local level, some German Jews did join German athletic clubs, singing societies, etc.

See earlier chapter 2 discussion and endnotes with regard to the young adulthood of Isaac Leeser. Many Central European immigrants came to America only after an extended stay in the British Isles.

Hans W. Gatzke, *Germany and the United States: A Special Relationship* (Cambridge, Mass., 1980), p. 32.

2. The first translations gradually began to appear, starting in 1855; see Rene Wellek, *Confrontations: Studies in the Intellectual and Literary Relations Between Germany, England and the United States During the Nineteenth Century* (Princeton, N.J., 1966), p. 204.

3. Walter J. Metzger, *Academic Freedom In the Age of the University* (New York, 1955), p. 102; Hans W. Gatzke, p. 38.

4. Walter Metzger, pp. 103–104.

5. See Jürgen Herbst, *The German Historical School in American Scholarship: A Study in the Transfer of Culture* (Ithaca, N.Y., 1965).

6. Michael A. Meyer, *Response to Modernity: A History of the Reform Movement in Judaism* (New York, 1988), p. 189; Gershon Greenberg, "Samuel Hirsch's American Judaism," *American Jewish Historical Quarterly,* Vol. 62, 1972/1973, pp. 373–74; Michael A. Meyer, "German-Jewish Identity in Nineteenth Century America," in Jacob Katz (ed.), *Toward Modernity: The European Jewish Model* (New Brunswick, 1987), pp. 252–54.

7. Their dates of arrival were: 1849 (Kalisch, Hocheimer); 1854 (Cohn, L. Adler, Felsenthal); 1856 (S. Adler); 1859 (Szold); 1865 (Mielziner); 1866 (Jastrow, Hirsch, Huebsch); 1869 (Kohler); 1870 (A. Moses, I. Moses); 1871 (Lansberg); and 1873 (Gottheil); see Eric E. Hirshler, *Jews From Germany in the United States* (New York, 1955), pp. 169–70.

8. Their years of study were: De Sola Mendes (1870–1873); Drachman (1881–1884); Kohut (1861–1867); Jastrow (1850s); Szold (1850s); Morais (1850s); F. Adler (early 1870s); E. Hirsch (mid-1870s); Sale (mid-1870s); Schulman (1880s); Schneeberger (1870s). This material was culled from Bertram Wallace Korn, "German-Jewish Intellectual Influences on American Jewish Life, 1824–1972," in A. Leland Jamison (ed.), *Tradition and Change in the Jewish Experience* (Syracuse, N.Y., 1978), pp. 109–11, 129–131.

9. Jack Wertheimer, *Unwelcome Strangers: Eastern European Jews in Imperial Germany* (New York, 1987), pp. 155–56; Michael A. Meyer, *Response to Modernity*, pp. 252–53.

10. A case study is provided by Benny Kraut, *From Reform Judaism to Ethical Culture: The Religious Evolution of Felix Adler* (Cincinnati, 1979), chap. 2, in which he describes Adler's student experiences among numerous aspiring American theological students in contact with German universities and German theological challenges; Frederick A. Norwood, *The Story of American Methodism* (Nashville, TN, 1974), p. 382.

11. Jay P. Dolan, *The American Catholic Experience: A History from Colonial Times to the Present* (New York, 1985), pp. 317–18, provides a discussion of liberal Catholic responses; Winthrop S. Hudson, *Religion in America: An Historical Account of the Development of American Religious Life* (New York, 1965), pp. 266–73 evaluates Protestant liberal trends of this nature; Jay P. Dolan, pp. 271, 353–53.

12. Frank. Adler, *Roots in a Moving Stream: The Centennial History of Congregation B'nai Jehudah of Kansas City, 1870–1970* (Kansas City, 1970), p. 72.

13. Cited in Joseph Blau, "The Spiritual Life of American Jewry," in Blau, Glazer, Handlin, and Stein, *The Characteristics of American Jews* (New York, 1965), p. 95.

The following fourteen rabbis attended: I. Aaron (HUC ordination), Dr. A. Guttman (German Ph.D.), Dr. E. G. Hirsch (German Ph.D.), Dr. K. Kohler (German Ph.D.), J. Krauskopf (HUC ordination), Dr. A. Moses (German Ph.D.), Dr. L. Mayer (German Ph.D.), D. Philipson (HUC ordination), Dr. S. Sale (German Ph.D.), Dr. M. Schlesinger (German Ph.D.), Dr. S. H. Sonneschein (German Ph.D.), M. Sessler, S. W. Bradford, and I. M. Wise (each of the final 3 were European trained). Information was gathered from a variety of biographical sources regarding each of these participants, notably in Moshe Davis, *The Emergence of Conservative Judaism: the Historical School in the Nineteenth Century*, (Philadelphia, 1963), pp. 329 ff.

14. See the texts of these remarks within Walter Jacob (ed.), *The Changing World of Reform Judaism: The Pittsburgh Platform in Retrospect* (Pittsburgh, 1985).

15. Samual Cohen, "Kaufman Kohler," in Simon Noveck (ed.), *Great Jewish Thinkers of the Twentieth Century* (Washington, D.C., 1963), p. 237.

16. Cited in Joseph L. Blau, *Modern Varieties of Judaism* (New York, 1966), p. 57.

17. Marc Lee Raphael, "Rabbi Jacob Voorsanger of San Francisco on Jews and Judaism: The Implications of the Pittsburgh Platform," *AJHQ*, Vol. 63, No. 2, December 1973, p. 192; Stuart Rosenberg, "Some Sermons in the Spirit of the Pittsburgh Platform," *AJHQ*, Vol. 63, No. 2, December 1973, p. 70.

18. Melvin I. Urofsky, *American Zionism From Herzl to the Holocaust* (New York, 1975), p. 76.

19. Ben Halpern, "The Americanization of Zionism, 1880–1930," in Nathan

Kaganoff (ed.), *Solidarity and Kinship: Essays on American Zionism* (Waltham, Mass., 1980), p. 40.

20. Kaufman Kohler, Conference Paper, 1885 Pittsburgh Conference, provided in Walter Jacob (ed.), *The Changing World of Reform Judaism: The Pittsburgh Platform in Retrospect* (Pittsburgh, 1985).

21. Aaron I. Abell, *Urban Impact on American Protestantism* (Hamden, Conn., 1962), pp. 90–91.

22. See discussions regarding Max Weber, *Bureaucracy*, in Nicos P. Mouzelis, *Organization and Bureaucracy: An Analysis of Modern Theories* (New York, 1968), pp. 7–75; Peter Berger, *The Sacred Canopy* (New York, 1969), p. 139.

23. Samuel Haber, *Efficiency and Uplift, Scientific Management in the Progressive Era, 1890–1920* (Chicago, 1964), chap. 4, entitled, "A Normal American Madness."

24. William McGuire King, "The Role of Auxiliary Ministries in Late Nineteenth-Century Methodism," In Russell E. Richey and Kenneth E. Rowe (eds.), *Rethinking Methodist History* (Nashville, 1985), p. 167, as well as pp. 168–72; Ben Primer, *Protestants and American Business Methods* (Ann Arbor, Mich., 1979), pp. 73–74.

25. Lawrence A. Cremin, *American Education: The Metropolitan Experience: 1876–1980* (New York, 1988), pp. 87–88; UAHC *Proceedings*, Vol. 13, 1885, p. 1874; also refer to Steven A. Fox, "On the Road to Unity: The Union of American Hebrew Congregations and American Jewry, 1873–1903," *American Jewish Archives*, November 1980, pp. 184–85.

26. *American Israelite*, 27 November 1885.

27. *The Proceedings of the Hebrew Sabbath School Union, 1886–1900*, especially 1889, pp. 2491–502; 1891, pp. 2662 ff; 1892, pp. 3063–69; 1896, pp. 3714–26.

28. James G. Heller,*I. M. Wise: His Life, Work and Thought* (New York, 1965), p. 588.

29. UAHC *Proceedings*, Vol. 7, 1879, pp. 793, 785; also refer to Steven A. Fox, p. 178.

30. UAHC *Proceedings*, Vol. 7, 1879, p. 680.

31. UAHC *Proceedings*, Vol. 11, 1883, pp. 1157–58, 1406–1407; UAHC *Proceedings*, Vol. 13, 1885, pp. 1600 ff (President Loth's Report).

32. UAHC *Proceedings*, 1896, p. 3665; 1898, p. 3991; and aforementioned KI materials regarding Krauskopf and Rabbi Martin Beifeld's HUC-JIR rabbinical thesis, 1975, "Rabbi Joseph Krauskopf."

33. These techniques were formalized by the creation of the Church Extension Society in 1864; see Frederick A. Norwood, p. 331.

34. UAHC *Proceedings*, Vol. 10, 1882, pp. 1155–56; UAHC *Proceedings*, Vol. 11, 1883, pp. 1445–46.

35. Robert E. Fierstien, *A Different Spirit: The Jewish Theological Seminary of America, 1886–1902* (New York, 1990), pp. 56–57.

36. UAHC *Proceedings*, Vol. 22, 1894, pp. 3381–82; Vol. 24, 1896, pp. 3653–59.

37. UAHC *Proceedings*, Vol. 24, 1896, pp. 3653–59.

38. UAHC *Proceedings*, Vol. 25, 1897, pp. 3851 ff; Vol. 26, 1898, pp. 4007–4009.

39. Richard Hofstadter, *The Age of Reform* (New York, 1955), p. 151.

40. Wilbert Moore, *The Professions: Roles and Rules* (New York, 1970), pp. 167–73.

41. Burton J. Bledstein, *The Culture of Professionalism: The Middle Class and the Development of Higher Education in America* (New York, 1976), p. 80.

42. The years of formation of these associations were AOS (1864), ANS (1875), ACS (1876), and ASCE (1880); Burton J. Bledstein, pp. 84–86.

43. Robert Michaelsen, "The Protestant Ministry in America: 1850 to the Present," in H. R. Niebuhr (ed.), *The Ministry in Historical Perspective* (New York, 1964), p. 272.

44. Conference of Rabbis of Southern Congregations, *Proceedings*, 1885, p. 4.

45. Conference of Rabbis of Southern Congregations, *Proceedings* 1885, p. 9.

46. Conference of Rabbis of Southern Congregations, *Proceedings*, 1885, pp. 44–57; Conference of Rabbis of Southern Congregations, *Proceedings*, 1886, pp. 58–59.

47. Jewish Ministers Association (JMA), *Proceedings*, 1885, p. 39, "The JMA: Its Origins and Meetings," initial paragraph.

48. JMA *Proceedings* 1885, p. 70, "Constitution," see "Object," of the JMA.

49. UAHC, *Proceedings*, 1886; JMA, *Proceedings*, 1885, pp. 46–53.

50. JMA, *Proceedings*, 1885, pp. 49–51.

51. James G. Heller, p. 472.

52. *CCAR Yearbook*, 1894.

53. James G. Heller, pp. 473–74.

54. James G. Heller, p. 474; Sidney Regner, "The History of the Conference," in B. W. Korn (ed.), *Retrospect and Prospect: Essays in Commemoration of the Seventy-Fifth Anniversary of the Founding of the Central Conference of American Rabbis, 1889–1964* (New York, 1965), p. 5.

55. *CCAR Yearbook*, Vol. 1, 1890–1891.

56. *CCAR Yearbook*, 1895, p. 45 ff; Vol. 8, 1897–1898, pp. 29 ff and 89 ff.

57. *CCAR Yearbook*, 1898, pp. 59–60.

58. *CCAR Yearbook*, 1898, Henry Berkowitz paper, p. 10; pp. 48–49; CCAR Constitution Article V, included in each volume of the *CCAR Yearbook of the 1890s*.

59. *CCAR Yearbook*, 1894, p. 95; Michael A. Meyer, *Response to Modernity*, pp. 279–80, shows how these liturgical publications represented the victory once again of German intellectual influences (Einhorn's earlier prayerbook was their primary source) over I. M. Wise's earlier, more moderate and Anglo-American *Minhag America*.

60. Burton J. Bledstein, p. 84.

61. Burton J. Bledstein, p. 241.

62. Burton J. Bledstein, p. 271.

63. Robert T. Handy, *A History of Union Theological Seminary in New York* (New York, 1987), p. 106; also see Robert L. Kelly, *Theological Education in America* (New York, 1924), in which Kelly's comprehensive survey of seminary curricula throughout America reveals this same pattern evident in most urban theological schools by the late 1890s.

64. Richard Hofstadter and C. DeWitt Hardy, *The Development and Scope of Higher Education in the United States* (New York, 1952), p. 11.

65. Burton J. Beldstein, pp. 287–331; Robert S. Michaelsen, "The Protestant Ministry in America," in H. R. Niebuhr and D. D. Williams (eds.), *The Ministry in Historical Perspective* (New York, 1956), p. 274.

66. Michael A. Meyer, *HUC-JIR: At One Hundred Years*, p. 59.

67. UAHC *Proceedings*, 6, pp. 4977 ff.

68. Michael A. Meyer, p. 60.

69. Cited in Michael A. Meyer, p. 59.

70. Michael A. Meyer, p. 61.

71. Robert S. Michaelsen, pp. 283–84; Burton J. Bledstein, p. 176; these data were gathered from correlating the HUC graduating lists with the placements listed within the annual UAHC *Proceedings*, 1883–1900.

72. *American Israelite*, 20 November 1924, p. 4, in which the editor praises the trend to compensate Reform rabbis generously in the range of $10,000 and $15,000 or more; on 29 January 1925, *American Israelite*, p. 4, cites the envy of America's Methodists with regard to the fine fashion in which rabbis are treated financially in contrast to Methodist ministers.

73. *Historical Statistics of the United States: Colonial Times to 1970, Part I*, U.S. Department of Commerce, 1970, Series D 779–93; *American Israelite*, 3 February 1888, p. 2.

74. *American Israelite*, 3 February 1888.

75. *Jewish Ledger*, 3 June 1910, p. 23.

76. I calculated these data from the information available within the UAHC Annual *Proceedings* from 1873 to 1900; David Philipson, *The Reform Movement in Judaism* (New York, 1907), p. 379.

77. Winthrop S. Hudson, *Religion in America: An Historical Account of the Development of American Religious Life* (New York, 1965), pp. 318–19.

5. Further Americanization of the Local Temple

1. Walter LeFeber, *The New Empire* (Ithaca, N.Y., 1963), p. 176; Mira Wilkins, *The Emergence of Multinational Enterprise: American Business Abroad from Colonial times to 1914* (Cambridge, Mass., 1970), pp. 66, 72–73.

2. Jay P. Dolan, *The American Catholic Experience: A History from Colonial Times to the Present* (New York, 1985), pp. 155–57.

3. Marc Lee Raphael, "Rabbi Jacob Voorsanger of San Francisco on Jews and Judaism: The Implications of the Pittsburgh Platform," *AJHQ*, Vol. 63, No. 2, December 1973, p. 199.

4. Martin J. Beifield, "Joseph Krauskoph and Zionism: Partners in Change," *AJH*, Vol. 75, No. 1, September 1985, p. 53.

5. *American Israelite*, 29 August 1895, p. 4.

6. Cited in Naomi W. Cohen, *Encounter With Emancipation*, pp. 690–91.

7. Will Herberg, *Protestant, Catholic, Jew* (New York, 1955), p. 181.

8. Stuart Rosenberg, "Some Sermons in the Spirit of the Pittsburgh Platform," *Historia Judaica*, Vol. 17, 1956, p. 62.

9. Michael A. Meyer, "German-Jewish Identity in Nineteenth-Century America," in Jacob Katz (ed.), *Toward Modernity: The European Jewish Model*, p. 262.

10. *American Israelite*, 17 March 1898, p. 4; Michael A. Meyer, p. 263; Bertram W. Korn, "German-Jewish Identity . . . ," p. 117; also see Naomi Cohen, pp. 204 ff, that credits Cyrus Adler with attempting to make American Jewry a major world center for Jewish scholarship via the Jewish Publication Society, Dropsie College (established in 1907), and the American Jewish Historical Society (1893); Michael A. Meyer, p. 59, offered a similar view; Jonathan Sarna, *JPS, the Americanization of Jewish Culture, 1888–1988* (Philadelphia, 1989), p. 14, suggested that this process was already emerging in the late 1880s and into the 1890s as evidenced by the creation of the JPS (1888), the JTS (1886), the American Jewish Historical Society

(1893), the Jewish Chautauqua Society (1893), Gratz College (1893), and the National Council of Jewish Women (1893).

11. Walter LeFeber, pp. 324–25.

12. *American Israelite*, 4 July 1918, p. 1.

13. Henry F. May, "Europe and the American Mind," in Henry F. May, *Ideas, Faiths and Feelings: Essays on American Intellectual and Religious History, 1952–1982* (New York, 1983), p. 200; John Higham, *Strangers in the Land: Patterns of American Nativism 1860–1925* (New York, 1967), p. 196.

14. John Higham, pp. 196–97. Jay P. Dolan, pp. 356–57, notes that by the 1920s large numbers of new immigrants had joined existing Catholic parish churches albeit at the lower rungs of influence.

15. Sydney E. Ahlstrom, *A Religious History of the American People* (New Haven, Conn., 1972), pp. 749–804.

16. Winthrop S. Hudson, *Religion in America: An Historical Account of the Development of American Religious Life* (New York, 1965), p. 245.

17. James G. Heller, *As Yesterday When It Is Past: A History of the I. M. Wise Temple, KKBY 1842–1942* (Cincinnati, 1942), p. 134.

18. Steven A. Fox, "On the Road to Unity: The Union of American Hebrew Congregations and American Jewry, 1873–1903," *AJA*, November 1980, pp. 177–78.

19. Kaufman Kohler, "Conference Paper," Pittsburgh Platform, Walter Jacobs (ed.), p. 95.

20. Max Heller, *Jubilee Souvenir of Temple Sinai, 1872–1922* (New Orleans, 1922), pp. 67–69.

21. KKBY Minute Books, President's Report of 1884, at the congregation's archives.

22. John Sutherland, *A City of Homes: Philadelphia Slums and Reformers, 1880–1913*, Ph.D. dissertation, Temple University, 1973, pp. 104–106.

23. Mary Agnes Dougherty, "The Social Gospel According to Phoebe," in Hilah F. Thomas and Rosemary Skinner Keller (eds.) *Women in New Worlds* (Nashville, 1981), pp. 206–13; also see Jay P. Dolan, pp. 328–29, for Catholic examples among Sisters' groups; William McGuire King, "The Role of Auxiliary Ministries in Late Nineteenth-Century Methodism," in Russell E. Richey and Kenneth E. Rowe (eds.), *Rethinking Methodist History* (Nashville, 1985), p. 170.

24. Jay P. Dolan, p. 328; Myron Berman, "A New Spirit on the East Side: The Early History of the Emanu-El Brotherhood, 1903–1920," *AJHQ*, Vol. 54, No. 1, September 1964, p. 61, 68–69, 73; Berman mentions related projects of religious outreach to Eastern European Jews by the national UAHC's "People's Synagogue" in South Philadelphia in cooperation with Keneseth Israel and Roseph Shalom temples, p. 61.

25. Fred Rosenbaum, p. 53; KKBY, Talmud Yelodim Institute, Annual Meeting Report of 1905, Archives at the Isaac Mayer Wise Temple, Cincinnati, Ohio.

26. Gibson Winter, *The Surburban Captivity of the Churches* (New York, 1962), pp. 15–66, which attributes the growth of American Protestant denominations in the 1920s to the expansion of the suburbs and of the middle class, precisely the factors that impacted upon the UAHC, as well as upon the emerging United Synagogue of America, and the Union of Orthodox Jewish Congregations; Jay P. Dolan, pp. 357–58; Deborah Dash Moore, *At Home in America: Second Generation New York Jews* (New York, 1981), pp. 15, 6–24; Robert D. Cross describes this same process for non-Jewish groups of various national-origins (for example,

Lutherans) as well during this same era, see Robert D. Cross (ed.), *The Church and the City* (New York, 1967), "Introduction," p. xxiv; see Milton Gordon, *Assimilation in American Life*, chaps. 2 and 3, especially pp. 51–54 on his notion of "ethclass," a convergence of class and ethnic factors.

27. For information regarding the impact of nativism following World War I, see John Higham, *Strangers in the Land: Patterns of American Nativism, 1860–1925*, pp. 194–330.

28. Martin E. Marty, *Modern American Religion, Volume I: The Irony of It All, 1893–1919* (Chicago, 1986), pp. 208–209.

29. Egal Feldman, *Dual Destinies: The Jewish Encounter With Protestant America* (Chicago, 1990), pp. 152–53.

30. I am indebted to Professor Jonathan D. Sarna for this observation as well as the following reflection: "Clearly, the decline of liberal religion at the end of the nineteenth century and the religious revival in Protestant circles had its analog in American Jewish circles—indeed, the very term revival dates back to the late 1870s, really before mass East European Jewish immigration could have had an influence."

31. *Jewish Ledger* (New Orleans), 30 September 1904, p. 6; CCAR *Yearbook*, Vol. 15, 1905, p. 60; Vol. 17, 1907, pp. 144 ff.
Jewish Ledger (New Orleans), 4 October 1912, p. 4.

32. Fred Rosenbaum, p. 71; Howard Fineshriber, pp. 35–40.

33. William Fineshriber, "The Decay of Theology in Popular Religion," CCAR *Yearbook*, Vol. 30, 1920, pp. 315–16.

34. *American Israelite*, 31 May 1929, p. 4; Cited in Marc Lee Raphael, p. 39.

35. D. Max Eichhorn, "The Student Body—Today and Yesterday" (comparison of 1900 and 1930) in Howard R, Greenstein (ed.), *Turning Point: Zionism and Reform Judaism* (Providence, R.I., 1981), Appendix A, pp. 173–76; *American Israelite*, 15 June 1916.

36. See 1927 survey results published in the *Jewish Layman*, the publication of the National Federation of Temple Brotherhoods; "An Intimate Portrait of the UAHC: A Centennial Documentary," *AJA*, Vol. 25, No. 1, April 1973, p. 32; and see *Reform Judaism in the Large Cities: A Survey* (Cincinnati, 1931), p. 47.

37. Cited in Fred Rosenbaum, pp. 72, 109; Arthur L. Reinhart, *The Voice of the Jewish Laity: A Survey of the Jewish Layman's Religious Attitudes and Practices* (Cincinnati, 1928), pp. 31, 34, 41.

38. Such efforts to attract second-generation, adult offspring of Russian and Polish Jews is assessed in great detail in Deborah Dash Moore, *At Home in America*, describing the emergence of the Jewish community in the Bronx in the 1920s.

39. Cited in Lawrence A. Cremin, p. 74. Church activities included church basketball, library, concerts, lectures, adult classes, women's home mission society, men's club or brotherhood, women's club, Boy Scouts, boys club, Campfire Girls, young people's society, mission study class, dramatic club, orchestra band, church athletic league, and church baseball. H. Paul Douglass, *The St. Louis Survey* (New York, 1924), p. 314.

40. Cited in Fred Rosenbaum, p. 83.

41. Fred Rosenbaum, p. 83.

42. James G. Heller, pp. 193–96.

43. UAHC *Proceedings*, 1900, 1930, 1932.

44. See the summary of H. Paul Douglass's surveys of church patterns in his *The City's Church* (New York, 1929); Jenna Weisman Joselit, "The Middle-Class

American Jewish Woman," in Jack Wertheimer (ed.) *The American Synagogue: A Sanctuary Transformed* (New York, 1987), p. 210.

45. Jenna Weisman Joselit, p. 212; Linda Gordon Kuzmack, *Woman's Cause: The Jewish Woman's Movement in England and the United States, 1881–1933* (Columbus, Ohio, 1990), pp. 172–73, suggests that temple Sisterhoods were also created in order to attract Jews of Eastern European descent to the Reform temple structure in a less threatening fashion.   ·

A description of the suffrage battle is provided by Carl N. Degler, *At Odds: Women and the Family in America from the Revolution to the Present* (New York, 1980), pp. 328–61. This granting of rights by the KKBY Temple in Cincinnati, for example, ultimately occurred in 1922; see James G. Heller, p. 183.

46. Max Heller, pp. 96–100.

47. Cited in Jenna Weisman Joselit, p. 211; James G. Heller, pp. 205–206.

48. Michael A. Meyer, *Response to Modernity*, p. 306; Jay P. Dolan, p. 328.

49. Ronald Sobel, *A History of New York's Temple Emanu-El: The Second Half Century*, Ph.D. dissertation, 1980, New York University, p. 219.

50. H. Paul Douglass, *The City's Church* (New York, 1929), refers to numerous discussions regarding the function of Protestant Men's Clubs or Brotherhoods; *American Israelite*, 22 January 1903, p. 4.

51. Ronald Sobel, p. 216.

52. Cited in Ronald Sobel, p. 291.

53. I. Jordan Kunik, "History of the Men's Club: 1918–1968."

54. Arthur Reinhart, "The National Federation of Temple Brotherhoods," *Universal Jewish Encyclopedia*, Vol. 8, 1942, p. 121; also refer to *American Hebrew* (New York), 26 January 1923, p. 390; 2 May 1924, p. 779; 1 May 1925, p. 805; *American Israelite*, 4 January 1923, p. 4; Michael A. Meyer, p. 306: "Not only did women predominate at services, but nationally the Sisterhoods outnumbered the Brotherhoods in chapters and individual membership by more than three to one." Leon A. Jick, "The Reform Synagogue," in Jack Wertheimer (ed.), *The American Synagogue: A Sanctuary Transformed* (New York, 1987), p. 97.

55. Paula S. Fass, *The Damned and the Beautiful: American Youth in the 1920s* (New York, 1977), pp. 13–14.

56. William McGuire King, "The Role of Auxiliary Ministries in Late Nineteenth-Century Methodism," in Russell E. Richey and Kenneth E. Rowe (eds.), *Rethinking Methodist History* (Nashville, 1985), p. 170; *Jewish Ledger* (New Orleans), 15 March 1912, p. 14.

57. *American Israelite*, 20 April 1916, p. 4.

58. Fred Rosenbaum, p. 90; Max Heller, p. 119.

59. Jacob D. Schwartz, "The Synagogue in Action: In Its Rabbinical and Social Phases," p. 9., results of the 1932/1933 national survey, available in the American Jewish Archives.

60. Deborah Dash Moore, *B'nai Brith and the Challenge of Ethnic Leadership* (Albany, N.Y., 1981), pp. 141–42.

61. Arthur L. Reinhart, *The Voice of the Jewish Laity: A Survey of the Jewish Layman's Religious Attitudes and Practices* (New York, 1928), p. 89.

62. James G. Heller, pp. 212-13; Jacob D. Schwartz, UAHC "Survey of Congregations," 1932/1933, pp. 42–44, American Jewish Archives.

63. Jay P. Dolan, pp. 297–300; Melvin I. Urofsky, *A Voice That Spoke For Justice: The Life and Times of Stephen S. Wise* (Albany, N.Y., 1982) chap. 9; Marc Lee Raphael, *Abba Hillel Silver: A Profile in American Judaism* (New York, 1989), pp.

25–31; Max Heller, pp. 92, 115; Fred Rosenbaum, pp. 74–76. The majority of the CCAR was dominated by anti-Zionism until the 1930s.

64. Gary P. Zola, "Reform Judaism's Pioneer Zionist: Maximilian Heller," *AJH*, Vol. 73, No. 4, June 1984, pp. 376–78; *Reform Judaism in the Large Cities: A Survey (conducted during 1930)*, p. 48; D. Max Eichhorn, "The Student Body—Today and Tomorrow (the results of a comparative study of the HUC student bodies of 1900 and 1930) in Howard R. Greenstein, *Turning Point: Zionism and Reform Judaism* (Providence, R.I., 1981), Appendix, p. 175; Anti-Zionism remained strong and vocal through World War II among Reform rabbis, producing the American Council for Judaism in 1942. Many Reform lay leaders remained passionate anti-Zionists until the Six-Day War of 1967.

65. J. D. Schwartz UAHC survey of 1932/1933, entitled "The Synagogue in Action: In Its Rabbinical and Social Phase," p. 4, American Jewish Archives.

66. *American Israelite*, 4 January 1923, p. 4.

67. *American Israelite*, 22 April 1926, p. 4; *Jewish Ledger* (New Orleans), 22 November 1929, p. 4, 4 July 1930, p. 4.

68. *Jewish Exponent* (Philadelphia), 4 June 1926, p. 4.

69. KKBY Archives, 1929 Annual Report of the President.

70. KKBY *Yearbook*, 1929/1930. Report of the Rabbi, pp. 13–14.

71. KKBY *Yearbook*, 1929/30, Report of the Rabbi, pp. 13–14.

72. UAHC *Proceedings* 1910–1915 offer references to these pioneering individuals.

73. Jenna Weisman Joselit, "Modern Orthodox Jews and the Ordeal of Civility," *AJH*, Vol. 74, No. 2, December 1984, p. 139.

74. Jenna Weisman Joselit, *New York's Jewish Jews: The Orthodox Community in the Interwar Years* (Bloomington, Ind.), pp. 139–40, 65.

75. Deborah Dash Moore, "A Synagogue Center Grows in Brooklyn," in Jack Wertheimer (ed.), *The American Synagogue: A Sanctuary Transformed*, pp. 303, 301.

76. Michael A. Meyer, pp. 297–98.

77. Deborah Dash Moore, *At Home In America: Second Generation New York Jews* (New York, 1981), p. 138.

78. Deborah Dash Moore, *At Home in America*, p. 134.

79. Jeffrey S. Gurock, "The Orthodox Synagogue," in Jack Wertheimer (ed.), *The American Synagogue: A Sanctuary Transformed*, pp. 62–63; Henry L. Feingold, *The Jewish People in America, Vol. IV: A Time for Searching: Entering the Mainstream, 1920–1945* (Baltimore, Md., 1992), p. 105.

80. See chapter 3 and the innovations of the Reform temples in the 1880s in order to retain the loyalties of the adult offspring of temple founders.

Examples of this institutional borrowing include the following: The (Reform) National Federation of Temple Sisterhoods established in 1913 offered a context for the creation in 1918 of the National Women's League for Conservative Judaism. Similarly, the 1921 establishment of its Young People's League for Conservative synagogue youth groups offered a precedent for the ultimate formation of the Reform movement young adult initiatives of the late 1920s. At the same time, both the Reform and Conservative movements were influenced by OU programming for Jews of East European descent, such as the Jewish Endeavor Society (JES) of 1901 and the Young Israel and Institutional Synagogue movements (JES's successors of the 1910s and 1920s); see Jeffrey S. Gurock, "The Orthodox Synagogue," in Jack Wertheimer (ed.), *The American Synagogue: A Sanctuary Transformed* (New York, 1988), pp. 55–57; Arthur L. Reinhart, *The Voice of the Laity: A Survey of the Jewish Layman's Religious Attitudes and Practices*, NFTB, 1928, p. 89.

81. Henry L. Feingold, p. 96.

82. H. S. Linfield, "Jewish Congregations in the U.S. of A.: Preliminary Statement," *American Jewish Year Book*, Vol. 30 1928–1929, pp. 200 ff; Michael A Meyer, p. 304.

6. American Corporate Culture Prevails

1. Arthur C. Bining and Thomas C. Cochran, *The Rise of American Economic Life* (New York, 1964), p. 498; Walter LeFeber, *The New Empire: An Interpretation of American Expansion, 1860–1898* (Ithaca, N.Y.), 1963), chaps. 5–8; Robert Handy, *A Christian America: Protestant Hopes and Historical Reality* (New York, 1971), p. 117–18 and the remainder of chap. 5; also see William T. Stead, *The Americanization of the World: The Trend of the Twentieth Century* (London, 1902), pp. 102–104, which points out examples of American religious innovations for the first time passing from the United States to Europe rather than vice versa.

2. Mira Wilkins, p. 72, indicates that a major reason for the expansion of American trade abroad is related to the aftermath of the 1893–1897 economic depression and instability within the United States. As a consequence, those American businesses that survived did so on the basis of an "economy of scale," for example, making profit by dramatically increasing their scope and functions at home and abroad.

Craig Dykstra and James Hudnut-Beumler, "The National Organizational Structures of Protestant Denominations: An Invitation to a Conversation," in Milton J. Coalter, John M. Mulder, and Louis B. Weeks (eds.) *The Organizational Revolution: Presbyterians and American Denominationalism* (Louisville, Ky., 1992), pp. 312–18.

3. Walter LeFeber and Richard Polenberg, *The American Century: A History of the United States Since the 1890's* (New York, 1975), p. 4; James Oliver Robertson, *American Myth, American Reality* (New York, 1980), pp. 176–77, 183.

4. Mira Wilkins, *The Emergence of Multinational Enterprise: American Business Abroad from the Colonial Era to 1914* (Cambridge, Mass., 1970), p. 70.

5. Glenn Porter, *The Rise of Big Business, 1860–1910* (Arlington Heights, Ill., 1973), pp. 4–22, for a review of these techniques and of the scholarly literature that assesses them.

6. Raymond Callahan, p. 1; also see Richard Hofstadter, *The Age of Reform* (New York, 1955), pp. 149–53, indicating the low status of clergy and of religion in general at the turn of the century; see Oliver Zunz, *Making America Corporate, 1870–1920* (Chicago, 1990), especially his review of existing literature in this field of study contained in the Introduction; Ben Primer, *Protestants and American Business Methods* (UMI Research Press, 1979), p. 55.

7. Ben Primer, *Protestants and American Business Methods*, devotes the second half of his study to tracing these trends within the major American Protestant denominations; William T. Stead, p. 104, points to Christian Endeavor Societies, model programs of such Church Extension, as prime examples of American religious innovations that were being transported to Europe, in contrast with the nineteenth-century reverse pattern of cultural transference.

8. Raymond E. Callahan, pp. 25–30, 56–57.

9. Raymond E. Callahan, pp. 43, 23.

10. Ralph Henry Gabriel, *The Course of American Democratic Thought* (New York, 1940), p. 336.

11. Daniel J. Elazar, p. 163, provides a chart of the date and city for each establishment of a Jewish Federation on a city-wide basis from 1895 to 1934.

12. Boris D. Bogin, *Jewish Philanthropy: An Exposition of Principles and Methods of Jewish Social Service in the United States* (New York, 1917), p. 49.

13. *Jewish Ledger*, 15 April 1910, p. 27, an open letter from George Zepin of the UAHC identifying such efficiency as a primary goal within the Union; *American Israelite*, 13 January 1916; UAHC *Proceedings*, Vol. 51, pp. 9606 ff.

14. Seftin Temkin, "Reform Judaism in America," *AJYB*, 1973, pp. 43–44; UAHC *Annual Report*, 1890, Financial Statement for the fiscal year ending 31 May 1890; Steven A. Fox, pp. 164–65.

15. Cincinnati in 1896, and Philadelphia in 1901; see Daniel J. Elazar, p. 163; *American Jewish Yearbook*, 1904, Directory of Local Organizations, p. 229; for further details see National Conference of Jewish Charities, *Proceedings*, 1902–1906.

16. Jonathan D. Sarna, "'A Sort of Paradise for the Hebrews': The Lofty Vision of Cincinnati Jews," in Henry D. Shapiro and Jonathan D. Sarna (eds.), *Ethnic Diversity and Civic Identity: Patterns of Conflict and Cohesion in Cincinnati since 1820* (Chicago, 1992), p. 144.

17. Charles S. Bernheimer, *The Russian Jew in the United States* (Philadelphia, 1905), p. 82.

18. *American Israelite*, 4 January 1901, p. 4. It is important to keep in mind that this was the heyday of the American business notion of the "stewardship of wealth," in which the "captains of industry," and local businessmen emulating these role models subscribed to the concept that successful entrepreneurs should take a leadership role in financing nonprofit educational, cultural, and religious institutions of the community-at-large; Ben Primer, p. 95.

19. Ben Primer, pp. 103–104.

20. KKBY (Cincinnati) Minute Book, 25 January 1924, which mentions the efforts of K.K. B'nai Yeshurun to implement this "uniform system of financing." Ben Primer, pp. 94–103.

21. Robert H. Bremner, *American Philanthropy* (Chicago, 1960), pp. 140–41.

22. Ben Primer, p. 115.

23. UAHC *Annual Report*, 1913 and 1931, providing the fiscal statements for 1912 and 1930; Oscar Handlin, *A Continuing Task: The American Jewish Joint Distribution Committee, 1914–1964* (New York, 1964), pp. 19–32; Daniel J. Elazar, *The Organizational Dynamics of American Jewry* (Philadelphia, 1976), pp. 180–94.

24. Marc Lee Raphael, "The Origins of Organized National Jewish Philanthropy in the United States, 1914–1939," in Moses Rischin (ed.), *The Jews of North America* (Detroit, 1987), p. 217.

25. KKBY *Yearbook*, 1927, included a series of purchased memorials and dedications with regard to the construction and funding of their new building.

26. KKBY (Cincinnati) Annual *Yearbook*, 1928, "Annual Report of the President of KKBY for Year 1928," p. 5, available at the Isaac Mayer Wise Temple Archives in Cincinnati.

27. *American Israelite*, 17 August 1899, p. 4, pointing out the successful "fair share" dues program of tiny and isolated Anshe Emeth of Peoria, Ill.

28. KKBY *Yearbook*, 1928, p. 17; also see the *American Israelite*, 17 August 1899,

p. 4, which indicated that such concepts were being considered, if not widely implemented, almost thirty years earlier.

29. UAHC *Proceedings*, January 1902, pp. 4386–87.

30. UAHC *Proceedings*, February 1903, pp. 4692–93.

31. CCAR *Yearbook*, 1903, pp. 27–28; discussion of a movement-wide "membership card" is provided in the UAHC *Proceedings*, Vol. 49, p. 9332.

32. UAHC *PROCEEDINGS*, February 1903, pp. 4710–13.

33. A prime example of the shortcomings of these ambitious plans was the failure of the UAHC's efforts on campuses. As Michael A. Meyer has assessed: "By 1923 . . . [with] about 23,000 Jewish [students on campus] . . . the UAHC was supporting twenty student congregations, but they languished for lack of resident professional guidance . . . B'nai Brith . . . Hillel Fundations soon drove the sporadic Reform endeavors to the sidelines" (Michael A. Meyer, p. 307).

34. Oliver Zunz, pp. 4, 6, 9, 65; Ben Primer, pp. 68–69; Lee K. Frankel, Jacob Billikopf, and other executives pioneered in management techniques for the United Hebrew Charities field of service; see Herman D. Stein, "Jewish Social Work in the United States," in Joseph L. Blau, et al., *The Characteristics of American Jews* (New York, 1965), pp. 185–94.

35. John Simons (ed.), *Who's Who in American Jewry* (New York, 1938), p. 1170.

36. UAHC *Proceedings*, March 1905, p. 5277; Aaron I. Abell, *The Urban Impact on American Protestantism, 1865–1900* (New York, 1962), p. 168.

37. Naomi Cohen, *Not Free To Desist* (Philadelphia, 1972), pp. 3–36.

38. George Zepin, "Jewish Religious Conditions in Scattered Communities," manuscript available at American Jewish Archives in Cincinnati, Box No. 2486, George Zepin; UAHC *Proceedings*, January 1906, p. 5478.

39. UAHC *Proceedings*, March 1905, pp. 5272 ff; January 1906, pp. 5477–79; March 1907, pp. 5559 ff, pp. 5753–55.

40. Raymond E. Callahan, p. 42; *The Churchman*, 15 October 1910, p. 561.

41. *Jewish Ledger (New Orleans)*, 15 April 1910, p. 27.

42. George Zepin, Annual Report of the Director of Synagogue and School Extension," 1910, pp. 1–2, American Jewish Archives, Box No. 1158, George Zepin.

43. Discussion of similar trends for serving Christians within institutions and other isolated settings is described in Robert S. Michaelsen, "The Protestant Ministry in America: 1850 to the Present," in H. R. Niebuhr (ed.), *The Ministry in Historical Perspective*, p. 271.

44. UAHC *Proceedings*, December 1916, p. 8018.

45. UAHC *Proceedings*, December 1916, p. 8019.

46. All of this material regarding the four rabbis can be found in George Zepin's Annual Report, UAHC *Proceedings*, December 1916, pp. 8020–68; Rabbi Martin Meyer's special commitment to this work is described in Fred Rosenbaum, *Architects of Reform*, pp. 76–78.

47. David M. Potter, *People of Plenty: Economic Abundance and the American Character* (Chicago, 1966), p. 169.

48. George Zepin, 1910 Annual Report, American Jewish Archives, Box No. 1158, George Zepin, pp. 3–4; KI Annual *Yearbook* 1896, p. 14; James G. Heller, p. 181; Fred Rosenbaum, p. 98.

49. *Jewish Ledger* (New Orleans), 10 January 1913, p. 23.

50. William T. Stead, pp. 103–104, credits American Protestantism for

creating and exporting this Christian Endeavor concept; for further details regarding Christian Endeavor work, see Aaron I. Abell, pp. 211–15.

JTS was founded in 1886 in response to the Pittsburgh Platform. JTS's failure to meet the needs of Yiddish-speaking immigrants led to its reorganization in 1901 by Reform Jews like Jacob Schiff, who engaged Solomon Schechter from Cambridge to secure a Yiddish-speaking faculty.

Modeled after the Christian Endeavor Societies popular among urban Protestants in this period, see Robert S. Michaelson, "The Protestant Ministry in America: 1850 to the Present," in H. R. Niebuhr (ed.), p. 265. The creation of Orthodox Jewish Endeavor Societies in New York City is discussed by Jeffrey S. Gurock, *The Men and Women of Yeshiva: Higher Education, Orthodoxy, and American Judaism* (New York, 1988), pp. 27–32.

51. Michael A. Meyer, p. 293.

52. George Zepin, 1910 Annual Report, pp. 1–2.

53. UAHC *Proceedings*, December 1916, p. 8042.

54. CCAR *Yearbook*, Vol. 14, 1904, pp. 64 ff; Vol. 15, 1905, pp. 199 ff and 264 ff.

55. *Jewish Ledger* (New Orleans), 10 January 1913, p. 23.

56. Herbert Parzen, *Architects of Conservative Judaism* (New York, 1964), pp. 63–66, describes some of aspects of Reform temple life which first and second generation Eastern Europeans found attractive.

57. Aaron I. Abell, pp. 188–93, describes the rise of the federation concept within Protestant circles from 1895 onward; Lawrence A. Cremin, *American Education: The Metropolitan Experience, 1876–1980* (New York, 1988), pp. 85–86.

Major cities in which such Jewish federations arose within this era are Boston (1895), Cincinnati (1896), Detroit (1899), Chicago, (1900), Philadelphia (1901), Cleveland (1903), Atlanta (1905), San Francisco (1910), Dallas (1911), Los Angeles (1912), New Orleans (1913), New York City (1917, replacing the Kehillah), Baltimore (1920). A complete list including smaller cities is available in Daniel J. Elazar, *The Organizational Dynamics of American Jewry* (Philadelphia, 1976), p. 163.

58. Roy Lubove, *The Professional Altruist: The Emergence of Social Work as a Career, 1880–1930* (New York, 1965), p. 183, and see the remainder of chap. 7; Charlotte Baum, Paula Hyman, and Sonya Michel, *The Jewish Woman in America* (New York, 1976), pp. 46–53.

The WCTU was established in 1874; see William T. Stead, pp. 103–104; Carl Degler, *At Odds: Women and the Family in America from the Revolution to the Present* (New York, 1980), p. 317.

59. UAHC *Proceedings*, 1913 pp. 7081–82.

60. UAHC *Proceedings*, January 1915, pp. 7680 ff; October 1913, pp. 7405–7407.

61. *American Israelite*, 4 January 1923, p. 4.

62. Emory Stevens Bucke et al. (eds.), *The History of American Methodism* Vol. 3 (Nashville, 1964), pp. 152–57.

CCAR *Yearbook*, 1910, p. 330; the larger societal educational trend in this direction is evaluated in great detail by Raymond E. Callahan, pp. 95–170; CCAR *Yearbook*, 1914, pp. 312 ff ("Symposium on Recent Progress in Religious Education").

63. Meir Ben-Horin, "From the Turn of the Century to the Late Thirties," in Judah Pilch (ed.), *A History of Jewish Education in America* (New York, 1969), pp. 72–73, 76.

64. Michael A. Meyer, *Response to Modernity*, p. 286; Meir Ben-Horin, p. 84.

65. Emory Stevens Bucke et al., p. 154.

66. Michael A. Meyer, p. 301.

67. H. Paul Douglass, *The City's Church* (New York, 1929), summarizes much of the research that Douglass conducted and published in the early 1920s, including discussions regarding Young People's Societies.

Established in 1921, USYPL attracted 119 local synagogue young adult groups by the end of the decade; see Pamela Nadell, pp. 332–33.

NFTS *Proceedings*, 18 January 1927, cited in Robert F. Goldman's unpublished paper, "The History of the National Federation of Temple Youth," American Jewish Archives, Cincinnati, p. 3.

68. Robert F. Goldman paper, p. 4.

69. Michael Meyer, *Response to Modernity*, pp. 306–307.

70. Marc Lee Raphael, *Abba Hillel Silver: A Profile in American Judaism* (New York, 1989), p. 22, describes how in 1917 when Rabbi Silver arrived in Cleveland, his Reform Temple included "the finest elements of wealthy and cultured Jewish Cleveland."

Melvin I. Urofsky, *A Voice That Spoke For Justice: The Life and Times of Stephen S. Wise* (Albany, N.Y., 1982), p. 64, describes the appeal of Wise's eloquent and sophisticated sermons for the children of the immigrants.

71. Herbert Parzen, p. 65.

72. Cited in Abraham J. Karp, "The Conservative Rabbi—Dissatisfied But Not Unhappy," *American Jewish Archives*, November 1983 p. 206.

73. Abraham J. Karp, "The Conservative Rabbi—Dissatisfied But Not Unhappy," p. 209; Herbert Rosenblum, "Ideology and Compromise: The Evolution of the United Synagogue Constitutional Preamble," *JSS*, Vol. 35, 1973, pp. 30–31.

74. Herbert Rosenblum, "The United Synagogue of America," Ph.D. dissertation, Brandeis University, 1970, p. 150.

75. Herbert Rosenblum, p. 27. This "Conservative Union" for non-Reform American Jews was not intended to be modeled on the British United Synagogue that included only a very limited programmatic and "extension services" dimension; United Synagogue of America, *Report of the Annual Convention*, 1913, p. 22.

76. Jeffrey S. Gurock, "The Orthodox Synagogue," in Jack Wertheimer (ed.), *The American Synagogue: A Sanctuary Transformed* (New York, 1987), p. 80, note 85.

77. Marshall Sklare, *Conservative Judaism: An American Religious Movement* (New York, 1955), p. 75. Michael Stanislawski also has suggested that the appeal of Conservative Judaism for Jews of Russian and Polish descent was related to "an innate East European approach to the reform of Judaism that was stymied at home [in Europe] by social reality but realizable in conditions of political freedom and cultural pluralism [in American]"; see Michael Stanislawski, *For Whom Do I Toil? Judah Leib Gordon and the Crisis of Russian Jewry* (New York, 1988), p. 229.

78. Jack Wertheimer, "The Conservative Synagogue," in Jack Wertheimer (ed.), *The American Synagogue: A Sanctuary Transformed* (New York, 1987), p. 118.

79. Jenna Weisman Joselit, *New York's Jewish Jews: The Orthodox Community in the Interwar Years* (Bloomington, Ind., 1990), pp. 6, 7; Jeffrey S. Gurock, "The Orthodox Synagogue," in Jack Wertheimer (ed.), *The American Synagogue: A Sanctuary Transformed* (New York, 1987), p. 63.

80. Jeffrey S. Gurock, "The Orthodox Synagogue," p. 60.

Conclusion

1. Michael A. Meyer, *Response to Modernity: A History of the Reform Movement in Judaism* (New York, 1988), p. ix.

2. E. Brooks Holifield, "Review of Recent Studies of the American Synagogue," *Religious Studies Review*, Vol. 17, No. 3, July 1991, p. 201.

3. Marjorie Hyler, "How Many Ways Can You Look at a Congregation?," *Progressions: A Lilly Endowment Occasional Report*, Vol. 3, Issue 1, January 1991, p. 6.

4. An example of acculturation as a theme in evaluating a period of Jewish history is Elias Bickerman, *From Ezra to the Last of the Maccabees* (New York, 1962), p. 181, in which Bickerman concludes that "ideas and concepts of the new age and the new culture were taken over without thereby surrendering spiritual values."

5. Gerson D. Cohen, *The Blessing of Assimilation in Jewish History* (Boston, 1966), p. 7.

6. A similar qualification is offered by Jay P. Dolan in his study of American Catholic revivalism in the nineteenth century, in the context of its similarities to American Protestant initiatives; see Jay P. Dolan, *Catholic Revivalism: The American Experience, 1830–1900* (South Bend, Ind., 1978), p. 188.

7. Michael A. Meyer, p. 304. Meyer points out that as early as 1924 Rabbi Abram Simon, President of the CCAR, advocated the creation of a Synagogue Council; also see original constitution and by-laws of the Synagogue Council of America, available at the American Jewish Archives in Cincinnati; Michael A. Meyer, p. 298.

8. Michael A. Meyer, p. 297. Meyer points out that Reform rabbis often lamented about this growing alienation.

Michael A. Meyer, *Hebrew Union College-Jewish Institute of Religion*, (Cincinnati, 1976), p. 119; also see Lawrence Hoffman, *Beyond the Text: A Holistic Approach to Liturgy* (Bloomington, Ind., 1987), pp. 127–28. Hoffman asserts that the affiliation drive among the second generation had been spent, and the third generation would only come to the fore as a major portion of temple membership during the 1950s, the next major period of UAHC growth.

Union of American Hebrew Congregations *Proceedings*, 1929, p. 27; United Synagogue of America, *Proceedings*, 1928, p. 21. For a discussion regarding the even greater financial difficulties of the Orthodox Union, see UOJCA, *33rd Annual Convention*, July 1933, p. 17.

United Synagogue Recorder, October 1928, pp. 4–5.

9. The first layman to be president of the United Synagogue was S. Herbert Golden in 1928; see Abraham J. Karp, *A History of the United Synagogue of America 1913–1963* (New York, 1964), p. 59.

Bernard Martin, "Conservative Judaism and Reconstructionism," in Bernard Martin (ed.), *Movements and Issues in American Judaism: An Analysis and Sourcebook of Developments Since 1945* (Westport, Conn., 1978), pp. 113–14.

By 1937 the membership of the United Synagogue had surpassed that of the UAHC. The 1937 edition of the *American Jewish Year Book* lists 290 Reform temples representing 50,000 families affiliated with the Union, while 250 synagogues with 75,000 families were associated with the United Synagogue of America; Robert Gordis, *The Jew Faces A New World* (New York, 1941), p. 199.

Bibliography

Archival Sources

American Jewish Archives in Cincinnati, Ohio

Archival Collection of the Talmud Yelodim Institute of Congregation K.K. B'nai Yeshurun of Cincinnati.
Hebrew Union Agricultural Society Minutes, 1882–1884.
Hebrew Sabbath School Union Proceedings, 1897–1903.
Sangerman, Jay J. "The Jewish Chautauqua Society, 1893–1939."
George Zepin Papers.
Jacob D. Schwartz Papers.
Robert F. Goldman (NFTB leader) Papers.
Board of Delegates of American Israelites, Census Cards, 1878.

American Jewish Historical Society Archives in Waltham, Massachusetts

Papers of the Board of Delegates of American Israelites.
Census of the Jews of the United States, 1878, conducted by the Board of Delegates of American Israelites.

Dropsie College Archives in Philadelphia, Pennsylvania

Isaac Leeser Papers.

Individual Congregational Archives

Minute Books and Archival Collection of Congregation Keneseth Israel in Philadelphia, Pennsylvania.
Minute Books and Archival Collection of Congregation K.K. B'nai Yeshurun in Cincinnati, Ohio.
Minute Books and Archival Materials of Temple Sinai of New Orleans, Louisiana.

New York Public Library

City Directories: Cincinnati (1850), Philadelphia (1850), San Francisco (1860), and New Orleans (1870).

Philadelphia Social History Project at the University of Pennsylvania

Finklestein, James. "The German Jewish Immigrants to Philadelphia, 1850–1880," 1984.

Western Jewish Historical Society Archives in Berkeley, California

Minute Books and Archival Collection of Temple Emanu-El of San Francisco.

Newspapers

American Israelite (Cincinnati, Ohio), 1873–1930
Emanu-El (San Francisco), 1895–1930
Jewish Exponent (Philadelphia), 1887–1930
Jewish Ledger (New Orleans), 1890–1930
Occident, 1843–1850

United States Census Data

1850 U.S. Census for Philadelphia
1850 U.S. Census for Cincinnati
1860 U.S. Census for San Francisco
1870 U.S. Census for New Orleans
1880 U.S. National Census
1900 U.S. Census for Philadelphia
1900 U.S. Census for Cincinnati
1900 U.S. Census for San Francisco
1900 U.S. Census for New Orleans
1900 U.S. National Census
Historical Statistics of the United States: Colonial Times to 1970, Part I. U.S. Department of Commerce, 1970.
Edwards, Alba. *Population: Comparative Occupational Statistics for the United States, 1870–1940.* U.S. Bureau of the Census, 1943.
Engelman, Uriah Zevi. "Jewish Statistics in the U.S. Census of Religious Bodies (1850–1936)." *Jewish Social Studies* (1947).
Sulzberger, David. "The Growth of American Jewish Population." *Proceedings of the American Jewish Historical Society*, 1898.

Reports and Yearbooks

Board of Delegates of American Israelites *Proceedings*, 1859–1878
CCAR *Yearbook*, 1890–1930
CCAR *Bulletin*, 1920–1930
UAHC *Proceedings*, 1873–1930, including the Proceedings of the HUC (1875–1930)
Proceedings of the NFTS (1913–1930)
Proceedings of the NFTB (1923–1930)
Jewish Ministers Association *Proceedings*, 1885–1887
Conference of Rabbis of Southern Congregations *Proceedings*, 1885–1887
United Synagogue of America *Annual Reports*, 1913–1930

Proceedings of the Rabbinical Assembly, 1919–1930
Rabbinical Literary Association *Proceedings*, 1881–1884
American Jewish Yearbook, 1899–1930
American Jewish Annual, 1880–1889
The Union (UAHC) *Bulletin*, 1911–1923
Union (UAHC) *Tidings*, 1919–1930
The Union (Home Study Magazine of UAHC), 1919–1922
Young Israel (Home Study Magazine of UAHC), 1922–1930
Jewish Chautauqua Society *Annual Reports*, 1893–1930
Hebrew Sabbath School Union *Annual Reports*, 1886–1900
National Council of Jewish Women *Annual Reports*, 1893–1900
Recent Social Trends in the United States: Report of the President's Committee on Social Trends, New York, 1933.
HUC Monthly, 1913–1930.
The Jewish Layman, 1926–1930.
Hebrew Union College *Jubilee Volume* (1875–1925)
Reform Judaism: Essays by Hebrew Union College Alumni, 1949.

Analyses of Data

Franzblau, Abraham N. "Is There An Oversupply of Rabbis?" *HUC Monthly* (1 June 1932).
Franzblau, Abraham N. "A Quarter Century of Rabbinic Training," 1929 (at the American Jewish Archives).
Reinhart, Arthur L., *The Voice of the Jewish Laity: A Survey of the Jewish Layman's Religious Attitudes and Practices*. UAHC. Cincinnati, 1928.
Schwartz, Jacob D. *The Synagogue in Action: In Its Rabbinical and Social Phrases*. 1932/1933 survey by UAHC.
Schwartz, Jacob D. *Survey of Congregations*. 1932/1933 survey by UAHC. Cincinnati, 1931.
UAHC. *Reform Judaism in the Large Cities: A Survey Conducted During 1930*. Cincinnati, 1931.
UAHC. *Statistics of the Jews of the United States*. Philadelphia, 1880.

Congregational Histories

Fineshriber, Howard. *Reform Congregation Keneseth Israel—Its First 100 Years, 1847–1947*. Philadelphia, 1950.
Heller, James G. *As Yesterday When It Is Past: A History of the Isaac M. Wise Temple K. K. B'nai Yeshurun, 1842–1942*. Cincinnati, 1942.
Heller, Max. *Jubilee Souvenir of Temple Sinai, 1872–1922*. New Orleans, 1922.
Kahan, Edgar. "The Saga of the First Fifty Years of Congregation Emanu-El." *Western Jewish Historical Society Quarterly* (April 1971).
Korros, Alexandra Shecket, and Jonathan D. Sarna. *American Synagogue History: A Bibliography and State-of-the-Field Survey*. New York, 1988.
Rosenbaum, Fred. *Architects of Reform: Congregational and Communal Leadership, Emanu-El of San Francisco, 1849–1980*. Berkeley, Ca., 1980.
Sobel, Ronald. *A History of New York's Temple Emanu-El: The Second Half Century*. Ph.D. dissertation. New York University, 1980.
Voorsanger, Jacob. *The Chronicles of Emanu-El*. San Francisco, 1900.

Wertheimer, Jack (ed.). *The American Synagogue: A Sanctuary Transformed.* New York, 1988.
Various other congregational histories among those listed in the *American Jewish Historical Quarterly* (December 1973): 126 ff.

Other Primary Sources

Bogen, Boris D. *Jewish Philanthropy: An Exposition of Principles and Methods of Jewish Social Service in the United States.* New York, 1917.
Hirsch, Emil. *My Religion.* 1925.
Philipson, David. *My Life As An American Jew.* Cincinnati, 1941.
Stead, William T. *The Americanization of the World: The Trend of the Twentieth Century.* London, 1902.
Stelzel, Charles. *Christianity's Storm Center: A Study of the Modern City.* 1907.
———. "The Institutional Church, 1907." In *The Church and the City*, edited by Robert D. Cross. New York, 1967.
de Tocqueville, Alexis. *Democracy in America.* 1833.
Wise, Isaac Mayer. *Reminiscences.* Cincinnati, 1901.

Secondary Sources

Abell, Aaron I. *The Urban Impact on American Protestantism, 1865–1900.* New York, 1962.
Adler, Cyrus and Margalith. *With Firmness in the Right.* New York, 1946.
Ahlstrom, Sydney E. *A Religious History of the American People.* New Haven, 1973.
Albert, Phyllis Cohen. *The Modernization of French Jewry: Consistory and Community in the Nineteenth Century.* Waltham, MA, 1977.
Albright, Raymond W. *History of the Protestant Episcopal Church.* New York, 1964.
Altmann, Alexander. "The New Style of Preaching in Nineteenth Century German Jewry." In *Essays in Jewish Intellectual History*, edited by Alexander Altmann. Waltham, Mass., 1977.
Ashkenazi, Elliot. *The Business of Jews in Louisiana, 1840–1870.* Tuscaloosa, Ala., 1988.
Barker, Leo V. *Lay Leadership in the Protestant Churches.* New York, 1934.
Bauer, Yehuda. *My Brother's Keeper: A History of the American Jewish Joint Distribution Committee, 1929–1939.* Philadelphia, 1974.
Baum, Charlotte, Paula Hyman, and Sonya Michel. *The Jewish Woman in America.* New York, 1976.
Beifield, Martin J. "Joseph Krauskopf." Rabbinical thesis. Hebrew Union College, 1975.
———. "Joseph Krauskopf and Zionism: Partners in Change." *American Jewish History* 75, no. 1 (September 1985).
Ben-Horin, Meir. "From the Turn of the Century to the Late Thirties." In *A History of Jewish Education in America*, edited by Judah Pilch. New York, 1969.
Berger, Peter. *The Sacred Canopy.* New York, 1969.
Berman, Myron. "A New Spirit on the East Side: The Early History of the Emanu-El Brotherhood, 1903–1920." *American Jewish Historical Quarterly* 54, no. 1 (September 1964).
Bernheimer, Charles S. *The Russian Jew in the United States.* Philadelphia, 1905.

Bernstein, Louis. *Challenge and Mission: The Emergence of the English-Speaking Orthodox Rabbinate*. New York, 1982.

———. "Generational Conflict in American Orthodoxy: The Early Years of the Rabbinical Council of America." *American Jewish History* 69, no. 2 (December 1969).

Bernstein, Seth. "The Economic Life of the Jews in San Francisco During the 1960s as Reflected in the City Directories." *American Jewish Archives* (April 1975).

Bining, Arthur C., and Cochran, Thomas C. *The Rise of American Economic Life*. New York, 1964.

Blau, Joseph. *Modern Varieties of Judaism*. New York, 1966.

———. "The Spiritual Life of American Jewry." In *The Characteristics of American Jews*, edited by Joseph Blau, et al. New York, 1965.

Bledstein, Burton J. *The Culture of Professionalism: The Middle Class and the Development of Higher Education in America*. New York, 1976.

Bode, Carl. *American Lyceum*. New York, 1953.

Bonner, Thomas N. *American Doctors and German Universities: A Chapter in International Intellectual Relations, 1870–1914*. Omaha, Neb., 1963.

Borne, Carl. "Early American Preaching." *Historia Judaica* 15 (1953).

Bremner, Robert H. *American Philanthropy*. Chicago, 1960.

Brickner, Barnett R. "The Jewish Community of Cincinnati, History and Description, 1817–1933." Ph.D. dissertation. University of Cincinnati, 1933.

Brown, Richard D. "Modernization: A Victorian Climax." In *Victorian America*, edited by Daniel Walker Howe. Philadelphia, 1976.

Buell, Lawrence. "The Unitarian Movement and the Art of Preaching in Nineteenth Century America." *American Quarterly*. 24, no. 2 (May 1972).

Burns, Michael. "The Rural Exodus of Alsatian Jews, 1791–1848." In *Living With Anti-Semitism: Modern Jewish Responses*, edited by Yehuda Reinharz. Hanover, N. H., 1987.

Calhoun, Daniel H. *Professional Lives in America*. Cambridge, Mass., 1965.

Callahan, Raymond E. *Education and the Cult of Efficiency: A Study of the Social Forces That Have Shaped the Administration of the Public Schools*. Chicago, 1962.

Carr-Saunders, Alexander. *The Professions*. New York, 1933.

Chafe, William H. *The American Woman: Her Changing Social, Economic and Political Roles, 1920–1970*. New York, 1972.

Chambrun, Clara. *Cincinnati: Story of the Queen City*. New York, 1939.

Cohen, Naomi W. *A Dual Heritage: The Public Career of Oscar S. Straus*. Philadelphia, 1969.

———. *Encounter With Emancipation: The German Jews in the United States, 1830–1914*. Philadelphia, 1984.

———. *Jews in Christian America: The Pursuit of Religious Equality*. New York, 1992.

———. *Not Free To Desist: The American Jewish Committee*. Philadelphia, 1972.

Cohon, Samuel. "Kaufman Kohler." In *Great Jewish Thinkers of the Twentieth Century*, edited by Simon Noveck. Washington, D.C., 1963.

———. "The History of the Hebrew Union College." *American Jewish Historical Society* (September 1950).

Cohn, Bernard N. "Early German Preaching in America." *Historia Judaica* 15 (1953).

Cole, Charles C. *The Social Ideas of the Northern Evangelicals, 1825–1860.* New York, 1954.

Cooke, George Willis, *Unitarianism in America: A History of its Origin and Development.* Boston, 1902.

Cremin, Lawrence A. *American Education: The Metropolitan Experience, 1876–1980.* New York, 1988.

———. *American Education: The National Experience, ,1783–1876.* New York, 1980.

Cross, Robert D. (ed.). *The Church and the City.* New York, 1967.

Davis, Allen F. *Spearheads for Reform: The Social Settlements and the Progressive Movement, 1890–1914.* New York, 1967.

Davis, Moshe. *The Emergence of Conservative Judaism: The Historical School in the Nineteenth Century.* Philadelphia, 1965.

Decker, Peter. *Fortunes and Failures: White-Collar Mobility in Nineteenth-Century San Francisco.* Cambridge, Mass., 1978.

———. "Jewish Merchants in San Francisco: Social Mobility on the Urban Frontier." *American Jewish History* 67 (June 1978).

Degler, Carl. *At Odds: Women and the Family in America from the Revolution to the Present.* New York, 1980.

———. *Out of Our Past.* New York, 1970.

Diner, Hasia R. *A Time for Gathering: The Second Migration, 1820–1880.* Baltimore, 1992.

Ditzion, Sidney. *Arsenals of a Democratic Culture: A Social History of the American Public Library Movement in New England and the Middle States from 1850 to 1900.* Chicago, 1947.

Dolan, Jay P. *The American Catholic Experience: A History From Colonial Times to The Present.* New York, 1985.

———. *Catholic Revivalism: The American Experience, 1830–1900.* London, 1978.

———. *The Immigrant Church: New York's Irish and German Catholics, 1815–1865.* Baltimore, 1975.

Dorn, Jacob. "Religion and the City." In *The Urban Experience*, edited by Mohl and Richardson. Belmont, Mass., 1973.

Douglass, H. Paul. *The City's Church.* New York, 1929.

———. *The Protestant Church as a Social Institution.* New York, 1935.

———. *The St. Louis Church Survey.* New York, 1924.

———. *The Suburban Trend.* New York, 1925.

Dunn, David, et al. *The History of the Evangelical and Reformed Churches.* Philadelphia, 1961.

Dykstra, Craig, and James Hudnut-Beumler. "The National Organizational Structures of Protestant Denominations: An Invitation to a Conversation." In *The Organizational Revolution: Presbyterians and American Denominationalism*, edited by Milton J. Coalter, et al. Louisville Ky., 1992, pp. 307–31.

Edwards, Alba. *Population: Comparative Occupational Statistics for the United States, 1870–1940.* Washington, D.C., 1943.

Eichhorn, Max. "The Student Body—Today and Yesterday (comparison to 1900 and 1930)." In *Turning Point: Zionism and Reform Judaism*, edited by Howard R. Greenstein. Providence, R.I., 1981.

Elazar, Daniel J. *The Organizational Dynamics of American Jewry.* Philadelphia, 1976.

Engleman, Uriah Z. "Jewish Statistics in the U.S. Census of Religious Bodies (1850–1936)." *Jewish Social Studies* 9, no. 2 (April 1947).

Fass, Paula S. *The Damned and the Beautiful: American Youth in the 1920s*. New York, 1977.

Faust, Albert B. *The German Element in the United States*. New York, 1909.

Feibelman, Julian B. *A Social and Economic Study of the New Orleans Jewish Community*. Philadelphia, 1941.

Fein, Isaac M. *The Making of an American Jewish Community: The History of Baltimore Jewry from 1723 to 1920*. Philadelphia, 1971.

Feingold, Henry. *Zion In America*. New York, 1974.

———. *A Time for Searching: Entering the Mainstream, 1920–1945*. Baltimore, 1992.

Feinstein, Marnin. *American Zionism, 1884–1904*. New York, 1965.

Feldman, Abraham. "The Changing Functions of the Synagogue and the Rabbi." In *Reform Judaism: Essays by H.U.C. Alumni*. Cincinnati, 1949.

Feldman, Egal. *Dual Destinies: The Jewish Encounter with Protestant America*. Chicago, 1990.

Fierstien, Robert. *From Foundation to Reorganization: The Jewish Theological Seminary of America, 1886–1902*. New York, 1989.

Fineshriber, Howard. *Reform Congregation Keneseth Israel: Its First Hundred Years, 1847–1947*. Philadelphia, 1950.

Fineshriber, William. "The Decay of Theology in Popular Religion." *CCAR Yearbook*. Vol. 30, 1920.

Foster, Charles I. *An Errand of Mercy: The Evangelical United Front, 1790–1837*. Chapel Hill, N.C., 1960.

Fox, Steven A. "On the Road to Unity: The Union of American Hebrew Congregations and American Jewry, 1873–1903." *American Jewish Archives* (November 1980).

Frankel, Jonathan. "Crisis as a Factor in Modern Jewish Politics, 1840, 1881–1882." In *Living With Anti-Semitism: Modern Jewish Responses*, edited by Yehuda Reinharz. Waltham, Mass., 1980.

Friedenberg, Robert V. *Hear O Israel: The History of American Jewish Preaching, 1654–1970*. Tuscaloosa, Ala., 1989.

Friedman, Murray (ed.). *Jewish Life in Philadelphia, 1830–1940*. Philadelphia, 1983.

Gabriel, Ralph Henry. *The Course of American Democratic Thought*. New York, 1940.

Gartner, Lloyd P. "Temples of Liberty Unpolluted: American Jews and Public Schools, 1840–1875." In *A Bicentennial Festschrift for Jacob Rader Marcus*, edited by B. W. Korn. Cincinnati, 1976.

Gatzke, Hans W. *Germany and the United States: A Special Relationship*. Cambridge, Mass., 1980.

Gerson, Louis L. *The Hyphenate in Recent American Politics and Diplomacy*. Lawrence, Kans., 1964.

Glanz, Rudolph. *The Jews of California: From the Discovery of Gold until 1880*. New York, 1960.

Glazer, Nathan. *American Judaism*. Chicago, 1957.

———. "The Jews." In *Ethnic Leadership in America*, edited by John Higham. Baltimore, 1978.

Goldberg, Martin Lloyd. *Fluctuation Between Traditionalism and Liberalism in*

American Reform Judaism from 1855 to 1937. Ph.D. dissertation. University of Pittsburgh, 1955.

Goldstein, Israel. *A Century of Judaism in New York: A History of B'nai Jeshurun.* New York, 1930.

Gordon, Milton, *Assimilation in American Life.* Oxford, 1964.

Goren, Arthur A. *Dissenter In Zion: From the Writings of Judah Magnes.* Cambridge, Mass., 1982.

———. "The Jewish Press." In *The Ethnic Press in the United States: A Historical Analysis and Handbook,* edited by Sally M. Miller. New York, 1987, pp. 203–228.

———. *New York Jews and the Quest for Community: The Kehillah Experiment, 1908–1922.* New York, 1970.

Greenberg, Gershon. "Samuel Hirsch's 'American Judaism.'" *American Jewish Historical Quarterly* 62 (1972/1973).

Greene, Theodore P. (ed.). *American Imperialism in 1898.* Boston, 1959.

Grinstein, Hyman. "The American Synagogue and Laxity of Religious Observance." M.A. thesis. Columbia University, 1936.

———. *The Rise of the Jewish Community of New York, 1654–1860.* Philadelphia, 1947.

Gurock, Jeffrey S. *The Men and Women of Yeshiva: Higher Education, Orthodoxy, and American Judaism.* New York, 1988.

———. "The Orthodox Synagogue." In *The American Synagogue: A Sanctuary Transformed,* edited by Jack Wertheimer. New York, 1987.

———. "Resisters and Accomodators: Varieties of Orthodox Rabbis in America, 1886–1983." *American Jewish Archives* (November 1983).

Gustafson, James M. "The Voluntary Church: A Moral Appraisal." In *Voluntary Associations: A Study of Groups in Free Societies,* edited by D. B. Robertson. Richmond, Va., 1966.

Haber, Samuel. *Efficiency and Uplift: Scientific Management in the Progressive Era, 1890–1920.* Chicago, 1964.

Halpern, Ben. "The Americanization of Zionism, 1880–1930." In *Solidarity and Kinship: Essays on American Zionism,* edited by Nathan Kaganoff. Waltham, Mass., 1980.

Handlin, Oscar. *A Continuing Task: The American Jewish Joint Distribution Committee, 1914–1964.* New York, 1964.

Handy, Robert. T. *A Christian America: Protestant Hopes and Historical Reality.* New York, 1971.

———. *A History of Union Theological Seminary in New York.* New York, 1987.

——— (ed.). *The Social Gospel in America, 1870–1920.* New York, 1966.

Hansen, Marcus L. "The Third Generation Immigrant." *Proceedings of the Massachusetts Historical Society,* 1939.

Harris, George. *A Century's Change in Religion.* Boston, 1914.

Heinze, Andrew R. *Adapting to Abundance: Jewish Immigrants, Mass Comsumption, and the Search for American Identity.* New York, 1990.

Heller, James G. *As Yesterday When It Is Past: A History of the I. M. Wise Temple, KKBY 1842–1942.* Cincinnati, 1942.

———. *Isaac Mayer Wise: His Life, Works and Thought.* New York, 1965.

Heller, Max. *Jubilee Souvenir of Temple Sinai, 1872–1922.* New Orleans, 1922.

Herberg, Will. *Protestant, Catholic, Jew.* New York, 1955.

Herbst, Jürgen. *The German Historical School in American Scholarship: A Study in the Transfer of Culture.* Ithaca, N.Y., 1965.

Hertzberg, Arthur. *The French Enlightenment and the Jews.* New York, 1970.
———. *The Jews in America: Four Centuries of an Uneasy Encounter.* New York, 1989.
Hertzberg, Steven. *Strangers Within the City: The Jews of Atlanta, 1845–1915.* Philadelphia, 1978.
Higham, John (ed.). *Ethnic Leadership in America.* Baltimore, 1978.
———. *Send These to Me: Jews and Other Immigrants in Urban America.* New York, 1975.
———. *Strangers in the Land: Patterns of American Nativism, 1860–1925.* New York, 1967.
Hirschler, Eric E. (ed.). *Jews From Germany in the United States.* New York, 1955.
Hoffman, Lawrence A. *Beyond the Text: A Holistic Approach to Liturgy.* Bloomington, Ind., 1987.
Hofstadter, Richard. *The Age of Reform.* New York, 1955.
Hofstadter, Richard, and C. DeWitt Hardy. *The Development and Scope of Higher Education in the United States.* New York, 1952.
Holifield, E. Brooks. *A History of Pastoral Care in America.* Nashville, 1983.
———. "Review of Recent Studies of the American Synagogue." *Religious Studies Review* 17, no. 3 (July 1991).
Holland, Dewitte, et al. (eds.). *Preaching in American History: Selected Issues in the American Pulpit, 1630–1967.* New York, 1969.
Hopkins, C. H. *The Rise of the Social Gospel in American Protestantism, 1865–1915.* New Haven, 1967.
Hopkins, C. H., et al. (eds.). *The Social Gospel: Religion and Reform in a Changing America.* Philadelphia, 1976.
Howe, Daniel Walker. *Victorian America.* Philadelphia, 1976.
Hudson, Winthrop. *Religion in America: An Historical Account of the Development of American Religious Life.* New York, 1965.
Hurlbut, Jesse L. *The Story of Chautauqua.* New York, 1921.
Idelsohn, A. Z. *Jewish Music in its Historical Development.* New York, 1929.
Jackson, Kenneth T. *Crabgrass Frontier: The Suburbanization of the United States.* New York, 1985.
Jackson, Kenneth T. and Schultz, Stanley K. (eds.). *Cities in American History.* New York, 1972.
Jacob, Walter (ed.). *The Changing World of Reform Judaism: The Pittsburgh Platform in Retrospect.* Pittsburgh, 1985.
Jick, Leon A. *The Americanization of the Synagogue, 1820–1870.* Waltham, MA, 1976.
———. "The Reform Synagogue." In *The American Synagogue: A Sanctuary Transformed,* edited by Jack Wertheimer. New York, 1987.
Joselit, Jena Weissman. "The Middle-Class American Jewish Woman." In *The American Synagogue: A Sanctuary Transformed,* edited by Jack Wertheimer. New York, 1987.
———. "Modern Orthodox Jews and the Ordeal of Civility." *American Jewish History* 74, no. 2 (December 1984).
———. *New York's Jewish Jews: The Orthodox Community in the Interwar Years.* Bloomington, Ind., 1990.
———. "Of Manners, Morals and Orthodox Judaism: Decorum Within the Orthodox Synagogue." In *Ramaz: School, Community, Scholarship and Orthodoxy,* edited by Jeffrey Gurock. Hoboken, N.J. 1989.

Joseph, Samuel. *Jewish Immigration to the United States, 1881–1910*. New York, 1914.

Karp, Abraham J. *A History of the United Synagogue of America*. New York, 1964.

———. "Overview: The Synagogue in America." In *The American Synagogue: A Sanctuary Transformed*, edited by Jack Wertheimer. New York, 1987.

Katz, Jacob. *Out of the Ghetto: The Social Background of Jewish Emancipation, 1770–1870*. New York, 1978.

Kelly, Robert L. *Theological Education in America*. New York, 1924.

Kennedy, Paul. *The Rise and Fall of the Great Powers: Economic Change and Military Conflict from 1500 to 2000*. New York, 1987.

Kennedy, William Bean. *The Shaping of Protestant Education: An Interpretation of the Sunday School and Development of Protestant Educational Strategy in the United States, 1789–1860*. New York, 1966.

Kessner, Thomas J. *The Golden Door: Italian and Jewish Immigrant Mobility in New York City, 1880–1915*. New York, 1977.

Kett, Joseph. "The History of Age Grouping in America." In *Rethinking Childhood*, edited by Arlene Skolmick. Boston, 1976.

———. *Rites of Passage: Adolescence in America from 1750 to the Present*. New York, 1977.

King, William McGuire. "Denominational Modernization and Religious Identity: The Case of the Methodist Episcopal Church." *Methodist History* 20, no. 2 (January 1982).

———. "The Role of Auxiliary Ministries in Late Nineteenth-Century Methodism." In *Rethinking Methodism*, edited by Russell E. Richey and Kenneth R. Rowe. Nashville, 1985.

Kirkland, Edward. *Industry Comes of Age: 1860–1897*. Chicago, 1961.

Klaperman, Gilbert. *The Story of Yeshiva University: The First Jewish University in America*. New York, 1969.

Knox, Israel. *Rabbi in America: The Story of Isaac M. Wise*. Boston, 1957.

Kober, Adolph. "Jewish Preaching and Preachers: A Contribution to the History of the Jewish Sermon in Germany and America." *Historia Judaica* 7 (1945).

Korn, Bertram Wallace. "American Jewry in 1849." In *Eventful Years and Experiences: Studies in Nineteenth Century American Jewish History*, edited by B. W. Korn. Cincinnati, 1958.

———. *The American Reaction to the Mortara Case*. Cincinnati, 1957.

———. "The First American Jewish Theological Seminary: Maimonides College, 1867–1873." In *Eventful Years and Experiences*, edited by B. W. Korn. Cincinnati, 1954.

———. "German-Jewish Intellectual Influences on American Jewish Life, 1824–1972." In *Tradition and Change in the Jewish Experience*, edited by A. Leland Jamison. Syracuse, N.Y., 1978.

———. "Isaac Leeser: Centennial Reflections." *American Jewish Archives* 19 (1967).

——— (ed.). *Retrospect and Prospect: Essays in Commemoration of the Seventy-Fifth Anniversary of the Founding of the Central Conference of American Rabbis, 1889–1964*. New York, 1965.

———. "The Temple Emanu El Theological Seminary of New York City." In *Essays in American Jewish History*, edited by J. R. Marcus. New York, 1975.

Krauskopf, Joseph. "A Half Century of American Judaism." *American Jewish Annual*. Vol. 6, 1884.

Kraut, Benny. "American Jewish Leaders: The Great, Greater and Greatest." *American Jewish History* 78, no. 2 (December 1988).

————. *From Reform Judaism to Ethical Culture: The Religious Evolution of Felix Adler.* Cincinnati, 1979.

————. "Judaism Triumphant: Isaac Mayer Wise on Unitarianism and Liberal Christianity." *AJS Review* 7–8 (1982/1983).

Kuzmack, Linda Gordon. *Woman's Cause: The Jewish Woman's Movement in England and the United States, 1881–1933.* Columbus, Ohio, 1990.

Lamberti, Marjorie. *Jewish Activism in Imperial Germany.* New Haven, 1978.

LeFeber, Walter and Polenberg, Richard. *The American Century: A History of the United States Since the 1890's.* New York, 1975.

LeFeber, Walter. *The New Empire: An Interpretation of American Expansion, 1860–1898.* Ithaca, N.Y., 1963.

Levy, Beryl H. *Reform Judaism in America.* New York, 1933.

Liberles, Robert. *Religious Conflict in Social Context: The Resurgence of Orthodox Judaism in Frankfurt am Main, 1838–1877.* Westport, Conn., 1985.

Littell, Franklin H. *From State Church to Pluralism: A Protestant Interpretation of Religion in American History.* New York, 1962.

Low, Alfred D. *Jews in the Eyes of the Germans: From the Enlightenment to Imperial Germany.* Philadelphia, 1979.

Lowenstein, Steven M. "The 1840's and the Creation of the German-Jewish Religious Reform Movement." In *Revolution and Evolution: 1848 in German Jewish History,* edited by W. E. Mosse, A. Paucker, and R. Rump. Tübingen, 1981.

Lubove, Roy. *The Professional Altruist: The Emergence of Social Work as a Career, 1880–1930.* New York, 1965.

Luccock, Halford E., and Paul Hutchinson. *The Story of Methodism.* New York, 1926.

Lynn, Kenneth S. (ed.). *The Professions in America.* Boston, 1965.

Lynn, Robert W., and Elliot Wright. *The Big Little School: Sunday Child of American Protestantism.* New York, 1971.

Mahler, Raphael. *A History of Modern Jewry, 1780–1815.* London, 1971.

Marcus, Jacob R. *Early American Jewry,* 2 vols. Philadelphia, 1951, 1953.

Markowitz, Eugene. "Henry Pereira Mendes: Architect of the Union of Orthodox Jewish Congregations of America." *American Jewish Historical Quarterly* (March 1966).

Marrus, Michael R. *The Politics of Assimilation: A Study of the French Jewish Community at the Time of the Dreyfus Affair.* Oxford, 1971.

Martin, Bernard (ed.). *Movements and Issues in American Judaism: An Analysis and Sourcebook of Developments Since 1945.* Westport, Conn., 1978.

Marty, Martin. *Righteous Empire: The Protestant Experience in America.* New York, 1970.

May, Mark. *The Education of American Ministers: Volume II—The Profession of the Ministry.* New York, 1933.

May, Max B. *Isaac Mayer Wise: The Founder of American Judaism.* New York, 1916.

May, Henry F. "Europe and the American Mind." In *Ideas, Faiths and Feelings: Essays on American Intellectual and Religious History, 1952–1982,* edited by Henry F. May. New York, 1983.

————. *Protestant Churches and Industrial America.* New York, 1949.

McKelvey, Blake. *The Urbanization of America, 1860–1915.* New Brunswick, N.J., 1963.

McNeill, John T. *Unitive Protestantism: A Study of One Religious Response.* Nashville, 1930.

Mead, Sidney. "The Rise of the Evangelical Conception of the Ministry in America, 1607–1850." In *The Ministry in Historical Perspective,* edited by H. R. Niebuhr and Daniel Williams. New York, 1956.

Mervis, Leonard. "The Social Justice Movement and the American Reform Rabbi," *American Jewish Archives* 7 (June 1955).

Metzger, Walter J. *Academic Freedom in the Age of the University.* New York, 1961.

Meyer, Michael A. "Christian Influences on Early German Reform Judaism." In *Studies in Jewish Bibliography, History and Literature in Honor of I. Edward Kiev,* edited by Charles Berlin. New York, 1971.

———. "German-Jewish Identity in Nineteenth-Century America." In *Toward Modernity: The European Jewish Model,* edited by Jacob Katz. New Brunswick, N.J., 1987.

———. *Hebrew Union College—Jewish Institute of Religion: At One Hundred Years.* Cincinnati, 1976.

———. *The Origins of the Modern Jew: Jewish Identity and European Culture in Germany, 1749–1824.* Detroit, 1967.

———. *Response to Modernity: A History of the Reform Movement in Judaism.* New York, 1988.

Michael, Ann Deborah. "The Origins of the Jewish Community of Cincinnati, 1817–1860." *Cincinnati Historical Society Bulletin,* 1922.

Michaelsen, Robert S. "The Protestant Ministry in America: 1850 to the Present." In *The Ministry in Historical Perspective,* edited by H. R. Niebuhr and Daniel Williams. New York, 1956.

Miller, William. *Men In Business.* Cambridge, Mass., 1952.

Moore, Deborah Dash. *At Home in America: Second Generation New York Jews.* New York, 1981.

———. *B'nai Brith.* New York, 1987.

———. "A Synagogue Center Grows in Brooklyn." In *The American Synagogue: A Sanctuary Transformed,* edited by Jack Wertheimer. New York, 1987.

Moore, Wilbert. *The Professions: Roles and Rules.* New York, 1970.

Morais, Henry S. *The Jews of Philadelphia.* Philadelphia, 1894.

Mostov, Steven G. "Dun and Bradstreet Reports as a Source of Jewish Economic History: Cincinnati 1840–1875." *American Jewish History* (March 1983).

———. *A "Jerusalem" on the Ohio: The Social and Economic History of Cincinnati's Jewish Community, 1840–1875.* Ph.D. dissertation. Brandeis University, 1981.

Mouzelis, Nicos P. *Organization and Bureaucracy: An Analysis of Modern Theories.* New York, 1968.

Nadel, Stanley. "Jewish Race and German Soul in Nineteenth Century America." *American Jewish History* 77, no. 1 (September 1977).

Nadell, Pamela S. *Conservative Judaism in America: A Biographical Dictionary and Sourcebook.* New York, 1988.

Nathan, Marvin. *The Attitude of the Jewish Student in the Colleges and Universities toward His Religion.* Philadelphia, 1932.

Nelsen, Ralph L. *Merger Movements in American Industry, 1895–1956.* Princeton, 1959.

Nelson, E. Clifford (ed.). *The Lutherans in North America.* Philadelphia, 1975.

Neufeldt, Harvey George. *The American Tract Society, 1825–1865: An Examination of its Religious, Economic, Social and Political Ideas.* Ph.D. dissertation. Michigan State University, 1971.

Neusner, Jacob. "The Role of English Jews in the Development of American Jewish Life, 1775–1850." *YIVO Annual.* Vol. 12, 1958/1959.

Norwood, Frederick A. *The Story of American Methodism: A History of the United Methodists and Their Relations.* Nashville, 1974.

Nussenbaum, Max Samuel. "Champion of Orthodox Judaism: A Biography of the Reverend Sabato Morais." D.H.L. dissertation. Yeshiva University, 1964.

Olitzky, Kerry. "Sundays at Chicago Sinai Congregation, Paradigm for a Movement." *American Jewish History* (January 1985).

———. "The Sunday Sabbath Movement in American Reform Judaism, Strategy or Evolution?" *American Jewish Archives* (April 1982).

Ostrander, Gilman M. *American Civilization in the First Machine Age, 1890–1940.* New York, 1970.

Panitz, Esther L. "In Defense of the Jewish Immigrant (1891–1924)." In *The Jewish Experience in America, Volume V: At Home in America,* edited by Abraham J. Karp. New York, 1969.

———. "The Polarity of American Jewish Attitudes toward Immigration (1870-1891)." In *The Jewish Experiences in America, Vol, IV: The Era of Immigration,* edited by Abraham J. Karp. New York, 1969.

———. *Simon Wolf: Private Conscience and Public Image.* Rutherford, N.J., 1987.

Parzen, Herbert. *Architects of Conservative Judaism.* New York, 1964.

Petuchowski, Jakob. *Prayerbook Reform in Europe: The Liturgy of European Liberal and Reform Judaism.* New York, 1968.

———. "Reform Judaism: Evolution or Revolution?" In *Jews in a Free Society,* edited by Edward A. Goldman. New York, 1978.

Philipson, David. *My Life as an American Jew.* Cincinnati, 1941.

———. *The Reform Movement in Judaism.* New York, 1931.

Pinson, Koppel. *Modern Germany: Its History and Civilization.* New York, 1966.

Plaut, W. Gunther. *The Growth of Reform Judaism.* New York, 1965.

———. *The Rise of Reform Judaism.* New York, 1963.

Pochman, Henry A. *German Culture in America: Philosophical and Literary Influences, 1600–1900.* Madison, Wisc., 1957.

Porter, Glenn. *The Rise of Big Business, 1860–1910.* Arlington Heights, Ill., 1973.

Potter, David M. *People of Plenty: Economic Abundance and the American Character.* Chicago, 1966.

Primer, Ben. *Protestants and American Business Methods.* Ann Arbor, Mich., 1979.

Raisin, Jacob S. *The Haskalah Movement in Russia.* Philadelphia, 1913.

Raphael, Marc Lee. *Profiles in American Judaism: The Reform, Conservative, Orthodox and Reconstructionist Traditions in Historical Perspective.* New York, 1984.

———. "The Origins of Organized National Jewish Philanthropy in the United States, 1914–1939." In *The Jews in North America,* edited by Moses Rischin. Detroit, 1987, pp. 213–23.

———. "Rabbi Jacob Voorsanger of San Francisco on Jews and Judaism: The Implications of the Pittsburgh Platform." *AJHQ* 63, no. 2 (December 1973).

Rausch, Eduardo L. "Jewish Education in the United States, 1840–1920." Ed.D. thesis. Harvard University, 1978.

Regner, Sidney. "The History of the Conference." In *Retrospect and Prospect: Essays in*

Commemoration of the Seventy-Fifth Anniversary of the Founding of the Central Conference of American Rabbis, 1889–1964, edited by B. W. Korn. New York, 1965.

Reichel, Aaron I. *The Maverick Rabbi: Herbert S. Goldstein.* Norfolk, Va., 1984.

Reinhart, Arthur L. "The National Federation of Temple Brotherhoods." In *Universal Jewish Encyclopedia.* Vol. 8, 1942.

———. *The Voice of the Jewish Laity: A Survey of the Jewish Layman's Religious Attitudes and Practices.* Cincinnati, 1928.

Rice, Edwin Wilbur. *The Sunday-School Movement and the American Sunday-School Union.* Philadelphia, 1927.

Richey, Russell E. (ed.). *Denominationalism.* Nashville, 1977.

———. "Evolving Patterns of Methodist Ministry," *Methodist History* 22, no. 1 (October 1983).

Riley, Glenda. "'Not Gainfully Employed': Women on the Iowa Frontier, 1833–1870." In Friedman, Jean E. and Shade, William G. *Our American Sisters: Women in American Life and Thought*, edited by Jean E. Friedman and William G. Shade. Lexington, MA, 1982.

Rischin, Moses (ed.), *The Jews of North America.* Detroit, 1987.

Robertson, James Oliver. *American Myth, American Reality.* New York, 1980.

Rockaway, Robert. "Ethnic Conflict in an Urban Environment: The German and Russian Jew in Detroit, 1881–1914." *AJHQ* 60, no. 2 (December 1970).

Rosenbaum, Fred. *Architects for Reform: Congregational and Community Leadership, Emanu-El of San Francisco, 1849–1980.* Berkeley, Ca., 1980.

Rosenberg, Stuart. "Some Sermons in the Spirit of the Pittsburgh Platform." *Historia Judaica* 17 (1956).

Rosenbloom, Joseph. "Some Conclusions about Rebecca Gratz." In *Essays in American Jewish History*, edited by Jacob Rader Marcus. New York, 1975.

Rosenblum, Herbert. *The Founding of the United Synagogue of America.* Ph.D. dissertation, Brandeis University, 1970.

———. "Ideology and Compromise: The Evolution of the United Synagogue Preamble." *Jewish Social Studies* 35 (1973).

———. "The Shaping of an Institution: The 1902 Reorganization of the Seminary." *Conservative Judaism* (1973).

Rothkoff, Aaron. *Bernard Revel: Builder of American Jewish Orthodoxy.* Philadelphia, 1972.

Rothman, Sheila M. *Woman's Proper Place: A History of Changing Ideas and Practices, 1870 to the Present.* New York, 1980.

Rudolph, Frederick. *The American College and University: A History*, New York, 1962.

Ryback, Martin B. "The East-West Conflict in American Reform Judaism." *American Jewish Achives* (January 1952).

Sarna, Jonathan D. "The American Jewish Response to Ninteenth-Century Christian Missions." *Journal of American History* 68 (1981/1982).

———. "The Debate over Mixed Seating in the American Synagogue." In *The American Synagogue: A Sanctuary Transformed*, edited by Jack Wertheimer. New York, 1987.

———. *JPS: The Americanization of Jewish Culture.* Philadelphia, 1989.

———. *Mordecai M. Noah: Jacksonian Politician and American Jewish Communal Leader—A Biographical Study.* New Haven, 1979.

———. "The 'Mythical Jew' and the 'Jew Next Door.'" In *Anti-Semitism in American History*, edited by David A. Gerber. Chicago, 1986.

―――. "'A Sort of Paradise for the Hebrews': The Lofty Vision of Cincinnati Jews." *In Ethnic Diversity and Civic Identity: Patterns of Conflict and Cohesion in Cincinnati since 1820*, edited by Henry D. Shapiro and Jonathan D. Sarna. Chicago, 1992, pp. 131–64.

―――. The Spectrum of Jewish Leadership i Ante-Bellum America." *The Journal of American Ethnic History.* (1982), pp. 59–67.

Scherer, Ross. *American Denominationalism: A Sociological View.* New York, 1975.

Schieber, Clara Eve. *The Transformation of American Sentiment towards Germany, 1870–1914.* Boston, 1923.

Schlesinger, Arthur. *The Rise of the City.* New York, 1933.

Schmidt, H. D. "The Terms of Emancipation, 1781–1812." *LBIYB.* Vol. 1, 1956.

Schorsch, Ismar. "Emancipation and the Crisis of Religious Authority: The Emergence of the Modern Rabbinate." In *Revolution and Evolution: 1848 in German Jewish History*, edited by W. E. Mosse, A. Paucker, and R. Runp. Tübingen, 1981.

―――. *Jewish Reactions to German Anti-Semitism,1870–1914.* New York, 1972.

―――. *Thoughts From 3080: Selected Addresses and Writings.* New York, 1988.

―――. "Zecharias Frankel and the European Origins of Conservative Judaism." *Judaism.* 30 (1981).

Scott, Donald M. *From Office to Profession: The New England Ministry, 1750–1850.* Philadelphia, 1978.

Scudder, M. L. *American Methodism.* New York, 1870.

Seller, Maxine S. *Isaac Leeser: Architect of the American Jewish Communtiy.* Ph.D. dissertation. University of Pennsylvania, 1965.

Sharfman, I. Harold. *The First Rabbi: Origins of Conflict Between Orhtodox and Reform.* New York, 1988.

Shelemay, Kay Kaufman. "Music in the American Synagogue: A Case Study of Houston." In *The American Synagogue: A Sanctuary Transformed*, edited by Jack Wertheimer. New York, 1987.

Silcox, Claris Edwin, and Galen M. Fisher. *Catholics, Jews and Protestants: A Study of Relationships in the United States and Canada.* New York, 1934.

Simon, E. Yechiel. "S. M. Isaacs: A Ninettenth Century Jewish Minister in New York City." D.H.L. dissertation. Yeshiva University, 1974.

Simons, John (ed.). *Who's Who in American Jewry.* New York, 1938.

Skard, Sigmund. *The American Myth and the European Mind, 1776–1960.* Philadelphia, 1961.

Sklare, Marshall. *Conservative Judaism: An American Religious Movement.* New York, 1972.

Slobin, Mark. *Chosen Voices: The Story of the American Cantorate.* Urbana, Ill., 1989.

Smith, Henry Nash. *Virgin Land: The American West as Symbol and Myth.* Cambridge, Mass., 1978.

Smith, Timothy L. *Revivalism and Social Reform: American Protestantism on the Eve of the Civil War.* Baltimore, 1980.

Solomon, Sidney. "The Conservative Congregational School as a Response to the American Scene." D.H.L. thesis. Jewish Theological Seminary, 1982.

Sorin, Gerald. *A Time for Building: The Third Migration, 1880–1920.* Baltimore, 1992.

Sorkin, David. *The Transformation of German Jewry, 1780–1840*, New York, 1987.

Stampfer, Joshua. *Pioneer Rabbi of the West: The Life and Times of Julius Eckman.* Portland, Ore., 1988.

Stanislawski, Michael. *Tsar Nicholas I and the Jews: The Transformation of Jewish Society in Russian, 1825–1855.* Philadelphia, 1983.

Starr, Paul. *The Social Transformation of American Medicine.* New York, 1982.

Stern, Harriet Kohn. "Origins of Reform Judaism in New Orleans." M.A. thesis, University of New Orleans, 1977.

Sulzburger, D. "The Growth of the Jewish Population in the U.S." *Publication of the American Jewish Historical Society.* No. 6, 1897.

Sussman, Lance J. "Another Look at Isaac Leeser and the First Jewish Translation of the Bible in the United States." *Modern Judaism* (May 1988).

———. "Isaac Leeser and the Protestanization of American Judaism." *American Jewish Archives* (April 1986).

———. *The Life and Career of Isaac Leeser, 1806–1868: A Study of American Judaism in its Formative Period.* Ph.D. dissertation. Hebrew Union College, 1987.

Sutherland, john. *A City of Homes: Philadelphia Slums and Reformers, 1880–1913.* Ph.D. dissertation. Temple University, 1973.

Sweet, William W. *Religion in the Development of American Culture, 1765–1840.* New York, 1952.

———. *The Story of Religion in America.* New York, 1950.

Szajkowski, Zosa. "The Attitude of American Jews to Eastern European Jewish Immigration (1881–1893)." *PAJHS* 40 (March 1951).

Tabak, Israel. "Rabbi Abraham Rice of Baltimore." *Tradition* (1965).

Tarshish, Allan. "The Board of Delegates of American Israelites." Rabbinical Thesis. HUC-JIR, 1932.

———. "The Economic Life of the American Jew." In *Essays in American Jewish History*, edited by J. R. Marcus. New York, 1975.

Temkin, Sefton. *Isaac Mayer Wise.* Ph.D. dissertation. Hebrew Union College, 1970.

———. "Isaac Mayer Wise: A Biographical Sketch." In *A Guide to the Writings of Isaac Mayer Wise*, edited by Doris C. Sturzenberger. Cincinnati, 1981.

———. *The New World of Reform.* London, 1971.

———. "Reform Judaism in America." *AJYB* (1973).

Teplitz, Saul. *Synagogue Life and Thought In Nineteenth Century America As Reflected In The English Sermon.* D.H.L. dissertation. Jewish Theological Seminary,

Tewksbury, Donald G. *The Founding of American Colleges and Universities Before the Civil War: With Particular Reference to the Religious Influences Bearing Upon the College Movement.* New York, 1932.

Thislethwaite, Frank. *The Anglo-American Connection in the Early Nineteenth Century.* Philadelphia, 1959.

Thwing, Charles F. *The American and the German University: One Hundred Years of History.* New York, 1928.

Toll, William. "The 'New Social History' and Recent Jewish Historical Writing." *American Jewish History* 69 (March 1980) pp. 325–41.

Torbet, Robert G. *A History of the Baptists.* Valley Forge, Pa., 1975.

Tyack, David B. "Bureaucracy and the Common School: The Example of Portland, Oregon, 1851–1913." In *Education in American History*, edited by Michael Katz. New York, 1983.

———. *The One Best System.* Cambridge, Mass., 1974.

Urofsky, Melvin I. *American Zionism from Herzl to the Holocaust.* New York, 1975.

———. *A Voice That Spoke For Justice: The Life and Times of Stephen S. Wise.* Albany, N.Y., 1982.

Van Deusen, Glyndon G. *The American Democracy: Its Rise to Power.* New York, 1964.

Vogel, Stanley M. *German Literary Influences on the American Transcendentalists.* New Haven, 1955.

Walker, Mack. *Germany and the Emigration, 1816–1885.* Cambridge, Mass., 1964.

Wall, Bennett. "Leon Gadchaux and the Godchaux Business Enterprises." *AJHQ* 66 (September 1976).

Warner, Samuel Bass. *The Private City: Philadelphia in Three Periods of its Growth.* Philadelphia, 1968.

Waxman, Chaim I. *American Jews in Transition.* Philadelphia, 1983.

Wechman, Robert J. *Emanuel Gamoran: Pioneer in Jewish Religious Education.* Ph.D. dissertation. Syracuse University, 1970.

Weisenburger, Francis P. *Ordeal of Faith: The Crisis of Church-Going America, 1865–1900.* New York, 1959.

Weissbach, Lee Shai. "The Jewish Communities of the United States on the Eve of Mass Migration: Some Comments on Geography and Bibliography." *American Jewish History* 78, no. 1 (September 1988).

Wellek, Rene. *Confrontations: Studies in the Intellectual and Literary Relations Between Germany, England and the United States During the Nineteenth Century.* Princeton, 1966.

Wentz, Abdel Ross. *A Basic History of Lutheranism in America.* Philadelphia, 1955.

———. *Samuel S. Schmucker.* Philadelphia, 1964.

Wertheimer, Jack. "The Conservative Synagogue." In *The American Synagogue: A Sanctuary Transformed,* edited by Jack Wertheimer. New York, 1987.

———. "The Conservative Synagogue Revisited." *American Jewish History* 74, no. 2 (December 1984).

———. *Unwelcome Strangers: Eastern European Jews in Imperial Germany.* New York, 1987.

Whiteman, Maxwell. "Isaac Leeser and the Jews of Philadelphia." *PAJHS* 48 (1959).

———. "The Legacy of Isaac Leeser." In *Jewish Life in Philadelphia 1830–1940,* edited by Murray Friedman. Philadelphia, 1983, pp. 26–47.

Wilkins, Mira. *The Emergence of Multinational Enterprise: American Business Abroad from Colonial Times to 1914.* Cambridge, Mass., 1970.

Williams, William Appleman. *The Contours of American History.* Chicago, 1966.

Wind, James P., Carl S. Dudley, and Jackson W. Carroll (eds.). *Carriers of Faith: Lessons from Congregational Studies.* Louisville, Ky., 1991.

Winter, Gibson. *The Surburban Captivity of the Churches.* New York, 1962.

Winter, Nathan. *Jewish Education in a Pluralist Society: Samson Benderly and Jewish Education in the United States.* New York, 1966.

Wischnitzer, Mark. *To Dwell In Safety: The Story of Jewish Migration Since 1800.* Philadelphia, 1948.

Wischnitzer, Rahel. *Synagogue Architecture in the United States: History and Interpretation.* Philadelphia, 1955.

Wolf, Simon. *The American Jew as Patriot, Soldier and Citizen.* Philadelphia, 1895.

Zola, Gary P. "Reform Judaism's Pioneer Zionist: Maximilian Heller." *AJH* 73, no. 4 (June, 1984).

Zucker, Jeffrey. "Cantor Edward Stark At Congregation Emanu El." *Western States Jewish History* (April 1985).

———. "Cantor Edward Stark at Congregation Emanu El, Part II." *Western States Jewish History* (July 1985).

Zunz, Oliver. *Making America Corporate, 1870–1920.* Chicago, 1992.

Index

UNIVERSITY PRESS OF NEW ENGLAND publishes books under its own imprint and is the publisher for Brandeis University Press, Brown University Press, University of Connecticut, Dartmouth College, Middlebury College Press, University of New Hampshire, University of Rhode Island, Tufts University, University of Vermont, Wesleyan University Press, and Salzburg Seminar.

Library of Congress Cataloging-in-Publication Data

Silverstein, Alan.
  Alternatives to assimilation : the response of Reform Judaism to
American culture, 1840–1930 / Alan Silverstein.
    p.   cm. — (Brandeis series in American Jewish history,
culture, and life)
  Includes bibliographical references and index.
  ISBN 0-87451-694-3 (cl.)—ISBN 0-87451-726-5
    1. REFORM JUDAISM—UNITED STATES—HISTORY. 2. JEWS—CULTURAL
ASSIMILATION—UNITED STATES. 3. SYNAGOGUES—UNITED STATES—
ORGANIZATION AND ADMINISTRATION—CASE STUDIES. I. TITLE.
II. SERIES.
BM197.S49   1994
296.8'346'0973—dc20   94-29489
∞